MARTIN BUBER

NEW JEWISH PHILOSOPHY AND THOUGHT
Zachary J. Braiterman

MARTIN BUBER

CREATURELY LIFE AND SOCIAL FORM

EDITED BY
Sarah Scott

INDIANA UNIVERSITY PRESS

This book is a publication of

Indiana University Press
Office of Scholarly Publishing
Herman B Wells Library 350
1320 East 10th Street
Bloomington, Indiana 47405 USA

iupress.org

© 2022 by Indiana University Press

All rights reserved
No part of this book may be reproduced or utilized in any form or by any means, electronic or mechanical, including photocopying and recording, or by any information storage and retrieval system, without permission in writing from the publisher. The paper used in this publication meets the minimum requirements of the American National Standard for Information Sciences—Permanence of Paper for Printed Library Materials, ANSI Z39.48-1992.

Manufactured in the United States of America

First printing 2022

Cataloging information is available from the Library of Congress.

ISBN 978-0-253-06363-2 (hardback)
ISBN 978-0-253-06364-9 (paperback)
ISBN 978-0-253-06365-6 (ebook)

CONTENTS

1. Introduction: A Martin Buber Renaissance / Sarah Scott   1

PART I: *Religious Dialogue*

2. Martin Buber and Catholic-Atheist Dialogue / Peter A. Huff   13
3. Reading Martin Buber's Bible: Translation and Commentary / Claire E. Sufrin   42

PART II: *Theopolitics*

4. Is the Dialogue between Heaven and Earth an I-Thou Relation? / Samuel Hayim Brody   65
5. The Hasidic Zaddik as Theopolitical Leader / Yemima Hadad   95

PART III: *Zionism and Binationalism*

6. Exile and Alienation in Martin Buber's Philosophical Anthropology / William Plevan   129
7. Martin Buber, Metaphysics, and the Aesthetics of Binationalism / Zachary Braiterman   151

PART IV: *Philosophy*

8. *Chaos, Abgrund,* and *Wirbel*: On Buber's Notion of Ambivalence / Asaf Ziderman   181
9. The Eloquent Muteness of Creatures: Affect and Animals in Martin Buber's Dialogical Writings / Dustin Atlas   202

10. Monologue Disguised as Dialogue: Almodóvar's *Talk to Her* and
    Buber on the "Lovers' Talk" / Sarah Scott   233

List of Contributors   261

Index   263

MARTIN BUBER

ONE

INTRODUCTION

A Martin Buber Renaissance

SARAH SCOTT

I. BEYOND BUBER, THE LEGEND

The reputation of Martin Buber (1878–1965) as one of the most prominent and prolific public intellectuals of his day is illustrated in an anecdote about Buber's presence at a lecture given by the founder of phenomenology, the philosopher Edmund Husserl: "'My name is Buber,' Buber said. Husserl was taken aback for a moment and asked, 'The real Buber?' Buber hesitated to give any further explanation, whereupon Husserl exclaimed: 'But there is no such person! Buber—why he's a legend!'"[1] Like most legends, Buber's life and work has often been understood through the lens of a single defining characteristic. For many readers, Buber is the author of his 1923 book *I and Thou*, which laid out his distinction between dialogic, I-Thou (*Ich-Du*) relations and monologic, I-It (*Ich-Es*) relations. In making this distinction, Buber formalized his lifelong engagement with the ontological, epistemic, and moral aspects of being in relation with another. This project, which he began a good twenty years prior to the work of Jean-Paul Sartre, Simone de Beauvoir, and Frantz Fanon on "the Other," influenced Emmanuel Levinas and caused "dialogue" to become a ubiquitous term. Yet Buber's activities were remarkably prolific and diverse. As an anthologist, translator, and author, he contributed to some seven hundred books and papers, including collections of Hasidic tales and the first major translation of the Hebrew Bible into German since Martin Luther. Buber was also quite active in the movements of his day, such as cultural Zionism, Jewish adult education, interreligious dialogue, and binationalism.[2] For other readers, the legend of Buber is this inauguration of Jewish studies. Thus, Hannah Arendt wrote in 1935, "Buber is German Judaism's incontestable guide. He is the official and actual head of all educational and cultural institutions. His personality is recognized by all parties and all groups. And furthermore he is the true leader of the youth."[3]

This collection aims to move beyond the legend of Buber—that is, to resist turning Buber into an "It," his contributions reduced to a few static ideas that we now take for granted. All legends distort, and when the figure behind the legend is seen to be just another person, legends disappoint. Rather than reading Buber through a single disciplinary lens or the lens of by now well-established stories—for example, his turn from mysticism or intervention in German neo-Kantianism—or focusing exclusively on the notion of dialogue or his Jewishness, this collection brings together scholars with diverse methodological backgrounds and expertise in different facets of his oeuvre. These include his engagement with anarchism and influence on Christianity and the role of language, imagination, affect, aesthetics, theopolitics, animals, and embodiment in his thought. Through this juxtaposition of frameworks and interests, the collection aims to make the case for Buber as a thinker of continuing relevance and controversy. Moreover, the contributions engage the range of his life and work, from his early lectures from the 1910s to his final commentaries from the 1960s. Many of these texts have been little studied or appreciated, and these analyses are a notable contribution to scholarship on Buber.

In many ways Buber was both behind and ahead of his time. When pressed to explain himself, he demurred, "I have no teaching. I only point to something. I point to reality. I point to something in reality that had not or had too little been seen. I take him who listens to me by the hand and lead him to the window. I open the window and point to what is outside. I have no teaching, but I carry on a conversation."[4] To what does Buber direct our attention, and why do we still need to carry on this conversation? The simplest answer is that he directs us to consider ourselves as relational beings. Fashioning his work as "spiritual resistance" against the extreme antisemitism, totalitarianism, and partitioning of peoples of the twentieth century, he could not have foreseen the new forms in which bigotry, excess state power, and spiritual despair would occasionally burst forth in the twenty-first century. Yet while his insistence on the significance of language, embodiment, affectivity, and holistic and interdependent subjects looked back to correct the dualism that characterized both the enlightenment and the mystical parentage of his day, these themes have now become central for current thinkers working in continental philosophy, religious studies, gender studies, and social and political philosophy. Similarly, his imagistic thinking and use of language harken back to romantic and mystical thinkers, yet in directing our attention to methods of communication he speaks to readers in the media-saturated twenty-first century. This twentieth-century legend, who often seemed more at home in the nineteenth century of his youth, ought to be an exemplary resource for twenty-first-century thinkers. This presupposes, however, that the phenomena to which Buber pointed have not, in the meantime, become so covered over by the lexicon and frameworks he helped inaugurate that we are no longer capable of genuine engagement.

This collection emerged from a conference marking the occasion of the fiftieth anniversary of Buber's death.[5] The same year of the memorial conference that led to this volume, a photograph of graffiti in Tel Aviv was posted on Twitter. The graffiti stated, "Martin Buber was right[;] Google it," accompanied by Muslim, Christian, and Jewish religious symbols.[6] While the graffiti had been up for some time, it seemed a fitting image for a year that saw numerous celebrations of Buber's life and work. However, in thinking of Buber as "right," we should keep in mind a cautionary story he told. Buber describes giving a public talk in an industrial city, in which university students dominated the questions while the workers in attendance remained silent. Finally a worker asked Buber a religious question. The secure tone of the question led Buber to assume he ought to challenge the man's worldview, and he replied at length with great passion. At the end of his reply, a "stern silence" ruled the room, and the worker simply replied, "You are right." To his chagrin, Buber realized he had confidently given a speech based on his preconceptions, without having truly conversed with this specific man and grappled with his specific reality.[7] Much as Buber realized he erred in giving a speech instead of having a conversation, we need to be open to setting aside what we think we know in order to really grapple with the fundamental problems of relationship. The humor (or pathos?) of the graffiti notwithstanding, Buber would be the last person to celebrate the statement that he "was right."

Every generation, indeed, every person, has to learn anew how to enter into relationship. If we read Buber as if he is "right," and giving us a list of concepts or theories to memorize and apply, we substitute the pointing activity itself for that to which he points. Here the technical language, methodological constraints, and historicism of scholars can dangerously lock us into an I-It relationship with that which we seek to understand. This collection aims to correct this by going back in our genealogy and reengaging one of the originators of twenty-first-century frameworks for understanding. By showing different approaches to reading and working with Buber's insights, we find the new or unseen in what seemed to be familiar; in breathing new life into the past, we give ourselves new ways of moving into the future. This is of a piece with another simple answer to the question to what does Buber direct our attention: renaissance. Buber first made his mark by calling for a "Jewish Renaissance."[8] Throughout his life he embodied the spirit of renaissance by showing what can be gained by breathing new life into what appears to be fixed or merely historical (e.g., biblical texts, Hasidic tales, language, and philosophic concepts) and using this rebirth to show that there is a way through the deadlocks of his age. By reengaging both the content and the methods of Buber's work, we may be able to enliven static ideas and find a way through the deadlocks of our age.

II. THE CONTRIBUTIONS

The collection explores four interconnected strains of Buber's relevance for the twenty-first century: religious dialogue, theopolitics, Zionism and binationalism, and philosophy. These are organizational rather than essential divisions, for the four strains coalesce to reveal the parallel structures and conversations that engaged Buber throughout his multifaceted life. For each section, two or three chapters are paired together, to encourage the reader to think through different perspectives and link texts or ideas that might not normally be treated together. Part one, "Religious Dialogue," begins with Peter A. Huff's "Martin Buber and Catholic-Atheist Dialogue," which challenges the notion that Buber is of interest only for Jewish studies by demonstrating the profound influence Buber had on Christianity. Drawing on the twin anniversaries of 1965—Buber's death and the Second Vatican Council—Huff presents the hitherto untold story of Buber as the "Jewish father of Vatican II," "on par with Plato and Augustine as a shaper of the Western Christian mind." Moving between vignettes about the reception of Buber, Buber's statements about his own struggles with faith, and Buber's more general claims about atheism as a distinctively modern mode of spiritual existence, Huff humanizes the legend of Buber as the paradigmatic thinker of dialogue and argues for Buber's continuing relevance for interreligious and religious-atheist dialogue.

While Huff presents the story of Buber's reception by Christian thinkers, Claire E. Sufrin focuses on Buber's work on the Bible and his understanding of revelation. In "Reading Martin Buber's Bible: Translation and Commentary," Sufrin charts three stages of Buber's thought: his early addresses and lectures, his translation of the Hebrew Bible into German with Franz Rosenzweig in the late 1920s, and his biblical commentaries from the 1930s and 1940s. Sufrin shows that Buber's analysis of historical revelation went hand in hand with his concern for developing methods for modern readers to approach the Bible—for example, in the use of *cola* (the number of syllables that can be spoken aloud within the span of a breath) and *Leitworte* (leading-words)—and his proposal for speech and presence as models for interacting with the text and ultimately God. Suffrin's methodological emphasis on shifts across texts mirrors the aspect of Buber that she illuminates, while Huff's methodological emphasis on biography and dialogue across communities mirrors the aspect he illuminates. Read together, they challenge us to grapple with Buber's understanding of how to approach religious phenomena and how he was and ought to be received as a religious thinker and translator.

Buber's political writings and controversial political stances are often mentioned, but they have been rarely studied. To correct this, Samuel Hayim Brody starts off part two, "Theopolitics," with "Is the Dialogue between Heaven and Earth an I-Thou Relation?" Brody analyzes some of the same biblical writings as Sufrin but with an eye toward understanding Buber's social and political thought. Against conventional readings that focus on his philosophy of dialogue, Brody develops an alternate intellectual history for Buber, one that focuses on his biblical writings and the positive and enduring influence of Buber's friend, the anarchist-socialist Gustav Landauer. As he traces the features of Buber's theopolitical vision, Brody shows the relationship between Buber's scholarly work and his social and political engagements, for example, his teaching for the Freies Jüdisches Lehrhaus, endorsement of the kibbutz movement, and defense of binationalism. In Brody's analysis, Buber's biblical writings are a form of Landauerian anarchism, while his Zionist and binational projects are best understood as fulfilling the biblical dynamic of election and response.

While Brody lays out the broad features of Buber's intellectual and political trajectory, Yemima Hadad zeroes in on the nature of leadership in Buber's theopolitical narrative in "The Hasidic Zaddik as Theopolitical Leader." Hadad reconstructs Buber's notion of leadership by analyzing his presentation of the biblical figures of the judge, king, prophet, and messiah. While commentators have tended to focus on Buber's study of biblical politics or his cultural Zionism, Hadad draws on Buber's study of Hasidism to bridge these two strains of thought. Ultimately she argues that, for Buber, the zaddik is the successor of the figure of the biblical prophet as well as an original theopolitical leader. Brody and Hadad both demonstrate the fruitfulness of decentering *I and Thou* when approaching Buber's biblical and Zionist writings and holistically considering the integral relationship between his scholarly religious work and his political commitments. Read together, they significantly advance the understanding of the way Buber challenged hierarchical structures of governance by developing a vision of radical human equality and powerless leadership.

Part three, "Zionism and Binationalism," begins with William Plevan's "Exile and Alienation in Martin Buber's Philosophical Anthropology," which explores Buber's universalization of a Jewish understanding of exile in order to diagnose the spiritual crisis of the modern West. Plevan shows how in Buber's philosophical writing, particularly his 1938 lectures "The Problem of the Human Being" (published as "What Is Man?"), Buber articulated this "Hebrew Humanism" in his critique of the views of exile found in Reform Judaism and political Zionism and in his critique of philosopher Max Scheler's neo-Gnostic views of alienation. In Plevan's analysis, Buber argues that it is a mistake to accept alienation without seeking to transform or overcome it but that this cannot be done through political achievement alone. Continuing to flesh out the holistic vision presented by Brody and Hadad, Plevan presents Buber's claim that what is needed is a third alternative to the dichotomies of the material and the spiritual, the secular and the sacred, and the philosophic and the religious.

Zachary Braiterman's "Martin Buber, Metaphysics, and the Aesthetics of Binationalism" argues that Buber's work is fundamentally theo-aesthetic, not theo-political. This complements Plevan's study of exile and alienation and the relationship between the spiritual and material while providing a different perspective on the political vision studied by Brody and Hadad. Although Buber is often approached through the lens of politics, ethics, and dialogue, Braiterman calls our attention to Buber's long history of visual thinking and emphasis on unity, the perfected image, and *Gestalt*. Buber's Zionism and endorsement of a binational compact between Arabs and Jews in Palestine are best understood, Braiterman argues, as stylized projects shaped by metaphysical and aesthetic desires for unity and a sense of belonging to a sacred landscape. Braiterman weaves together his analysis of Buber with readings of Meron Benvenisti, Tawfik Canaan, Meir Shalev, and Jean-Luc Nancy, ultimately questioning if Buber's aestheticism, complicated relationship to Orientalism, and emphasis on unity are the right way to approach political conflict. Read together, Plevan and Braiterman illuminate Buber's lifelong project to confront the spiritual significance of exile and partition and the vision of unity that underlies his critiques of political responses.

In part four, "Philosophy," three essays reconstruct notorious yet underdeveloped aspects of Buber's philosophical anthropology and dialogic ethics. While Buber has often been lumped in with existentialist thought, all three essays expand Buber's relevance by reading Buber alongside other twentieth- and twenty-first-century philosophers and movements. In "*Chaos, Abgrund,* and *Wirbel*: On Buber's Notion of Ambivalence," Asaf Ziderman develops Buber's philosophy of action, which previous commentators have touched on by employing terms such as *holy insecurity, narrow ridge,* and *demarcation line.* Ziderman points out that these terms were little used by Buber himself and instead identifies three terms Buber did consistently use when talking about the challenge of facing a genuine dilemma: *Chaos, Abgrund* (abyss), and *Wirbel* (vortex or whirlpool). Ziderman unpacks Buber's use of these three metaphors in texts such as "Images of Good and Evil," showing that there is a tension in Buber's writing between negative ambivalence, which is an accelerating downward spiral of self-doubt, and positive ambivalence, in which uncertainty is a virtue. Mapping James Bugental's distinction between sequential and simultaneous states of ambivalence onto Buber's account of ambivalence, Ziderman argues that this tension is resolved when we are able to fully embrace all options simultaneously.

In "The Eloquent Muteness of Creatures: Affect and Animals in Martin Buber's Dialogical Writings," Dustin Atlas explores how human-animal dialogue is possible, what affects are discovered in animal dialogue, and what these affects tell us about dialogue in general. To do this, Atlas uses affect theory (e.g., Sara Ahmed, Brian Massumi, and Charles Sanders Peirce) to illuminate Buber's puzzling and often glossed-over passages on nature and nonhuman animals, such as Buber's description of encountering a tree in *Daniel* and Buber's reflections on learning about dialogue from a cat in *I and Thou*. In Atlas's analysis, these remarks on dialogue with nonhumans are not a mere quirk but clarifications of important features of Buber's philosophical anthropology and philosophy of dialogue, including his insistence that dialogue need not be linguistic and that dialogic relations are permeated by anxiety and melancholy.

In my "Monologue Disguised as Dialogue: Almodóvar's *Talk to Her* and Buber on the 'Lovers' Talk,'" I use Pedro Almodóvar's 2002 film *Talk to Her* to illustrate and explore two often overlooked aspects of Buber's philosophy of dialogue: his use of embodied relations, particularly sexual encounters, to explain dialogue and his claim that much "dialogue" is actually monologue disguised as dialogue. Bringing Buber into relation with contemporary feminism, I argue that Buber's account of dialogue provides a foundation for the communicative model of sexuality proposed by later feminist theorists. I defend this claim by reconstructing Buber's criteria for genuine dialogue, paying special attention to his account of moral imagination and the moral criteria of mutuality versus symmetry. Read together, the final three essays develop a nuanced understanding of Buber's philosophic work by analyzing often ignored metaphors, examples, passages, and texts, demonstrating his continuing philosophic relevance and inviting reflection beyond Buber's thought.

With this collection serving as a guidebook to Buber's thought and different approaches to working with Buber, the reader is invited to move beyond legends, reach across disciplinary boundaries, and reengage with the fundamental problems of relationship he identified. We hope that this encourages wider engagement with Buber's range of works beyond whatever first brought the reader to Buber so that his advice may be heeded: "When we really understand a poem, all we know of the poet is what we learn of him in the poem—no autobiographical wisdom is of value for the pure understanding of what is to be understood: the I which approaches us is the subject of this single poem. But when we read other poems by the poet in the same true way their subjects combine in all their multiplicity, completing and confirming one another, to form the one polyphony of the person's existence." In seeking to understand the depth and complexity of Buber's thought by taking up his various interests together, in their polyphony, we draw on Buber not necessarily as "right" but as a source to sustain us as we rethink religion, politics, language, alienation, and embodied and affective existence. In this renaissance of the major questions and frameworks found in Buber's work, we point the way toward future guiding images of renewed relationship that we as yet only dimly perceive. As Gershom Scholem said at Buber's funeral, "He was a teacher who wanted his pupils not to do as he had done, but to follow their own paths. His pupils were rebels, which was exactly what he wanted."[9]

NOTES

I am grateful to Zachary Braiterman, Gary Dunham, Paul Mendes-Flohr, and the anonymous reviewers for their helpful comments and encouragement.

1. Maurice Friedman, *Martin Buber's Life and Work* (Detroit: Wayne State University Press, 1988), 121. For a more up-to-date biography, see Paul Mendes-Flohr, *Martin Buber: A Life of Faith and Dissent* (New Haven, CT: Yale University Press, 2019).

2. See *Martin Buber: A Bibliography of His Writings 1898–1978*, comp. Margot Cohn and Rafael Buber (Jerusalem: Magnes Press; Munich: K. G. Saur, 1980). See also the German critical text edition of Buber's writings: *Martin Buber Werkausgabe*, ed. Paul Mendes-Flohr, et al. (Gütersloh, Germany: Gütersloher Verlagshaus, 2001–2020), which is already at twenty-one volumes.

3. Hannah Arendt, "A Guide for Youth: Martin Buber," in *The Jewish Writings*, ed. Jerome Kohn and Ron. H. Feldman (New York: Schocken, 2007), 31.

4. Martin Buber, "Replies to My Critics," in *The Philosophy of Martin Buber*, ed. Paul Arthur Schilpp and Maurice Friedman (La Salle, IL: Open Court, 1967), 693.

5. "Dialogue in the Twenty-First Century: A Martin Buber Memorial Conference," April 23, 2015, Center for Ethics, Manhattan College, Riverdale,

New York. Chapters 2, 4, 6, 7, 8, and 10 are revisions of papers given at the conference. Chapters 3, 5, and 9 were solicited after the conference. I thank Manhattan College for the financial support and my colleagues for the logistical and moral support for the conference.

6. Orli Fridman, Twitter, July 30, 2015, 6:06 a.m., https://twitter.com/orlifridman/status/626695397973622786.

7. Martin Buber, "Interrogation of Martin Buber," conducted by M. S. Friedman, in *Philosophic Interrogations*, ed. S. Rome and B. Rome (New York: Holt, Rinehart and Winston, 1964), 28. I give a brief analysis of the moral significance of this story in Sarah Scott, "From Genius to Taste: Martin Buber's Aestheticism," *Journal of Jewish Thought and Philosophy* 25, no. 1 (2017): 110–30.

8. For Buber's call for a "Jewish Renaissance," see Martin Buber, *The First Buber: Youthful Zionist Writings of Martin Buber*, ed. and trans. Gilya G. Schmidt (Syracuse, NY: Syracuse University Press, 1999). Adjacent to these early writings, Buber completed a dissertation on the Renaissance philosophers Nicholas of Cusa and Jakob Böhme and planned to pursue advanced study of Renaissance art history. For an analysis of his use of Nicholas of Cusa, see Sarah Scott, "Knowing Otherness: Martin Buber's Appropriation of Nicholas of Cusa," *International Philosophical Quarterly* 55, no. 4 (2015): 399–416. On the notion of "renaissance," see Asher D. Biemann, *Inventing New Beginnings: On the Idea of Renaissance in Modern Judaism* (Stanford CA: Stanford University Press, 2009).

9. Gershom Scholem, quoted in Aubrey Hodes, *Martin Buber: An Intimate Portrait* (New York: Viking Press, 1971), 222.

PART I

RELIGIOUS DIALOGUE

TWO

MARTIN BUBER AND CATHOLIC-ATHEIST DIALOGUE

PETER A. HUFF

THE ANNIVERSARY OF THE CATHOLIC Church's Second Vatican Council (1962–65) sparked a new and intense season of reflection on the meaning of the council and its legacy. The council, which brought some 2,500 Catholic bishops to Rome during four consecutive autumn sessions, has often been described as "the most important religious event in the twentieth century."[1] It was certainly the most important event in the modern history of the Catholic Church and arguably the most important event in Western Christian experience since the Reformation. Vatican II's allegedly primary objective of *aggiornamento* (popularly understood as updating or modernizing) commanded world attention during the years of the council and has consistently driven debates about the council and the implementation of its mandates for nearly six decades.

One major reason for Vatican II's significance is its unparalleled emphasis on the place of dialogue in the Catholic worldview and the Catholic way of life. As a premier historian of the council has put it, "No single word, with the possible exception of *aggiornamento*, would be more often invoked to indicate what the council was all about."[2] New studies of the council highlight the centrality of dialogue in conciliar literature and in the memories of council participants.[3] The bishops' call to dialogue with Orthodox and Protestant Christians, with Jews, and with members of all the world's religious creeds and communities fired the imagination of the Vatican II generation of Catholics, both clerical and lay. Had the council not happened, the massive enterprise of Catholic-sponsored events, organizations, and initiatives currently shaping the international interfaith and intercultural dialogue scene would be unimaginable. The institutionalization of dialogue in the Vatican's bureaucracy (in dicasteries, or departments, such as the Pontifical Council for Christian Unity, the

Commission for Religious Relations with the Jews, and the Pontifical Council for Interreligious Dialogue); the continual proliferation of Vatican documents on dialogue (such as the 2015 publication "The Gifts and the Calling of God Are Irrevocable" on Catholic-Jewish relations); and the historic gatherings of world religious leaders in Assisi, organized by the church's papal office in 1986, 2002, 2011, 2016, and 2020, powerfully confirm the perception of dialogue as a core and indispensable component of the Vatican II heritage.[4]

On its own, the council's document *Nostra Aetate* embodied the church's new dialogic impulse and represented a sea change in Catholic views of and interactions with other traditions, especially the Jewish tradition.[5] As Yaakov Ariel has put it, the revolutionary Vatican text "signaled a new chapter in interfaith relations in general and a breakthrough in Christian-Jewish relations in particular."[6] The declaration repudiated stock features of Christian anti-Judaism, such as the charge of deicide and the theology of supersessionism, long imagining Judaism as obsolete in light of Christian revelation. It also opened the door to a postmissionary concept of Catholicism and stimulated cautious optimism among Jewish observers around the world. Activist Rabbi Marc Tanenbaum, a witness to and catalyst in the transformation of Catholic-Jewish understanding at the time, summed up many Jewish responses to *Nostra Aetate* and the council in his 1966 lecture at the University of Notre Dame: "Vatican II: An Interfaith Appreciation: A Jewish Viewpoint." The Catholic Church, he said, "took a great and historic leap forward in ... affirming on the highest levels of its teaching authority the indebtedness of Christianity and the Christians to Judaism and the Jewish people, the rejection of anti-Semitism, and all unprecedented calls for fraternal dialogue between Christians and Jews."[7] Today, despite setbacks and missteps, post–Vatican II Catholic-Jewish dialogue is one of the success stories in global interreligious engagement.

Another landmark document from the Second Vatican Council, *Gaudium et Spes*, the Pastoral Constitution on the Church in the Modern World, called for "honest and prudent dialogue" between Catholics and a group or population in modern society previously overlooked in ecumenical and interfaith dialogue circles: unbelievers.[8] Pope Paul VI, who after the death of the convener Pope John XXIII shepherded the council from 1963 to its conclusion, personally endorsed dialogue with atheists in his midcouncil encyclical *Ecclesiam Suam* (1964). Well known before the council for his support for dialogue with communists and after his papal election for promotion of *Ostpolitik* détente with nations in the Soviet bloc, Paul took practical steps to make Catholic-atheist dialogue a reality. He established an unprecedented Vatican department to oversee the extraordinary exchange between Catholics and unbelievers (the now-defunct *Secretaria Pro Non Credentibus*) and commissioned the Society of Jesus to make examination of and engagement with atheism high priorities for the Jesuit order's intellectual apostolate. In various ways, the post–Vatican II popes—John Paul II, Benedict XVI, and Francis—have also acknowledged the urgent need to address the existence of and concerns of a growing global atheist community. Pope Francis's news-making "Letter to a Non-Believer" (2013), seeking "a dialogue that is open and free of preconceptions," represents the current status of this arm of Catholic outreach, only ratified by scores of subsequent public statements from the pope, including his 2020 encyclical *Fratelli Tutti*, which he describes as an invitation to dialogue without borders.[9] Still, ecumenical affairs with other Christians and interreligious ventures with believers in traditions outside of Christianity largely define the Catholic commitment to dialogue. Nearly sixty years after the world-changing council, Catholic-atheist dialogue remains a conspicuous part of Vatican II's unfinished agenda.

In this chapter, I will attempt to make the case that Martin Buber, often identified as one of the Jewish "fathers" of Vatican II, may serve as the unofficial patron of this long-deferred dialogue. Based on a close reading of his private and published writings, especially *I and Thou* and articles and speeches in volumes such as *Eclipse of God* and *Between Man and Man*, this essay seeks to argue for both Buber's originality and his enduring relevance in what Pope Francis has dubbed not an "age of change" but a historic moment defined by an unprecedented "change of age."[10] Given his uniquely privileged place in Catholic thought, his undogmatic appreciation of the varieties and value of modern atheism, and his matchless record in Jewish-Christian dialogue and Arab-Israeli dialogue, Buber is uniquely qualified to serve as a guiding spirit for what may be the next great challenge facing the Catholic Church in world history: an authentic Catholic quest for dialogue (and at times even partnership) with unbelievers in what many are calling the age of atheism.[11]

I. PERSPECTIVE AND APPRECIATION

By way of preface, I "must speak of myself," as Buber himself famously said in his "History of the Dialogical Principle."[12] In other words, I must expose something of my perspective and my appreciation for the life and thought of Buber. I write as a Catholic theologian dedicated to the apostolate of ecumenical and interreligious dialogue—the kind of dialogue that, in the words of Pope John Paul II, functions as a "path toward the kingdom."[13] I have not always been a Catholic or a proponent or practitioner of dialogue, though. Raised in the evangelical subculture of the American South, I knew nothing about Catholic popes, Jewish philosophers, or honest unbelievers for many years. Needless to say, during the churchgoing years of my childhood and youth, dialogue never surfaced as a significant theme in my spiritual experience or a familiar term in my theological vocabulary.

An undergraduate encounter with Buber via the work of Princeton philosopher Malcolm Diamond changed all that. Diamond's *Contemporary Philosophy and Religious Thought* was the first serious piece of academic philosophy I ever read, and his chapter entitled "Martin Buber: On Meeting God" was nothing less than a vehicle of revelation for me. Malcolm quoted Martin, and the voice of Buber spoke to me like an intelligence from another dimension: "'To be sure,' Buber writes, 'whoever knows God also knows God's remoteness and the agony of drought upon a frightened heart, but not the loss of presence.'"[14] Acquainted at the time with little more than devotional literature and Billy Graham tracts, I was profoundly struck by the new voice and compelling message.

By the late 1970s, I had joined the ranks of those malaise-ridden young people who, as Walter Kaufmann put it, went about clasping *I and Thou* "to their bosoms."[15] I even carried my paperback copy of the Kaufmann translation of *I and Thou* on a senior-year trip to Israel. But since I grew up among a peculiar people who did indeed "know the verb forms Thou commands" (thanks to immersion in the semantic world of the King James Bible and Protestant hymnody), I have never shared Kaufmann's pronominal phobia.[16] A brilliant philosopher, translator, and writer, Kaufmann was nevertheless wrong to dismiss University of Glasgow professor Ronald Gregor Smith (1913–1968), translator of not only *Ich und Du* but also the essays in *Between Man and Man* and author of one of the first critical introductions to Buber's thought in English, as simply "the clergyman"—in effect banishing the equally brilliant Christian theologian, not two years after his death, to the unwelcome netherworld of "It."[17] *Thou* is much more than "a preachers' word."[18] Arguably every continued use of the word, in the shrinking linguistic zone shared by Buber, Shakespeare, the Book of Common Prayer, the Book of Mormon, and a Quaker meeting here or there, ought to make us marvel at the losses suffered by the English language in the last half millennium.[19]

For me, as for many readers, I suspect, the meeting with Buber represented entrance into an unexpected new world, a world that demanded confrontation with the limitations of my experience and called me to explore new horizons far beyond my creed and ken. I was intrigued by Buber's attraction to his "great brother" Jesus, unsettled by his "unwished-for God," enthralled by the "eternal *Thou* with many names," and convicted by his prophetic judgment on religion heedless of the everyday.[20] His leitmotifs of "holy insecurity," "fearful grace," and the person "endangered before God" stirred mixed emotions of awe and anxiety.[21] More importantly, Buber served as my initial escort into (for me) uncharted realms of living Jewish tradition and Jewish-Christian relations. After Buber, I could no longer endorse the tragically skewed arithmetic of the Sunday school classroom and the uninformed Christian pulpit: "Judaism = Christianity − Jesus." One of the greatest lessons I have learned from Buber is that neither God nor Judaism—nor atheism, for that matter—can be found "by subtraction."[22]

II. BUBER AND CHRISTIAN THOUGHT

In any event, my experience cannot be that unusual. It shows in microcosm what had been and still is happening in macrocosm. Untold numbers of Christians have been transformed by Buber's insights into the biblical message and the dynamics of faith, not to mention the mystery of the human person and humanity's capacity for transcendence. Buber's contribution to a multi-faceted and far-reaching theology of dialogue has been enormous and well documented. His extraordinary impact on specifically Christian theologies of dialogue, acknowledged by virtually every historian of the last one hundred years of Christian intellectual endeavor, is beyond question and almost beyond measure.[23] What Anglican divine John Macquarrie once called the "remarkable debt" owed to Buber by Christianity becomes quite evident when we survey the full sweep of the contemporary Christian theological project, from neoclassical pillars such as Karl Barth and Emil Brunner to their late modern disciples and their feminist, liberation, and postmodern critics.[24] Paul Tillich's assessment of "what Protestant theology has received and should receive" from Buber—his verdict was "much"—captured the theological consensus at midtwentieth-century. The appearance of his article on "Martin Buber and Christian Thought" in the journal *Commentary*, inaugurated by the American Jewish Committee in 1945, itself did much to advance what he called "the 'I-Thou' encounter of Judaism and Christianity."[25] In *The Self and the Dramas of History* (1955), Tillich's colleague Reinhold Niebuhr had already argued that Buber perceived the true nature of historical experience "more acutely than any Christian theologian."[26] Martin Luther King's references to Buber in "Letter from Birmingham Jail" (1963) and *Why We Can't Wait* (1964), aiming at a broader audience, forcefully demonstrated Buber's significance for mainstream Christianity and his relevance for its social challenges and causes.[27]

By the 1960s, a joke was circulating in certain Protestant sectors naming Buber one of the most influential "Christian" theologians of the day.[28] He was the sole Jewish thinker represented in the highly acclaimed Makers of the Modern Theological Mind series published in the 1970s by the Baptist firm Word Books. Today, another Alfred North Whitehead (who spoke memorably of Plato) or another Jaroslav Pelikan (who detected the long arm of Augustine in Western religious life) could fittingly describe the Christian theological conversation from the Great War to the twenty-first century as a "series of footnotes" to Martin Buber. More than once Buber has been portrayed as "the foremost Jewish teacher of Christians."[29] Karen Armstrong echoed a sentiment shared by many when she said Buber "has been more popular with Christians than with Jews."[30] The uncontended position of Buber in a standard textbook within today's mainstream Protestant educational establishment—Alister McGrath's *Christian Theology* (now in its twenty-fifth anniversary and sixth edition)—provides some indication of Buber's permanent place in the Christian canon.[31]

Buber's impact on Roman Catholic approaches to dialogue has been particularly profound. The prolific Swiss theologian Hans Urs von Balthasar, who once named Buber one of the "founding fathers of our age," ensured that Buber and responses to Buber would become permanent features of mainstream Catholic theological experience for many years.[32] Numerous commentators have seen Balthasar's *Einsame Zweisprache: Martin Buber und das Christentum* (1958), an expanded version of arguments presented in "Martin Buber und das Christentum" (1957), as a milestone in Catholic intellectual culture and one of the principal catalysts for the Catholic Church's reassessment of its relationship with Judaism and the Jewish people after the Second World War.[33] Trappist monk and spiritual writer Thomas Merton, responsible for so much of the vitality in Catholicism's culture of dialogue, referred to Buber's insights as "among the wisest religious truths written in our century."[34]

A Buber-inspired aspiration for dialogue remains a keynote of contemporary Catholic intellectual life at all levels, including the highest ranks of magisterial teaching. Buber was part of a trinity of Jewish thinkers, including historian Jules Isaacs and theologian Abraham Joshua Heschel, who contributed to the Second Vatican Council's discernment of its world-historical vocation.[35] Ann Michele Nolan's important analysis of dialogue in the documents of Vatican II begins—on the very first page—with a discussion of the impact of *I and Thou*.[36] Though he declined the invitation to meet in private audience with Pope John XXIII, the convener of Vatican II, Buber helped make "dialogue with the world and with people of every persuasion" one of the principal themes of the church's unforgettable twenty-first ecumenical council.[37]

Echoes of Buber reverberate throughout at least six of Vatican II's sixteen official documents—all of them among the most significant produced by the gathering of bishops: the decree on Christian unity (*Unitatis Redintegratio*), the declaration on religious freedom (*Dignitatis Humanae*), the declaration on the church and other world religions (*Nostra Aetate*), and the major constitutions on the church (*Lumen Gentium*), on divine revelation (*Dei Verbum*), and on the church's interface with modernity (*Gaudium et Spes*). Arguably, the declaration on Catholicism and world religions (*Nostra Aetate*)—what John Paul II referred to as "the Magna Carta of interreligious dialogue for our times"[38]—reveals the greatest extent of Buber's influence on the conciliar generation of Catholic leadership. For the first time in history, largely thanks to Buber, Catholic authorities in solemn assembly identified dialogue—along with worship, education, service, and evangelization—as an essential task at the heart of the church's mission in the modern world. From that moment on, it has been an uncontestable point of magisterial teaching that dialogue is not a preference or an option contingent on mood or any other nontheological factor such as social status, educational level, or political bent. Respectful "dialogue with other religions, with philosophy and science, as well as with unbelievers and atheists," as the post–Vatican II *Catechism of the Catholic Church* plainly states, is an integral part of the fabric of Catholic moral obligation.[39] As Pope Francis has made clear, dialogue is a "duty."[40] His declaration of the Extraordinary Jubilee of Mercy (2015–16) included a clarion call for "even more fervent dialogue so that we might know and understand one another better ... eliminate every form of closed-mindedness and disrespect, and drive out every form of violence and discrimination."[41]

Accordingly, Martin Buber occupies a singular place in papal discourse. Popes John Paul II and Benedict XVI each testified to Buber's influential role in the formation of their respective theological visions and spiritual orientations. John Paul, whose personalism was influenced by Edmund Husserl, Max Scheler, and Emmanuel Levinas, regularly highlighted Buber's significance in the catechetical messages delivered at his general audiences and in his publications for a popular audience, such as the best-selling *Crossing the Threshold of Hope* (1994).[42] Pope Benedict's major books and essays represent a career-long dialogue with the Jewish thinker—the figure who, as Benedict confessed in his autobiography, left an "essential mark" on the trajectory of his spiritual outlook.[43]

Pope Francis—a student of Buber admirer Romano Guardini (1885–1968), the German priest-philosopher who received both the Peace Prize of the German Book Trade and the Erasmus Prize prior to Buber—has granted Buber even greater status in Catholic thought and church teaching.⁴⁴ Francis cited Buber specifically in *Lumen Fidei* (2013), his first encyclical, the so-called four-handed document written in collaboration with Pope Emeritus Benedict.⁴⁵ Francis also invoked Buber's most recognizable contribution to intellectual culture in *Laudato Si'* (2015), the pope's second (and first solo) encyclical on the topic of the environmental crisis and the need for a global "ecological conversion."⁴⁶

Two passages from *Laudato Si'* demonstrate the extent to which Buber's thought patterns have been absorbed into papal discourse, receiving what amounts to an unprecedented (and unofficial) pontifical *imprimatur*—so much so that they may be employed virtually as code for an identifiable philosophical point of view without the necessity of commentary, defense, or, at times, even citation. The first passage appears in the context of Francis's affirmation of the uniqueness of the human being, even, as he says, "if we postulate a process of evolution":

> Each of us has his or her own personal identity and is capable of entering into dialogue with others and with God himself. Our capacity to reason, to develop arguments, to be inventive, to interpret reality and to create art, along with other not yet discovered capacities, are signs of a uniqueness which transcends the spheres of physics and biology. The sheer novelty involved in the emergence of a personal being within a material universe presupposes a direct action of God and a particular call to life and to relationship on the part of a "Thou" who addresses himself to another "thou."⁴⁷

The second passage strikes a comparable theme in the context of Francis's critique of "misguided anthropocentrism": "Christian thought sees human beings as possessing a particular dignity above other creatures; it thus inculcates esteem for each person and respect for others. Our openness to others, each of whom is a 'thou' capable of knowing, loving and entering into dialogue, remains the source of our nobility as human persons. A correct relationship with the created world demands that we not weaken this social dimension of openness to others, much less the transcendent dimension of our openness to the 'Thou' of God."⁴⁸ Buber's colleague Rabbi Heschel was the first living Jewish scholar to appear by name in an official papal document. During the 1970s, Paul VI, great humanist and ecumenical pioneer in his own right, made reference to Heschel several times in his public addresses and formal audiences.⁴⁹ Martin Buber is the first nonbiblical Jewish writer ever mentioned in an encyclical letter, the most authoritative sort of text produced by the Catholic Church's supreme pastoral office.⁵⁰

III. CATHOLICISM AND ATHEISM

Within the texts of official Catholic documents, then, especially within the publications of the Second Vatican Council, Buber and the Catholic imagination meet in creative and history-making encounter. The conciliar texts represent much more than the inauguration of a new chastened, self-aware, and relatively optimistic Catholic reengagement with Jewish tradition and the Jewish people. Jewish intellectual life, itself shaped significantly by Buber, now plays an equally active role in the development of Catholic thought and spirituality. As Harold Kasimow and John Merkle have stated, the deep reevaluation of Catholic-Jewish relations inaugurated at and signified by Vatican II "has fostered renewal of Catholic life and theology based on, among other things, a newfound appreciation of the Hebrew Bible, the Jewishness of Jesus and his ministry, and Jewish approaches to God, covenantal life with God, the relationship of the physical and spiritual dimensions of life, and redemption in and of this world."[51]

Perhaps even more astonishingly, an implicit trialogue occurs within the structure of the Vatican II texts, for atheist perspectives are given significant breathing room in the intellectual cosmos of Catholic teaching, too. There is nothing new about this state of affairs. In the thirteenth century, Saint Thomas Aquinas advanced as many arguments against theism as for it. In contrast to the long prejudice against the Bible's most famous "fool" (Pss. 14 and 53, RSV), Thomas begins his "five ways" in the *Summa Theologica* with an unexpected level of respect for the intuitive genesis of unbelief: "It seems that God does not exist."[52] As Malcolm Diamond reminds us, "apologetic theologians, such as Aquinas, address the nonbelievers as well as the faithful."[53] Within Catholic thought at its best, apologetically oriented from the earliest centuries, we often find a curious empathy for atheist observations and objections. Like Buber, the "young Nietzsche" appears in Francis's *Lumen Fidei* and not just as a foil or straw person—certainly another "first" in papal literature.[54] Unbelief is a built-in component of the contemporary Catholic theological horizon.

Interconnected themes in the Christian worldview such as biblical iconoclasm, apophatic mysticism, and the tropes of *deus absconditus* (the hidden God), *agnosto theo* (the unknown God), and the "dark night of the soul" have fueled a widespread scholarly quest for not only the historical and cultural relationship between Christianity and atheism but what we might call the deep chemical or cellular relationships that tie the two realities together as well. Ernst Bloch and Hans Urs Von Balthasar, independent of each other, each spoke provocatively of "atheism in Christianity."[55] More recently, at least two generations of historians, arguing for the inescapably modern credentials of atheism, have set forth multiple claims for the roots of modern unbelief in theology itself. Jesuit scholar Michael Buckley in his erudite *At the Origins of Modern Atheism* (1987) and *Denying and Disclosing God* (2004), Gavin Hyman in *A Short History of Atheism* (2010), and Dominic Erdozain in *The Soul of Doubt: The Religious Roots of Unbelief from Luther to Marx* (2016) have advanced what is perhaps the most arresting thesis: the specifically Christian sources of atheism.[56]

A parallel question, raised only occasionally by sentiments such as composer Ralph Vaughn Williams's remark about a "good mass" written by an atheist, reminds us that the true story of Christianity's multimillennial career will always remain elusive and ultimately incomprehensible if atheist contributions to Christian life and thought—including, but not limited to, the fields of music, art, architecture, literature, and philosophy—are never fully recognized or honestly accounted for.[57] At the very least, one has to admit the possibility of cross pollination, if not outright genetic kinship. Ancient Rome's depiction of the early Christians as *atheoi*, mirroring Saint Paul's portrayal of Hellenistic pagans (see Ephesians 2:12), may be much more than an ironic first-century case of mistaken identity. The correlation between Christianity and the increasingly "catholic" impulse of atheism in today's global culture is one of the most underinvestigated topics in theological studies—a topic of great relevance for the integrity and coherence of the discipline and the self-identity of its contemporary practitioners.[58]

A remarkable passage from the work of German theologian Joseph Ratzinger (later Pope Benedict XVI) illustrates this fascinating and unexpected convergence within Catholic thought. In a section of his classic *Introduction to Christianity* (German original, 1968), just before he relates a "Jewish story told by Martin Buber," Ratzinger offers a breathtakingly frank assessment of the interpenetration of belief and unbelief in the contemporary mind, one that merits full citation here:

> If, on the one hand, the believer can perfect his faith only on the ocean of nihilism, temptation, and doubt, if he has been assigned the ocean of uncertainty as the only possible site for his faith, on the other hand, the unbeliever is not to be understood undialectically as a mere man without faith. Just as we have already recognized that the believer does not live immune to doubt but is always threatened by the plunge into the void, so now we can discern the entangled nature of human destinies and say that the nonbeliever does not lead a sealed-off, self-sufficient life, either. However vigorously he may assert that he is a pure positivist, who has long left behind

him supernatural temptations and weaknesses and now accepts only what is immediately certain, he will never be free of the secret uncertainty about whether positivism really has the last word. Just as the believer is choked by the salt water of doubt constantly washed into his mouth by the ocean of uncertainty, so the nonbeliever is troubled by doubts about his unbelief, about the real totality of the world he has made up his mind to explain as a self-contained whole. He can never be absolutely certain of the autonomy of what he has seen and interpreted as a whole; he remains threatened by the question of whether belief is not after all the reality it claims to be. Just as the believer knows himself to be constantly threatened by unbelief, which he must experience as a continual temptation, so for the unbeliever faith remains a temptation and a threat to his apparently permanently closed world. In short, there is no escape from the dilemma of being a man. Anyone who makes up his mind to evade the uncertainty of belief will have to experience the uncertainty of unbelief, which can never finally eliminate for certain the possibility that belief may after all be the truth.[59]

To a significant extent, this state of affairs is observable in the experience of Vatican II itself. We distort the meaning of the historical Vatican II when we read the council phenomenon (both its alleged "spirit" and its so-called "letter") solely through the lens of the conciliar theme of *aggiornamento*, couching the council event and its much storied aftermath exclusively and uncritically in the context of a midcentury modern narrative of inevitable liberalization and progress. We cannot forget that one of the most significant features of the Second Vatican Council was its appearance during the era of the death of God. Vatican II was the first council to reckon seriously with modern unbelief. Never before had the denial or rejection of God been so widespread and seemingly so normal. Other councils have contended with competing faiths. Vatican II was the first to face squarely the reality of no faith.[60]

Vatican II's *Gaudium et Spes*, calling for dialogue with unbelievers, identified atheism as "one of the most serious of contemporary phenomena," meriting "close consideration."[61] Today, record-breaking demographic changes argue for the relevance of new ventures in Catholic-atheist dialogue. In the last century and a half, atheism has become an increasingly prominent force in a world where once it was only an eccentric, or even hypothetical, frame of mind. According to Stephen Bullivant, a leading figure in Christian-atheist dialogue, "Atheism today is a large, pervasive, growing and—by now—perfectly 'ordinary' feature of a great many societies."[62] Recent studies show that anywhere from a quarter to a third of all American young people self-describe as atheist or agnostic or religiously unaffiliated, and some estimates place the global atheist population close to one billion.[63] These new developments signal something of an "atheist moment" in contemporary experience. Though the number of atheists worldwide may have been higher during the time of Vatican II, when state-mandated atheism held sway, virtually all of today's atheism is voluntary—and, since based on greater intellectual conviction, arguably of much greater consequence. In such a context, Catholics face an auspicious opportunity to implement the directives of Vatican II and initiate a dialogue that is truly "catholic" in scope and spirit.

IV. BUBER AND ATHEISM

Here Buber's relevance emerges in full relief and with full force. His advancement of the perennial debate on the existence of God shaped an entire period in philosophy and theology and continues to challenge uncritical views of atheism, antitheism, nontheism, agnosticism, and nonreligion in all their variety and fertility. Tillich spoke of Buber's positive contribution to Christian theology as threefold: his "existential interpretation of prophetic religion, his rediscovery of mysticism as an element within prophetic religion, and his understanding of the relation between prophetic religion and culture."[64] In a similar vein, we can identify at least three ways in which Buber has significantly enhanced our understanding of atheism, not just its ideas, but also its fundamental ideals and identity.

First, Buber understood atheism in world-historical terms. His recognition of the "eclipse of God" as a distinctive sign of the era scarred by global war, genocide, and the "gigantically swollen" I-It relation provides a useful vantage point for critical investigation into the multiple forces generating and informing ever new strains of doubt and disbelief.[65] The essays united under the title *Eclipse of God* (1952), based largely on Buber's lectures in the United States during the academic year 1951–52, reveal a philosophical project sensitive to not only the distinctive forms of belief and unbelief constitutive of modern life but their interlocking natures, migrations, and destinies as well. Just as the bishops of Vatican II would later acknowledge that atheism "covers a range of things," that it is "the result of a variety of causes," and that believers, especially Christian believers, bear "no small part" of the responsibility for its genesis and growth, Buber respected the diverse species of disbelief and attempted critically to come to terms with their intricately overdetermined quality.[66] Focusing on figures dominant in the intellectual debates of his time, he differentiated between Jean-Paul Sartre's protest atheism and rival "materialistic" styles of unbelief, distinguished Albert Camus's strategic iconoclasm from dogmatic antitheism, and identified Carl Jung's psychological "gnosticism" as "the real antagonist of the reality of faith."[67] Often overlooked is the fact that Buber places both theist and atheist in the same existential position, each experiencing in his or her own way a felt attenuation of the sense of transcendence and each somehow at least partially culpable for the seemingly universal phenomenon: "Eclipse of the light of heaven, eclipse of God—such indeed is the character of the historic hour through which the world is passing."[68] According to Buber, the theist today enjoys no discernable advantage over the atheist: "For one who believes in the living God, who knows about Him, and is fated to spend his life in a time of His hiddenness, it is very difficult to live."[69] Confrontation with the horror and mystery of the Shoah, Buber was convinced, especially exposes the vulnerability of belief: "How is a life with God still possible in a time in which there is an Oswiecim? The estrangement has become too cruel, the hiddenness too deep. One can still 'believe' in the God who allowed those things to happen, but can one still speak to Him? Can one still hear His word? Can one still . . . enter at all into a dialogic relationship with Him? . . . Dare we recommend to . . . the Job of the gas chambers: 'Call to Him, for He is kind, for His mercy endureth forever'?"[70]

Second, Buber saw atheism as a distinctively modern mode of spiritual existence, not the antagonist or antithesis of religious faith but a startling new way to pursue humanity's age-old spiritual vocation. He was among the first observers in Western culture to perceive the deeply spiritual and at times even mystical potency driving modern unbelief. Doubt, he said, is a function of the life of faith, "almost part of the genuine privilege of believing," "one of the most important factors in the development of faith."[71] And prayer, he admitted, is "so difficult" for citizens of the present-day secular city.[72] Atheism itself, then, can be a prelude to an encounter with or a rediscovery of the living God. Buber's grasp of the prophetic and even purifying dimension of humanist atheisms and his deep insight into unbelief as an uncommon type of nonreligious rite of devotion point to a remarkable mind willing to take seriously the modern atheist imagination and understand it principally in terms of experience. Drawing obliquely from the long legacy of reflection on Paul's improvised *agnosto theo* sermon at the Areopagus in Athens (recorded in Acts 17:22–34), discerning previously untapped continuity between biblical faith and pagan cult (reminiscent of the ancient Israelite encounter with "holy pagans"), Buber discovered within at least certain expressions of atheism instincts and aspirations that approximated the quest for holiness and the mystery of prayer itself.[73] "Critical 'atheism' (*Atheoi* is the name which the Greeks gave to those who denied the traditional gods) is the prayer which is spoken in the third person in the form of speech about an idea. It is the prayer of the philosopher to the again unknown God. It is well suited to arouse religious men and to impel them to set forth right across the God-deprived reality to a new meeting."[74]

Third, Buber detected in modern atheism a radically new way to enforce or at least raise awareness about the ancient taboo against profanation of "the name of the LORD your God" (Exod. 20:7, JPS). In a unique modification of the classical Talmudic impulse, he interpreted the atheist critique as a protective hedge about genuine theism, baring the shortcomings of ineffective and dehumanizing models of God and clearing the ground for a fresh openness to revelation. He also consistently rejected inordinately intellectualist and third-person views of both the affirmation of God and the denial of God, abandoning all efforts to prove (and disprove) the existence of God and repudiating all but dialectical speech about the sacred.[75] Whether or not he sought to create a "humanistic religion," as Kaufmann claimed, or promote a "religious secularism," as Donald Moore has maintained, Buber's judgment of what he called "theomania" as the ultimate convergence of idolatry and authentic atheism (not placed in inverted commas) calls into question the routine God-talk of both traditional piety and the theological establishment—the use of "God," as he said, as a "sublime convention of the cultured person."[76] As he put it so memorably in *I and Thou*, whoever relegates God to "It"—"and not the 'atheist' [again, inverted commas] who from the night and longing of his garret window addresses the nameless"—is the truly "godless" person.[77] Historically Christian tradition has tended to categorize atheism *sub ratione dei* as either cognitive error or volitional revolt. In contrast to fideist and rationalist responses to atheisms old and new, Buber's approach offers an empathetic and richly nuanced assessment of atheist experience ideally suited to fulfill Vatican II's dream of a dialogue reaching far beyond the boundaries of belief.

V. BUBER AND THE PROBLEM OF GOD

Another triad, this time rooted in Buber's personal experience, discloses the deep sources of these original and distinctive insights. As all his biographers have testified, Buber tended to view his life episodically. From his perspective, watershed moments—some "mismeetings" (*Vergegnungen*), others moments of conversion—profoundly influenced the course and contours of his life.[78] In the rich tapestry of his life, he isolates symbolic turning points such as a boyhood encounter with an older girl who bluntly informed him his absent mother would never return, a poignant encounter with a "broad dapple-gray horse" when he was first struck by the evanescence of the I-Thou relation, an unforgettable wartime meeting with an unknown young man who later perished at the front, and the brutal murder of his friend and colleague Gustav Landauer, socialist, anarchist, mystic, and nonviolent pioneer.[79] Three additional episodes in Buber's life, self-narrated sometimes more than once in his letters and the autobiographical sections of his published works, especially capture his evolving sensitivity to the problem of God and the virtual necessity of atheism of one sort or another in the context of modern life.

The first notable episode is his encounter with the Anglican minister and missionary William H. Hechler (1845–1931), Christian Zionist and associate of the father of modern Zionism, Theodor Herzl.[80] Hechler visited Buber in Berlin before the outbreak of the First World War, seeking to win support for his proto-fundamentalist reading of biblical prophecy, especially the book of Daniel and its alleged prediction of modern global catastrophe. His point-blank question to Buber—"Tell me: Do you believe in God?"—thrust Buber into a crisis of conscience. Buber's response, fully constructed only after the departure of his eccentric guest, inaugurated a lifelong project of reflection on the hubris often present at the core of conventional belief and the chastened sense of reverence frequently fueling expressions of unplanned and sometimes uncontrollable unbelief. "If to believe in God," Buber said to himself, "means to be able to talk *about* him in the third person, then, I do *not* believe in God. But if to believe in him means to be able to talk *to* him, then I do believe in God."[81]

Buber's wrestling with Hechler's challenge amounted to an unexpected personal recalibration of one of the most radical and surprising insights at the heart of biblical monotheism. At its core, Buber discovered, genuine theism inescapably contains an undeniable germ of atheism, the unique strain of unbelief that drove ancient Israel's prophets to critique both the "alien deities" of the surrounding cultures and false notions of the self-revealing and self-concealing "living God" operative in the Hebrew mind (and, as we have suggested, the comparable impulse that inspired Roman pundits to christen upstart apostles and apologists as atheists).[82] This realization entails more, though, than just the recognition of the dialectical nature of belief and unbelief—that belief in something necessarily depends on denial of something else, that every conversion is also by definition a deconversion or negative metanoia fleeing an outworn creed or failed god. Israel's invisible and celibate (if not asexual) God, whose name is shrouded in mystery and whose Holy of Holies is best known for its kataphatic emptiness, stumped the imagination of ancient civilizations, not because those peoples were religiously impoverished, but precisely because they were "extremely religious" (Acts 17:22, NRSV). From one perspective, Israel's lone, transcendent, and virtually unimaginable YHVH bears a striking resemblance to a nonexistent God. Mathematically, the number one seems a giant leap away from zero. Theologically, or rather experientially, what has perennially haunted the monotheist is the short distance from one God to none. As William Hamilton put it on the eve of the death of God controversy some sixty years ago, "It is a very short step, but a critical one, to move from the otherness of God to the absence of God."[83]

The "Jewish story told by Martin Buber" that would later so fascinate future pope Joseph Ratzinger explores this very point. It narrates an exchange between an "adherent of the Enlightenment" and Rabbi Levi Yitschak of Berditchev (1740–1809), one iteration of the classic faith-doubt contest that has assumed innumerable forms in modern experience and almost functions as a definition of the essence of modernity itself. Only in Buber's story, however, the rabbi puts forth no arguments in reply to the scholar's attacks on old-fashioned truth claims. He finds it futile to "lay God and His kingdom on the table" and chooses to bring the one-sided debate to a sudden conclusion with the statement: "But think, my son, perhaps it is true after all." This "terrible 'perhaps,'" Buber submits, could after all be faith's only even moderately effective response to the near dogmatic skepticism of modernity.[84] Buber's acquaintance with real-life atheism (including the unbelief of colleagues and members of his own family), however, suggests that he also knew very well that this "terrible 'perhaps'" could work both ways. Outside the realm of traditional myth and legend, faith and doubt live in unpredictable symbiosis, and neither seems to have the final word.

The second event in Buber's life moving him toward a reassessment of atheism, narrated in the "Prelude" to *Eclipse of God*, involved a late-night conversation with a relatively inarticulate factory worker—the "man with the shepherd's face," as Buber described him—who after much hesitation proposed a theory of naturalism of the popular and uncritical sort, parroting with great solemnity Laplace's legendary dismissal of the God-hypothesis. According to his own account, Buber proceeded to "shatter the security" of the man's naively empiricist *Weltanschauung* but stopped short in the process, aghast as he realized he was ushering the now virtually brow-beaten blue-collar listener to a narrow and lifeless theism. The workman capitulated to the professor, "You are right." But Buber asked himself, "What had I done?": "I had led the man to the threshold beyond which there sat enthroned the majestic image which the great physicist, the great man of faith, Pascal, called the God of the Philosophers. Had I wished for that? Had I not rather wished to lead him to the other, Him, whom Pascal called the God of Abraham, Isaac, and Jacob, Him to whom one can say Thou?"[85]

The third incident, chronicled originally in a letter to his colleague Franz Rosenzweig and then later in the same "Prelude" to *Eclipse of God*, was a visit during 1923, the year of the release of *I and Thou*, to the Marburg neo-Kantian philosopher Paul Gerhard Natorp, described in *Eclipse* as simply "a noble old thinker." Once again, the event revolves around a question posed to Buber and a reply composed after the fact. In this case, the response had been brewing for nearly three decades. The question: "How can you bring yourself to say 'God' time after time?" The answer, one of Buber's finest moments when he transformed a personal experience into a parable for his age:

> "Yes," I said, "[God] is the most heavy-laden of all human words. None has become so soiled, so mutilated. Just for this reason I may not abandon it. Generations of men have laid the burden of their anxious lives upon this word and weighed it to the ground; it lies in the dust and bears their whole burden. The races of men with their religious factions have torn the word to pieces; they have killed for it and died for it, and it bears their finger-marks and their blood.... Certainly, they draw caricatures and write 'God' underneath; they murder one another and say 'in God's name.' But when all madness and delusion fall to dust, when they stand over against Him in the loneliest darkness and no longer say 'He, He' but rather sigh 'Thou,' shout 'Thou,' all of them the one word, and when they then add 'God,' is it not the real God whom they all implore, the One Living God, the God of the children of man?... We must esteem those who interdict it because they rebel against the injustice and wrong which are so readily referred to 'God' for authorization. But we may not give up.... We cannot cleanse the word 'God' and we cannot make it whole; but, defiled and mutilated as it is, we can raise it from the ground and set it over an hour of great care."[86]

VI. THE LIFE OF DIALOGUE

What we observe in these biographical episodes, crafted by Buber over his career as signposts in his spiritual pilgrimage, is the development of a process of candid self-examination and dialectical reflection that became the master stroke in his intellectual signature. Dissident Catholic theologian Hans Küng, the youngest *peritus* or theological advisor at Vatican II, whose *Does God Exist?* (German, 1978) still defines the sum and scope of Catholic approaches to atheism, said this of Buber: "More than anyone else he gave expression to the tremendous misuse—but also the indispensability—of the word God."[87] For a Catholic church often identified by its critics (internal and external) as the virtual archetype of theomaniacal addiction to a "logicized God," the "God of the theologians," Buber's almost unintentional internalization of the dialogue between believer and unbeliever functions as an invitation to construct a more expansive Catholic theology of atheism and in the process reach out to the growing global community of unbelievers in the sincerity and prudence mandated by the Vatican II bishops—but not without generosity, curiosity, and humility.[88]

Ultimately, of course, the question of method arises. Nothing has nagged ecumenical or interreligious dialogue more than questions of procedure and praxis. For Buber, though, from the outset dialogue always surpassed theory or ideal; before all else, it was a principled way of life, one that often frustrated observers or half-hearted participants who sought less than the full-scale interface whose goal for Buber was always "healing through meeting."[89] Buber's life of dialogue, attested to by a wide variety of colleagues, disciples, biographers, and interpreters, provides a model for Catholic believers who would follow the call of the Second Vatican Council to pursue the final frontier of dialogue: Catholic engagement with citizens of the world of unbelief.

Two areas of Buber's participation in the adventure of dialogue possess special relevance for Catholic-atheist dialogue: his investment in Jewish-Christian dialogue and his leadership in fostering Arab-Israeli understanding. Maurice Friedman and Paul Mendes-Flohr have amply documented Buber's crucial role in initiating and guiding dialogue between Jews and Christians.[90] Buber commenced his academic career immersing himself in the literature of the Christian intellectual tradition, writing his dissertation on Christian mystics Nicholas of Cusa and Jacob Böhme. He collaborated with Christian theologians in the founding of *Die Kreatur*, one of the first scholarly journals devoted to Jewish-Christian dialogue. And despite war, genocide, and geographical separation, he corresponded extensively with a variety of figures intent on forging a Christian faith responsive to the needs of twentieth-century people. After World War II, Buber was in frequent contact with Christian thinkers. Many cherished the memory of their first encounter with Buber as a moment of *kairos* in their Christian vocations. His willingness to accept honors and awards in Europe after the Holocaust and to lecture in the United States during the final decade of his life embodied his invitation to dialogue and solidified opinion in the theological community regarding the significance of his insights and the sincerity of his efforts. Witnesses to his personal engagement with professors and students after formal lectures were especially impressed by his penetrating attentiveness to individuals and their specific inquiries. Unfortunately, the degree of Jewish-Christian exchange implicit in Buber's relationship with his wife Paula Winkler, a self-described "philozionist" who converted from Catholicism to Judaism, will likely never be fully known.[91]

Buber's chief literary contribution to Jewish-Christian understanding, *Two Types of Faith* (1950), a testament to a deeply internalized and carefully cultivated dialogue between Judaism and Christianity, is remarkable to the Christian reader for more than its fruitful comparison of *emunah* (existential trust in the divine) and *pistis* (intellectual assent to propositions about the sacred). The book's admiration for Jesus, a "great son of Israel," its appreciation for the "fiery centre" of Christian spiritual life, and its skillful exposure of the complex interplay of ideas and attitudes in the history-heavy relationship between Jews and Christians speak to the limitations of a merely comparative theology and the great promise of a richly dialogic theology.[92] What is most striking—and most relevant to our topic—is the text's unapologetic grounding of dialogue in an unconditional acceptance of difference, an acknowledgment of inextricable connection, and an openness to an unscripted future:

> The faith of Judaism and the faith of Christendom are by nature different in kind, each in conformity with its human basis, and they will indeed remain different, until mankind is gathered in from the exiles of the "religions" into the Kingship of God. But an Israel striving after the renewal of its faith through the rebirth of the person and a Christianity striving for the renewal of its faith through the rebirth of nations would have something as yet unsaid to say to each other and a help to give to one another—hardly to be conceived at the present time.[93]

In an earlier publication, "The Two Foci of the Jewish Soul" (1930), addressed to a Christian audience, Buber advanced this same point—explicitly and forcefully invoking the theme of respect for a faith not one's own: "It behooves both you and us to hold inviolably fast to our own true faith, that is to our own deepest relationship to truth. It behooves both of us to show a religious respect for the true faith of the other. This is not what is called 'tolerance,' our task is not to tolerate each other's waywardness but to acknowledge the real relationship in which both stand to the truth."[94]

Similarly, Buber's sacrificial work on behalf of Jewish-Arab reconciliation represented an enactment of this respect for the Other in dramatic and exceptional terms. Few members of his generation knew more profoundly the unique place of the "stranger" in biblical teaching, rooted as it is squarely in the context of ancient Israel's living memory of slavery and its understanding of the independent and unbounded character of YHVH: "For the LORD your God is God supreme and Lord supreme, the great, the mighty, and the awesome God, who... befriends the stranger, providing him with food and clothing—You too must befriend the stranger, for you were strangers in the land of Egypt" (Deuteronomy 10:17–19, JPS).[95] Buber's nonconformity in the Zionist community and later among the Israeli intelligentsia, paralleling the vulnerable social status of the Hebrew patriarchs, demonstrated the extraordinary degree to which he appropriated some of the most fundamental themes of the Bible—in spite of, or perhaps because of, his controversial unorthodox religious stance.

For decades, Buber laced his dream of Hebrew Humanism with advocacy for peaceful Jewish-Arab coexistence in Palestine.[96] He took leading roles in groups such as Brit Shalom (Covenant of Peace), the League for Jewish-Arab Rapprochement and Cooperation, and Ihud (Unity), promoting—before and after the establishment of the state of Israel, and often in conflict with Jewish, Arab, and world opinion—a rare vision of binational identity and cooperation. He defended unpopular causes and spoke out on controversial matters when many kept silent. Convinced that "politicization" in his day was fast approaching a "pathological" level, Buber persistently emphasized the spiritual dimension of the Zionist hope, convinced that only a "community of otherness" could lead the multifaith Middle East to a providential appointment with greatness.[97]

Buber's work in the fields of Jewish-Christian and Jewish-Arab relations vividly underscored his grasp of another core teaching of scripture: the uniqueness of the human person. His very practical appreciation for *humanitas* as a "center of surprise in creation" served as the underlying conviction supporting his countercultural activity in dialogue initiatives and his most seasoned statements on the subject: "Authentic Bilingualism," "Genuine Dialogue and the Possibility of Peace" (his speech on the occasion of his reception of the 1953 Peace Prize of the German Book Trade) and "Believing Humanism" (his 1963 Erasmus Prize address).[98] These publications make it clear that for Buber authentic engagement rests on neither common ground nor moral compromise but on fundamental respect for difference itself: "In a genuine dialogue each of the partners, even when he stands in opposition to the other, heeds, affirms, and confirms his opponent as an existing other."[99] Using the image of marriage as a heuristic device to spark creative reflection on this kind of relationship, Buber's summary of the life of dialogue—nearly a hymn to difference—in his classic "The Question to the Single One" (1936) may serve as a miniature primer for pioneers in the next stages of Catholic-atheist dialogue. Its sheer and frankly stunning genius merits full quotation:

> This person is other, essentially other than myself, and this otherness of his is what I mean, because I mean him; I confirm it; I wish his otherness to exist, because I wish his particular being to exist. That is the basic principle of marriage and from this basis it leads, if it is real marriage, to insight into the right and the legitimacy of otherness and to that vital acknowledgement of

many-faced otherness—even in the contradiction and conflict with it—from which dealings with the body politic receive their religious ethos. That the men with whom I am bound up in the body politic and with whom I have directly or indirectly to do, are essentially other than myself, that this one or that one does not have merely a different mind, or way of thinking or feeling, or a different conviction or attitude, but has also a different perception of the world, a different recognition and order of meaning, a different touch from the regions of existence, a different faith, a different soil: to affirm all this, to affirm it in the way of a creature, in the midst of the hard situations of conflict, without relaxing their real seriousness, is the way by which we may officiate as helpers in this wide realm entrusted to us as well, and from which alone we are from time to time permitted to touch in our doubts, in humility and upright investigation, on the other's "truth" or "untruth," "justice" or "injustice." But to this we are led by marriage, if it is real, with a power for which there is scarcely a substitute, by its steady experiencing of the life-substance of the other as other, and still more by its crises and the overcoming of them which rises out of the organic depths, whenever the monster of otherness, which but now blew on us with its icy demons' breath and now is redeemed by our risen affirmation of the other, which knows and destroys all negation, is transformed into the mighty angel of union of which we dreamed in our mother's womb.[100]

VII. CONCLUSION

Today, virtually no one would deny that some kind of "angel of union" has attended Buber's one-of-a-kind relationship with the world of late modern and contemporary Christianity. For nearly a century, the "wisest religious truths" that Merton found in Buber's works have sparked a series of renewal movements in various areas of Christian life and thought. Thanks largely to Buber, generations of Christian thinkers and leaders have rediscovered the Jewishness of their savior and the enduring relevance of his Jewish Bible. Many have encountered a luminous Jewish tradition that casts a searing light on all too resilient prejudices and calls into serious question some of the most basic assumptions of Christian habit and hope. Above all, Buber's central and undeviating focus on dialogue, encoded in the eminently suggestive and now nearly canonical phrase "I and Thou," has opened new horizons for fresh investigation into perennial questions of God and human existence, forcing the best of Christian theologians to reexamine the very ground and purpose of their craft.

The proof is in the footnotes—many of them footnotes to new *Confessions* and modern *Summas* that are themselves footnotes to Buber, now arguably on par with Plato and Augustine as a shaper of the Western Christian mind. The imprint on the Roman Catholic mind, including the papal mind, is particularly astonishing, especially when we consider the minor role assigned to dialogue in the Catholic tradition before the Second Vatican Council. If John O'Malley is correct about dialogue's cardinal place in the definition of "what the council was all about," we can be sure that Catholic theology, in both its critical and constructive forms, will remain for the foreseeable future a series of references to and reflections on Buber's extraordinary achievement.[101]

Even accounting for Buber's influence on Catholic experiments in ecumenical and interreligious outreach, the riches embedded in his legacy have not been sufficiently tapped for the sake of new types of dialogue with one of the great products of the Christian mind: atheism. Unbelief and nonaffiliation sweep the globe, and "eclipse of God" increasingly captures the spiritual experience of millions of people both without and within the world's religious traditions. Efforts to implement Vatican II's call for "honest and prudent" dialogue with the ever-widening community of unbelievers, however, lag far behind other aspects of Catholic mission. Buber's distinctive insights into the causes and character of modern atheisms, along with his deep and abiding appreciation for "meeting" as the hallmark of "all real living," arguably provide the theoretical and practical resources needed to transform the church's deferred dialogue into a robust expression of engaged Catholicism rightly calibrated for what Pope Francis has called a "change of age."[102]

In his introduction to the original edition of *Between Man and Man*, Ronald Gregor Smith spoke of Buber's "wisdom" as "the power to step over artificial boundaries, for the sake of true humanity."[103] Smith's recognition is even more relevant today, as the boundary lines between belief and unbelief are in constant flux and appears increasingly difficult to identify. Some critics might dispute the artificiality of such a border, but few would dismiss the urgent need for mutual understanding—and the self-understanding that accompanies it. Long dubbed the "absent father" of the Second Vatican Council's theology of dialogue, Martin Buber, more than a half century after the council and more than a half century after his death, points the way toward the next great chapter in the story of human boundary crossing.

NOTES

Portions of this chapter first appeared in online journals associated with the International Society for Universal Dialogue and the Collegeville Institute for Ecumenical and Cultural Research.

1. John W. O'Malley, *What Happened at Vatican II* (Cambridge, MA: Belknap Press of Harvard University Press, 2008), 1.
2. Ibid., 80.
3. See Ann Michele Nolan, *A Privileged Moment: Dialogue in the Language of the Second Vatican Council 1962–1965* (Bern, Switzerland: Peter Lang, 2006), and Catherine E. Clifford, "Learning from the Council: The Church in Dialogue," *Theoforum* 44/1 (2013): 23–42.
4. See Maria Diemling and Thomas J. Herbst, eds., *Interpreting the "Spirit of Assisi": Challenges to Interfaith Dialogue in a Pluralistic World* (Phoenix, AZ: Tau Publishing, 2013).
5. See Edward Idris Cassidy, *Ecumenism and Interreligious Dialogue: Unitatis Redintegratio, Nostra Aetate* (New York: Paulist Press, 2005).
6. Yaakov Ariel, "Jewish-Christian Dialogue" in *The Wiley-Blackwell Companion to Inter-Religious Dialogue*, ed. Catherine Cornille (Malden, MA: Wiley-Blackwell, 2013), 205.
7. Marc H. Tanenbaum, "Vatican II: An Interfaith Appreciation: A Jewish Viewpoint" in *A Prophet for Our Time: An Anthology of the Writings of Rabi Marc H. Tanenbaum*, ed. Judith H. Banki and Eugene J. Fisher (New York: Fordham University Press, 2002), 87. See John Connelly, *From Enemy to Brother: The Revolution in Catholic Teaching on the Jews, 1933–1965* (Cambridge, MA: Harvard University Press, 2012).
8. *Gaudium et Spes*, section 21 in *Vatican II: Essential Texts*, ed. Norman Tanner (New York: Image, 2012), 213.
9. Pope Francis, "Letter to a Non-Believer" (2013), https://www.vatican.va/content/francesco/en/letters/2013/documents/papa-francesco_20130911_eugenio-scalfari.html. Accessed April 18, 2022; Pope Francis, *Fratelli Tutti* (2020), Francis: Encyclicals, Holy See, website of the Vatican, https://www.vatican.va/content/francesco/en/encyclicals/documents/papa-francesco_20201003_enciclica-fratelli-tutti.html. See especially paragraphs 74 and 281. Accessed April 18, 2022.
10. Pope Francis, "Address to Bishops of Brazil (28 July 2013)," https://wwwvatican.va/content/francesco/en/speeches/2013/july/documents/papa-francesco_20130727_gmg-episcopato-brasile.html. See section 2. Accessed April 18, 2022.
11. See Peter Watson, *The Age of Atheists: How We Have Sought to Live since the Death of God* (New York: Simon and Schuster, 2014), and Terry Eagleton, *Culture and the Death of God* (New Haven, CT: Yale University Press, 2014).
12. Martin Buber, *Between Man and Man*, trans. Ronald Gregor-Smith (New York: Routledge, 2002), 254. Kenneth Paul Kramer emphasizes the importance of a first-person understanding of Buber in *Martin Buber's Dialogue: Discovering Who We Really Are* (Eugene, OR: Cascade Books, 2019).

13. Pope John Paul II, *Redemptoris Missio* (1990), John Paul II: Encyclicals, Holy See, website of the Vatican, https://www.vatican.va/content/john-paul-ii/en/encyclicals/documents/hf_jp-ii_enc_07121990_redemptoris-missio.html. See section 57. Accessed April 18, 2022.

14. Malcolm L. Diamond, *Contemporary Philosophy and Religious Thought: An Introduction to the Philosophy of Religion* (New York: McGraw-Hill, 1974), 114.

15. Walter Kaufmann, *Discovering the Mind*, vol. 2 (New York: McGraw-Hill, 1980), 258.

16. Walter Kaufmann, "I and You: A Prologue," in *I and Thou*, by Martin Buber, trans. Walter Kaufmann (New York: Touchstone, 1996), 14.

17. Kaufmann, *Discovering the Mind*, 2:252. See Ronald Gregor Smith, *Martin Buber* (London: Carey Kingsgate Press, 1967). See also Keith W. Clements, *The Theology of Ronald Gregor Smith* (Leiden: E. J. Brill, 1986), and John A. Williams, "Ronald Gregor Smith, Critical Faith and the Practice of Religion," *Scottish Journal of Theology* 42 (1989): 85–100.

18. Kaufmann, "I and You," 15.

19. For a full treatment of Kaufmann's relationship with Buber's thought, see Stanley Corngold, *Walter Kaufmann: Philosopher, Humanist, Heretic* (Princeton, NJ: Princeton University Press, 2019).

20. Martin Buber, *Two Types of Faith: A Study of the Interpretation of Judaism and Christianity*, trans. Norman P. Goldhawk (New York: Harper and Row, 1961), 12; Martin Buber, *Eclipse of God: Studies in the Relation between Religion and Philosophy* (New York: Harper and Brothers, 1957), 73; Martin Buber, *I and Thou*, trans. Ronald Gregor Smith, 2nd ed. (New York: Charles Scribner's Sons, 1958), 75.

21. See Maurice Friedman, *Martin Buber's Life and Work: The Early Years 1878–1923* (New York: E. P. Dutton, 1981), 123, 304, and Maurice Friedman, *Encounter on the Narrow Ridge: A Life of Martin Buber* (New York: Paragon House, 1993), 85.

22. Buber, *Between Man and Man*, 67.

23. See Maurice Friedman, *Martin Buber: The Life of Dialogue* (Chicago: University of Chicago Press, 1955), chapter 27.

24. John Macquarrie, *Twentieth-Century Religious Thought* (London: SCM Press, 1988), 350.

25. Paul Tillich, *Theology of Culture*, ed. Robert C. Kimball (New York: Oxford University Press, 1959), 188, 199. See also Paul Tillich, "Martin Buber and Christian Thought: His Threefold Contribution to Protestantism," *Commentary* 5/6 (June 1948): 515–21.

26. Reinhold Niebuhr, *The Self and the Dramas of History* (New York: Charles Scribner's Sons, 1955), 88.

27. Martin Luther King Jr., "Letter from Birmingham Jail," in *The Essential Writings of Martin Luther King, Jr.*, ed. James M. Washington (San Francisco: HarperSanFrancisco, 1986), 293; Martin Luther King Jr., *Why We Can't Wait* (New York: Mentor, 1964), 82.

28. Aubrey Hodes, *Martin Buber: An Intimate Portrait* (New York: Viking Press, 1971), 185.

29. Stephen M. Panko, *Martin Buber* (Waco, TX: Word Books, 1979), 28.

30. Karen Armstrong, *A History of God: The 4000-Year Quest of Judaism, Christianity, and Islam* (New York: Alfred A. Knopf, 1993), 387.

31. See Alister E. McGrath, *Christian Theology: An Introduction*, 6th ed. (Wiley-Blackwell, 2016).

32. Nahum N. Glatzer and Paul Mendes-Flohr, eds., *The Letters of Martin Buber: A Life of Dialogue*, trans. Richard Winston, Clara Winston, and Harry Zohn (Syracuse, NY: Syracuse University Press, 1996), 57.

33. See Hans Urs Von Balthasar, *Martin Buber and Christianity: A Dialogue between Israel and the Church*, trans. Alexander Dru (New York: Macmillan, 1961), and Hans Urs Von Balthasar, "Martin Buber and Christianity" in *The Philosophy of Martin Buber*, ed. Paul Arthur Schilpp and Maurice Friedman (La Salle, IL: Open Court, 1967), 341–60. See also Virgil Nemoianu, "Voice of Christian Humanism: The Achievement of Hans Urs Von Balthasar," *Crisis Magazine*, September 1, 1988, www.crisismagazine.com/1988/voice-of-christian-humanism-the-achievement-of-hans-urs-von-balthasar.

34. Quoted in Roger Lipsey, *Make Peace before the Sun Goes Down: The Long Encounter of Thomas Merton and His Abbot, James Fox* (Boston: Shambhala, 2015), 105.

35. See Gary Spruch, *Wide Horizons: Abraham Joshua Heschel, AJC, and the Spirit of Nostra Aetate* (New York: American Jewish Committee, 2008), https://www.ajc.org/sites/default/files/pdf/2017-09/Project_Highlight_Wide_Horizons.pdf. Accessed April 18, 2022. . See also Norman C. Tobias, *Jewish Conscience of the Church: Jules Isaac and the Second Vatican Council* (New York: Palgrave Macmillan, 2017).

36. See Nolan, *Privileged Moment*, 1.

37. Friedman, *Encounter on the Narrow Ridge*, 439–40; *Gaudium et Spes*, section 43 in Tanner, *Vatican II*, 238.

38. Pope John Paul II, *Ecclesia in Asia* (1999), John Paul II: Apostolic Exhortations, Holy See, website of the Vatican, https://www.vatican.va/content/john-paul-ii/en/apost_exhortations/documents/hf_jp-ii_exh_06111999_ecclesia-in-asia.html. See section 31. Accessed April 18, 2022.

39. *Catechism of the Catholic Church* (Liguori, MO: Liguori Publications, 1994), section 39. See also section 856.

40. Pope Francis, *The Joy of the Gospel: Evangelii Gaudium* (New York: Image, 2013), paragraph 250. Francis calls the entirety of his third encyclical, *Fratelli Tutti* (2020), an "invitation to dialogue" (paragraph 6). See Francis, *Fratelli Tutti*.

41. Pope Francis and Andrea Tornielli, *The Name of God Is Mercy*, trans. Oonagh Stransky (New York: Random House, 2016), 146.

42. See George Huntston Williams, *The Mind of John Paul II: Origins of His Thought and Action* (New York: Seabury Press, 1981); George Weigel, *Witness to Hope: The Biography of Pope John Paul II* (New York: HarperCollins, 2001); and Pope John Paul II, *Crossing the Threshold of Hope*, ed. Vittorio Messori, trans. Jenny McPhee and Martha McPhee (New York: Alfred A. Knopf, 1994), 36, 210.

43. Joseph Ratzinger, *Milestones: Memoirs 1927–1977*, trans. Erasmo Leiva-Merikakis (San Francisco: Ignatius Press, 1998), 44. See also Joseph Ratzinger, *Truth and Tolerance: Christian Belief and World Religions*, trans. Henry Taylor (San Francisco: Ignatius Press, 2004), 10, 46, 192.

44. See Robert Anthony Krieg, *Romano Guardini: A Precursor of Vatican II* (Notre Dame, IN: University of Notre Dame Press, 1997).

45. Pope Francis, *The Light of Faith: Lumen Fidei* (San Francisco: Ignatius Press, 2013), paragraph 13. The Buber reference, showcasing a definition of idolatry from *Tales of the Hasidim*, comes in the context of a discussion of the "temptation of unbelief."

46. Pope Francis, *Praise Be to You: Laudato Si'; On Care for Our Common Home* (San Francisco: Ignatius Press, 2015), paragraphs 216–21.

47. Ibid., paragraph 81.

48. Ibid., paragraph 119.

49. See, for example, Pope Paul VI, "General Audience (31 January 1973)," *Paolo VI: Udienze*, Holy See, website of the Vatican, https://www.vatican.va/content/paul-vi/it/audiences/1973/documents/hf_p-vi_aud_19730131.html. Accessed April 18, 2022.

50. In his third encyclical, *Fratelli Tutti* (2020), Francis does not mention Buber but does quote from Buber's teacher Georg Simmel (see paragraph 150)—a papal "first."

51. Harold Kasimow and John Merkle, "Did Rabbi Heschel Influence Pope Francis?" in Harold Kasimow, *Interfaith Activism: Abraham Joshua Heschel and Religious Diversity* (Eugene, OR: Wipf and Stock, 2015), 83–93.

52. Thomas Aquinas, *Summa Theologica*, 1.2.3.

53. Malcolm Diamond, *Martin Buber: Jewish Existentialist* (New York: Oxford University Press, 1960), 43.

54. Pope Francis, *Light of Faith*, paragraph 2.

55. See Ernst Bloch, *Atheism in Christianity: The Religion of the Exodus and the Kingdom*, trans. J. T. McSwann (London: Verso, 2009), and Hans Urs Von Balthasar, *A Short Primer for Unsettled Laymen*, trans. Mary Theresilde Skerry (San Francisco: Ignatius Press, 1985), 87.

56. See Michael J. Buckley, *At the Origins of Modern Atheism* (New Haven, CT: Yale University Press, 1987), and *Denying and Disclosing God: The Ambiguous Progress of Modern Atheism* (New Haven, CT: Yale University Press, 2004). See also Gavin Hyman, *A Short History of Atheism* (London: I. B. Tauris, 2010), and Dominic Erdozain, *The Soul of Doubt: The Religious Roots of Unbelief from Luther to Marx* (Oxford: Oxford University Press, 2016).

57. Paul A. Bertagnolli, "Music," in *The Oxford Handbook of Atheism*, ed. Stephen Bullivant and Michael Ruse (Oxford: Oxford University Press, 2013), 719.

58. See Stephen Bullivant, *Faith and Unbelief* (New York: Paulist Press, 2013).

59. Joseph Ratzinger, *Introduction to Christianity*, trans. J. R. Foster (San Francisco: Ignatius Press, 2004), 44–45.

60. See Peter A. Huff, *The Voice of Vatican II: Words for Our Church Today* (Liguori, MO: Liguori Publications, 2012), 65.

61. *Gaudium et Spes*, section 19 in Tanner, *Vatican II*, 210.

62. Bullivant, *Faith and Unbelief*, xiv.

63. See Phil Zuckerman, "Atheism: Contemporary Numbers and Patterns," in *The Cambridge Companion to Atheism*, ed. Michael Martin (Cambridge: Cambridge University Press, 2007), 47–65, and "'Nones' on the Rise: One-in-Five Adults Have No Religious Affiliation," Pew Research Center, 2012, https://www.pewresearch.org/religion/2012/10/09/nones-on-the-rise/. See also Jerome P. Baggett, *The Varieties of Nonreligious Experience: Atheism in American Culture* (New York: New York University Press, 2019), Elizabeth Drescher, *Choosing Our Religion: The Spiritual Lives of America's Nones* (New York: Oxford University Press, 2016); and Peter A. Huff, *Atheism and Agnosticism: Exploring the Issues* (Santa Barbara, CA: ABC-CLIO, 2021).

64. Tillich, *Theology of Culture*, 188.

65. Buber, *Eclipse of God*, 129.

66. *Gaudium et Spes*, 19 in Tanner, *Vatican II*, 210–11.

67. Buber, *Eclipse of God*, 66, 136; Friedman, *Encounter on the Narrow Ridge*, 342.

68. Buber, *Eclipse of God*, 23.

69. Friedman, *Encounter on the Narrow Ridge*, 339.

70. Quoted in Panko, *Martin Buber*, 32–33.

71. Glatzer and Mendes-Flohr, *Letters of Martin Buber*, 390; Maurice Friedman, *My Friendship with Martin Buber* (Syracuse, NY: Syracuse University Press, 2013), 84.

72. Martin Buber, *A Believing Humanism: My Testament 1902–1965*, trans. Maurice Friedman (New York: Simon and Schuster, 1967), 201.

73. See Jean Danielou, *Holy Pagans of the Old Testament*, trans. Felix Faber (London: Longmans, Green, 1957).

74. Buber, *Eclipse of God*, 46.

75. Buber, *I and Thou*, trans. Kaufmann, 182; Buber, *Between Man and Man*, 63.

76. Buber, *I and Thou*, trans. Kaufmann, 164; Buber, *Believing Humanism*, 172. See Kaufmann, *Discovering the Mind*, 2:274, and Donald J. Moore, *Martin Buber: Prophet of Religious Secularism* (New York: Fordham University Press, 1996).

77. Buber, *I and Thou*, trans. Kaufman, 156.

78. See Paul Mendes-Flohr, *Martin Buber: A Life of Faith and Dissent* (New Haven, CT: Yale University Press, 2019).

79. See Friedman, *Martin Buber's Life and Work: The Early Years*, 5, 14–15, 188–89, 232–58.

80. No critical biography of Hechler exists. See Victoria Clark, *Allies for Armageddon: The Rise of Christian Zionism* (New Haven, CT: Yale University Press, 2007), 98–109.

81. Friedman, *Martin Buber's Life and Work: The Early Years*, 186; Friedman, *Encounter on the Narrow Ridge*, 78.

82. Buber, *Eclipse of God*, 66.

83. William Hamilton, *The New Essence of Christianity* (New York: Association Press, 1961), 55.

84. Ratzinger, *Introduction to Christianity*, 45–46.

85. Buber, *Eclipse of God*, 5–6.

86. Ibid., 7–9. See Glatzer and Mendes-Flohr, *Letters of Martin Buber*, 302.

87. Hans Küng, *Judaism: Between Yesterday and Tomorrow*, trans. John Bowden (New York: Crossroad, 1992), 452.

88. Buber, *Between Man and Man*, 67.

89. See Martin Buber, *Pointing the Way: Collected Essays*, trans. Maurice Friedman (Atlantic Highlands, NJ: Humanities Press International, 1957), 93–97.

90. See Friedman, *Martin Buber: The Life of Dialogue*, chapter 27; Martin Friedman, *Martin Buber's Life and Work: The Middle Years 1923–1945* (New York: E. P. Dutton, 1983), chapters 6 and 10. See also Mendes-Flohr, *Martin Buber*, especially chapters 4 and 8, and Hodes, *Martin Buber*, 176–89.

91. Friedman, *Martin Buber's Life and Work: The Early Years*, 49.

92. Buber, *Two Types of Faith*, 9, 96.

93. Ibid., 174.

94. Martin Buber, *Israel and the World: Essays in a Time of Crisis* (Syracuse, NY: Syracuse University Press, 1997), 40.

95. See Gen. 23:4; Exod. 2:22, 22:21, 23:9; Lev. 19:9–10, 33–34, and 23:22; and Num. 9:14. See also Ezek. 47:22–23.

96. See Friedman, *Encounter on the Narrow Ridge*, chapter 14.

97. Martin Buber, "Two Peoples in Palestine" in *A Land of Two Peoples: Martin Buber on Jews and Arabs*, ed. Paul Mendes-Flohr (New York: Oxford University Press, 1983), 200. Friedman, *Encounter on the Narrow Ridge*, 417.

98. Buber, *Pointing the Way*, 198; Buber, *Believing Humanism*, 80–84, 117–22, 195–201.

99. Buber, *Believing Humanism*, 202.
100. Buber, *Between Man and Man*, 71–72.
101. O'Malley, *What Happened at Vatican II*, 80.
102. Buber, *I and Thou*, trans. Smith, 11.
103. Quoted in Hodes, *Martin Buber*, 228.

THREE

READING MARTIN BUBER'S BIBLE

Translation and Commentary

CLAIRE E. SUFRIN

DESCRIBING THE CULTURE OF CENTRAL and western European Jews in the modern period and, in particular, Jewish efforts to attain civic emancipation in the nineteenth century, Richard I. Cohen argues that "as the roots of Jewish identification were being attacked from within and without, and as Jewish cohesiveness was weakened by integration, negotiation with the biblical text helped Jews enunciate another form of belonging and erect new boundaries with their cultural habitat."[1] That is, active engagement with the Hebrew Bible allowed Jews to articulate their place within a broader gentile society at the very same time that they were also gaining greater acceptance in that society than they had ever had before. In the context of a modernizing Europe—and within it, a rapidly modernizing Jewish population—the Hebrew Bible was cast by Jewish leaders as a cultural artifact that Jews could proudly hold up as their people's contribution to the development of civilization and culture. It offered proof of the people's moral and ethical foundations, their monotheistic religious instincts, and their poetic sensibilities. This turn to the Bible was in part a rejection of Christian modes of understanding the text, whether in overtly theological and devotional contexts or in the more subtly anti-Jewish work of Christian biblical scholars whose theological commitments influenced their historical critical work.[2] At the same time, renewed attention to the biblical text reflected and promoted the liberalization of Judaism itself, a process that unfolded within Jewish communities across western and central Europe (and in the United States) throughout the nineteenth century and into the twentieth as liberal-minded rabbis and others turned to the rabbinic tradition with a critical lens, seeking to bring Jewish religious beliefs and practices in line with Enlightenment values of rationality and reason. Rituals and beliefs that could not be understood on these terms were rejected. With the rise of the Wissenschaft des Judentums movement in 1819 and the academic study of Judaism it promoted, rabbinic texts were historicized and largely stripped of any immediate relevance for Jewish life. As the importance of rabbinic literature and custom declined, the biblical text became a new focus both for those who advocated a liberal Judaism and for those who sought to combat it in the name of tradition.[3]

These demographic, political, and religious shifts shaped the environment that nurtured Jewish thinker Martin Buber from birth. Born in Vienna in 1878, Buber grew up with his grandparents in Polish Galicia, in a household that was not only liberal but also devoted to the Wissenschaft des Judentums. (His grandfather Solomon Buber was a prominent Wissenschaft des Judentums scholar and edited a critical edition of *Midrash Rabbah* that remains the standard today, more than a century later.) What made Buber's upbringing truly unusual was that he and his grandfather were also participant-observers in the traditional Jewish life of the Galician Hasidim that surrounded them. The spirited prayers and imaginative storytelling of these pietistic communities and courts influenced Buber's thinking throughout his life. Over his lifetime, he was an anthologizer, a translator, a sociologist, and a Zionist; above all, he was a public intellectual, pursuing scholarship in service to the Jewish communities of modernity: the emancipated Jews who found themselves unsure of what their Jewishness might have to offer them as a source of meaning and values in the modern world. The Bible was central to this pursuit and Buber returned to it over and over again through his life, developing different hermeneutic approaches to reading and understanding it.

Neither liberal nor orthodox in his orientation toward Judaism, Buber's engagement with the Bible was driven by his desire to understand and articulate the relationship between the past of the biblical Israelites and the present of modern Jews. In particular, what Buber pursued in his many writings about the Hebrew Bible was, first, a better understanding of how the historical relationship between the biblical Israelites and God might inform the religiosity of the modern Jew and, second, how the modern Jew might access that understanding and then act on it to enrich her own existence. In short, history and hermeneutics were for Buber interwoven as he hoped that together they might motivate a renewal of Jewish spirituality in the modern world.

In this chapter, I focus on Buber's understanding of revelation—both as an abstract concept and as an event described in the biblical text—as his thinking matured in the years from 1909 through 1945. I show how his basic definition of revelation as divine presence and not divine speech grew more complex over this time as he became an increasingly careful reader of the Hebrew Bible. The chapter is divided into three sections, each one devoted to a particular period of Buber's writings. The first section addresses the 1910s and early 1920s, years that include Buber's *Early Addresses on Judaism*, his "Religion as Presence" lectures, and *I and Thou*. The second section examines Buber's thinking about revelation in the context of his translation of the Hebrew Bible into German with his friend and colleague Franz Rosenzweig (1886–1929) in the late 1920s. Finally, the third section considers the books of biblical commentaries Buber wrote in the 1930s and 1940s. As I move through these writings, I focus in particular on Buber's discussions of two biblical scenes of human-divine encounter that might be seen as prototypical moments of revelation: Moses meeting God at the burning bush in Exodus 3 and the Israelites encountering God at Mount Sinai in Exodus 19. Each of these scenes challenges the modern reader seeking to understand how it is that God might speak to human beings.

I. RELIGION, REVELATION, AND THE BIBLE IN BUBER'S WRITINGS OF THE 1910S AND EARLY 1920S

After the First World War and until he left for Jerusalem in 1938, Buber lived in Heppenheim, a short train ride from Frankfurt. Frankfurt's Freies Judisches Lehrhaus, then under Franz Rosenzweig's direction, was the site of Buber's "Religion as Presence" lectures, a series of eight talks he delivered in early 1922. Buber and Rosenzweig had become friendly in the wake of Rosenzweig's criticism of Buber's understanding of revelation in talks he delivered and published between 1909 and 1919. This criticism and the conversation it engendered set the stage for our understanding of the significance of the "Religion as Presence" lectures and Buber's definition of revelation and human-divine encounter therein.

In his *Early Addresses on Judaism* of the 1910s, Buber defines Judaism as a struggle to overcome the difference between religiosity and religion.[4] By religiosity, he means the actual and immediate experience of connection with God or even the pursuit of that experience, while by religion he means stable forms of religious expression such as literature, ritual, or law. These forms are necessary, but there is always a danger that they will replace the original religiosity that gave rise to them. In line with liberal critics of traditional Judaism, this is exactly Buber's diagnosis of the neo-Orthodoxy advocated by followers of Samson Raphael Hirsch (1808–1888). But Buber is also critical of liberal Judaism, accusing its defenders of stifling the dynamism of Jewish teaching by limiting it to ethical monotheism, little more than a dogmatic insistence on God's oneness and an emphasis on the importance of love of one's neighbor and other moral commandments.[5]

Though Buber is not named in Rosenzweig's "Atheistic Theology" (1914), the essay is a sharp critique of views Buber expresses in his first three *Early Addresses on Judaism*, which were published in 1911. In his essay, Rosenzweig compares modern Jewish thought to the Life of Jesus movement that had swept through liberal Christianity in the nineteenth century. He argues that a parallel "Jewish People's Theology" began with the view of the scholars of the Wissenschaft des Judentums, who, in their efforts to portray Judaism as a rational religion, emphasized the experience and the creativity of the Jewish people as the forces that had shaped Judaism and not the activity of God in human history. They saw myth as the process by which human beings created the divine. But in doing so, Rosenzweig argues, these thinkers deny the reality of revelation: "The distinctness of God and man, this frightful scandal for all new and old paganism, seems to be removed; the offensive thought of revelation, this plunging of a higher content into an unworthy vessel, is brought to silence."[6] In contrast, Rosenzweig insists that revelation consists of the exposure of something true about human experience by a divine force beyond the realm of human beings. It has happened and will happen again; the reality of revelation as a historical event cannot be denied, and revelation will reassert itself against all attempts to explain it away in rational terms. To those who would attempt a rational understanding of revelation, Rosenzweig warns: "Let his theology be as scientific as it wants to be and can be: it cannot circumvent the notion of revelation."[7]

The last of Buber's *Early Addresses on Judaism*, the 1919 "Herut," already reveals the influence of Rosenzweig's "Atheistic Theology." In this essay, Buber focuses on youth, which he defines as the time of life in which one is open to the call of the "Unconditioned," that is, God. If the call of God is the defining moment of youth, responding to the call is the defining challenge of youth, and Buber describes resources available to the young Jew seeking to respond with authenticity and creativity. In the Hebrew Bible, a youth finds that "mankind's wordless dialogue with God is condensed for him into the language of the soul, which he is not merely able to understand, but to which he himself can add new expressions, as yet unspoken. Without this language, he could do no more than stammer and falter."[8] The biblical text portrays human beings responding to God's call. In studying the biblical text, a young person does not find a script for responding to God but a set of images and words that might inspire her own response, in her own language and her own context: a response to divine presence that is, in short, creative and just barely derivative.

"Herut" marks an important transition in Buber's thinking about religion.[9] His emphasis has moved from the tension between living religiosity and stale religious forms that dominated his thinking a decade earlier to God as an immediate presence. The pursuit of the Absolute that defined religiosity fades, and the religious challenge is the recognition of the divine and response to it. Revelation is a reality insofar as every human being—at some point or another in her life—has the opportunity to respond to God as an immediate presence in this way. Furthermore, in "Herut" Buber recognizes a connection between the record of past revelations found in the Hebrew Bible and the present-day divine callings that characterize youth. The biblical text preserves the responses made by earlier generations to God's calling. The text does not preserve the calls themselves, a distinction that will grow sharper as Buber's thinking about the Bible matures over the next two decades.

The transition in Buber's thinking about religion that we observe in "Herut" develops more fully in the "Religion as Presence" lectures he delivers at Frankfurt's Freies Jüdisches Lehrhaus in early 1922. The presence of religion to which Buber refers is the presence of God, universally available at any moment and in any place, but only to those human beings who turn toward it. As he tells his audience in the first lecture, "presence is a concept of the soul; every presence is a moment of the human soul that is followed by another moment. An absolute present that did not become past would have to be one that did not merely exist in man as a moment of his soul, but one in which man stood, something in which man lived, yet which he could fulfill only in his inner being, by the dedication of his entire inner being."[10] In the seventh lecture, he acknowledges that this absolute presence is God: "religion . . . is presence, is a present that by its nature does not and cannot become past. And when we comprehend this correctly, when we feel that here is something that is no longer time-bound . . . when we feel this we also feel that this present of which we speak is the presence of God."[11] Religion is thus not an attitude but an experience. As such, it relies on openness, emotion, and intuition. To encounter God in this way is difficult, even violent; Buber calls it a confrontation with God. But in this confrontation, "I am the I when I confront the Thou." Or as he says just a few sentences later, "we speak, when we truly speak, out of presence, in presence."[12]

In the final lecture, Buber recognizes the confrontation between the divine and the human as revelation. As he writes here, understood as confrontation, revelation is "something that happens everywhere and all the time, that can happen to every human being, every human being who opens himself up completely, being completely collected and unified in himself. The basic meaning, therefore, of this revelation and of all revelation is a sending forth of the human being.... This calling, this sending forth to the test, to the deed, to humanity, into the world, into the We, to the place of actualization—that is the strength, that is what revelation gives."[13] Revelation as confrontation is a transformative event in the life of the individual, an assurance of divine presence that sets one on a path toward meaningful relationships among human beings who themselves can now be present within a community.

As Rivka Horwitz has demonstrated, large parts of the "Religion as Presence" lectures can be read as a rough draft for *I and Thou* (1923), Buber's most well-known work and the centerpiece of his dialogical philosophy. With this in mind, I turn now to *I and Thou* for a brief consideration of Buber's presentation of revelation as a form of dialogue before returning to the "Religion as Presence" lectures. The central argument of *I and Thou* is that human beings interact with others in the world within either instrumental "I-It" relationships or dialogical "I-Thou" encounters. While an I-It orientation is often necessary to support life and society, taking on an I-Thou orientation enriches human engagement with the world and lifts it above a purely animal existence. A second piece of this argument is that these two orientations toward the world are "word-pairs": dialogue for example is an *I-Thou* encounter, not a Thou encounter. The idea of word-pairs captures Buber's claim that the "I" is always constituted in relationship to an Other, whether that Other is used as an It or encountered as a Thou. My "I" is never alone but exists, from moment to moment, in orientation toward an It or toward a Thou. For Buber, there can be no solitary individual, for our way in the world will always be shaped by the presence of others and our interactions with them. While the I of I-Thou may be called a person (*Mensch*), the I of I-It is but an ego. No person is solely one or the other, though each of us tends in one direction or the other.[14]

In the book's third and final section, Buber describes God as the Eternal Thou and revelation as a particular sort of I-Thou dialogue. As in the "Religion as Presence" lectures, the defining feature of revelation in *I and Thou* is the presence of God, here called the Eternal Thou. Buber insists that revelation has no content; God does not speak to human beings in human language. Revelation is instead divine presence: "I do not believe in God's naming himself or in God's defining himself before man. The word of revelation is I am there as whoever I am there. That which reveals is that which reveals. That which has being is there, nothing more. The eternal source of strength flows, the eternal touch is waiting, the eternal voice sounds, nothing more."[15] Though Buber does not formally acknowledge it, this passage from *I and Thou* builds on Exodus 3:14 and the Hebrew phrase "ehyeh asher ehyeh" ("I will be who I will be" or "I am that I am") that appears therein.[16] These words are spoken by God to Moses at the site of a burning bush, offered in response to Moses's concern that the enslaved Israelites will ask the name of the deity who has all of a sudden arrived to redeem them. Here, in his unmarked reference to Exodus 3:14, Buber begins with "Ich bin da als ich bin da," which is a reasonable, more or less literal translation of the Hebrew. He then parses the phrase to define divine existence ("Ich bin," I am) as divine presence ("da," here). Divine language enacts that which it describes, and God's saying "ehyeh asher ehyeh" is God's presence.[17]

Buber's rendering of *ehyeh asher ehyeh* within his discussion of revelation in *I and Thou* allows him to imply subtly that his understanding of revelation has a biblical basis. But divine speech—substantive words issued by God or through a divine messenger in human language to human beings in their own particular situations—is an essential part of the biblical narrative and would seem to contradict Buber's insistence that God does not speak actual words to human beings. Within *I and Thou*, Buber does not address how revelation might have come to be recorded as the divine speech found in the Hebrew Bible. Ironically, Buber's reference to *ehyeh asher ehyeh*, though it is itself a citation of divine speech as recorded in the Hebrew Bible, serves to limit divine speech and deny it everywhere else it appears within the biblical text. Furthermore, by not acknowledging that he is drawing from the Hebrew Bible, Buber makes a claim about God that can be understood in terms that are less particularly Jewish than might be the case if he had acknowledged it. Comparison with the "Religion as Presence" lectures makes this point all the more apparent: in the equivalent passage of the "Religion as Presence" lectures, which were addressed to a specifically Jewish audience at the Frankfort Lehrhaus, Buber cites Exodus 3:14 in Hebrew.

In both *I and Thou* and the "Religion as Presence" lectures, what is revealed in revelation is that there is a revealer, that is, that God is present. In the latter, Buber uses distinctly sensual imagery to capture this idea: "The voice, the eternal voice, becomes word through contact with the human being, with the surface of the human being that it touches, so to speak, with the skin, the ear, the living person that it touches. Through contact with the human being the voice becomes the Word; it becomes God's word. But only in the human being does the voice become a word of God, a word that speaks of God."[18] Touch serves as a metaphor for the process that transforms the divine voice into Word, which immediately suggests sacred text. Stressing the multiplicity of religions that have existed over time, Buber writes of the "forms of God" created by human beings emerging from confrontation with God. Multiple forms of God reflect different encounters and motivate different religions; so long as human beings remain open, any religion might guide them anew into the encounter with God that is revelation.

The relationship between revelation and sacred text becomes pressing for Buber as he and Rosenzweig begin translating the Hebrew Bible into German in 1925. Over the next four years, until Rosenzweig's death in 1929, the pair sit together weekly, making their way from Genesis through Psalms. (Buber later finishes the translation on his own in Jerusalem.) The translation work pushes Buber to read the text more carefully, with attention both to its language and grammar and to its theological message, and this change is reflected in his writings about the Bible from this time.[19]

II. THE BUBER-ROSENZWEIG TRANSLATION (1925–1929)

Buber and Rosenzweig's (B-R) translation of the Hebrew Bible relies on a unique method of translation they devise based on literary principles they called *cola* and *Leitworte* (leading-words), both of which they consider to be essential features of the Hebrew text. A *cola* is a "breath unit," or the number of syllables that can be spoken aloud within the span of a breath. They argue that the physical limitations breathing places on speech reflect the inner movements of a person's soul. As Rosenzweig summarizes,

> Breath is the stuff of speech; the drawing of breath is accordingly the natural segmenting of speech. It is subject to its own law: that we cannot speak more than twenty, at most thirty words without taking a deep breath (and not just a catch-breath)—often indeed we can say only five to ten words. But within this boundary the distribution of breath-renewing silences follows the inner order of speech, which is only occasionally determined by its logical structure, and which for the most part mirrors directly the movements and arousals of the soul itself in its gradations of energy and above all in its gradations of time.[20]

The principle of cola assumes that there is a deeper meaning of the text that is in line with the reader's "movements and arousals of the soul." Earlier translations, which ignore the cola of the biblical text, increase the distance between the text and the reader's soul and thus limit its potential to transform the reader on a spiritual or soulful level.

The translation was published in colometric lines, each line representing the length of a single breathing unit. The difference is visually apparent with the briefest glance at a page of the translation, as we can see in comparing the opening lines of Genesis in the standard Luther translation and in the B-R translation. In Luther's translation, the first five verses appear as follows: "(1) Am Anfang schuf Gott Himmel und Erde. (2) Und die Erde war wüst und leer, und es war finster auf der Tiefe; und der Geist Gottes schwebte auf dem Wasser. (3) Und Gott sprach: Es werde Licht! Und es ward Licht. (4) Und Gott sah, daß das Licht gut war. Da schied Gott das Licht von der Finsternis (5) Und nannte das Licht Tag und die Finsternis Nacht. Da ward aus Abend und Morgen der erste Tag." Each verse in the German corresponds to a verse in the original text. A particular edition will divide the verses into different lines to fit within certain margins or other printing limitations, but such changes are not considered to have an effect on the meaning of the text or the reader's experience of it. In contrast, in the B-R Bible, the verses appear as follows:

> Im Anfang schuf Gott den Himmel und die Erde.
>
> Die Erde war Wirrnis und Wüste.
> Finsternis allüber Abgrund.
> Braus Gottes brütend allüber den Wassern.
>
> Da sprach Gott: Licht werde! Und Licht ward.
> Und Gott sah das Licht: dass es gut war.
> So schied Gott zwischen dem Licht und der Finsternis.
> Dem Licht rief Gott: Tag! und der Finsternis rief er:
>   Nacht!
> Abend ward und Morgen ward: Ein Tag.[21]

The significance of the colometric arrangement is immediately apparent. The division of the text into short lines and stanzas slows the rhythm of the text. The second stanza is lined up so that each of God's four actions is distinct. One is forced—whether reading silently or aloud—to proceed more slowly, and each act receives focused attention. Furthermore, printed editions of the B-R translation do not include potentially distracting verse numbers or chapter markers within the text itself; they appear only at the top of the page for those seeking a particular passage.

Beyond cola, Buber and Rosenzweig argue that the biblical text is shaped by the redactor's purposeful use of *Leitworte*. A *Leitwort* is "a word or word root that is meaningfully repeated within a text or sequence of texts or complex of texts; those who attend to these repetitions will find a meaning of the text revealed or clarified, or at any rate made more emphatic."[22] Together all the text's many *Leitworte* produce what Buber calls "the circulatory system of a great text."[23] Buber and Rosenzweig attempt to reproduce this feature of the biblical text by treating German as though it were Hebrew, namely, by identifying word-roots shared between related verbs and nouns. Each time a particular Hebrew word appears, Buber and Rosenzweig render it with the same German word. They insist as well that Hebrew words linked by a shared word-root be translated with German words that are similarly linked. At times, this works well; at other times, this principle of translation stretches the limits of the German language, forcing the creation of neologisms and even obscuring the meaning of the text. The words of the biblical text, of course, appear within particular verses and contexts that help determine their meaning. While one appearance of a word might be well translated by a particular German word, it is not necessarily the case that the same German word will capture the word's contextual meaning elsewhere in the text. The translation that results from Buber and Rosenzweig's strict reproduction of the text's *Leitworte* is distinctly different from the standard German translation completed by Luther in the early sixteenth century. It was also distinctly different from translations by other German Jews in the modern period, including Moses Mendelssohn (1729–1786) and Leopold Zunz (1794–1886).[24]

"Ich werde dasein, als der ich dasein werde." This is how Buber and Rosenzweig translate Exodus 3:14. It is Rosenzweig, not Buber, who writes about the particular choices they make in translating this verse, but his explanation is in line with Buber's thinking as we have seen it so far: "In the narrative context, then, the only justifiable translation is one that makes prominent not God's being eternal but his being present, his being present for and with you now and in time to come."[25] Rosenzweig references grammatical and lexical technicalities and contrasts his version with earlier translations ranging from the Septuagint and the Vulgate to Mendelssohn and other German Jewish translators. But the grammatical evidence ultimately serves a theological argument in line with Buber's account of revelation in both the "Religion as Presence" lectures and *I and Thou*, namely, that God is defined by presence and that *ehyeh asher ehyeh* is an expression of this. Rosenzweig presents divine presence not in contrast to divine speech, as Buber does, but in contrast to a more commonsense understanding of the verse as an indication of God's eternal nature.

Buber addresses biblical revelation in his 1926 essay, "People Today and the Jewish Bible."[26] This essay expands beyond a discussion of the technicalities of the B-R translation into an account of the connection between revelation as an event and the record of God's words in the biblical text. This account also goes far beyond what we saw in Buber's earlier works and thus merits our careful attention here. In "People Today," Buber defines the central theme of the biblical text as "the encounter of a group of people with the Nameless Being whom they, hearing his speech and speaking to him in turn, ventured to name; their encounter with him in history, in the course of earthly events."[27] It is not the burning bush but the revelation at Sinai in Exodus 19 that serves here to illustrate the concept of a revelatory event. This episode raises several specific questions and issues. First and foremost, the Sinaitic revelation is a collective revelation: God appears before the Israelites to enter a covenant with them as a nation. How is this like or unlike Buber's description of revelation within the terms of I-Thou dialogue? Second, when the Israelites are overwhelmed by the divine presence, they send Moses as their emissary to receive the rest of God's message. Moses delivers commandments, which he presents as God's expectations of what the Israelites will do to uphold their side of the covenant. Because it is presented by Moses as part of the revelation, this content poses a second major challenge to Buber's account of contentless revelation. In addition to this verbal content, the biblical account of the scene at Sinai includes sensory imagery, such as thunder, trumpets, fire, and smoke. This imagery—and the fear it engenders in the Israelites—poses a third challenge to Buber's definition of revelation. Can revelation be accompanied by signs such as these? If so, are they necessary? If not, why does the text include them?

In "People Today," Buber describes the biblical account of revelation at Sinai as "the verbal trace of a natural event, i.e., an event having occurred in the common sensory world of humankind and having fitted into its patterns, which the assemblage that experienced it experienced as God's revelation to it and so preserved it in the inspired and in no way arbitrary formative memory of generations."[28] This description is multilayered, describing both the text of Exodus—the "verbal trace"—and the event itself. In regard to the latter, Buber makes several points: first and foremost, whatever the revelation at Sinai was, it was not supernatural. It did not break any of the laws of nature but happened within the ordinary world in which we continue to live. Second, it was the people present who experienced this natural event as something special and, in particular, as revelation. Because they experienced it in this way, they felt they should take extra efforts to record an account of it. The text that we have represents that attempt; it is inherently inadequate and—particularly because the authors suggest it was supernatural when it cannot have been—should not be read as a literal or complete account. Nevertheless, though as a description it is inadequate, the Torah's account of Sinai offers a model of revelation as an intense event that demands response. It changes the lives of those who were there, and it plays an important role in the Jewish people's collective self-understanding.

Buber engages briefly with some of the commandments that appear within the biblical text as God's articulation of the covenant. But it is the building of the Ohel Mo'ed—the Tent of Meeting—that is commanded in Exodus 25 and then actualized in Exodus 36 that Buber presents as an illustration of the sort of action demanded by divine presence: "history at least is a dialogue. People learn to build [the Tent]; but their hands are not guided."[29] Buber develops this point through comparison of God's creation of the world in Genesis and the Israelites' construction of the Ohel Mo'ed in Exodus. In particular, and in line with the theory of *Leitworte*, Buber highlights repetition of the verb '*asah* throughout the two passages and the verbs *yaḥal* and *ra'ah* at the conclusion of both the divine creation and the human construction. These *Leitworte* call the reader to examine these passages together; in the examination, the differences between them that emerge reveal a deeper meaning.

More specifically, Buber argues that the *Leitworte* shared between these two passages alert us to the differences between creation and revelation as two distinct epochs within the biblical conception of history. In creation, God's words are answered by the "dumb genesis of things"—that is, God speaks and the things he names are created and appear.[30] In the epoch of revelation—the epoch of human history—it is human beings, not things, that must respond, and they must do so with intention and purpose. In the case of the Ohel Mo'ed, specifically, God's revelation calls for the tent and human beings respond by collecting the necessary materials, taking up their tools and creating the tent themselves. Buber argues that the Ohel Mo'ed illustrates more broadly that human response is a necessary element of revelation. This is in line with his discussion of revelation in *I and Thou* and his other earlier works, but at the same time, the Ohel Mo'ed is by far the most specific and concrete example of response to revelation to be found in Buber's writings about the Bible up to this point.

As his discussion of the Ohel Mo'ed illustrates, Buber's translation work makes explicit the tension between his definition of revelation as divine presence and the claims of the biblical text to be a record of divine speech. But Buber does not retreat from his insistence that revelation in biblical times was no different from the revelations possible in other times and other places. He continues to argue that revelation and decisive response are possible and real for any human being at any time; it "is lived in the fearful and magnificent full decisiveness of the moment—of the historical moment, which in its actualities is everywhere a moment of biography, yours and mine no less than Alexander's or Caesar's, but not your moment of yourself but of your encounter."[31]

III. COMMENTARIES

Buber's biblical commentaries provide a final case for our examination of his understanding of revelation. *Kingship of God* (1933), *Prophetic Faith* (1942), and

Moses (1945) are argument-driven treatises about the nature of the biblical text, suffused with footnotes. Furthermore, in his commentaries Buber approaches the text with a methodology he calls "Tradition Criticism." Though he does not directly reference German biblical scholar Hermann Gunkel (1862–1932), who developed the more standard methodologies of Form Criticism and Tradition Criticism, Buber's method overlaps with Gunkel's in important ways. In particular, Buber and Gunkel both assume that the text's stories and ideas record an earlier, oral tradition, and Buber reads the text as a collection of these oral traditions that was later written down rather than as a collection of disparate written sources redacted into a single whole. Beyond this, Buber relies on the concept of *Leitworte* he developed while translating as a key for unlocking deeper meanings embedded in the written text.[32]

In line with his description of the text in "People Today," in his commentaries Buber reads the Bible as a record of encounters between the Israelites and God. He argues further that the written accounts of these events simultaneously represent stages in the development of a distinctive Israelite theology. Determining stages in the development of the human-divine relationship through particular historical events becomes the reader's primary challenge. This is markedly different from the task of making the text present that Buber had set before the readers of the B-R translation when he told them to "place themselves anew before the renewed book, hold back nothing of themselves, let everything happen between themselves and it, whatever may happen."[33]

Buber wrote the first of his commentaries, *Kingship of God*, in the hope of attaining a position in a German university as a biblical scholar.[34] The rise of the Nazi regime made this impossible not long after the book was published. Buber was later hired as chair of the new Department of the Sociology of Culture (now Sociology and Anthropology) at the Hebrew University in Jerusalem, where he moved in 1938 and lived until his death in 1965. Though his position was in sociology, not biblical studies, Buber wrote the latter two commentaries in Jerusalem. They were among his first book-length publications in Hebrew (though in both cases, the books were published in German translation within just a few years).

The central argument of *Kingship of God* is theopolitical, namely, that the Israelites understood God to be their king and that the Hebrew Bible preserves both the development of this theology and the efforts of Israelites to realize it within the structure of their society.[35] In seeking support for his argument from the Pentateuch in particular, Buber focuses on the name of God and illustrations of God's omnipresence, understanding both as departures from pagan beliefs that gods are located in specific places and can be summoned by name. *Ehyeh asher ehyeh*, Exodus 3:14, again serves as a locus point for Buber's discussion of divine presence and divine-human interaction in *Kingship of God*: "The first *ehye* simply gives the assurance: I shall be there (ever and ever with My host, with My people, with you)—and thus you do not need to conjure me. And the following *asher ehye*, according to all parallels, can only mean: as I Who will always be there, as I ever and ever will be there, that is, as I ever and ever will want to appear.... In short: you do not need to conjure Me, but you cannot conjure Me either."[36] Yet again, Buber uses the theophany at the burning bush to define revelation as divine presence rather than divine speech. His specification that divine presence need not be and cannot be summoned is intended to separate the one God of the Israelites from the multiple gods of the pagan traditions the Israelites were rejecting. These gods could be conjured or summoned to respond to specific human needs. The God of the Israelites *is* presence and is thus *always present*. This is in line with Buber's account of revelation in *I and Thou* and also reflects Rosenzweig's grammatical argument in the context of the B-R translation.

As I discussed previously, in the context of translating, Buber describes the text of Exodus 19 as the "verbal trace" of an actual, natural event in the collective history of the Israelites. In *Moses*, Buber looks beyond the drama of the revelation at Sinai to focus on Exodus 24, where Moses completes the process of covenant making. Buber focuses on the rituals Moses performs at the base of the mountain to turn the twelve Israelite tribes into the one nation of Israel. According to Buber, it is Moses who articulates the commandments that make up the covenant as a way of marking or preserving the relationship between the Israelites and God. The commandments are a human response to revelation, not revelation itself. Revelation itself remains contentless, defined by God's presence and not God's words.

Why does Moses undertake the task of transforming the Israelites from a group of tribes into a nation in a covenantal relationship with God? Buber turns to God's revelation to Moses at the burning bush in Exodus 3 to explain Moses's conviction that the people need a covenant. Buber's discussion of *ehyeh asher ehyeh* in *Moses* is far more detailed than any of his earlier discussions of Exodus 3:14, as he takes care to understand the verse within the larger chapter in which it appears. He begins with Exodus 3:6, where God identifies himself as the "God of the Fathers" who was known to Abraham, Isaac, and Jacob. Buber argues that connections between God, the ancestors, and the Israelites enslaved in Egypt is further underscored by the *Leitworte 'ami* (my people) and *Mitsrayim* (Egypt). Using these *Leitworte*, Buber argues that God's connection to the ancestors is stronger than God's connection to the enslaved

Israelites themselves, for the latter connection will only truly be established at Mount Sinai: "With this repeated 'my people' [*'ami*] at the commencement and close of the passage, YHVH recognizes Israel in a fashion more powerful and unequivocal than would have been possible by any other verbal means. To be sure, he has not yet designated himself their God. He will become the God of Israel as a people solely through the revelation to the people; now he wishes to be known only as the God of their forefathers, to whom he had once promised the land whither he would lead Israel."[37] Buber's emphasis on the connection between the God of the Fathers and the God speaking at the burning bush seems intended to build on his earlier arguments that *ehyeh asher ehyeh* represents a refutation of pagan traditions that associated gods with particular places. But more significantly for our inquiry, in this discussion Buber seems to suggest that God revealed a specific content to Moses, namely, the connection between this revealing God, the Israelites, and the Israelite forefathers. The alternative, that it was Moses who assigned this meaning to his encounter with God's presence at the burning bush, is possible but further from the simple meaning of Buber's text.

As Buber's analysis of the burning bush encounter continues, he describes Moses and God's conversation as "the great [dialogue] in which the God commands and the man resists."[38] He then describes several moments in which God "states" something or makes a particular promise. It is hard to believe that Buber is claiming that God spoke specific words aloud for Moses to hear, but he also does not indicate that the words that the text ascribes to God were Moses's interpretation of his experience of revelation, as they would have to be within the model of revelation as divine presence that runs through so much of his work. In his concluding statement on *ehyeh asher ehyeh*, Buber writes that the account "does not belong to literature but to the sphere attained by the founders of religion. If it is theology, it is that archaic theology which, in the form of a historical narrative, stands at the threshold of every genuine historical religion. No matter who related that speech or when, he derived it from a tradition which, in the last resort, cannot go back to anybody other than the founder."[39] Even if it was not Moses himself who recorded the words we have, by the nature of what they describe, we can be certain that they point to an actual event in his life and thus in history. At the same time, Moses is responsible for the content of the revelation. That is to say, even while we can be certain that something happened at the burning bush, we must give credit to Moses for his response, namely, the covenant he brings to the Israelites and its many theological implications. But the line between the revelation of divine presence and the human response is notably blurred in Buber's discussion of the event. Without the background of Buber's earlier discussions of revelation, it is possible, even likely, that the separation between the two would barely be noticed at all.

IV. CONCLUSION

In the preceding pages, I traced Buber's discussions of revelation in three distinct stages of his thinking about the Bible. By looking in particular at his discussions of Exodus 3:14 and the phrase *ehyeh asher ehyeh* and then at the Sinaitic revelation in Exodus 19, I tried to show how Buber developed his understanding of revelation in connection with the biblical text. In the case of Exodus 3:14, the biblical text offered support for Buber's contention that revelation is a dialogical relationship between a human being and God. From the human side, that relationship is a sense of divine presence. *Ehyeh asher ehyeh* expresses divine presence; though the biblical text presents it as God's response when Moses asks for God's name, Buber argues that the meaning of the words themselves indicate that what Moses received in response to his question was divine presence, not these words or any others. Buber explores this statement of divine presence several times in his writings of the late 1910s and early 1920s, but his analysis consistently makes this same point.

It is when Buber becomes a translator of biblical text that we begin to see him wrestling more closely with the biblical text's claims to be a record of events as they happened, including events of divine speech. As noted previously, the revelation at Sinai in Exodus 19 presents challenges Buber's earlier account of revelation in several specific ways. It is a collective revelation experienced by the entire people, challenging Buber's earlier description of human-divine encounters as intimate I-Thou relationships. The extraordinary nature of the revelation as it is described in Exodus underscores this challenge. For the question of divine speech, the extensive content of the covenant formed at Sinai challenges Buber's insistence that God does not speak.

To answer the challenges of the Sinaitic revelation to his account of human-divine encounter, Buber looks beyond Exodus 19 to the building of the Ohel Mo'ed, the Tent of Meeting. This account becomes a model for Buber's argument that revelation of divine presence is a demand for human response, a response that must come in the form of decisive, purposeful action. Buber's emphasis on human response continues in his commentaries, where he accounts for both the covenant and the commandments that define it as Moses's own response to his initial encounter with divine presence at the burning bush of Exodus 3. This analysis begins with Buber's earlier understanding of revelation as divine presence while also offering an account of where the words that the biblical text places into God's mouth originated. It is striking that in discussing Moses in his commentaries Buber occasionally repeats the biblical language of "God said" to explain how the divine presence moved Moses to draw the tribes of Israel together through a covenant. I do not think that Buber's view changed or that he means to accept the Bible's claim that God speaks in human language. Rather, his slippage into this language reveals the power of speech as a model for interaction, an essential point of Buber's *I and Thou* and his emphasis there on the word-pairs that define human existence in the world from moment to moment. And, ultimately, whatever words Moses used to describe his encounter with God at the burning bush and whatever words the Israelites used to describe what happened at Sinai, what seems to matter most in Buber's view is that they chose to create a record of their momentary encounter with and response to divine presence.

NOTES

1. Richard I. Cohen, "Urban Visibility and Biblical Visions: Jewish Culture in Western and Central Europe in the Modern Age," in *Cultures of the Jews: A New History*, ed. David Biale (New York: Schocken Books, 2002), 764.

2. Jon D. Levenson, *The Hebrew Bible, the Old Testament, and Historical Criticism* (Louisville, KY: Westminster/John Knox Press, 1993).

3. Regarding the development of a Jewish exegetical theology in the nineteenth century, see Alexandra Zirkle, "Biblical Hermeneutics: Between Wissenschaft and Religion," *Daat: A Journal of Jewish Philosophy & Kabbalah* 88 (2019): 11–32.

4. On dualism in Buber's thought in general, see Avraham Shapira, *Hope for Our Time: Key Trends in the Thought of Martin Buber* (Albany: State University of New York Press, 1999). On Buber's adoption of the terms *religion* and *religiosity* from the sociologist George Simmel, see Paul Mendes-Flohr, *From Mysticism to Dialogue: Martin Buber's Transformation of German Social Thought* (Detroit: Wayne State University Press, 1989).

5. Buber writes that with the liberal version of Judaism, "Judaism appears to be a curious awkward detour to some modern philosophical theorems—as, for instance, the idea of God as a postulate of critical reason, or the categorical imperative.... The originators of such theories overlook the fact that religious truth is not a conceptual abstraction but has existential relevance; that is, that words can only point the way, and that religious truth can be made adequately manifest only in the individual's or the community's life" (Martin Buber, "Herut: On Youth and Religion," in *On Judaism*, ed. Nahum N. Glatzer [New York: Schocken, 1996], 161; also published as "Cheruth: Eine Rede Über Jugend und

Religion," in *Reden Über Das Judentum* [Frankfurt am Main: Literarische Anstalt Rütten und Loening, 1923], 217).

6. Franz Rosenzweig, "Atheistic Theology," in *Philosophical and Theological Writings*, ed. Paul W. Franks and Michael L. Morgan (Indianapolis: Hackett, 2000), 19; also published as "Atheistische Theologie," in *Zweistromland*, ed. Reinhold Mayer and Annemarie Mayer (Derdrecht, Netherlands: Martinus Nighoff, 1984), 693.

7. Rosenzweig, "Atheistic Theology," 24; "Atheistische Theologie," 697.

8. Buber, "Herut," 155; "Cheruth," 209.

9. Hugo Bergman reads "Herut" as an anticipation of *I and Thou*. In light of Horwitz's work on the "Religion as Presence" lectures, I think this is an overreading. See Hugo Bergman, "Martin Buber and Mysticism," in *The Philosophy of Martin Buber*, ed. Paul A. Schilpp and Maurice Friedman (La Salle, IL: Open Court, 1967).

10. Rivka Horwitz, *Buber's Way to "I and Thou": The Development of Martin Buber's Thought and His "Religion as Presence" Lectures* (Philadelphia: Jewish Publication Society, 1988), 20. The original German text for these lectures may be found in an earlier edition of the book: Rivka Horwitz, *Buber's Way to I and Thou: An Historical Analysis and the First Publication of Martin Buber's Lectures "Religion Als Gegenwart"* (Heidelberg, Germany: Lambert Schneider, 1976). All later references are to the 1988 English edition.

11. Horwitz, *Buber's Way*, 106–7.

12. Ibid., 106.

13. Ibid., 121.

14. "No human being is pure person, and none is pure ego.... But some men are so person-oriented that one may call them persons, while others are so ego-oriented that one may call them egos" (Martin Buber, *I and Thou*, trans. Walter Kaufmann [New York: Scribner, 1970], 114–15; published in German as *Ich und Du*, 8th ed. [Heidelberg, Germany: Lambert Schneider, 1974], 79).

15. Buber, *I and Thou*, 160; *Ich und Du*, 132.

16. Robert Alter, *The Five Books of Moses: A Translation with Commentary* (New York: W. W. Norton, 2004), 321n14.

17. For a different perspective on Exodus 3:14 in German Jewish thought, see Francesca Albertini, "Èhyeh Asher Èhyeh: Ex 3, 14 According to the Interpretations of Moses Mendelssohn, Franz Rosenzweig, and Martin Buber," in *Jewish Studies at the Turn of the Twentieth Century*, ed. Judit Targarona Borrás and Angel Sáenz-Badillos (Boston: Brill, 1999), 19–26.

18. Horwitz, *Buber's Way*, 150.

19. On Rosenzweig's hermeneutics, see Mara H. Benjamin, *Rosenzweig's Bible: Reinventing Scripture for Jewish Modernity* (Cambridge: Cambridge University Press, 2009).

20. Franz Rosenzweig, "Scripture and Word: On the New Bible Translation," in *Scripture and Translation*, trans. Lawrence Rosenwald and Everett Fox (Bloomington: Indiana University Press, 1994), 43; originally published as "Die Schrift und Das Wort," in *Die Schrift und Ihre Verdeutschung* (Berlin: Schocken, 1936), 81.

21. Martin Buber and Franz Rosenzweig, trans., *Das Buch im Anfang* (Berlin: Lambert Schneider, n.d.), 7. This is the text that appears in an early edition of Genesis (*Das Buch Im Anfang*). For this particular passage, later editions are significantly revised. (The particular text I am working with has no date but appears to me to be the original edition.)

22. Martin Buber, "Leitwort Style in Pentateuch Narrative," in *Scripture and Translation*, 114; originally published as "Leitwortstil in Der Erzählung des Pentateuchs," in *Die Schrift und Ihre Verdeutschung*, 211.

23. Martin Buber, "Leitwort and Discourse Type: An Example," in *Scripture and Translation*, 150; originally published as "Das Leitwort und Der Formtypus der Rede," in *Die Schrift und Ihre Verdeutschung*, 275.

24. On the phenomenon of Jews translating the Hebrew Bible into German, see Abigail E. Gillman, "Between Religion and Culture: Mendelssohn, Buber, Rosenzweig, and the Enterprise of Biblical Translation," in *Biblical Translation in Context*, ed. Frederick W. Knobloch (Bethesda: University Press of Maryland, 2002), 93–114; Abigail Gillman, *A History of German Jewish Bible Translation* (Chicago: University of Chicago Press, 2018); Maren Ruth Niehoff, "The Buber-Rosenzweig Translation of the Bible within Jewish-German Tradition," *Journal of Jewish Studies* 44, no. 2 (1993): 258–79; W. Gunther Plaut, *German-Jewish Bible Translations: Linguistic Theology as a Political Phenomenon* (New York: Leo Baeck Institute, 1992); and Naomi Seidman, *Faithful Renderings: Jewish-Christian Difference and the Politics of Translation* (Chicago: University of Chicago Press, 2006), 153–98.

25. Franz Rosenzweig, "'The Eternal': Mendelssohn and the Name of God," in *Scripture and Translation*, 105; "'Der Ewige,'" in *Die Schrift und Ihre Verdeutschung*, 194.

26. The original title, "Der Mensch von Heute und die Jüdische Bibel," has also been translated as "The Man of Today and the Jewish Bible." The German *mensch* is more gender neutral than *man* suggests, and I follow Everett Fox and Lawrence Rosenwald in referring to the essay as "People Today and the Jewish Bible." See Martin Buber, "People Today and the Jewish Bible," in *Scripture and Translation*, 4n1.

27. Ibid., 4; originally published as "Der Mensch von Heute und Die Jüdische Bibel," in *Die Schrift und Ihre Verdeutschung*, 13.

28. Buber, "People Today," 10; "Der Mensch von Heute," 25.

29. Buber, "People Today," 19; "Der Mensch von Heute," 42.

30. Buber, "People Today," 19; "Der Mensch von Heute," 42.

31. Buber, "People Today," 9; "Der Mensch von Heute," 22.

32. For further consideration of Buber's hermeneutic method in his commentaries, see Claire Sufrin, "History, Myth, and Divine Dialogue in Martin Buber's Biblical Commentaries," *Jewish Quarterly Review* 103, no. 1 (2013): 74–100.

33. Buber, "People Today," 7; "Der Mensch von Heute," 19.

34. Paul Mendes-Flohr, ed., *Martin Buber: A Contemporary Perspective* (Syracuse, NY: Syracuse University Press, 2002), 1–2.

35. Samuel Hayim Brody, *Martin Buber's Theopolitics* (Bloomington: Indiana University Press, 2018).

36. Martin Buber, *Kingship of God*, 3rd ed., trans. Richard Scheimann (Amherst, NY: Humanity Books, 1990), 106; originally published as *Königtum Gottes* (Berlin: Schocken, 1932), 84.

37. Martin Buber, *Moses: The Revelation and the Covenant* (New York: Harper Torchbooks, 1957), 45–46; published in Hebrew as *Mosheh*, ed. Avraham Shapira (Jerusalem: Schocken, 1999), 68.

38. Buber, *Moses*, 46; *Mosheh*, 69.

39. Buber, *Moses*, 55; *Mosheh*, 78.

PART II

THEOPOLITICS

FOUR

IS THE DIALOGUE BETWEEN HEAVEN AND EARTH AN I-THOU RELATION?

SAMUEL HAYIM BRODY

I. INTRODUCTION: BUBER AND BRANDING

I and Thou (*Ich und Du*, 1923) has often been taken to be Martin Buber's masterwork. This judgment has frequently implied several corollaries: that *I and Thou* is a work of philosophy and, therefore, that Buber is a philosopher; that his philosophy contains the fundamental ontological and ethical orientation that informs all his other writing; and that both earlier and later texts of Buber's, regardless of genre, should hence be refracted through the lens of *I and Thou* and thus considered as contributions to a larger project of constructing a "philosophy of dialogue." This larger project, the philosophy of dialogue, is then understood as Buber's primary life's work, with *I and Thou* its major statement and other works being applications or elaborations of this philosophy.[1]

The desire behind this interpretive strategy is to be able to bring together the vast range of Buber's writing on Hasidism, biblical topics, education, aesthetics, philosophy, and Zionism under a single, coherent rubric; "dialogue" presents itself as a candidate for such a rubric since it is sufficiently capacious to include a wide variety of genres and sufficiently flexible to account for Buber's constant evolution as a thinker. For some texts, this reading comes easily: for example, 1929's "Dialogue" (*Zwiesprache*), explicitly billed as an expansion and clarification of matters left unresolved in *I and Thou*. For others, however, especially Buber's large corpus of writings on the Bible, scholars have arguably had to reach with more difficulty for an interpretation that makes sense in terms of "dialogue." Nonetheless, readers have sensed over the years that there is some common thread that lends its color to everything Buber writes, and "dialogue" is the most common name they have given to that thread. It is not the only one; "Jewish existentialism" and "Hebrew Humanism" have also served this function, even when it is specifically acknowledged that Buber denied having a single intellectual "system" or profile.[2]

Most likely none of these terms suffices to incorporate *all* of Buber's work, even if each nonetheless captures some significant portion. Buber himself did his part to promote the centrality of "dialogue"; in the afterword to the 1957 edition of *I and Thou*, he wrote that attempts to clarify what he had said in that work had brought "several shorter works ... into being," in which he emphasized "the central significance of the close association of the relation to God with the relation to one's fellow-men, which is my most essential concern." The afterword itself he described as the result of his decision to move from answering individual queries and criticisms toward an effort not to "restrict the dialogical relationship to those readers who decide to speak up: perhaps some of those who remain silent deserve special consideration."[3] Note that here Buber describes his "most essential concern" as embodied in *I and Thou* and "several shorter works," namely, the ones mentioned previously as elaborations on the dialogical philosophy. And yet, surely Buber did not mean that only a few of his works ever addressed his most essential concern! I would propose reading these statements as a comment on genre: the works on "dialogue," with their ontological vocabulary and poetic-philosophical argumentation, are simply one genre in which Buber wrote about his most essential concern.

Buber vacillated between offering these catchwords and slogans, as if engaged in a branding campaign, and saying that he had no coherent "teaching" at all. He clearly had a keen sense of the stakes in coining a phrase. In the early 1940s, he reflected on his use of the term *Jewish Renaissance* at the turn of the century, as well as his later terms *Biblical Humanism* and *Hebrew Humanism*, expressing the care that went into the choice of each word in these terms as well as the fear that such care could nonetheless be thwarted by careless misinterpretation. He also describes the way in which the "full meaning" of a term could dawn "only gradually," even over the course of decades of usage, as "the basic consequences deriving from our choice of this term" became clear.[4] I would describe this attitude as a pragmatic experimentalism with respect to sloganeering. Over time, Buber took note of the effects that a particular slogan or catchphrase had had in the world, who had been drawn to it and who repelled by it, and how it had been understood and misunderstood and then modified the terms as he thought appropriate. In keeping with the occasionalist tendency of his thought that has sometimes itself been subsumed under the name of "dialogue," he offered these catchwords to particular audiences in particular contexts for particular purposes and was always willing to discard or replace them when they became irrelevant or counterproductive.

It is in that spirit that I consider the possibility that Buber's biblical writings, which form a large proportion of his total corpus, beginning with *Königtum Gottes* (*Kingship of God*, 1932) and continuing with its unfinished sequel *Der Gesalbte* (*The Anointed*, 1936), *Torat Hanevi'im* (*The Prophetic Faith*, 1942), and *Moshe* (*Moses*, 1945), are not best considered as a species of "dialogical thought" or an attempt to "apply dialogical principles" to the Bible. Not only do we overgeneralize if we imagine the idea of "dialogue" to be relevant in the same way to all areas of Buber's work, but we also miss the unique contribution of the biblical writings to Buber's oeuvre if we classify them as simply lengthy exercises or applications of a well-known, previously articulated principle. Rather, it seems to me that Buber's "encounter" with the Hebrew Bible (to use a "dialogical" term) generated its own categories and its own patterns, which certainly share commonalities with Buber's other ideas but which should not be treated as reducible to them.

Buber himself was aware that the better part of his international renown inhered in his title as "philosopher of dialogue," and if we keep in mind his pragmatic and strategic attitude toward his own slogans, we notice the ways he tries to leverage this popularity. So, indeed, in his biblical writings Buber occasionally refers to the relationship between God and the people Israel as a "dialogue between heaven and earth." Overall, however, the fact is that I-Thou language is used sparingly in these works. Moreover, when I-Thou language *is* used, it seems to indicate a type of dialogue very different from the relation to the Eternal Thou as described in *I and Thou*. Again, my aim here is neither to fault Buber for failing to adhere slavishly to his own technical terms nor to expose him as somehow insufficiently systematic. Quite the contrary—even the greatest supporters of the idea of reading everything Buber ever wrote through the lens of "dialogue," such as Maurice Friedman, would not claim this type of consistency for him, even as a goal.[5] What I hope to show is that if we start from the biblical writings, and treat them on their own terms, we end up with an intriguingly distinct constellation of key concepts and values, orbiting around the central idea of "theopolitics," which can be used as an alternative lens to examine other elements of Buber's work, most prominently including his engagement in the Zionist-Arab conflict. This lens, in its turn, suggests a slightly different reading of Buber's intellectual trajectory and career for its own proper contextualization. What follows will present that alternative context and reading first, before turning to the biblical texts themselves.

II. THEOPOLITICS: ANARCHISM AND THEOCRACY

My primary claim is that the term *theopolitics*, which Buber develops and uses throughout his writings on the Bible and which I offer here in the manner described previously as a catchword or slogan for the collective project of those works, should be understood as a cipher for a Landauerian anarchism, expressed in a Jewish vocabulary and encoded in a biblical-critical apparatus. Although Paul Mendes-Flohr's argument for the influence of the German anarchist Gustav Landauer (1870–1919) on Buber has been widely accepted, the reach of this influence has generally been understood primarily in terms of its impact on Buber's philosophy, namely, his movement "from mysticism to dialogue" during World War I.[6] In this narrative, Landauer's harsh criticism of Buber's war politics is the spark that snaps Buber out of his neo-Romantic reverie, leading him to understand the problematic nature of his support for the war and thereby (as a logical consequence, it is argued) of the neo-Romantic mystical worldview that had undergirded all his previous work, from the first collections of Hasidic tales (*Legend of the Baal Shem*, 1906, and *Tales of Rebbe Nachman*, 1908) to the Prague lectures on Judaism (1909–10) and *Daniel: Dialogues on Realization* (1913). Spurred on by this trauma, Buber sets out to rectify the problem, allotting an increasing place in his thought to encounter and to the position of the Other; this process culminates in the writing of *I and Thou* and the development of the dialogic.

I propose to modify this narrative in two ways: first, by considering the positive, rather than merely the negative, influence of Landauer on Buber. That is, I argue that Buber does not merely take Landauer's criticism as a sign that he needs to probe what he had previously gotten wrong—there is a positive impact as well, as he turns to a deeper examination of his friend's thought in order to understand why Landauer got World War I *right*. Second, I extend the narrative of this impact into the 1920s, beyond the publication of *I and Thou*, so that it encompasses the work with Franz Rosenzweig (1886–1929) on the German Bible translation, the adventure of the Frankfurt Lehrhaus, and Buber's increasing engagement with religious socialism and with the burgeoning centrality of the kibbutz idea to the Zionist movement. This approach allows me to consider *Kingship of God* as a different kind of culmination: one that expresses neither Buber's prewar mystical neo-Romanticism nor a "philosophy of dialogue" but, rather, a synthetic and idiosyncratic combination of all these interests as Buber worked them out from 1916 to 1932. *Kingship of God*, in turn, forms the basis for a new theopolitical treatment of the Hebrew Bible and the history of Israel as Buber pursues it in *The Anointed, The Prophetic Faith*, and *Moses*.

IIa. The Positive Impact of Landauer's Anarchism on Buber

To fully appreciate Landauer's influence on Buber, we have to form a clearer impression of Landauer himself. The years of his lifespan closely track the fate of socialism and anarchism in Germany. Gustav Landauer and the *Kaiserreich* were very nearly born twins—Landauer was older by one year—and he outlived the second Reich by a few months. He grew to maturity together with German socialism; 1875 saw the birth of the Sozialistische Arbeiterpartei Deutschlands (SAPD), the party that would eventually (as the SPD) become the largest political institution in Germany despite Bismarck's best efforts to ban it by means of the 1878 Sozialistingesetze (Socialist Laws).[7] And he would die, fatefully, at the dawn of the Weimar Republic, at the hands of right-wing Freikorps militiamen, hired by the new SPD leadership of Friedrich Ebert and Gustav Noske to put down the anarchist and communist rebellions of 1919 (despite the opposition of the Freikorps not just to anarchism and communism but also to liberalism and the republic itself).

As a young man studying classicism and romanticism at the University of Berlin, Landauer was initially more interested in poetry and Nietzsche than in Marxism. His only connection to radical politics was his work with the Freie Volksbühne, a theater company funded by the SPD to provide the working masses with access to high culture at low prices. Eventually, however, through friends in the company, Landauer came to affiliate with the Jungen, a group of dissident youth whose objections to the SPD's 1891 Erfurt Program led them to oppose any involvement in electoral politics. Thus, Landauer was later able to say of his own political autobiography that "I was an anarchist before I was a socialist, and one of the few who had not taken a detour via social democracy."[8] For Landauer, the expulsion of the Jungen from the Erfurt congress marked the SPD as rotten from the beginning, and in 1919, only weeks before his death, he declared, "In the entire natural history I know of no more disgusting creature than the Social Democratic Party."[9]

I lack space here to fully explore the contours of Landauer's thought. But as can be seen from this brief contextualization, it stands squarely within the tradition of left-wing revolutionary anarchism as theorized by nineteenth-century thinkers such as Pierre-Joseph Proudhon (1809–65), Mikhail Bakunin (1814–76), and Peter Kropotkin (1842–21) while also eventually contributing several important ideas that reframe and redirect that tradition. Anarchism of this type considered itself coterminous with socialism or communism rightly construed; its differences from its Marxist rival centered less on ultimate goals (perfect freedom together with perfect equality, a classless society, the abolition of private property and the state) and more on means (the strategy of seizing the machinery of the state, establishing a dictatorship of the proletariat in order to place the means of production under the control of a vanguard party operating in the name of the oppressed class). Anarchists were skeptical that the Marxist state would wither away and argued that a radicalized and mobilized working class would be better served to immediately constitute decentralized and dehierarchized organizations of the type they would want to see in a free society. Rather than imagine transition phases, or the achievement of "full communism" only "after the revolution," anarchists typically sought, in the words of the Industrial Workers of the World (IWW), to prefigure "the new society within the shell of the old."[10]

Landauer, through his newspaper *Der Sozialist* (its very title a polemical thrust against authoritarian socialism) as well as through his books and pamphlets, promoted a "romantic," Nietzschean version of anarchism that sought to unite revolutionary, class-based, and industrial politics with a focus on the importance of individual freedom and creativity as well as a more rural orientation and a recovery of certain features of medieval society. He was criticized for this last emphasis by radicals to whom it seemed conservative and nostalgic. However, Landauer always insisted that he was merely objectively assessing what was liberty- and equality-promoting, without the burden of the progressivist and rationalist bias that distorted Marxist theories of history (and which he thought, in a manner presaging contemporary postmodernism, to be itself a product or symptom of the system Marxism understood itself as attacking).[11] This also enabled Landauer to take a somewhat more positive view of religion than many of his comrades; while in prison, he translated the Christian mystic Meister Eckhart into modern German alongside the writings of Shakespeare and Oscar Wilde.

It was thus as a proponent of a mystically informed, "unorthodox" anarchism that a young Buber would have first encountered Landauer, at a meeting of the Neue Gemeinschaft organization around the turn of the century.[12] The two men quickly formed a connection, perhaps over their shared appreciation for Nietzsche and for neo-Romantic religiosity over organized religion. Over the coming decades, Buber would help renew Landauer's interest in his own Judaism through his publications on Hasidism, which may themselves in turn have been at least partially influenced by Landauer's explorations of Christian mysticism. Buber would join Landauer's Sozialistische Bund; Landauer would publish a book, *Die Revolution*, in Buber's Die Gesellschaft series. They wrote articles about each other.[13] Ultimately, however, it turned out that the two men had assumed more *political* closeness between them than there turned out to be; it seems to have come as a shock to both when they found themselves at loggerheads over Buber's support for Germany in the world war.

How could this have happened? This is not the place to present a fine-grained analysis of the differences between the two men on matters of aesthetics or ontology that may have undergirded their eventual difference on the war yet also managed to escape the attention of both men during their many intellectual exchanges.[14] For our purposes it is enough to note that Landauer had articulated a principled opposition to violence, and not just to violence perpetrated by the state on a mass scale but also to that committed by his ideological fellow travelers, the anarchists. In a 1901 essay called "Anarchic Thoughts on Anarchism," Landauer invoked Tolstoy in support of his claim that "any kind of violence is dictatorial... a goal can only be reached if it is already reflected in its means."[15] The claim that violence was needed to bring freedom to the world, Landauer argued, proved the dictatorial tendencies of its advocates: "This is yet another crucial fallacy: that one can—or must—bring anarchism to the world; that anarchy is an affair of all of humanity; that there will indeed be a day of judgment followed by a millennial era. Those who want 'to bring freedom to the world'— which will always be *their* idea of freedom—are tyrants, not anarchists."[16] Buber lavishes praise on this article in his 1904 essay on Landauer's thought, calling it "one of the most beautiful documents of human self-liberation."[17] Yet he seems to have failed to grasp its Tolstoyan lesson—namely, the necessary consonance of ends and means—and to have completely ignored its antimessianic politics when he writes in 1914 of the "solemn exaltation" of the imminent conflagration of Europe, enthusing that force and spirit would henceforth be joined together, exclaiming, "Incipit vita nova"![18] It was these failures that led Landauer to accuse his friend of "aestheticism and formalism" and of publishing "what the Hapsburgs, the Hohenzollerns, and the interests allied with them want to hear" in addition to telling him that he "had no right ... to publicly take a stand on the political events of the present day" and predicting that Buber would "have to analyze, add, qualify, retract, and regret.... In the future you will not take part in the German war against the other peoples of Europe, nor in the war of Europe against itself, as you do now in your profound confusion and bewilderment."[19]

As noted previously, it is often argued that this criticism provoked Buber to embark on a process of self-searching that led him to revise his previous worldview and commitments.[20] What I now want to emphasize is the extent to which he did not merely revise his previous ideas to correct for what had allowed him to get the war so wrong but that he also took into consideration what had allowed Landauer to be among the few people in Germany to get the war *right*, to resist and refuse to succumb to the *Kriegserlebnis* that swept the country in 1914: Landauer's anarchism. The first evidence of this emerges almost immediately, later in the summer of 1916, during Buber's public debate with philosopher Hermann Cohen (1842–1918) over Zionism. In response to Cohen's claim that the state precedes and constitutes the nation (an anti-Zionist point in its context, since it supports the popular liberal conception of German Jews as "Germans of the Mosaic faith"), Buber writes,

> just as the state in general is not the determining goal of mankind, so the "Jewish state" is not the determining goal for the Jews.... [Our argument] does not concern the Jewish state, that, yes, were it to be founded today would be built upon the same principles as any other modern state. It does not concern the addition of one more trifling power structure.... Zion restored will become the house of the Lord for all peoples and the center of the new world ... in which "the blood-stained garment of war is burned" and "the swords are turned into plowshares."[21]

Many scholars have noted that Buber and Cohen fail to appreciate each other's positions in the course of this debate, at times even failing to accord each other the respect one would expect from two such eminent Jewish intellectual leaders. It seems justified to speculate that Buber wanted to demonstrate, as soon as possible, his public allegiance to principles Landauer would approve. And indeed, Landauer wrote to Buber twice to express his appreciation for the tack Buber took in this debate; one of these letters is the first one postdating May 1916 to be included by Buber in his two-volume edition of Landauer's correspondence.[22]

Two years later, during the chaotic period of mutiny and revolution following the end of the war, we find more evidence of Buber's "Landauerian" turn. In December 1918, one month after socialist leader Kurt Eisner declared Bavaria an independent republic, effectively ending hundreds of years of monarchy without firing a shot, Buber seems to have traveled to Munich to deliver an address.[23] He had been invited there by Landauer, who was in Munich at the behest of Eisner himself, engaged in "transforming the souls through lecturing."[24] And this was what Buber attempted to do, although Landauer would surely have liked it even better had he stayed in Munich and aided the revolution further through developing curricula for "people's education." The lecture that Buber gave in Munich was entitled "Das Judentum und die wahre Gemeinschaft" ("Judaism and True Community") and was eventually published as *Der Heilige Weg: Ein Wort an die Juden und an die Völker* (*The Holy Way: A Word to the Jews and to the Nations*), with a dedication to Landauer (who had been killed in the interim).[25] The text bears the stamp of Landauer's ideas throughout but especially when Buber addresses himself to the contemporary political situation: "Nothing new can be established by stripping an autocratic constitution off a country and superimposing on it a communist one instead when life between man and man remains unchanged, and so too the methods of government."[26]

Of even greater interest in this text is the significant shift that has occurred in Buber's thinking in contrast to his Prague "Lectures on Judaism," delivered only seven years earlier but on the other side of the war, the revolution, and the British conquest of Palestine. In those lectures, Buber had offered a fairly typical cultural Zionist reading of Jewish history: once, the Jewish people were vital and creative in their land; then, they were exiled and lost their vitality, which appeared only occasionally in subterranean movements outside the norm; now, the Jews return to Zion and to the land and so restore their original creative genius. In "The Holy Way," however, the loss of the Jewish commonwealth is no longer the event that "split Judaism's history in two."[27] Rather, "the true turning point in Jewish history" is declared to be *the moment of the establishment of the Israelite monarchy*.[28] It is the turn to institutional human authority, portrayed (after I Samuel 8) as an idolatrous impulse and not the loss of sovereignty over the land that marks the eternal before and after in Jewish life. By restricting God's rule to spiritual matters, the Israelite monarchy trades heaven for earth and essentially creates the idea of the purely political sphere for the first time, secularizing the originary unity of the divine covenant. Over the course of the 1920s, Buber hones and fine-tunes his understanding of the Bible, so that by 1932, when he publishes *Kingship of God*, he has his philology and biblical history better squared away. But the basic claim—the *theopolitical* claim—remains the same as in 1918, where it emerges under the sign of Landauer's revolution.

IIb. The 1920s: Buber's Bible Work and Landauer's Legacy

In 1923, the Munich Anarchosyndikalistische Vereinigung (Anarcho-Syndicalist Association) erected an obelisk at Landauer's grave, and Buber published *I and Thou*. The two events are only superficially unrelated. As executor of Landauer's literary estate, Buber spent much of the 1920s building a different kind of monument to Landauer—one that would last longer than the obelisk, which was torn down ten years later upon the Nazi rise to power. First, he issued Landauer's lectures on Shakespeare, *Shakespeare: Dargestellt in Vorträgen* (*Shakespeare: Presented in Lectures*, 1920). That same year, Buber gave a short address to the world conference of the Zionist socialist movement, *Ha'poel Ha'tzair* (The young worker), eulogizing Landauer as "the hidden leader" that the Zionist movement had never known—a claim we will return to.[29] In 1921, he followed up with *Der werdende Mensch: Aufsätze über Leben und Schrifttum* (*The Evolving Man: Essays on Life and Literature*), and in 1924, he published *Beginnen: Aufsätze über Sozialismus* (*Beginning: Essays on Socialism*). In 1929, Buber brought out the aforementioned two-volume edition of Landauer's correspondence, *Gustav Landauer: Sein Lebensgang in Briefen* (*Gustav Landauer: His Life in Letters*). This edition contains only Landauer's own letters, not the responses, but Buber provides context, background, and extensive commentary. Finally, on the tenth anniversary of Landauer's murder, Buber published "Erinnerung an einen Tod" ("Recollection of a Death"). At this point, his urge to commemorate his friend seems to have finally subsided, and he did not pick up his pen to discuss Landauer for another ten years.[30]

Usually, other projects are emphasized in discussions of Buber's 1920s activity. And it is these to which I intend to devote the remainder of this discussion. The purpose of the foregoing is to serve as a reminder that Buber pursued all these plans simultaneously; in keeping with the value he placed philosophically on unity and wholeness, he did not separate these spheres in his life or work. Thus, he commemorated Landauer *while* he embarked on the Bible translation with Rosenzweig; he edited Landauer's letters *while* he taught at the Lehrhaus.

Take the new translation of the Bible into German, undertaken with Franz Rosenzweig from 1925 until the latter's death in 1929 and afterward continued by Buber alone. Much has been written about the hermeneutic approaches shared by the two men, and about their desire to revitalize the spoken, aural element of biblical language. And yet there was a political element to the project as well. When the reactionary antisemitic writer Wilhelm Stapel, editor of the *Deutsches Volkstum*, accused Buber and Rosenzweig of exemplifying a "Jewish nervous agitation" leading to an unwarranted "renovation" of the German language, Buber responded that despite Stapel's "total ignorance of the text," he was nonetheless "the most perceptive of our antagonists" because he "had seen clearly what danger to his conception of a 'Christian statesman'— i.e., a sham Christian offering religious sanction to all the violences of the state—would be entailed among the German people by the dissemination of the actual Scriptures, which demand the shaping of society on the basis of belief."[31] In other words, Buber considers the "demand" of the scriptures to cut clearly against the kind of political theology with which Stapel was aligned and proudly considered his translation efforts, in and of themselves, to pose a threat to such projects.

One might well ask how Buber knew that this was the case—after all, did not Stapel, like other right-wing political theologians, also advocate "the shaping of society on the basis of belief"? This question is what moved no less a theologian than Karl Barth to conclude that the religious socialist movement led by Leonhard Ragaz—although he was far more sympathetic to it than to right-wing and nationalist political theologies—was nonetheless overly prone to simply using theology to legitimate existing political positions rather than deriving the positions out of a serious encounter with revelation.[32] For Buber, however, while it was clear that there could be "no legitimately messianic, no legitimately messianically-intended, politics," nevertheless "that does not imply that the political sphere may be excluded from the hallowing of all things."[33] False political theology could be detected by the criterion of whether it just so happened to agree with ordinary political realism about the proper sphere of politics and then allowed (in the manner of Carl Schmitt) that the political was its own sphere with its own rules, simultaneously seeking to immunize that sphere from criticism by divinizing it. "As it is presumption to 'believe' in something without—however inadequately—living that in which one believes, so it is presumption to wish to 'accomplish' something without—however inadequately—living what one wants to accomplish."[34] The necessary consonance of ends and means, the central principle of Landauer's anarchism, became the criterion of Buber's "religious socialism." In his biblical studies, he would foreground it again, under the name of theopolitics.

Before turning to those studies, however, it is important to mention one more sphere in which Buber hoped to see the hallowing of the political sphere in the 1920s. In his essay "Three Theses of a Religious Socialism," Buber had argued that "religion and socialism are essentially directed to each other.... Religion without socialism is disembodied spirit, therefore not genuine spirit; socialism without religion is body emptied of spirit, hence also not genuine body." And yet he had also carved out a special place for secular socialist activism that aimed at social justice: "But—socialism without religion does not hear the divine address, it does not aim at a response, still it happens that it responds; religion without socialism hears the call but does not respond."[35] Here we have an echo of the praise offered by Rabbi Abraham Isaac Kook (1865–1935), often considered the father of religious Zionism, for the secular Zionist activists whom he considered to be unwitting tools of the divine despite their defiance of Torah and *halakha*. And it may be that, in fact, Buber had the very same secular socialist activists in mind.

Buber considered Landauer's death to have robbed Zionism of someone whose destiny it was to set an example for it. He had attempted to enlist Landauer in the service of Zionism many times and been rebuffed. Landauer saw Germany as the place to realize his dreams of a nonhierarchical, directly democratic socialist society made up of a network of nested workers', peasants', and soldiers' councils. He worried, further, that the growing British interest in Palestine meant that it would become yet another site of colonial domination and that this agenda would override whatever independent projects small groups of idealistic Zionists might attempt to realize there, as he wrote to Buber in 1918:

"The more Germany and Turkey on the one side, England, America, and the political Zionists on the other, take an interest in Palestine, the more my attitude cools toward this region, to which my heart has never drawn me and which for me is not necessarily the site for a Jewish community."[36] A few months later, he wrote, "Don't take it amiss, Buber, if I cannot participate in one or the other of your undertakings; everyone needs his own forms and springboards. That doesn't affect our harmony and community, which has grown much deeper in the course of these years."[37] Buber did not cease to attempt to involve him, however. As late as March 1919, he inspired Zionist Nahum Goldmann (1895–1982) to ask Landauer to speak at a conference in Berlin for German socialist Zionists. Goldmann also convinced Landauer to take part in a small preliminary convention in Munich, planned by Buber for April 1919; he specifically asked him to draft statements on decentralized society, nationalization of land, and worker control of industry.[38] The Bavarian Council Republic interrupted these plans and neither conference ever took place, but the correspondence shows that Landauer's utopian ideas were taken seriously by socialist Zionists at the time, who expected to apply them immediately in building nonhierarchical socialist settlements in Palestine.[39] As mentioned earlier, the German branch of Ha'poel Ha'tzair, a non-Marxist socialist Zionist group, held its founding conference in 1920 in Prague, at which Buber spoke and proclaimed that "Landauer's idea was our idea... and in accordance with this idea, Landauer was to have participated in the building of a new land and a new society as guide and mentor."[40] The legendary farmer-philosopher A. D. Gordon (1856–1922), a leader of Ha'poel Ha'tzair in Palestine, returned from this conference claiming to have "found his ideas" in Landauer's writing, and Chaim Arlosoroff (1899–1933), a young leader of Ha'poel Ha'tzair who would later be instrumental in the founding of the Mapai, declared to the conference that "in our views as to building up our economy in Palestine and in the Exile the Weltanschauung of Gustav Landauer has served us as a foundation."[41]

It was the fact that the kibbutz model was being *put into practice* in Palestine, and not simply being drafted in utopianist blueprints, that drew Buber to it as the potential kernel of a new type of society. There was no single model kibbutz, but certain broad principles dominated the movement. As stated by the founding group of Kibbutz Degania in a letter to Arthur Ruppin, the director of the Palestine Land Development Company, these aimed at "a cooperative community without exploiters or exploited."[42] This objective would be realized through the collective ownership of property, including the means of production; free distribution of consumer goods, according to need; the abolition of wage labor; decisions to be made by a general assembly of all the kibbutz members, with each member having an equal vote; the integration of manual and intellectual labor; a rotation of roles and duties with the equal distribution of routine, monotonous tasks; the abolition of hierarchy in workplace management, with no "bosses" with power to inspect worker output or restrict worker movement; and the provision for health care for the sick and elderly.[43] Kibbutzim were occasionally, though not always, explicit about the sources of this form of communal organization in anarchism.[44] And kibbutz members were blithely untroubled by "realists" who worried that their ideas were impossible or contrary to human nature. When a Degania member was asked what would happen when a worker refused to pull his share, or took too much from the collective treasury, the response was "we would not love him."[45]

Landauer feared that Buber was signing on to a Zionist project of which he was not in control and in which he was doomed to be little more than a dissenting minority voice. This fear turned out to be correct. But given the strength of labor ideology and of the kibbutz movement in the 1920s, it was hardly completely romantic for Buber to see the cells of a new type of society forming in Palestine.[46] From the anarchist standpoint, arguably, what later transpired in Palestine was a mirror of what had happened in Germany—a labor-oriented but statist party (Ebert and the SPD in Germany, Ben-Gurion and the *Achdut Ha'avoda* in Palestine) first crowds out its more utopian, nonhierarchical ideological comrades and then, in turn, succumbs to forces to its own political right.

For Buber, however, this "experiment that did not fail" (as he put it in *Paths in Utopia*) was more than just a potentially successful revolutionary effort. Considered in light of its full significance, it was nothing less than the beginning of a Jewish renewal, and not just a "cultural" renewal of the type he had been interested in at the turn of the century. This renewal would be a return of the Jews to the very task of their election, neglected and obscured over millennia of exile and only now coming once again into view. That effort, though, entailed incredible risks, just as it had in the days of the judges and the prophets. That effort and those risks are the matter of biblical theopolitics, and concern for their contemporary resonance forms the unspoken background to all of Buber's biblical studies.

III. TWO TYPES OF DIALOGUE: THE ETERNAL THOU AND THE KINGLY COVENANT

Buber's biblical writings take the form of academic scholarly studies. They are far more heavily footnoted than his other works and involve more references to contemporary scholarship as well as (arguably) more attention to careful argumentation than his more poetically written philosophy. In the case of *Kingship of God*, there is a biographical reason for this: Buber was hoping to achieve academic appointment at the Hebrew University.[47] He maintained the style, however, for his subsequent works, even if at a lower intensity. The genre places constraints on what Buber can say and how he can say it, especially in terms of what counts as relevant to the topic at hand. Nonetheless, although they are rarely explicitly polemical, philosophical, or directed to current events, their relevance to all these areas is clear just under the surface.

The concept of theopolitics, for example, makes its first appearance in these writings in the preface to the first edition of *Kingship of God*, in the midst of a discussion of philological and literary-critical method. Buber, at some remove from standard scholarly procedure, asserts that he differs from the reigning versions of the Documentary Hypothesis in that he is "not able to believe in a separable, coherent original document to be regarded as 'Elohistic'" and that he regards the J and E sources not as "sources, but trends of literature, [which] originate plainly from two socially and spiritually separated circles":

> J from the circle of courtly, for the most part early courtly, compilers, poets, and chroniclers, cultivated but rejoicing in legend, resolutely attentive to religious tradition but in the treatment of contemporary or recent history prone to a profane-political tendency; E from the circle of the *nebiim*, who had some time earlier entered upon their Word-administrating and poetical office, but literarily active for a far longer time, independent of the court, supported by the people, less gifted in narration, but inspired in message, experiencing and portraying history as a theo-political occurrence, contending for the interpenetration of religion and politics against every principle of partition which would place them in opposition to one another.[48]

Buber has taken two views, which in his occasional writings of the 1920s he had identified with false political theology and with the attempt to negate that theology, and mapped them onto ancient Israelite writers and editors. Right away, we have a key indication that Buber is not simply going to be "encountering" the text purely pneumatically, reading it for some generic inspiration or advice. Rather, he intends to classify and sort the text into elements that display signs of "profane-political tendency" and those whose writers and transmitters tap into the sense of theopolitics.[49]

Buber is consistent about this emphasis in the biblical writings that follow *Kingship of God*, which are less explicitly academic in orientation. For example, in *Moses*, he writes that the figure of Moses cannot be understood according to "religious" or cultic categories (such as priest or prophet), since his idea is "the realization of the unity of religious and social life in the community of Israel, the substantiation of a ruling by God that shall not be culturally restricted but shall comprehend the entire existence of the nation, the theo-political principle."[50] Israel, in this sense, is Moses' *project*, and "until the present day Israel has really existed in the precise degree in which Moses has proved right."[51]

But what is this theopolitics, and what (if any) is its relationship to "dialogue"? Here, *Moses* plays an especially useful role. For *Kingship of God* is concerned primarily with elucidating the idea of the "kingly covenant" with YHVH as a literal, direct ruler in Israel, exclusive of human authority, and *The Prophetic Faith* narrates the history of the relationship of the people to the human authorities, the kings, whom they instituted in defiance of that exclusive lordship. In *Moses*, however, special attention is paid to what is often thought of as "legislation": the specific ordinances decreed by Moses for the people of Israel to follow, and the topic often considered the highest anathema to Buber's conception of Judaism.

In one of the most famous passages of *I and Thou*, Buber writes that in revelation "man receives, and what he receives is not a 'content' but a presence, a presence as strength."[52] This presence imparts the knowledge of being associated, rather than alone, and it conveys the inherent meaningfulness of existence and of this life. Notoriously, however, for Buber's reputation as a Jewish thinker, it does not convey a "content," anything that could be "transferred or expressed as a universally valid and generally acceptable piece of knowledge." It is not even possible to frame the "ought" of putting this ineffable meaning into practice in a general way: "The meaning we receive can be put to the proof in action only by each person in the uniqueness of his being and in the uniqueness of his life. No prescription can lead us to the encounter, and none leads from it."[53] This extreme antinomianism and occasionalism is often taken as exemplary of an entire cadre of German Jewish thinkers, including Rosenzweig, Walter Benjamin, Franz Kafka, and Gershom Scholem (though, in the case of Rosenzweig, the matter is qualified by his insistence on the possibility that traditional *halakha* may, at least, "lead us to the encounter" if we are inclined to let it).[54]

In the biblical writings, however, beginning with *Kingship of God*, we read of a "will to constitution," a continuing effort by the people of Israel to answer the call of a God enthroned as king and to measure up to their sense of being commanded. This is connected to one of the few uses of the term *Zwiegespräch* (dialogue) in the text:

> The kingship of God is a paradox, but an historical one: it consists in the historical conflict of the subjected person against the resisting one, a conflict

which, without its naïve, but on that very account most important, original form, cannot be grasped. It is the most visible appearance of that kingdom-dialectic [*Reichsdialektik*] which educated the Israelitish people to know history as the dialectic [*Zwiegespräch*] of an asking divinity and an answer-refusing, but nevertheless an answer-attempting humanity, the dialogue [*Zwiegespräch*] whose demand is an *eschaton*.[55] That this dialectic [*Dialektik*] has its quite earthly form, that it embodies itself not on theological heights, but in the midst of the whirl of political actualities, and that, robbed of these, the constant historical consciousness of a people, Israel, as bearer of the kingdom-message [*Reichsbotschaft*] could not be understood—all this allows, yes commands, us to recognize the will toward constitution (that is, to actualization) as an original constant [*ursprünglichen Bestand*] in the dynamic of this folk life, which functions in *historiography* because it has functioned in *history*.[56]

The "subjected person" and the "resisting one" are not simply people who have more or less success or fortune initiating I-Thou relationships; the "dialogue whose demand is an *eschaton*" is embodied in "will to constitution," in striving to make the kingship of God real. The normative thrust of the passage seems to run against Buber's earlier claim that actualization cannot be set up as an "ought."

In *Moses*, Buber arguably goes further, elaborating the "will to constitution" into an outright sympathetic discussion of "law"—if not positive law, then nonetheless something that endures beyond the existential situation of individuals hearing individual, content-less revelations of presence: "Naturally God rules through men who have been gripped and filled by His spirit, and who on occasion carry out His will not merely by means of instantaneous decisions but also through lasting justice and law [*überdauerndes Recht und Gesetz*] . . . without law [*Gesetz*] that is, without any clear-cut and transmissible line of demarcation between that which is pleasing to God and that which is displeasing to Him, there can be no historical continuity of divine rule upon earth."[57] Here we have a clear indicator that in the biblical context, at least, there is "content" to the call of revelation, and not merely "presence" as in the dialogical writings. But what does this content consist of? We seem to have come back around to the question of political theology as debated by Barth, Ragaz, Schmitt, and Stapel. If Buber has indeed abandoned the extreme antinomian position, is he returned to the maelstrom of divine politics, of proofs and counterproofs, of exegetical arguments for coercive political programs?

Buber's theopolitics emphasizes that Israel is elected to form the first decent society on earth, to become a "kingdom of priests and a holy nation." Although

Buber adheres to the most current trends in biblical criticism as he sees them and, of course, does not enumerate the rabbinic 613 commandments as the nature of the revelational content, nonetheless we find such institutions as the Sabbath and Jubilee, as well as others, sketched out in terms of how they serve the purpose of the divine election. I would argue that in almost every single one of these instances, which I lack the space to elaborate here, the divine purpose alluded to can best be understood as meaning "conducive to true community," in a sense that Landauer would have understood. In other words, whenever Buber allows "content" to revelation in the biblical writings, this "content" is theopolitical in nature, which means anarchistic. In line with Ragaz and the religious socialists, Buber holds that a transcendent vision of a kingly God does not underwrite an authoritarian political theology but rather undermines it, together with all unjustified human hierarchies, instead lending support to a radical vision of human equality—perhaps much more dependably than the fleeting I-Thou relation.[58] This has implications for his Zionism, since it casts fundamental doubt on the goal of statehood and sovereignty, or to be more precise, it casts fundamental doubt on the idea that a Jewish polity is best constituted according to modern Western political-theory ideas about sovereignty and security.

One significant example will have to suffice. *Moses* describes its title character as a founder of a very particular type of polity, one that seeks to carve out a middle ground between the authoritarian political theology of Egypt and the freedom of the Midianite shepherds and nomads among whom Moses had sojourned. Moses wants that Midianite freedom, but he wants it for a "people" that will constitute a stable political unit in a way that the Midianites do not. This shows up in much of his specific "legislation"—for example, in his attitude toward land tenure. In Egypt, "the King ... exercises a strict, unremittent supervision over all landed property, so that all landed property merges in that of the King. 'The land,' as the Bible expresses it in full accordance with the historical reality, 'became Pharaoh's'; and every worker-family was left with just as much of the yield of the soil as was required for bare subsistence."[59] One could easily imagine a system of private property as the appropriate contrast to this, empowering the smallholders to invest and undertake enterprises; Buber hints at this possibility in his discussion of the proclamation of Balaam, which portrays an ideal vision of Israel rather than an actually existing situation. Buber claims that this vision derives from Moses's own vision: "Moses had wished for such an Israel, he had desired life, marriage and property to be secure, and envy to be eradicated among the people."[60]

This quasi-Lockean formulation is undermined, however, by Buber's eventual description of the Mosaic alternative to Egyptian land-tenure practices.

Having rebelled against an aristocratic upbringing by marrying into a quasi-nomadic Midianite society, Moses would have had trouble imagining "all the external and internal transformations that were bound to be involved in a transfer to a predominantly agrarian form of life."[61] Buber imagines that Moses began to meditate on these matters at Kadesh, when the people first became involved in sustained agricultural endeavors. At this point, Moses "would have had to start out from his basic idea, that of the real and direct rule of God; which would necessarily have led to the postulate that God owns all land." The sabbatical is one expression of this conviction; Moses "conceived the idea of overcoming the continually-expanding social harm forever by ensuring the restoration, in each ensuing Sabbatical year, 'of the normal situation of the national community of Israel after all the deviations and wrong developments of the preceding six years.'"[62] God's ultimate ownership of the land facilitates the redistribution of that land after seven years of private accumulation, thus preventing any permanent class structure from developing.

This hearkens back to a discussion in *Kingship of God*, where Buber had argued against the claim, common in biblical scholarship, that Leviticus 25:23, "Mine is the land, for you are only guests and sojourners with Me," had to be a late text and a "theological utopia" rather than the reflection of an actual ancient view that could ever have become manifest in political practice. The ultimate consequence of this view is that all "private property is feudal tenure"—there is ultimately no right to hold property that cannot be undone after a number of years by redistribution or reequalization, since the true owner of the land has stated that this is how he wishes to dispose of it. Indeed, Buber sees the sabbatical year, whose purpose it was "to lead to a renewal of the organization of the society, in order to start afresh," as having the status of "a renewal of the Covenant" itself.[63] For Buber's Moses, the considerations for adopting social law are inseparable from the religious vision:

> Above all this there hovers the consecration to YHVH, to whom the earth belongs and who, by means of that earth, nourishes His dwellers and sojourners. They ought not to thrust one another aside, they ought not to impoverish one another permanently or enslave one another; they must again and ever again become equal to one another in their freedom of person and free relation to the soil; they must rest together and enjoy the usufruct together; the times dedicated to God make them free and equal again and again, as they were at the beginning. The land is given to them in common in order that in it and from it they may become a true national Community, a "Holy People" ... in order that they might become a *berakah*, a blessing power.[64]

The gift of the land is not simply a reminder to the Israelites of the author of their prosperity, to whom they owe gratitude, but also of the *purposes* for which the giver of the land intends it to be used. If they honor these purposes, their activity will serve as a "blessing power" to all the other peoples of the earth, who will have the opportunity to observe justice in action. If they fail, they will desecrate the name of God and bring dishonor to the very mission for which they were brought into existence as a people.

We are very far now from the idea that no "ought" may be generated by revelation ("dialogue" with the "Eternal Thou") beyond the unique meaning understood by each person in the uniqueness of their own encounter. We are very *close*, however, to the kind of vision that Landauer and his anarchist comrades laid out for Germany and that Buber hoped to transplant to contemporary Palestine via the kibbutz movement. "Law" and "content" are both admissible if they are conducive to true community (as in preventing the emergence of permanent economic classes); they are inadmissible if they are destructive of this end, a quality that is then defined as rebellion against the kingship of God. The theopolitical has become the criterion of the telos of the dialogic.

I will conclude this section by directly addressing the most overtly "dialogical" section in all of Buber's biblical writings. It occurs in *The Prophetic Faith*, a work of which Scholem said that in it Buber "seems to me to have reached the high point of his efforts to understand the Bible as a great dialogue."[65] *The Prophetic Faith* is a kind of narrative of the fate of the theopolitical principle after the institution of hereditary monarchy in Israel. We have already seen that Buber considered the *nevi'im*, or prophets, to be a kind of circle committed to the continued propagation of this principle even when this meant contesting royal power. The kings, of course, knew this as well, which was why they employed court prophets of their own. The line between true prophecy and false is once again the line between legitimation of human institutional hierarchy and the contestation of that hierarchy.

Jeremiah is perhaps the prophet who does the most dramatic battle against false prophets of YHVH (Buber is less interested in Elijah, however, for though he battled false prophets, they were those of Baal, not YHVH). Buber is not totally contemptuous of the court prophets, acknowledging that "certainly many of them are honest patriots" who may have found Jeremiah's oracles of doom to be offensive.[66] However, there is no doubt that for them, YHVH is experienced as an outgrowth and consequence of Israelite order in general as it existed under the late Judean monarchy. Prophecy for them is the reinforcing of the essential rightness and eternal perdurance of this order. This is in contrast to the experience of Jeremiah and other true prophets:

> The divine word, which suddenly descends into the human situation, unexpected and unwilled by man, is free and fresh like the lightning.... This is not the expression of a familiar deity, with whom man comes into regular contact in fixed places and at fixed times. He, Who speaks, is incomprehensible, irregular, surprising, overwhelming, sovereign. Therefore it is the virtue of this word, and of this alone, to lead, that is to say, to show the way.... Only Jeremiah of all the Israelite prophets has dared to note this bold and devout life conversation of the utterly inferior with the utterly superior— in such a measure is man here become a person. All Israelite relationship of faith is dialogic; here the dialogue has reached its pure form. Man can speak, he is permitted to speak; if only he truly speaks to God, there is nothing he may not say to Him.

The vocabulary of conversation, speaking, and dialogue is powerfully evident in this passage, which also contains a bit of the old Nietzschean neo-Romanticism ("free and fresh like the lightning") and occasionalism ("incomprehensible, irregular, surprising..."). At the same time, however, this word that Jeremiah receives is not pure power, not just some kind of saturated phenomenon. His obligation is to "show God's sway, the pulling down and building up of the world's architect, the rooting out and the planting of the world's gardener. God lets the prophet note His action, as such, in chronicles of the Spirit. That he is 'appointed' 'to root out,' means that he has to say of the rooting out that it is such. He has to *say* what God *does*."[67] And what God *does* is destroy the kingdom of Judah and the Temple, a "punishment for sins" that is also a natural consequence of the continued failure of the kings, who should never have been empowered to reign in the first place, to heed the prophetic word and enact a political and economic *teshuva*, or turning, toward the original anarcho-theocratic Mosaic vision.

IV. CONCLUSION: THEOPOLITICS, ZIONISM, AND DIALOGUE

To conclude, I will briefly restate my claims. The "dialogue between heaven and earth" of the biblical writings seems to differ from that presented in *I and Thou* and "Dialogue," since the relationship between God and Israel in the biblical writings is presented as both hierarchical and covenantal, laying insistent demands on the collectivity of Israel even if those demands may not be crystallized in the form of the rabbinic commandments. Instead, this demand requires *teshuva*, a turning to God that manifests in the organization of society according to a theopolitical impulse, which tends to map onto a Landauerian vision of anarchism: a society containing only nonhierarchical forms of organization, in which authority is granted only to those who (1) earn it, (2) to do particular things, (3) for a limited time.[68] It is this theopolitical vision that Buber deploys against traditional notions of political theology and hierocracy, and it is this vision that manifests in Buber's commitment to the kibbutz as the potential core of a new Jewish society in Palestine.

If I am right, Buber's continued adherence to Zionism, and its corollary commitment to a robust Jewish-Arab binationalism, may be better understood as a manifestation of the understanding of election and response derived from the biblical writings than of "dialogue." The temptation to carry dialogue over into the meeting between Jews and Arabs is even greater than the urge to read all Buber's work through the lens of *I and Thou*, if only because it is so easy to speak of the need for dialogue between two peoples in order for there to be peace. However, a survey of the range of Buber's editorials and occasional writing on Zionism, together with a consideration of his major statement in *Ben Am Le-Artzo* (*On Zion*, 1944), would appear to show that the later Buber understands the contemporary Zionist project as a renewal of the original attempt of the people of Israel to fulfill the terms of its election, and as such, it remains subject to the same specific dangers that inhered in this attempt the first time around. Buber thus assumes the role of the contemporary inheritor of the prophetic, anarcho-theocratic tradition, urging his Zionist fellow-travelers not to succumb once again to the monarchic, statist temptation. Buber's famous binationalism, then, should be seen as a pragmatic compromise, not with an ideal of *full* Jewish sovereignty in a homogeneous society, but with *any* idea of statehood at all.

Buber saw clearly that the so-called Arab question posed a threat to the viability of the only kind of Zionism he believed worth the name, not just because it raised general and fuzzy ethical quandaries about the use of power or the ability to live with others, but also because the fear of an external threat called Philistines was the very factor that first gave rise to the temptation of idolatrous human authority in Israel, undermining the rule of God, severing the political sphere from a now impotent realm of the spiritual, and leading eventually to destruction and exile. Buber's binationalism is, as he put it, "only a temporary adaptation of our path to the concrete, historical situation—it is not necessarily the path itself."[69] He does not arrive at it by taking the generally current ideas about liberal self-governance and nation-state structures and then adding one plus one, nor can it really be understood as some kind of extrapolation or generalization of the teachings of *I and Thou* and "Dialogue." Rather, the task of finding a modus vivendi for living with, and not merely alongside, the Palestinians is a necessary prerequisite for preventing the reemergence of the kind of fear and hypersecurity consciousness that is conducive to the deformation of an anarchistic theopolitics into an authoritarian political theology—and thus to the failure of the Jews to fulfill their side of the covenant. Binationalism, through establishing clear conduits for cooperation between Palestinians and Jews, counters the fear-security resonance machine that conduces idolatrous recourse to an authoritarian human power.

Scholars, theologians, clergy, and students will continue to show interest in Buber's ontology, his religious anthropology, and his philosophy of education. Here I have emphasized the potential fruitfulness of a decentering of *I and Thou* for the consideration of a fairly large percentage of Buber's corpus, namely, the biblical writings and the Zionist writings. Of dialogue, Buber writes that "an element of communication, however inward, seems to belong to its essence. But in its highest moments"—and we would surely expect any dialogue between heaven and earth to rank among these highest moments—"dialogue reaches out even beyond these boundaries. It is completed outside contents, even the most personal, which are or can be communicated."[70] And yet the *theopolitical* dialogue between heaven and earth has a clear content, not personal but collective, that is and can continue to be communicated.

NOTES

1. The weightiest example of this tendency is perhaps Maurice Friedman's three-volume biography, *Martin Buber's Life and Work* (Detroit: Wayne State University Press, 1988). Friedman structures his narrative, which he calls a "dialography," such that volume 1, *The Early Years, 1878–1923*, pivots around *I and Thou*; the second part of the text is entitled "The Threshold of Fulfillment," and this fulfillment or culmination is found in the final part, "I and Thou."

2. See the opening lines of Grete Schaeder, *The Hebrew Humanism of Martin Buber*, trans. Noah J. Jacobs (Detroit: Wayne State University Press, 1973), 11: "Buber's 'Hebrew Humanism' is not an ideology; it is a conception of man. Nor is it meant to be used as a formula to help us derive a doctrine from Buber's work. It is rather that 'narrow ridge' between systems which he regarded as his proper place. Even in the last years of his life he declared, 'I have no doctrine,' and described himself as 'atypical' and not confined to any particular intellectual system."

3. Martin Buber, afterword to *I and Thou*, trans. Walter Kaufmann (New York: Charles Scribner's Sons, 1970), 171.

4. Martin Buber, "Hebrew Humanism," in *Israel and the World: Essays in a Time of Crisis* (Syracuse: Syracuse University Press, 1997), 240. One could later

apply this same thinking to the term *Zionism*, as a brand that had already come to mean something very different from Buber's intentions by the time of the establishment of the State of Israel in 1948.

5. Though Friedman's definition of the *dialogic* is so elastic that it extends to cover literally any "response" Buber makes to his times, to his readers and critics, or to a text, this again is not entirely Friedman's fault as there are precedents for it in Buber's own writing, as with the aforementioned example of the dialogical relationship with his silent readers.

6. Paul Mendes-Flohr, *From Mysticism to Dialogue: Martin Buber's Transformation of German Social Thought* (Detroit: Wayne State University Press, 1989); originally published as *Von der Mystik zum Dialog: Martin Bubers geistige Entwicklung bis hin zu "Ich und Du"* (Athenäum: Jüdischer, 1978). The German title highlights the precise location of the "dialogical turn" with the publication of *I and Thou*.

7. The SAPD was created through a merger of Ferdinand Lasalle's Allgemeiner Deutscher Arbeiterverein (General German Workers' Association) with Wilhelm Liebknecht and August Bebel's Sozialdemokratische Arbeiterpartei Deutschlands (Social Democratic Workers' Party of Germany). The event provided the occasion for Karl Marx's "Critique of the Gotha Program," which warned his friend Liebknecht against too close an association with Lasalle. The Socialist Laws were allowed to lapse following Bismarck's death in 1890, after which the SPD could again organize openly.

8. Gustav Landauer, "Twenty-Five Years Later: On the Jubilee of Wilhelm II," in *Revolution and Other Writings: A Political Reader*, ed. and trans. Gabriel Kuhn (Oakland: PM Press, 2010), 62–67; originally published as "Vor fünfundzwanzig Jahren. Zum Regierungsjubiläum Wilhelms II," *Der Sozialist*, June 15, 1913.

9. Cited in Gabriel Kuhn and Siegbert Wolf, introduction to *Revolution and other Writings*, 21. The contradiction between holding this view and working for the Freie Volksbühne was shortly resolved through the creation in 1892 of the *Neue* Freie Volksbühne, which did not take money from the SPD.

10. For general histories of anarchism, see Peter Marshall, *Demanding the Impossible: A History of Anarchism* (Oakland: PM Press, 2010), and George Woodcock, *Anarchism: A History of Libertarian Ideas and Movements* (Toronto: University of Toronto Press, 2009). Buber himself provides an interesting overview of Proudhon and Kropotkin's work in his own *Paths in Utopia*, where he posits Landauer as the logical conclusion of the sequence. See Martin Buber, *Netivot Be'utopia* (Tel Aviv: Am Oved, 1947), trans. R. F. C. Hull as *Paths in Utopia* (Boston: Beacon Press, 1958).

11. Scholars have debated these elements of Landauer's thought, querying the possibility of a romantic or even *völkisch* left. Gabriel Kuhn and Siegbert

Wolf think any comparison to *völkisch* thought is a misnomer, since Landauer never defined the *Volk* in relation to biological or spiritual Germanness, and it was common for socialists to use *Volk* as a contrast to capitalists rather than to other nations: "Writing about *Volk* must not be confused with being *völkisch*" (Kuhn and Wolf, introduction, 19). Paul Breines supports this view in his review of Eugene Lunn's biography of Landauer: "A Völkisch Left?" *Reviews in European History* 1, no. 1 (June 1974): 133–38; cf. Eugene Lunn, *Prophet of Community: The Romantic Socialism of Gustav Landauer* (Berkeley: University of California Press, 1973). The debate has resonance for Buber's thought as well. See George L. Mosse, "The Influence of the *Völkisch* Idea on German Jewry," in *Studies of the Leo Baeck Institute*, ed. Max Kreutzberger (New York: Frederick Ungar, 1967), 83–114; Bernard Susser, "Ideological Multivalence: Martin Buber and the German Volkish Tradition," *Political Theory* 5, no. 1 (February 1977): 75–96; and, most recently, Yemima Hadad, "Hasidic Myth-Activism: Martin Buber's Theopolitical Revision of Volkish Nationalism," *Religions* 10, no. 2 (2019): 96.

12. Buber may have been present for Landauer's lecture "Durch Absonderung zur Gemeinschaft" ("Through Separation to Community"), if the similarities to be found in his own first talk to the Neue Gemeinschaft are any indication. Cf. Paul Flohr and Bernard Susser, "*Alte und Neue Gemeinschaft*: An Unpublished Buber Manuscript," *Association for Jewish Studies Review* 1 no.1 (1976): 41–56, and Gustav Landauer, "Through Separation to Community," in Kuhn and Wolf, *Revolution and Other Writings*, 94–108.

13. Martin Buber, "Gustav Landauer," *Die Zeit* 39, no. 506 (June 11, 1904): 127–28 (today, see *Martin Buber Werkausgabe*, Band 2.1, *Mythos und Mystik: Frühe religionswissenschaftliche Schriften*, ed. David Groiser [Gutersloh: Gutersloher Verlaghaus, 2013], 102–7); Gustav Landauer, "Die Legende des Baal Schem," *Das literarische Echo* 13 (October 1, 1910) (today see Gustav Landauer, *Philosophie und Judentum: Ausgewählte Schriften*, Band 5, ed. Siegbert Wolf [Hessen: AV, 2012], 345–47). Also see Gustav Landauer, "Martin Buber," in *Neue Blätter* (Hellerau/Berlin: Verlag der Neuen Blätter, 1913), 90–107, and Landauer, *Philosophie und Judentum*, 351–62.

14. For an elaboration of this analysis, see Samuel Hayim Brody, *Martin Buber's Theopolitics* (Bloomington: Indiana University Press, 2018).

15. Gustav Landauer, "Anarchische Gedanken über Anarchismus," *Die Zukunft*, October 26, 1901. English: "Anarchic Thoughts on Anarchism," in Kuhn and Wolf, *Revolution and Other Writings*, 84–91.

16. Ibid., 87. In some sense this is an avant la lettre critique of the macho-style contemporary anarcha-feminists have dubbed "manarchism."

17. The original German reads, "eines der schönsten Dokumente menschlicher Selbstbefreiung."

18. Martin Buber to Hans Kohn, September 30, 1914, in *The Letters of Martin Buber: A Life of Dialogue*, ed. Nahum N. Glatzer and Paul Mendes-Flohr, trans. Richard and Clara Winston and Harry Zohn (Syracuse, NY: Syracuse University Press, 1996), 160.
19. Gustav Landauer to Martin Buber, May 12, 1916, in Glatzer and Mendes-Flohr, *Letters of Martin Buber*, 188–92.
20. See Mendes-Flohr, *From Mysticism to Dialogue*, 93–126.
21. In the order of their appearance, the debate was conducted in these articles: Hermann Cohen, "Religion und Zionismus," *K. C. Blätter* 11 (May/June 1916), 643–46; Martin Buber, "Begriffe und Wirklichkeit: Brief an Herrn Geh. Regierungsrat Prof. Dr. Hermann Cohen," *Der Jude* 1, no. 5 (July 1916), 281–289; Hermann Cohen, "Antwort auf das Offene Schreiben des Herrn Dr. Martin Buber," *K. C. Blätter* 12 (July/August 1916), 683–88; Martin Buber, "Zion, der Staat und die Menschheit: Bemerkungen zu Hermann Cohens Antwort," *Der Jude* 1, no. 7 (October 1916), 425–433. The Buber pieces are available in *Werkausgabe 3*, 293–320; the Cohen pieces, in Hermann Cohen, *Jüdische Schriften, Zweiter Band*, ed. Bruno Strauss (Berlin: C.A. Schwetschke, 1924), 319–40. In English, the debate is unfortunately as yet only available in excerpts. See Martin Buber and Hermann Cohen, "A Debate on Zionism and Messianism (Summer 1916)," in *The Jew in the Modern World: A Documentary History*, 3rd edition, ed. Paul Mendes-Flohr and Jehuda Reinharz (New York: Oxford University Press, 2010), 651–55; Hermann Cohen, "A Reply to Dr. Martin Buber's Open Letter to Hermann Cohen," in *Reason and Hope: Selections from the Jewish Writings of Hermann Cohen*, ed. and trans. Eva Jospe (Cincinnati: Hebrew Union College Press, 1993), 164–70; and Martin Buber, "Zion, the State, and Humanity: Remarks on Hermann Cohen's Answer," in Cohen, *Jew*, 85–96.
22. Landauer to Buber, October 17, 1916, in *Gustav Landauer: Sein Lebensgang in Briefen*, vol. 2, ed. Martin Buber (Frankfurt: Rütten & Loening, 1929), 163.
23. Mendes-Flohr, *From Mysticism to Dialogue*, 175n159.
24. The letter in which Landauer invited Buber to Munich also included comments on his work with Eisner: "collaboration with Eisner functions very well. I am sure you have seen from his proclamations how 'anarchist' his understanding of democracy is: he favors the active participation of the people in all social bodies, not bleak parliamentarism" (Landauer to Buber, November 22, 1918, in Buber, *Sein Lebensgang in Briefen*, 2:299). Buber annotates this comment to provide evidence for Landauer's claim by directing the reader to certain of Eisner's speeches. Translation from Gabriel Kuhn, ed. and trans., *All Power to the Councils!: A Documentary History of the German Revolution of 1918–1919* (Oakland: PM Press, 2012), 172.
25. Martin Buber, *Der Heilige Weg: Ein Wort an die Juden und an die Völker* (Frankfurt: Rütten & Loening, 1919). Published after Landauer's death, the text

carries the dedication: "Dem Freunde Gustav Landauer aufs Grab." Translated in Martin Buber, *On Judaism*, ed. Nahum N. Glatzer (New York: Schocken Books, 1995), 108–48.

26. Ibid., in "The Holy Way," 147.

27. Martin Buber, "The Spirit of the Orient and Judaism," in *On Judaism*, 71–73. This lecture, the fourth of the "lectures on Judaism," was also one of the texts singled out by Landauer for criticism in his May 1916 letter, although not on this point in particular.

28. Martin Buber, "The Holy Way," in *On Judaism*, 117. ("Die eigentliche Wende der jüdischen Geschichte.")

29. "Der heimliche Führer," *Die Arbeit*, 2, no. 6 (1920), 36–37. A Hebrew translation of Buber's eulogy essay "Landauer und die Revolution" appeared in the Zionist paper *Ha'adama* in 1920.

30. Buber, "Erinnerung an einen Tod," *Neue Wege*, 23, no. 4 (April 1929): 161–65. Available in English as "Recollection of a Death," in Martin Buber, *Pointing the Way: Collected Essays*, ed. and trans. Maurice S. Friedman (New York: Schocken Books, 1974), 115–20. In 1939, Buber published a short piece entitled *Landauer b'sha'a zo* (*Landauer in This Hour*): *Ha'poel Ha'tzair* 10, no. 29 (June 27, 1929): 8–9. Also that year, Hebrew translations of "Landauer and the Revolution" and "The Hidden Leader" were collected with the new article into a Hebrew collection, *Al Gustav Landauer*, published by the Histadrut (the Federation of Hebrew Workers in the Land of Israel).

31. Martin Buber, "Letter to Herman Gerson" and "The How and Why of our Bible Translation," in *Scripture and Translation*, trans. Lawrence Rosenwald with Everett Fox (Bloomington: Indiana University Press, 1994), 201, 217. Stapel had published a book entitled *Der christliche Staatsmann* in 1932. In his oblique reference to other, "less perceptive" antagonists here, Buber may have intended critics from the left like Siegfried Kracauer; see Martin Jay, "Politics of Translation: Siegfried Kracauer and Walter Benjamin on the Buber-Rosenzweig Bible," *Leo Baeck Institute Year Book XXI* (London: Secker & Warburg, 1976), 3–24.

32. See, for instance, Christophe Chalamet, "Karl Barth and the Weimar Republic," in *The Weimar Moment: Liberalism, Political Theology, and Law*, ed. Leonard V. Kaplan and Rudy Koshar (Lanham, MD: Lexington Books, 2012), 255. See also, in the same collection, Gary Dorrien, "Barthian Dialectics: 'Yes' and 'No' on the Barthian Revolt and its Legacy," 217–40.

33. Martin Buber, "Gandhi, Politics, and Us (1930)," in *Pointing the Way*, 137.

34. Martin Buber, "Three Theses of a Religious Socialism (1928)," in *Pointing the Way*, 113.

35. Ibid., 112.

36. Landauer to Buber, February 5, 1918, in Glatzer and Mendes-Flohr, *Letters of Martin Buber*, 230.

37. Landauer to Buber, May 10, 1918, in Glatzer and Mendes-Flohr, *Letters of Martin Buber*, 231.

38. "Appendix II: Exchange of Letters: Goldmann-Landauer," in *A Living Revolution: Anarchism in the Kibbutz Movement*, by James Horrox (Oakland: AK Press, 2009), 133–37.

39. A point stressed by Ruth Link-Salinger, *Gustav Landauer: Philosopher of Utopia* (Indianapolis: Hackett, 1977), 52–53.

40. Horrox, *Living Revolution*, 43–44. This was the speech published as "Der heimliche Führer," *Die Arbeit* 2, no. 6 (June 1920): 36–37. This was a special issue of Ha'poel Ha'tzair's journal dedicated to Landauer.

41. Gordon quote: Michael Tyldesley, *No Heavenly Delusion? A Comparative Study of Three Communal Movements* (Liverpool, UK: Liverpool University Press, 2003), 48; Arlosoroff quote: Shalom Ratzabi, *Between Zionism and Judaism: The Radical Circle in Brith Shalom, 1925–1933* (Leiden, Netherlands: Brill, 2002), 413. Link-Salinger has argued that Arlosoroff's *Der Jüdische Volkssozialismus* (Jewish People's Socialism, 1919), "is so full of such Landauer 'chestnuts' as return to nature, the land as source of creativity, the importance of producers' and consumers' collectives, the importance of 'Gemeinschaftsgesinnung' over class hate or class rule ... that one can only marvel at the common core of their thinking or at the extraordinary strength of the 'Zeitgeist' as it informed equally German-Jewish and Jewish-Zionist thinking from the same inspiration and the same ideologies" (*Philosopher of Utopia*, 73). Arlosoroff was editor of the Ha'poel Ha'tzair paper, *Die Arbeit*, when Buber's article on Landauer was published; he also published Kropotkin's essay "Anarchist Communism," with his own commentary, in another Ha'poel Ha'tzair anthology, *Maabarot* (see Horrox, *Living Revolution*, 51). However, it must be said that either Arlosoroff's early commitments were compromised after he moved to Palestine in 1924, or else he had never believed that anarchist principles for communal settlement entailed consequences for other Zionist practices. His essay "On the Question of Joint Organization" (1927) argues that binational unions are impractical in light of Jewish workers' need for higher wages and that the wage depression caused by joint organization with Arabs would lead to decreased immigration and threaten the goal of a Jewish majority in Palestine. As shown in Zachary Lockman's *Comrades and Enemies: Arab and Jewish Workers in Palestine, 1906–1948* (Berkeley: University of California Press, 1996), 100–101, Arlosoroff opposed Buber's group, Brit Shalom, on the issues of economic segregation from Palestinian Arabs and the rate of Jewish immigration to Palestine.

42. Cited in Horrox, *Living Revolution*, 18.

43. Harry Viteles, *A History of the Co-operative Movement in Israel*, book 1, *The Evolution of the Co-operative Movement* (London: Vallentine, Mitchell & Co.,

1966). See also Henry Near, *The Kibbutz Movement: A History*, vol. 1, *Origins and Growth, 1909–1939* (Oxford: Oxford University Press, 1992).

44. Joseph Trumpeldor: "Like Kropotkin, I believe that only a very large, territorially extensive commune leads to anarchy," cited in Horrox, *Living Revolution*, 35; Meir Yaari: "[In the movement's early years] we were what is known as anarchists... We believed in a prototype of future society in which the individual's life would be free of coercion, while being autonomous"; Manes Sperber: "[we were interested] in the anarcho-communist theory of Kropotkin, the revolutionary prince, far more than in Marxism" (ibid., 45).

45. Cited in Horrox, *Living Revolution*, 71. Of course, the kibbutzim eventually played a crucial role in militarily dividing and conquering Palestine, and due to this prominent function in the *Nakba*, they are not usually cited as an inspiring precedent by contemporary Israeli anarchists. By the same token, Zionist educational programs that make mention of the military prowess of these "pioneers" may mention their socialist solidarity, but are unlikely to play up the specific radical theoretical sources of their practices.

46. Though to be sure, Buber lacked anything like a deep anticolonial analysis that would have been able to present even the best-intentioned "colonists" as harbingers of a project of dispossession. His real "utopianism" may have been his hope that he could convince the Zionist movement to give up its goal of tying numerical superiority to state sovereignty—though even here it is important to recall that Buber imagined a small movement, and no critical mass of Jewish refugees appeared imminent in Palestine in the 1920s.

47. Paul Mendes-Flohr, "The Kingdom of God: Martin Buber's Critique of Messianic Politics," *Behemoth: A Journal on Civilization* 1.2 (2008): 26–38.

48. Martin Buber, *Kingship of God*, trans. Richard Scheimann (Amherst, NY: Humanity Books, 1967), 16–17.

49. This project may itself involve a certain amount of "pneumatic" reading (it was Scholem who once used this word to describe Buber's romantic, Diltheyan hermeneutics). However, the point is that the *pneuma* here is directed into very particular channels.

50. Martin Buber, *Moses: The Revelation and the Covenant* (Amherst, NY: Humanity Books, 1998), 186.

51. Ibid., 189.

52. Buber, *I and Thou*, 158.

53. Ibid., 161.

54. See Franz Rosenzweig, "The Builders: Concerning the Law," in *On Jewish Learning* (Madison: University of Wisconsin Press, 2002), 72–92, and the Buber-Rosenzweig correspondence concerning it in ibid., 109–18.

55. Scheimann's translation here is slightly misleading. The 1932 edition reads, "Um die Geschichte als um das Zwiegespräch von fragender Gottheit

und antwortversagender, aber doch auch antwortversuchender Menschheit zu wissen, dessen Gefragtes ein Eschaton ist." Buber apparently worried that the object of *dessen* was unclear, since the 1956 edition, which Scheimann follows, adds an additional *das Zwiegespräch* between *wissen* and *dessen*. But in his translation Scheimann renders the first as "dialectic," a word Buber already used *Dialektik* for earlier in the paragraph and will presently use again, and the second as "dialogue." There might be some value in maintaining the distinctions between *paradox, dialectic,* and *dialogue* here, even if it is only to show the degree to which Buber treats them as interchangeable. The italicized *eschaton* is Scheimann's. The use of *dialectic* here seems non-Hegelian, in that the conflict does not produce "higher" stages that move along a teleological path *toward* the eschaton. It simply recurs.

56. I have restored these italicizations, omitted in Scheimann's English translation, from the 1932 edition of *Königtum Gottes*, p. 12, which reads "der in der Geschicht*schreibung* wirkt, weil er in der *Geschichte* gewirkt hat."

57. Buber, *Moses*, 187–88. Hebrew and German references are to *Moshe* (Tel-Aviv: Schocken Press, 1945) and to *Moses* (Zürich: Gregor Müller, 1948).

58. As Buber underlined many times throughout his dialogical writings, will and effort are not sufficient for the achievement of "You-saying," though the grace that makes You-saying possible may at times also attend on will and effort: "The You encounters me by grace—it cannot be found by seeking." Moreover, although "presence is not what is evanescent and passes but what confronts us, waiting and enduring," the I-Thou *relationship* always melts back into the I-It relationship at some point, and this is "our melancholy lot." See Buber, *I and Thou*, 62, 64, 75. This is not to say, however, that Buber would not have been *able* to reconcile the I-Thou relation (as the model of fulfilled relationship for a philosophical anthropology focused on the individual or dyad) with the kingship of God (as the model of true community combining freedom and equality). Such reconciliation should not be assumed to be simple or obvious, however.

59. Buber, *Moses*, 21.

60. Ibid., 171.

61. Ibid., 175.

62. Ibid., 179. The quotation here is from Albrecht Alt, *Die Ursprünge des israelitischen Rechts* (Leipzig, Germany: S. Hirzel, 1934), 65. In associating the sabbatical year not just with letting the land lie fallow but also with economic redistribution, Buber assumes as correct the view of some scholars that the sabbatical was originally as forceful as the Jubilee, which was only introduced later, after the Israelites persisted in viewing the sabbatical as impracticable and thus failed to observe it.

63. Buber, *Moses*, 179.

64. Ibid., 181.

65. Gershom Scholem, "Martin Buber's Conception of Judaism," in *On Jews and Judaism in Crisis*, ed. Werner J. Dannhauser (New York: Schocken Books, 1976), 159.

66. Martin Buber, *The Prophetic Faith*, trans. Carlyle Witton-Davies (New York: Collier Books, 1977), 179. Originally published as *Torat Ha-Nevi'im* (Tel Aviv: Mossad Bialik, 1942).

67. Ibid., 180.

68. For more on Landauer's approach in the German context, see his pamphlet "The United Republics of Germany and Their Constitution," in Kuhn, *All Power to the Councils!*, 199–204. Buber sees this model at work in the biblical book of Judges.

69. Martin Buber, "The Bi-National Approach to Zionism," in *Towards Union in Palestine: Essays on Zionism and Jewish-Arab Cooperation*, ed. Martin Buber, Judah Magnes, and Ernst Simon (Westport, CT: Greenwood Press, 1972), 10. Originally published in 1947 by the Ihud Association, Jerusalem.

70. Martin Buber, "Dialogue," in *Between Man and Man*, trans. Ronald Gregor-Smith (New York: Routledge, 2002), 5.

FIVE

THE HASIDIC ZADDIK AS THEOPOLITICAL LEADER

YEMIMA HADAD

THIS CHAPTER EXAMINES THE CONTRIBUTION of the Hasidic figure of the zaddik to Martin Buber's theopolitical vision.[1] Most scholarship on Buber's theopolitical thought concentrates on two aspects: biblical politics and Zionism. I would like to bridge these two domains, showing that Hasidism plays an important role in Buber's theopolitical narrative.[2] I will begin by highlighting the implicit connections between theopolitics and Hasidism in Buber's writings.[3] I will then continue to discuss the role of human leadership in biblical theopolitics, and finally, I will show the contribution of the figure of the zaddik to Buber's theopolitics. The focus of my study is not strictly historical; instead, it offers a philosophical conceptual analysis of Buber's own theopolitical theory.[4]

I. THE SIGNIFICANCE OF HASIDISM AS A THEOPOLITICAL MOMENT: FROM THE BIBLE THROUGH HASIDISM TO ZIONISM

It has been well established that Martin Buber's theopolitical idea reaches far beyond his exegetical work on the Bible, and that Buber himself considered theopolitics not only relevant but also applicable to modern times.[5] Research on Buber's theopolitics typically concentrates on two areas: his commentary on the Bible as representing ancient Hebrew times and his writings on twentieth-century Zionism, which he considered to be a historical moment and opportunity for the renewal of theopolitics in the land of Israel. According to Christoph Schmidt, theopolitics is seen by Buber as Zionism's true task: "If Zionism is actually supposed to be negation of the exile, then that means for Buber that it must not behave only as a geopolitical suspension, but rather a theological commission to overcome the division of politics and theology and to place Zionism under the theopolitical commission."[6] In what follows, I wish to argue that exile and Hasidism play significant roles in theopolitics, not solely in terms of negation (i.e., the negation of the "geopolitical" and the expansion of theology over politics), but also positively, allowing for the evolution of the Israelites toward the task of overcoming "the division of politics and theology" and creating unity between them (theopolitics) through Zionism.

Following the Maharal of Prague (Rabbi Liva ben Betzalel or Judah Loew, ca. 1512–1609), in *On Zion: The History of an Idea* (based on lectures from 1944), Buber views the punishment of *galut* (exile) as purgatory, a period of purification during which Israel undergoes an internal process of separation and selection from within. According to this view, destruction heralds a reconstruction of Israel.[7] Thus, *galut* is perceived not only as a dramatic event in history or merely as a punishment for sins but also as playing an important role in developing and evolving the people of Israel in preparation for theopolitical reconstitution. Indeed, the land of Israel plays a crucial role in the realization of theopolitics. The connection between the Israelites and the land of Israel is, according to Buber, one made with a particular vocation in mind: the land of Israel is given to the Israelites in order to fulfill divine justice there. For this fulfillment, there is a need for a concrete land: "In order that Israel may become the first-fruits of the divine harvest, it needs a real land as well as a real people."[8] In Buber's theopolitical plot, *galut*, the loss of the homeland in biblical times, occurred as the outcome of a continued deterioration of the theopolitical idea. The loss of the homeland demonstrates the violation of the conditional covenant.

The covenant stipulates that Eretz Israel is the holy place designated for the establishment of a theopolitical regime by the Israelites.[9] However, this covenant is only valid if the Israelites choose to fulfill the theopolitical vision on this land. In other words, the loss of the homeland demonstrates the *conditional* covenant between Israel and Eretz Israel: "Now, therefore, *if* ye will hearken unto My voice indeed and keep My covenant, then ye shall be Mine own treasure from among all peoples. For all the earth is Mine, and ye shall be unto Me a Kingdom of priests and a holy nation. These are the words which thou [Moses] shalt speak unto the children of Israel."[10] The land of Israel is not a free gift or a permanent property but an assigned piece of land for the assigned vocation by an assigned people. Thus, if the Israelites betray their mission, they are destined to lose the given land.

According to the theopolitical vision, the Israelites are designated to be *Mamlechet Kohanim*, a "kingdom of priests." That is to say, they are to be a nation that has no central human government but a decentered self-governance in which all members worship God as their sole leader, thus establishing a direct, dialogical relationship with God as well as direct, dialogical relations with each other.[11] These dialogical relations bind them together into one community of God, *goi kadosh*, a "holy nation." Theopolitics articulates the dialectical relationship between human anarchy and divine theocracy. Buber's theopolitical Zionism strives to establish religious anarchy in the land of Israel, where the one and only government is God's government. According to this vision, God shall eventually receive his kingship from the people, and they will follow the ethical dialogical principle on the land of Israel. This particular national vocation is the first step toward a universal vision—the dissemination of theopolitics among nations until the whole world becomes God's kingdom.[12]

It is especially in Hasidism that Buber recognizes the seeds for the renewal of the theopolitical vision during the times of *galut*. There exists, according to Buber, a connection between those seeds and the awakening of Zionism, in which he finds the opportunity to renew theopolitics. In *The Origin and Meaning of Hasidism* (1960), he writes,

> The Kingdom of God has remained [in Hasidism in contrast to Christianity] the same as it always was in the eyes of Judaism—to which Hasidism has remained faithful willingly and unwillingly—namely the establishment of the Kingship of God over the "human nation" as nation of nations; and this Kingdom will not come about until the nation, which has been destined for this purpose, shall begin to establish in its own way of living the will of God for the redemption of the world. . . . Hasidism announced with great enthusiasm that Israel, the heart of humanity, and Eretz Israel, the heart of the world, are required by each other, and without their unity redemption will not come.[13]

Buber views Hasidism as the first awakening since biblical times toward the theopolitical task: the task of establishing God's kingship in the world, which, according to this vision, must start within Israel before spreading among the nations. In this respect, Hasidism was not only a historical precedent for Buber. It was also a religious power that could restrain Zionism from following the general secular nationalist wave that was prevalent in the nineteenth and twentieth centuries. Whereas in modern nationalism nation and land ultimately become objects of worship, in theopolitics the nation and the land are justified only by submission to God and his moral law. Theopolitics, however, has a universal horizon: world redemption. It is to begin with Israel and to eventually encompass the world. The land and the nation are not understood as "ends in themselves" but only as a means for the realization of justice and peace in God's kingdom on earth. As Buber writes in *The Origin and Meaning of Hasidism*, "here in Hasidism we have something close to us in time, and its offshoots reach into our very age. Hasidism is a great revelation of spirit and life in which the nation appears to be connected by an inner tie with the world, with the soul, and with God. Only through such a contact will it be possible to guard Zionism against following the way of the nationalism of our age, which by demolishing the bridges which connect it with the world, is destroying its own value and its right to exist."[14] Modern nationalism is an antagonistic, oppositional, insular force that is cut off on all ends but one—the notion of the state; it is cut off from God, the world, and the soul. Hasidism, for Buber, must harness the secular-nationalist energy of Zionism and restore the severed ties to God, world, and soul. Only then can a nation-state claim its moral right to exist at all.

With this *spiritual-religious* Zionism, Buber strives to renew theocracy in the land of Israel through a twofold correction: the correction of Judaism's diasporic bias toward theology at the exclusion of politics and the correction of Zionism's tendencies toward a politics of nationalism at the exclusion of the theological.[15] Buber is convinced that "Hasidic Zionism" can safeguard mainstream Zionism against secularism and national egotism under the assumption that true religiosity submits itself to divine justice, peace, and coexistence out of religious love for God's creation.[16] However, given the fact that both Hasidism and Jewish orthodoxy were reluctant to engage with the actual world of the nations, it is likely that Buber derived his vision of national universalism, as suggested by Avraham Shapira, from Johann Gottfried Herder's pluralistic nationalism and that, in fact, he read Herder into Hasidism.[17]

We have now established that Buber's theopolitics contains three moments: the biblical, the Hasidic, and the Zionist. His writings on Hasidism stand between his writings on the Bible and Zionism. He sees in Hasidism a mediating movement of sorts between biblical and modern theopolitics to be reached by Zionism. The relation between Hasidism and theopolitics also shaped Buber's understanding of leadership. Thus, we will reflect in the following sections on the leadership of the zaddik in relation to biblical leadership and to the leader to come—to the theopolitical messiah.

II. LEADERSHIP IN THE BIBLE

Before observing the inner connections between the leaders of the past (the prophet and the zaddik) and the leaders to come (the messiah), it is useful to examine leadership in the Bible and its role in Buber's theopolitical vision. In the following section, I will reflect on utopian biblical leadership, namely, God as the leader of Israel or, in Buber's formulation, YHVH the king. I will then go on to examine the archetypes of human leadership in the Bible—the judge, the king, and the prophet—and their roles in theopolitics. Finally, I will discuss the Hasidic zaddik as a theopolitical leader through demonstrating a connection to the biblical prophet. I will argue that in Buber's vision, the Hasidic zaddik is both the successor of the biblical prophet and an original theopolitical leader in his own right.

IIa. YHVH the King: Theocracy and Religious Anarchy

The theopolitical utopia pronounces the idea that God is the leader and king of the Israelites. However, he is not only the king of the tribe; he is also the king of the world and all nations.[18] God's leadership has both a religious and political character. He is the lord of nature and the master of history. Though he is a universal God, he has elected one nation, the Israelites, as his firstborn to lead and disseminate the theopolitical message in the world.[19] Election, however, according to Buber, means that God has entrusted the Israelites with an office, not a rank.

Buber's theopolitical vision is based on two foundational stories from the book of Judges: the speech of Gideon, and Jotham's fable. Buber claims that Gideon's speech proves that theocracy exists—as the striving toward a constitution—early in the book of Judges and not, as argued by Julius Wellhausen, in the later times of the prophets or merely as an idealized concept.[20] Gideon's refusal to receive the kingdom from the Israelites pronounces the antithesis between human and divine rulership: "I will not rule over you, neither shall my son rule over you; The Lord shall rule over you."[21]

The *theopolitical utopia*, where God is the king, can be seen either as a *direct theocracy* or as *religious anarchy*. Both, in Buber's understanding, mean one and the same thing: *direct theocracy* means that only God ultimately rules and leads the Israelites (YHVH the king), whereas *religious anarchy* annihilates any kind of human rulership. Bernard Susser and Samuel Hayim Brody have labeled this conceptual unity "anarcho-theocracy."[22] Theocracy and anarchy, supposedly contradictory concepts, merge in Buber's theopolitics. This unification of direct theocracy and religious anarchy is arguably derived by Buber out of the Jewish mystical principle of coincidence of opposites, which is articulated both in Kabbalah and Hasidism through the ideas of *tikkun olam* (repairing the world) and *geula* (redemption), both of which imply a unification of opposite elements in the Godhead.[23]

In addition to Gideon's speech, Buber's interpretation of biblical theopolitics is also based on Jotham's fable.[24] Buber states, "The Jotham fable, the strongest anti-monarchical poem of world literature, is the counterpart of the Gideon passage. Independently of the latter it could [also] be understood anarchistically."[25] According to Buber's allegorical interpretation of Jotham's fable, no central human rulership besides God's is required. The members of this utopian community should become, according to this utopia, a kingdom of priests (*Mamlechet Kohanim*). *Kohanim* here, Buber explains, "does not mean 'Priests,' rather servants who 'stand ready' to carry out the orders of the King, His adjutants through whom He announces His will."[26]

The members of this community shall be in direct relationship with the divine leader and with each other. They shall be sustained as a community through mutual relationships with one another and their common relation to the center (i.e., God).[27] A broad observation of Buber's later writings shows that the relationship between God and the Israelites is dialogical in its nature and that God leads the people both as individuals and as a congregation through the personal dialogue each member holds with him (I-Eternal Thou relations).[28] This dialogue, as Buber emphasizes in *I and Thou* and other places, does not consist of a series of concrete commands but in an attentiveness to divine "presence." Buber trusts that the acknowledgment of the Eternal Thou as dialogical presence suffices as its own imperative and that our response becomes, in turn, responsibility.[29]

As a community, God leads the people—not to where they want to go but to where *he* wants them to go.[30] God leads them by bestowing his divine grace on pious members of the community (also called charismatic leaders), who now assume a temporary leadership role for the task assigned.[31] Their leadership comes to an end when their task is completed, a fluctuation that helps maintain religious anarchy. No human leadership exists permanently; rather, temporary leadership occasionally emerges in accordance with the needs of the hour. Hence, the theopolitical leader resembles an apostle more than a ruler or governor. In peaceful periods, the community functions without a dominant human leader, assuming, of course, that everyone knows and follows God's way on their own.

The essential point is that Buber denies any rulership of man over man. According to his interpretation of Jotham's fable, the members of a religious anarchy see no advantage in ruling, or being ruled, by a human. They deny the task of ruling, preferring instead to concentrate on the mutual utility they can each bring to the community by acting according to their own divinely ordained nature. The olive tree prefers to offer its fruits and oil than to rule, and so does the fig tree, the grapevine, and so on; only the thorn bush, which bears no fruit of its own, wishes to rule. Thus Buber writes, "the Kingship... is not a productive calling. It is vain, but also bewildering and seditious, that men rule over man. Everyone is to pursue his own proper business, and the manifold fruitfulnesses will constitute a community over which, in order that it endure, no one needs to rule—no one except God alone.... The 'commonwealth without government' is thought of by the author or the redactor of the antimonarchic Book of Judges as a commonwealth for which an invisible government is sufficient."[32] According to the utopian order described in the fable, all members are capable of taking on the role of leadership. However, the specific person to take the lead at a certain moment is elected according to their ability to listen and respond to the demands of the hour. Potentially, each member, at a certain time, can take on the role of leadership based on this situational ability rather than an innate ability to rule or lead. And each situation requires a different kind of leader. A single permanent leader, therefore, cannot bear the theopolitical mission alone. Leadership in religious anarchy (or direct theocracy) is but a task-specific office.[33] There are no permanent positions of governance but only a shared responsibility of leadership that shifts with the changes, challenges, and demands of the present moment. According to Buber's theopolitical utopia, the only permanent leader is God. The sustainability of anarchy depends on the temporality of human leadership.

The vocation of the Israelites is directed toward universal redemption. God shall eventually become the King of all nations. However, in order to fulfill this mission in relation to other nations, Buber maintains that Israel must start by achieving it within its own boundaries: "I am [says allegedly God] the King of the world, but I have chosen you for myself as my unmediated royal dominion. Therefore you shall establish my Kingdom over you—but as my messengers and helpers in order thus to begin the preparation of humanity for my Kingdom."[34] If God is to become the one and only King, then human leadership can indeed only be of preparatory significance. But how did this preparation manifest itself in biblical times? And why did it fail? Here we must look at three biblical archetypes of human leadership: the judge, the king, and the prophet.

IIb. The Judge as Theopolitical Leader

The utopian model of "God the leader" or "God the King" did not pass the test of reality in the ancient Hebrew community. The Israelites, argues Buber, were not yet ready to receive God's direct leadership.[35] Thus, the period of judges emerged as an intermediary stage of the theocratic ideal. Buber uses two distinct concepts, which set apart the *primitive theocracy* in the book of Judges from the *direct theocracy* described previously.[36] *Direct theocracy*, in which God has a direct relationship with each and every member of the community (i.e., the "kingdom of priests"), is not yet fully achieved in the book of Judges, though it depicts the highest stage in the fulfillment of this ideal up to our own times. In the period of the judges, God's nation was not yet mature enough for its theopolitical vocation, and the gap between abstract, divine leadership and the people's need for concrete leadership required mediation. The judge, therefore, becomes a theopolitical leader whose task it is to guide the people and pave the way for the preparation of the whole community to receive God's direct leadership.[37] As a mere guide, the judge does not wish for the people to follow his own ways, nor, as we recall from Gideon's speech, does he wish to rule the people. Rather, the judge has attained the level of leadership Buber compared to priesthood in the book of Exodus: He has become a "direct servant."[38]

The judge, then, is a charismatic leader who is chosen directly by God and leads by means of divine charisma. *Charisma* in ancient Greek means "the gift of God." Buber refers to the divine nature of charisma bestowed on leaders, which can be found in the scriptural verses claiming that God's spirit was empowered by resting on the leader.[39] Yet the nature of charisma is not permanent but is limited to a certain time or task: "The office of the *shophtim* [judges] on that account is understood not as a form of government... but as a mandatory vocation conditioned and limited by the situation—an exclusively charismatic office whose interruptions of tenure thus ultimately belong to its essence."[40] After completion of the task, the leadership role is fulfilled and religious anarchy thus maintained. The charismatic leader is always, according to Buber, a leader of the hour. God bestows on the leader the charismatic power to lead the people through times of danger or distress. When there are no pressing political or social demands, the community is maintained without central human leadership.

Buber's idea of temporary human leadership based on charisma is meant to abolish any claim for centralized human rule of man over man that would violate direct theocracy.[41] By temporarily bestowing the power of charisma on a leader, God remains the direct leader and indirectly participates in history. Rather than attributing power to himself, the "man of God" acknowledges the divine charismatic power given to him and admits it.[42] Since no man has permanent possession of divine charisma, it becomes impossible for the congregation to follow one permanent human leader. Even the righteous man—according to Buber—is exposed to sin and can fail and stumble in fulfilling the theopolitical task. This is the reason for Buber's criticism of the monarchic trend that emerges in the book of Judges and is established later in the books of Samuel and Kings. The monarchic trend becomes the first concrete deviation from the theopolitical vision.

Thus, Buber contrasts the *antimonarchic* period seen in the first part of the book of Judges, which is still *direct theocracy*, with the *monarchic* period starting with the second part of the book of Judges and continuing into the books of Samuel and Kings. In this later period, theocracy is designated as *indirect*, since it is mediated by a permanent figure, the king, whose leadership is beyond temporary divine charisma.[43] In other words, divine leadership is now mediated by a permanent human leader whose power, it seems, is independent of divine charisma.

IIc. The King as Theopolitical Leader

The book of Judges, as Buber sees it, introduces us to two competing trends: the monarchic and the antimonarchic. The trend of direct theocracy (which is antimonarchic) in the first part of the book gives way to the antithetical thesis that advocates the monarchic trend in the last part of the book. As often in the book of Judges, a lack of central leadership means, in practice, the decline from religious anarchy to a reality of chaotic anarchy.[44] From the monarchic perspective, the reason for this chaos and moral deterioration is a lack of successive leadership: "In those days there was no King in Israel; every man did that which was right in his own eyes."[45] According to the authors of the monarchic trend, permanent leadership, with a secure, successive, human kingdom of dynasty, would increase stability and security. Buber, however, does not share the feeling that social deterioration occurred because of a lack of human rule. He views this failure as a fact of immaturity: direct theocracy failed because it came ahead of its time and, therefore, instead of achieving religious anarchism, turned repeatedly into chaotic anarchism.[46] It was then only natural that with chaos and political instability, the need for permanent human leadership grew.[47] Buber thinks of this political transformation as nothing but compromise: "The institution of the judges passes over to that of the kingdom as soon as it becomes clear that the people now cannot actually acknowledge the divine representation except in the form of the continuity, that is to say, that from now on the people's order is only to be realized as a state order. The dynastic continuity implies a continuity of responsibility to fulfill the divine commission."[48] Without the guidance of God's leadership, in a word, the human kingdom cannot secure the order and stability it promises.

Indirect theocracy starts with the book of Samuel, when the Israelites demand that a king be nominated to them, as is practice in all other nations. God succumbs to their demand with the intention, however, of expanding (and spiritually enhancing) their wish.[49] Buber asserts that God "fulfill[s] the wish of the people [to have a king], while at the same time changing its grounds, by way of enhancing it to the divine will."[50] God accepts their demand on the condition that the Israelite kingdom become not "as all nations" but, rather, a continuation of established theocracy.[51] At this point, *direct theocracy* is exchanged for mediated theocracy, that is, *indirect theocracy*. We will meet this didactic compromise again when we discuss the leadership of the zaddik in Hasidism. What matters to us now is that the monarchic transformation is treated as an intermediate level in order to allow for the future establishment of *direct theocracy*.[52] In other words, indirect theocracy is still seen as part of the earlier antimonarchic tradition. The kingdom, Buber contends, was "strongly built into theocracy or theocratically undergirded."[53]

In indirect theocracy, the nominated human king, the anointed one, is expected to function as *eved Ha-Shem* (the servant of God). In contrast to other nations, the Israelite king cannot justify his rulership as a privilege given to him by the grace of God, nor can he justify his actions as the will of God. Buber explains that in kingdoms of ancient nations the "prince is looked upon as son of the god . . . [and] the King himself is divinized"—a disposition that secured his right to rule as entrusted to him by God.[54] His will was regarded as divine and his actions as faithful representations of divine power and will. The Israelite king, by contrast, has *obligations* toward God and will be held accountable by God for all his sins: "YHVH undertakes to deal with [the Israelite king] as with His son, chastising him as His son. Over against the Kings, who boast themselves to be sons of God to whom full power is given in accordance with the ancient Eastern conception of the King as adopted by the deity (cf. Ps. 2, 7), we have these words declaring that this sonship is meant as responsibility to the father, who time and again calls his son to account."[55] The position of the Israelite king is demanding: his leadership is not a way of ruling, but a way of serving; he should serve God on the one hand and the community on the other. Buber calls the book of Samuel the "Biblical Politeia."[56] However, unlike in the "Platonic Politeia," where the philosopher king subordinates himself to reason, in the Biblical Politeia, the anointed king subordinates himself to God not by reason but through revelation.[57]

The king differs from the judge in two crucial respects: the reception of charisma, and the permanence of his leadership. Whereas the judge's charisma is bestowed on him for the assigned task, the human king holds long-term, though not unlimited, charisma, which is given to him according to God's will and which could be given also to a different figure other than him.[58] The judge is appointed—according to Buber, though not necessarily according to the Bible—for a particular mission, while the king is appointed potentially for life with his leadership extending over generations. However, as the Israelite king is subordinated to the divine in indirect theocracy, the anointed king, or his dynasty, could be dethroned by God if they betray the divine mission.

As the theopolitical reality develops in the books of Samuel and Kings, the original theopolitical utopia gradually declines. The human kings begin to neglect their real task. *Avdey Ha-Shem*, the servants of God, become kings "like all nations" and lead Israel, ultimately, to the catastrophe of exile. Thus, the books of Samuel and Kings, according to Buber, depict a tension between the rule of God and the rule of man. The king restricts God's government to the sacramental and holy realms in order to earn and appropriate the political so that it can be considered profane and independent of the divine: "The functions of YHVH are to be reduced so that they do not bind the King: the cosmic spheres are left in His control, as is the Holy of Holies, whereas for the government of Israel full power has been given to His anointed one, and with this YHVH, so to speak, surrendered His influence in this domain."[59] The king, pursuing his own benefit, reduces the commitment to God to the realms considered as sacred (rites and rituals), leaving to himself all else. The profane becomes, from this point on, the secular and is removed from the divine. Ultimately, the king's all too human will for power dispenses with the dialogical obligation to the Eternal Thou.[60]

This secularization changed the original essence of Biblical Politeia. Instead of a king being anointed by God and subordinated to him as servant, the king declares *himself* a ruler appointed by the will of God and with the unlimited grace of God, claiming that his appointment and power are proof of God's will and divine approval.[61] Buber calls this the turn to the *mamrim* (obstinate), referring to those who, while not turning their backs on the tribal God, still refuse to follow his ways, wishing instead to worship him in their own way.[62] The king is not a heretic per se. He does not deny God, nor renounce the commitment to him; he merely distances himself from God's way and from direct dialogue with him by limiting God to the sacramental. And as the king, so his people: the Israelites, by means of sacrifices and offerings, which define the sacred as a separate sphere, seek to acquire the freedom of profane life.[63] Indeed, the greatest sin of Israel, as Buber sees it, becomes the separation of the sacred (*kodesh*) from the secular (*chol*). Up to this point, everything was sacred: everyday life, the political realm, and the sacramental were equally part of religious life. But with the rise of human kings, the Israelites distinguished the holy from the profane, limiting the divine to the holy, while appropriating the profane for themselves. This period could be seen as the first (ancient) secularization of Israel.

Though the human kingdom promised order, stability, and leadership to end the chaotic anarchy of the former period, it brought eventually nothing but a further decline from the ideal of divine theocracy. Indirect theocracy was supposed to bridge and prepare Israel for reestablishing a revised *direct theocracy* in the future. Instead, however, the Israelite kingdom took another step backward: not only from direct to indirect theocracy, but one that brought about a further decline of the theopolitical vision; it ultimately turned indirect theocracy into sheer monarchy, splitting religion from state and subordinating the priests to the rule of the king.[64] But it is at this junction in the theopolitical drama that a new charismatic leader appears: the prophet.

IId. The Prophet as Theopolitical Leader

As the kings and the priests betrayed their real mission to serve God, the prophets emerged as the true charismatic leaders and the true carriers of the theopolitical vocation. The prophet enters the theopolitical drama as a recipient of divine charisma who challenges the authority of the kings whenever they "did evil in the eyes of the Lord." Buber stresses that the existence of prophecy proves that the Israelite kingdom was rooted in the tradition of direct theocracy. After all, the authority of the prophets to "confront the possessor of power [the king] with the [divine] origin and significance of his power" was based on the presumption that a higher authority existed than the human king.[65]

According to Buber, the role of the prophet as the receiver of charisma is neither that of soothsayer nor that of seer but again that of *eved Ha-Shem*, a servant of God and a mediator between heaven and earth.[66] In this regard, the figure of the prophet is more similar to that of the judge than the king. One can say that Buber contrasts two types of leadership in the Bible: the judge and the prophet against the king and the priest. The judges and prophets Buber defines as "susceptible to the Spirit, uninhibitedly surrendered to the Spirit, those men receiving the working of the Spirit as Kingly rule for the life of Israel."[67] The priests and kings, on the other hand, he defines as holders of official positions, which are permanent and authoritative: "Kings rule, Priests minister in their office, while the man of the Spirit [the prophet], without power or office, hears the word of his Leader [God]."[68] Buber's critique of the priests and kings implies that they forgot that God does not bestow permanent positions but vocations: "He [God] will apportion to the one [human leader], for ever and ever chosen by Him, his tasks, but naked power without a situationally related task He does not wish to bestow."[69] Every man who holds a position is responsible for a specific vocation and held accountable when betraying it. In contrast to the priest, the prophet does not hold any formal position and fulfilled his divine mission without any material benefits.[70] What Buber seems to suggest is that true leaders are always officeless, and that charismatic leaders—who have no claim to material benefits—are more likely to remain faithful to the cause of social justice than those in office who enjoy and command stability. Within indirect theocracy, the prophet is tasked to remind the Israelites and the king who their real king is and to impress on them that God's realm encompasses *every* realm—the political, the ethical, the social, and the sacramental: "[God] is not content to be 'God' in the religious sense. He does not want to surrender to a man that which is not 'God's,' the rule over the entire actuality of worldly life: this very rule He lays claim to and enters upon it; for there is nothing which is not God's. . . . He makes known His will first of all as constitution—not constitution of cult and custom only, also of economy and society."[71] The prophet, then, must remind the Israelites and the king that the social and political are *religious* obligations and that the polarization between religious and secular is the main sin for which the Israelites need to be held accountable. He must remind the people and its leaders that the covenant of God with the Israelites does not purely concern ritual and sacramental obligations, but that it is first and foremost a political obligation, a theopolitical contract concerning every realm of human life. In this sense, the prophet's divine mission consists in a rebuke of Israel's forgetfulness of true vocation and renewal of its covenantal obligations.[72]

This mission became all the more urgent as indirect theocracy, in the book of Kings, declined not only into the rule of kings and priests but also into the abuse of religion to the advantage of centralizing a political government, where priests submitted to the rule of the kings.[73] Naturally, the king wished to neutralize the voice of the prophet, for the latter's independence of mind and speech undermined his authority. Therefore, he tried to bring the prophet closer to the political interests of the kingdom, offering him what few others would reject—an office with material benefits: "The early Kingdom strives to neutralize the Prophets by giving them an official status in the form of a court office."[74] However, this effort seemed in vain, for, unlike kings and priests, the power of the prophetic message was anchored in his independence. His authority to speak on behalf of justice and against evil, to criticize the government and the people for its moral failures and social corruption, was derived precisely from refusing any office while remaining active and involved in the nation's political and social life. In other words, the prophets were practicing an activism of powerlessness. Devoid of statutory might and egoistic interests, they stood vulnerable in face of kingly and priestly power, facing the public and rebuking them for their moral corruption. Only thus could the prophets, in good conscience, demand peace and justice.[75]

The prophet is the final and, perhaps, most ideal type of leader in Buber's theopolitical drama. This applies only to the Bible, however, not to the theopolitical plot itself. As I will argue in the next section, the principle of powerless leadership applies not only to the Bible, but also becomes a model for later periods, even for modernity.

III. THE ZADDIK AS THEOPOLITICAL LEADER

Whereas the prophet is active during the period of indirect theocracy and wishes to repair its flawed political reality by restoring it to the covenantal vision, the zaddik in Hasidism is active only after the destruction of the Israelite kingdom, when the possibility of restoration seems indefinitely postponed. He acts in the time of exile long after Israel, having failed to keep its part in the covenant, had lost the Promised Land—the very land designated for the actualization of direct theocracy. The great mistake Israel made in ancient times, as we have seen previously, was divorcing the secular from the holy. Biblical "secularism" means the restriction of the divine realm to the sacramental and ritual to the holy while appropriating all other realms to the profane life of man. The separation of the secular from the holy implied also the *reduction* of the holy that gave rise to Israel's deviation from the theopolitical vision. This deviation deepened during the periods of exile, where politics and the profane remained strictly separated from religious life. It was Hasidism that, for Buber, brought a correction to this history. Reclaiming the realm of the secular as holy, it found holiness in every aspect of life. In Hasidism, "no deed is condemned by its nature to remain 'profane.'"[76] By sacralizing the secular, the Hasidic zaddik became the successor to his biblical twin—the prophet.

In the speech "Symbolic and Sacramental Existence," which he delivered in 1934 in Ascona, two years after publishing his major scientific work *Kingship of God*, Buber places the biblical prophet in explicit relation to the Hasidic zaddik, identifying a common root of these two figures: "The Zaddik of the early period of Hasidism, the classic Zaddik, is only an especially clear, theoretically delineated stamp of the same archetype, originating in the biblical world and pointing into a future one."[77] There exists, for Buber, an inner connection between the leadership roles of the prophet, the zaddik, and the coming messiah. I would like to argue that this connection traverses Buber's entire theopolitical plot and that each of these figures constitutes a stage of leadership toward the realization of the vision of God the king.

Indeed, there are many similarities between Buber's description of the biblical prophet and the Hasidic zaddik in his writings. Both are charismatic leaders, both are characterized as serving as leaders rather than as rulers and possessors of power, both play the role of mediator between God and the people, both are considered to be "the mouth of God," both establish truth through their existence and in their own ways of life, and both admonish the people against moral deterioration.[78] Yet despite these obvious similarities, one must look beyond them to recognize that the zaddik, for Buber, is not only a modern copy of the figure of the prophet but also an original figure in its own right. Here, I would like to demonstrate the unique contribution of this figure to the renewal of theopolitics.

In his earlier and later essays on Hasidism, as well as in his retelling of the Hasidic tales, one can identify the special emphasis Buber places on the zaddik as a *social leader* marked by his participation in communal life. The life of the Hasidim, Buber stressed, is founded on communal cooperation and mutual help. The Hasid knows himself "not as a whole but as a part," and "[the] purer and more perfect he is, so much the more intimately does he know that he is a part and so much the more actively there stirs in him the community of existence."[79] The zaddik, according to Buber, is not a leader who lives his life separate or isolated from the people in order to achieve a higher rank of spiritualism. Like his biblical counterpart, the zaddik, too, is a mediator between God and the people. He is a pillar, an axis mundi, who carries God's voice into the world and carries the people's grievances to God.[80] To be sure, the dialectical movement of the zaddik between the heights of spiritualism to the depths of reality is a characteristic also of the prophet. But only in Hasidism was it further developed into the doctrine of the "descent of the zaddik" (*yeridat ha-zaddik*).[81]

The doctrine of the descent of the zaddik was derived from the idea of the fallen sparks in the Lurianic Kabbalah: the zaddik is sent into the domains of sin, to the *kellipot* (husks), in order to release the sacred sparks and elevate them. The zaddik's task is, therefore, to help the people elevate themselves spiritually by separating the sparks from the *kellipot*.[82] The descent of the zaddik is an essential part of his mission to help the simple people achieve *tikkun azmi*, which is a precondition for *tikkun olam*.[83] In the *Tales of the Hasidim* (1946), Buber retells an episode called "Climbing Down" that illustrates this doctrine: "Rabbi Shelomo said: If you want to raise a man from the mud and filth do not think it is enough to keep standing on top and reaching down to him a helping hand. You must go all the way down into the mud and filth. Then take hold of him with strong hands and pull him and yourself out into the light."[84] The tale demonstrates the zaddik's obligation to descend from his high spiritual level in order to assist his community.⁸⁵ This is an essential part of his antiauthoritative leadership: the zaddik does not demand the people to ascend to him but demands of himself to descend to them. The zaddik's descent down to the public sphere is not for his own benefit—sometimes it is even to the contrary—and it is often accompanied by a deep resentment of the people. The descent is, as it were, a "compromise" the zaddik is obliged to make, in order for the community to elevate itself. As in the case of indirect theocracy, where God had to compromise and lower his demands on the people, the zaddik's descent also meant a *didactic compromise*. The zaddik must become a mere vessel. He must descend for the people to be elevated.

This also means that the zaddik must feel empathy toward the hardships, sorrow, and pain people experience in order to be able to connect with them and help them elevate and develop their spiritual level. Only by way of deep empathic engagement can the therapeutic process of *tikkun azmi*—or self-repair—be realized. The zaddik must reduce himself to, or pretend to be, one of the simple people so that they can relate to him and identify with him.⁸⁶ Thus, the zaddik loiters in the markets and streets and talks to the people, approaching them in order to help them lift themselves up to a higher level of spirituality. The zaddik's descent leads to *mutual elevation*: his engagement with simple people teaches the zaddik to know their plight and everyday hardships, and it is this experience that challenges his spiritual world, while the simple people learn about the spiritual world by associating with him, a glimpse into the higher spheres that allows them to raise themselves. They learn more by watching, imitating, and adopting the zaddik's ways than they would through receiving theoretical teachings.⁸⁷ Thus, by descending into the muddy and unclean world of the everyday, the zaddik becomes a hidden pillar to his fellow human beings. His spiritual self-restraint and self-concealment suggest elements of *zimzum* translated into the mundane world, but they also suggest elements of the hidden messiah.

Contrary to Sabbatianism, however, the zaddik's descent does not imply and glorify committing sins. Rather, his descent requires the zaddik's deep engagement with, and attachment to, the sinners he wants to elevate. The descent into the world of sin is described by Gershom Scholem as "the great adventure, without which he [the zaddik] cannot perform his mission."⁸⁸ The zaddik risks himself by descending for the sake of the community. But through that risk he elevates himself. This is the great paradox of the zaddik's descent: it is, ultimately, an ascent; or as Buber puts it: "This is the mystery of community: not only do the lower need the higher, but the higher also need the lower."⁸⁹

The political implications of Hasidism now become clearer. Buber recognizes Hasidism not only as an ideal community but also as a renewal of the theopolitical message. Through the unification of the realm of holiness with the realm of everydayness, Hasidism seeks a restoration of God's rule in every realm and every aspect of mundane life. Here, the whole of life is sanctified before God. Buber thinks that the

> Torah as law in the customary sense, that is, as the sum of commands of God that have no other aim than enabling man to fulfill God's incomprehensible will, is placed in question by Sabbatian antinomianism ... the Hasidic conception of the Torah is an elaboration of the traditional belief that God wants to win through man the world created by him. He wants to make it truly His world, His Kingdom, but through human deed. The intention of the divine revelation is to form men who work on the redemption of creation. By this is not meant an isolated Messianic action, but a deed of everyday that prepares the Messianic completion ... the mitzvoth, the commands designate the realm of things that are already explicitly given to man for hallowing ... [but] God wills that everything be hallowed until in the Messianic age the distinction between sacred and profane no longer exists because all has become holy.[90]

Observance, or *mizwot*, is not the only commitment of the Hasid. Each and every realm of life becomes a sacred duty (that is Buber's interpretation of *Avoda baGashmiyut*). The Hasid sees in every occurrence the presence of God, and in everything a sign or a word from God intended and directed at him. He hears the living word of God, and not only a word of the past. No more separation exists between the religious realm of worship and the everyday. All realms are considered to be religious, the political as well as the moral. Therefore, one obeys God not only through fulfilling the *mizwot* but also through every deed.[91] In this way, the Hasid, like the prophet and like the judge, remains attentive to God's word.

The task of the prophet and the zaddik, according to Buber, is not only to rebuke Israel for its failures but also to teach the nation to form a direct relationship to God and to become what it is designed to be: a nation of priests (*Am Kohanim*). If the prophet relentlessly criticized the leaders of the kingdom, the zaddik becomes a voice against rabbinic establishment and human authority. But his voice was also one of constructive affirmation. The zaddik emerges as a builder of community—a community under direct divine authority and of mutual relationships. In this sense, the zaddik conjoins the figure of the critical prophet and the affirmative figure of the judge who gathers together the community. He is not merely a successor to his biblical counterparts but also a synthesizer—a new kind of theopolitical leader.

But the zaddik, who was active in the period of exile, must himself be surpassed. He must be followed by new leaders to come, leaders whose theopolitical lineage extends from the prototype of the judge in the antimonarchic period, to the prophet in the period of indirect theocracy, to the zaddik of the exilic period. Rooted in this lineage, but not rigidly defined by it, are the zaddikim to come, who, according to Buber, will lay a new foundation of religious anarchy.

IV. THE LEADER TO COME AND THE MESSIAH

Buber traces the origins of the messianic idea to the Bible.[92] The roots of the idea of the messiah came from the figure of the anointed king in the books of Samuel and Kings. The messiah in the Bible is a real human being whose anointment signifies the beginning of his kingdom.[93] The transformation of messianism from a political idea into a theological one occurred, according to Buber, during the times of exile, as the hope for a political renewal was shattered. With the growing disappointment throughout history, messianism becomes purely eschatological. Buber viewed this kind of messianism as a decadent point of view, which sees no possibility for change in history: "For the 'eschatological' hope—in Israel...—is first always historical hope; it becomes eschatologized only through growing historical disillusionment."[94] Thus, Buber rejects the eschatological idea of a divine messiah bringing divine redemption into the world.[95] According to him, the original intention of messianism was to constitute the government of God *in* the world.[96] In the books of Samuel and Kings, the messiah is *a real human being* who is anointed, with anointment marking those who were elected to realize the theopolitical mission in the mundane world.[97] Like the king in the Bible, the zaddik in Hasidism is no "superman"; he is dormant in *every* human being who, in Grete Schaeder's words, "applies himself with greater soul energy to the task which confronts every man."[98]

Buber's interpretation of the Israelite leadership of "the leader to come" is understood as a process of *longue durée* rather than a miraculous arrival that marks the end of time: "It is a mistake to regard Jewish messianism as a belief in an event happening once at the end of time and in a single human figure created as the center of this event."[99] The messianic era, in other words, is neither more nor less than a reconstitution of the biblical theopolitical ideal of the rule of God on earth. The world to come, according to this view, shall not be conceived as transcending the mundane world. Rather, it should gradually become a reality in an ongoing eternal improvement. Buber stresses that "man can work toward the redemption of the world" rather than wait for the "Coming One." From this follows that each and every human being participates in redemption: "in reality ... each [man] can only be effective in his domain. Each man has a sphere of being, far extended in space and time which is allotted to him to be redeemed through him."[100] The completion of the never-ending task of perfecting the world is only possible, when the one leader becomes many, and the many become each and every one of us.

One should not expect in the future the renewal of prophecy or even the return of zaddikim or the appearance of a divine messiah. The future figure shall be, to use Buber's words, a "delineated stamp of the same archetype." That is, he will not be divine, but human; he will possess the archetypical components of biblical and Hasidic leaders, yet he shall be an original figure in his own right that suits the historical hour in which he is engaged. He will act by inner power (charisma) in fulfilling his portion of the never-ending task of *tikkun olam*, he will deny offices and act on terms of self-imposed powerlessness to remind those in power of their true duty for justice and peace, he will feel accountable for his deeds in face of the seen and unseen God, and he will not become a sole leader but join others in his specific actual demand for justice and peace.[101] Unlike in the case of the prophet rebuking the people and human rulership, the zaddik—and therefore the leader to come—cannot exhaust his actions by being a critic of society and governance but must be closely engaged with the people as a *builder*. Through his actions, the zaddik guides the people into a direct relationship with God no mediation and no intermediary can replace.[102]

Thus, the leader to come is *eventually* leaders in the plural, women and men, the community at large. Buber rejects the centralization of power in human hands. Only the messianic pretender seeks the concentration of power, for he is, by his nature, a single figure. The institution of the zaddik, however, consists— by its nature—in a multiplicity of contemporary living leaders among whom the labor of redemption, as it were, is divided and shared.[103] As merely religious and moral agents, the "power" of the religious leaders stems, much like the power of the zaddikim in Hasidism, from the legitimacy and faith accorded to them by the people. The leaders to come are not only intellectuals, or educated people, or people of spirit (*Anshey Ha-Ruach*); rather, they are *humble* activists, servants of God in the social sphere. The messianic era, therefore, can only be realized if each member of the community, much like in Jotham's fable, independently contributes to the whole society, and if the roles of leadership are based on temporary charisma, on a divine power not possessed by one of the members alone, but by many different members. The role of leadership is a limited task and not a permanent position. The leader is not a ruler, but only a mediator, and mediators can be, and should be, in the plural.

Buber's concept of anarchy, then, is based on temporary leadership; any permanent leadership (except God's) undermines religious anarchy. Religious anarchy, however, is very different from a secular vision of anarchy, as it considers itself accountable before God. In religious anarchy, there is a permanent leader, a King, who belongs to another order of hierarchy, an order no human can claim. Theocracy associates itself with religious anarchy insofar as it contradicts the human order of hierarchy. From the social point of view, a theocratic community functions as an anarchy, since no human ruler exists, but from the religious point of view, the community functions as a direct theocracy, since God is the one and only ruler who truly warrants authority and demands to be followed.

V. CONCLUSION: ANARCHISM AND MESSIANISM

This leaves us with many open questions concerning Buber's utopian vision: How can one differentiate between false and true leaders? How can one know God's will, and how are we to follow God's ways? What if different members claim to have received different—or even opposite—divine tasks? How is it possible to harmonize many different voices, each claiming to have a divine message? These questions occupied Buber throughout his life, and many of his critics have pointed out that his practical answers remained less than satisfying. But just as for Buber Zionism was not a fixed ideology but a task to constantly be adjusted to reality, so theopolitics remained a project that could only verify itself in the concrete situation.

Buber considered Zionism the opportunity to explore and implement religious anarchy in real life. My purpose was to show that Hasidism, and specifically the figure of the zaddik, plays a prominent part in Buber's theopolitical vision and his cultural Zionism. The zaddik's task is to prepare the hearts of Israel for their theopolitical mission by way of descending into the material world and, through his moral message, demanding the annulment of the profane realm and its sanctification. The historical figure of zaddik thus becomes a model to be followed by leaders to come, leaders whose theopolitical lineage runs from the prototype of the judge in the antimonarchic period, to the prophet in the period of indirect theocracy, to the zaddik in Hasidism in the period of exile. Rooted in this lineage, the zaddikim to come, according to

Buber, are leaders settling in the land of Israel, and contributing to the foundation of religious anarchy, which he considered to be the most enduring order of society. And just as there is a lineage of theopolitical leadership, so there is also an ideal pointing toward the future. The figure of the leader to come should serve as a model for the people until all learn to embody the qualities of righteous leadership. This figure, however, remains to be treated in greater detail in a different essay.[104]

NOTES

This essay is based on a paper given at the Association for Jewish Studies 2015 meeting in Boston. I thank Paul Mendes-Flohr and Hannan Hever for reading an early draft of this paper. I also thank Admiel Kosman, Menachem Lorberbaum, Benjamin Pollock, and the Rosenzweig Minerva Research Center at the Hebrew University in Jerusalem for being a supportive intellectual community.

1. On the concept of "theopolitics" see Samuel Hayim Brody, "Is Theopolitics an Antipolitics?," *Dialogue as a Transdisciplinary Concept*, ed. Paul Mendes-Flohr (Berlin: De Gruyter, 2015): 61–88, and Samuel Hayim Brody, *Martin Buber's Theopolitics* (Bloomington: Indiana University Press, 2018). I would like to thank Brody for sharing with me his manuscript prior to publication. See also Warren Zev Harvey, "Anarchism and Theocracy in the Thought of Martin Buber," in *Israeli Philosophy: A Selection of Articles on General and Jewish Philosophy*, ed. Moshe Hallamish and Asa Kasher (Tel Aviv: Papyrus Publications, 1983), 9–19 [Hebrew]. For Buber's *theopolitics* against Carl Schmitt's *political theology*, see Martin Buber, *Between Man and Man*, trans. Ronald Gregor-Smith (London: Routledge, 2002), 86–89; Nitzan Lebovic, "The Jerusalem School: The Theopolitical Hour," *New German Critique* 105 (2008): 97–120; Christoph Schmidt, "Martin Buber: The Theopolitical Hour," trans. Samuel Hayim Brody, in *Makers of Jewish Modernity: Thinkers, Artists, Leaders, and the World They Made*, ed. Jacques Picard et al. (Princeton, NJ: Princeton University Press, 2016), 187–303; Gregory Kaplan, "Power and Israel in Martin Buber's Critique of Carl Schmitt's Political Theology," in *Judaism Liberalism and Political Theology*, ed. Randi Rashkover and Martin Kavka (Bloomington: Indiana University Press, 2014), 166–77; Yoav Schaefer, "Between Political Theology and Theopolitics: Martin Buber's *Kingship of God*," *Modern Judaism—A Journal of Jewish Ideas and Experience* 37, no. 2 (2017): 231–55; and Charles H. T. Lesch, "Theopolitics Contra Political Theology: Martin Buber's Biblical Critique of Carl Schmitt," *American Political Science Review* 113, no. 1 (2019): 195–208.

2. I use discursively the terms *theopolitical narrative, plot,* and *drama* and *theopolitical idea, theory,* and *task*. I use the first set of terms when I want to refer

to the events and occurrences in the theopolitical story from the Bible through Hasidism to Zionism and up to future events. I use the second set of terms when I speak of the theoretical level of the structure and scheme beyond the particular biblical or Hasidic stories.

3. Methodological comment: Buber's complete and comprehensive theory of theopolitics was published in 1932 in his biblical exegesis *Kingship of God* and in his later biblical writings. However, some of the texts I use dealing with the theopolitical interpretation of Hasidism preceded this book. This notwithstanding, I argue that Buber's concern with theopolitics in Hasidism (especially leadership and community) preceded his biblical writings and shaped the way he read the Bible later on. Conversely, Buber's earlier theopolitical sensibilities, which appear in his interpretation of Hasidism, served him later in writing *Kingship of God*. The affinity and continuity between Buber's interpretation of Hasidism and his exegesis of the Bible is also acknowledged by Martina Urban, "Retelling Biblical Mythos Through the Hasidic Tale: Buber's 'Saul and David' and the Question of Leadership," *Modern Judaism* 24 (2004): 59–78; Claire E. Sufrin, "On Myth, History, and the Study of Hasidism: Martin Buber and Gershom Scholem," in *Encountering the Medieval in Modern Jewish Thought*, ed. James A. Diamond and Aaron W. Hughes (Leiden, Netherlands: Brill, 2012); and Yossef Schwartz, "The Politicizing of the Mystical in Buber and His Contemporaries," in *New Perspectives on Martin Buber*, ed. Michael Zank (Tübingen, Germany: Mohr Siebeck, 2006), 206. Schwartz views *Kingship of God* as a development from Buber's earlier interest in Hasidism and mysticism.

4. Buber's approach to the holy texts is never plainly historical. Buber distinguishes between the truth of myth and historical truth; see Martin Buber, *Kingship of God*, trans. Richard Scheimann (London: G. Allen and Unwin, 1967), 62–63.

5. See Brody, *Martin Buber's Theopolitics*; Lebovic, "Jerusalem School"; Schmidt, "Martin Buber: The Theopolitical Hour"; Paul Mendes-Flohr, "The Kingdom of God: Martin Buber's Critique of Messianic Politics," *Behemoth: A Journal on Civilization* 1, no.2 (2008): 26–38; Shalom Ratzabi, "Zionism as Theopolitics and the a-Naturalistic Character of Jewish Nationalism: Commentary on Martin Buber's National Thought and Its Origins," *Iyunim BiTkumat Israel: Studies in Zionism, the Yishuv and the State of Israel* 14 (2004): 97–129 [Hebrew]; Shalom Ratzabi, *Anarchism in Zion: Between Martin Buber and Aharon David Gordon* (Tel Aviv: am Oved, 2011) [Hebrew]; Kotaro Hiraoka, "The Bible and Political Philosophy in Modern Jewish Thought: Martin Buber's Theocracy and Its Reception in an Israeli Context," *Journal of the Interdisciplinary Study of Monotheistic Religions* 6 (2010): 53–66; and Dan Avnon, *Martin Buber: The Hidden Dialogue* (Boston: Rowman and Littlefield, 1998), 149–214.

6. Schmidt, "Martin Buber's Theopolitical Hour," 195.

7. Martin Buber, *On Zion: The History of an Idea*, trans. Stanley Godman (London: Horovitz, 1973), 84: "All the destruction which has befallen Israel and its land precedes the new reconstruction." See also Buber's comments about the "purificatory influence of the Exile" and about separation and selection in Judaism in ibid., 84, 88.

8. Ibid., 8. See also xix, xxi, 88–89, 117.

9. Ibid., xvii.

10. Exod. 19:5–6; emphasis added (JPS 1917 edition).

11. See Martin Buber, "The Dialogue between Heaven and Earth," in *On Judaism*, ed. Nahum N. Galtzer (New York: Schocken Books, 1995), 214–26. See also Avnon, *Martin Buber: The Hidden Dialogue*, 149–78.

12. Buber claims: "The messianic faith of Israel is . . . the being oriented toward the fulfilment of the relation between God and the world in a consummated Kingly rule of God" (*Kingship of God*, 14–15). By that, he also means to speak of the redemption of the whole world and all humanity, not Israel's redemption alone. See also Buber's words: God "does not want to compel the world to become His"; the divine kingdom means a community "out of free will" (ibid., 138–39).

13. Martin Buber, *The Origin and Meaning of Hasidism*, trans. and ed. Maurice Friedman (New York: Humanity Books, 1988), 206. This book was developed over the course of many years. The fourth chapter is the earliest part called "The Spirit and Body of the Hasidic Movement" and appeared in the introduction to *Der grosse Maggid und seine Nachfolge* (1921). The third chapter, "Spinoza, Sabbatai Zvi and the Baal-Shem," was introduced first in the *Chassidische Bücher* (1927). The fifth chapter "Symbolic and Sacramental Existence," which is discussed in detail in this essay, was written in 1934, two years after the publication of Buber's *Kingship of God*. The first chapter, "The Beginnings"; the second chapter, "The Founding Stone"; the sixth chapter, "God and Soul"; the seventh chapter, "Redemption"; and the eighth chapter, "The Place of Hasidism in the History of Religion," were written in Hebrew in Jerusalem between 1940 and 1943 and were later translated into English and German. For a detailed historiography of Buber's writing on Hasidism see Grete Schaeder, "The Message of Hasidism," in *The Hebrew Humanism of Martin Buber*, trans. Noah J. Jacobs (Detroit: Wayne State University Press, 1973), 287–338.

14. Buber, *Origin and Meaning of Hasidism*, 218.

15. Schmidt, "Martin Buber's Theopolitical Hour," 194–95. For Buber's criticism of Leo Pinsker and Theodor Herzl, see Buber, *On Zion*, 123.

16. Gershom Scholem disputed Buber's interpretation of Hasidism precisely for this kind of bias. See Gershom Scholem, "Martin Buber's Hasidism: A Critique," *Commentary* 32, no. 4 (1961): 305–16, and Rivka Schatz Uffenheimer, "Man's Relation to God and World in Buber's Rendering of the Hasidic

Teaching," in *The Philosophy of Martin Buber*, ed. Paul Arthur Schilpp and Maurice Friedman (La Salle, IL: Open Court, 1967), 403–34. For Buber's response, see Martin Buber, "Interpreting Hasidism," *Commentary* 36, no. 3 (1963): 218–25. On the Buber-Scholem controversy, see Steven D. Kepnes, "A Hermeneutical Approach to the Buber-Scholem Controversy," *Journal of Jewish Studies* 38, no. 1 (1987): 81–98; Moshe Idel, "Martin Buber and Gerschom Scholem on Hasidism: A Critical Appraisal," in *Hasidism Reappraised*, ed. Ada Rapoport-Albert (London: Liverpool University Press 1996), 389–403; Ron Margolin, *Mikdash Adam* (Jerusalem: Magnes Press, 2005), 16–18, 27–33, 428–32 [Hebrew]; Tsippi Kauffmann, *In All Your Ways Know Him* (Ramat Gan, Israel: Bar-Ilan University, 2009) [Hebrew]; and Hannan Hever, "Buber versus Scholem and the Figure of the Hasidic Jew: A Literary Debate between Two Political Theologies," in *Jews and the Ends of Theory*, ed. Shai Ginsburg, Martin Land, and Jonathan Boyarin (New York: Fordham University Press, 2019), 225–62. The liberty Buber took in interpreting Hasidism was also referred to as "creative freedom." See, for example, Grete Schaeder, "Realization," in Jacobs, *Hebrew Humanism of Martin Buber*, 76, and Laurence J. Silberstein, *Martin Buber's Social and Religious Thought: Alienation and the Quest for Meaning* (New York: New York University Press, 1989), 44.

My own understanding of I-Thou is that it is a formulation of a religious imperative about the love of divine creation. The love of the human Thou is derived from it; however, it is not the sole implication, and therefore, Buber speaks of I-Thou in terms that are not only human, such as nature, animals, plants, and spiritual entities. On Buber's *I and Thou*, see Admiel Kosman, "Mavo Le-Mishnat Buber," in *Ani Ve-Atah*, trans. Aharon Flashman (Mosad Bialik: Jerusalem, 2013), 160–220 [Hebrew]. See also Leora Batnitzky, "The Problem of Translation: Risking the Present for the Sake of the Past," in *Idolatry and Representation—the Philosophy of Franz Rosenzweig Reconsidered* (Princeton, NJ: Princeton University Press, 2000), 119–23. See also Asher D. Biemann, "Humanizing the It: Martin Buber on Technology and the Ethics of Things," *Religions* 13, no.2 (2022): 1–25. One can also try to understand the dialogue with nonhumans in terms of the Kabbalistic elevation of the sparks: see Buber, "The Life of the Hasidim" (1908), in *Hasidism and Modern Man*, ed. and trans. Maurice Friedman (New York: Horizon Press, 1958), 98–122. On I and Thou and Hasidism, see Israel Koren, *The Mystery of the Earth: Mysticism and Hasidism in the Thought of Martin Buber* (Leiden, Netherlands: Brill, 2010), esp. 187–314.

17. Avraham Shapira, "Buber's Attachment to Herder and German Volkism," *Studies in Zionism* 14, no. 1 (1993): 1–30. For more on Buber's concept of nationality and its roots in German romanticism, see Bernard Susser, "Ideological Multivalence: Martin Buber and the German Volkish Tradition,"

Political Theory 5, no. 1 (1977): 75–96; Manuel Duarte De Oliveira, "Passion for Land and Volk: Martin Buber and Neo-Romanticism," *The Leo Baeck Institute Year Book* 41, no. 1 (1996): 239–60; Ratzabi, *Anarchism in Zion*, 126–27; and Yemima Hadad, "Hasidic Myth-Activism: Martin Buber's Theopolitical Revision of Volkish Nationalism," *Religions* 10, no. 2 (2019): 1–33.

18. Buber, *Kingship of God*, 106.

19. Martin Buber, "The Election of Israel," in *On the Bible: Eighteen Studies*, ed. Nahum N. Glatzer (New York: Syracuse University Press, 2000), 84–85, 89.

20. Buber, *Kingship of God*, 64.

21. Judg. 8:23 (JPS 1917 edition).

22. Bernard Susser, "The Anarcho-Federalism of Martin Buber," *Publius* 9, no. 4 (1979): 103–15, especially 103, where Susser speaks of Buber's "anarcho-theocratic vision." Brody adopts Susser's term in *Martin Buber's Theopolitics*.

23. Sanford L. Drob, "The Doctrine of Coincidentia Oppositorum in Jewish Mysticism," *Kabbalah and Postmodernism: A Dialogue* (New York: Lang, 2009), 129. For the importance of the principle of unity in Buber's thought, see Elliot R. Wolfson, "The Problem of Unity in the Thought of Martin Buber," *Journal of the History of Philosophy* 27, no. 3 (1989): 423–44.

24. Judg. 19.

25. Buber, *Kingship of God*, 75.

26. Buber, "Election of Israel," 88.

27. In this interpretation, I follow Silberstein, *Martin Buber's Social and Religious Thought*, 177. Silberstein sees the center as the divine. Dan Avnon argues against that and tends to see the center as a human leadership; see Avnon, *Martin Buber: The Hidden Dialogue*, 155, 250. See also Avnon, "The 'Living Center' of Martin Buber's Political Theory," *Political Theory* 21, no.1 (1993): 55–77.

28. Buber, *Kingship of God*, 65, 67; Martin Buber, *I and Thou*, trans. Ronald Gregor Smith (New York: Charles Scribner's Sons, 1984), 86–120.

29. Buber argues in *I and Thou* that God does not speak to humans with words but with his presence. See, for instance, "God's speech to men penetrates what happens in the life of each one of us, and all that happens in the world around us, biographical and historical, and makes it for you and me into instruction, message, demand. Happening upon happening, situation upon situation, are enabled and empowered by the personal speech of God to demand the human person that he take his stand and make his decision. Often enough we think there is nothing to hear, but long before we have ourselves put wax in our ears" (*I and Thou*, 125–26). Elsewhere Buber states that "the biblical word preserves the dialogical character of living reality"; see Buber, "Biblical Humanism," in *On the Bible: Eighteen Studies*, 214–15. Buber argues that God does not speak with man "in riddles" but in "signs of what happens." See Martin Buber, *The Prophetic Faith*, trans. Carlyle Witton-Davies (New York: Harper and Row, 1960),

57. For more on the divine-human dialogue in the Bible, see Michael Fishbane, *The Garments of Torah: Essays in Biblical Hermeneutics* (Bloomington: Indiana University Press, 1992), 81–98. For a more critical reflection on dialogue, see Steven T. Katz, "Dialogue and Revelation in the Thought of Martin Buber," *Religious Studies* 14, no. 1 (1978): 57–68.

30. Buber, *Prophetic Faith*, 35.

31. On Buber's claim for the divine nature of the *charis*, see Buber, *Kingship of God*, 57. Charismatic leadership is temporal and not permanent; see ibid., 140. See also Sarah Scott, "Martin Buber's Notion of Grace as a Defense of Religious Anarchism," in *Essays on Anarchism and Religion*, vol. 3, ed. Alexandre Christoyannopoulos and Mathew Adams (Stockholm: Stockholm University Press, 2020), 189–222.

32. Buber, *Kingship of God*, 75.

33. Ibid., 76–77.

34. Buber, "Election of Israel," 89.

35. Buber, *Kingship of God*, 84.

36. See Buber's correspondence with Caspri about the primitive theocracy in ancient Israel in the prestate condition (ibid., 23, 83–84).

37. Buber says this about the prophets, but it seems to me applicable for the judges as well; see Buber, *Origin and Meaning of Hasidism*, 151–65.

38. Note that Buber made a distinction between *Kohanim* in Exodus as "direct servants" and *Kohanim* in Deuteronomy as holders of sacred positions and offices. When he speaks about Israel's vocation in establishing the religious anarchy, he refers to the first meaning (Buber, *Prophetic Faith*, 160).

39. See, for example, Exod. 24:2; and 1 Sam. 10:10, 11:6, and 19:20–23.

40. Buber, *Kingship of God*, 76–77.

41. Buber discerns between theocracy and hierocracy (ibid., 56–57).

42. The charismatic leader admits the dispenser of charisma (i.e., the divine); see ibid., 139.

43. Ibid., 66–84.

44. Ibid., 77–78. According to Buber's line of reasoning, direct theocracy is atonement for religious anarchy. Anarchy refers to a lack of human leadership, however, this may be possible only through direct theocracy, where the divine leads the community and individuals.

45. Judg. 17:6 (JPS 1917 edition).

46. Buber, *Kingship of God*, 83–84.

47. Ibid., 77–78.

48. Buber, *Prophetic Faith*, 152.

49. Buber, *Darko shel Mikra* [The Way of the Bible] (Jerusalem: Bialik Intitute, 1964), 170. Also see Akiva Ernst Simon, *Kav ha-Tikhum: Nationalism, Zionism*

and the Jewish-Arab Conflict in Martin Buber's Thought (Center for Arab Studies: Givat Haviva, 1973), 12–13.

50. Buber, "Maaseh Hamlachat Saul," *Darko shel Mikra*, 185 (my translation from the Hebrew).

51. See 1 Sam. 8:19, and Buber, *Darko shel Mikra*, 169–73.

52. I argue that Buber views this surrender from God's part to the demands of the Israelites in terms of Hasidic and Kabbalistic doctrines of "elevating the holy sparks." God as the leader of the people does here what the zaddik in Hasidism does: "Man come to him, and each desires his opinion, his help. And even though it [the demand of the people from the zaddik] is corporal and semi-corporal needs that they bring to him, in his world-insight there is nothing corporal that cannot be transfigured, nothing material that cannot be raised to spirit. And it is this that he does for all: *he elevates their need before he satisfies it*" (Buber, "My Way to Hasidism," in *Hasidism and Modern Man*, 69).

53. Buber, *Kingship of God*, 42. Buber distinguished *hierocracy*, which is often referred to in scholarship also as *indirect theocracy*, from the indirect theocracy of the Israelite Kingdom (ibid, 56–57). He insisted that "the equation: theocracy = rule of Priests, rests upon an error which is fatal for the knowledge of Biblical reality" (ibid., 30).

54. Ibid., 89.

55. Buber, *Prophetic Faith*, 84.

56. Buber, *Darko shel Mikra*, 170.

57. Buber does not think that a human can experience full penetration of pure reason or absolute truth. He thinks of truth as something that is revealed to humans in a dialogical process.

58. Buber, *Kingship of God*, 140.

59. Buber, *Prophetic Faith*, 83.

60. Buber criticized Friedrich Nietzsche's "will to power" in "Religion and Ethics," in *Eclipse of God: Studies in the Relation between Religion and Philosophy* (Princeton, NJ: Princeton University Press, 2016), 97. On Buber's critique of Nietzsche see Paul Mendes-Flohr, "Zarathustra's Apostle: Martin Buber and the Jewish Renaissance," in *Nietzsche and Jewish Culture*, ed. Jacob Golumb (New York: Routledge, 1997), and Paul Mendes-Flohr, "Nationalism as a Spiritual Sensibility: The Philosophical Suppositions of Buber's Hebrew Humanism," *Journal of Religion* 69, no. 2 (1989): 155–68. See also David Ohana, *Nietzsche and Jewish Political Theology* (New York: Routledge, 2018).

61. Buber, *Kingship of God*, 89–90.

62. Ibid., 110.

63. Buber, *Prophetic Faith*, 95.

64. Ibid., 82. See also Buber, *Darko shel Mikra*, 242.

65. Buber, *Kingship of God*, 42.

66. Buber, *Prophetic Faith*, 151–52.
67. Ibid., 157.
68. Ibid., 50.
69. Buber, *Kingship of God*, 119.
70. Buber, *Darko shel Mikra*, 250, 255. See Buber, *Prophetic Faith*, 108: "In his answer Amos says that true prophecy is not a human calling, but a mission of God, who takes a man from his work, 'from following the sheep,' and sends him to the people with his message." For the true and false prophecy in Buber's thought, see Warren Zev Harvey, "Buber on False Prophets and Nationalism," *Journal of World Philosophies* 4, no. 2 (2019): 1–7, and [Michael Walzer, Menachem Lorberbaum, and Noam J. Zohar, eds.], *The Jewish Political Tradition*, vol. 1, *Authority* (New Haven, CT: Yale University Press, 2000), 132.
71. Buber, *Kingship of God*, 119.
72. Ibid., 91: "the theocratic principle begins to lose its comprehensive power and to be limited merely religious." See also ibid., 151–52, and 139: "a world which does not want to be God's, and to a God who does not want to compel the world to become His." On Jewish forgetfulness in Buber's thought, see Yemima Hadad, "Fruits of Forgetfulness: Politics and Nationalism in the Philosophies of Martin Buber and Martin Heidegger," in *Heidegger and Jewish Thought: Difficult Others*, ed. Elad Lapidot and Micha Brumlik (New York: Rowman & Littlefield, 2017), 201–20.
73. Buber, *Darko shel Mikra*, 268.
74. Buber, *Prophetic Faith*, 82. See also Buber, *Darko shel Mikra*, 242.
75. Buber, *Darko shel Mikra*, 234. In this context, see Samuel Hayim Brody, "Prophecy and Powerlessness," *Political Theology* 21, no. 1 (2020): 43–55.
76. Buber, *Origin and Meaning of Hasidism*, 135.
77. Ibid., 173.
78. See Buber, "Symbolic and Sacramental Existence," in *Origin and Meaning of Hasidism*, 151–82. See also Admiel Kosman and Yemima Hadad, "The Societal Role of the Man of Spirit according to Martin Buber," *Hebrew Union College Annual* 91 (2020): 207–260.
79. Buber, "Life of the Hasidim," 112, 120.
80. See Arthur Green, "The Zaddiq as Axis Mundi," *Journal of the American Academy of Religion* 45, no. 3 (1977): 327–47, and Moshe Idel, "Zaddiq as 'Vessel' and 'Channel' in Hasidism," in *Hasidism: Between Ecstasy and Magic* (Albany: State University of New York Press, 1995), 189–208, especially 204.
81. See Norman Lamm, *The Religious Thought of Hasidism: Text and Commentary* (New York: Yeshiva University Press, 1999), 267–70; Rachel Elior, "Between 'Yesh' and 'Ayin'; the Doctrine of the Zaddik in the Works of Jacob Isaac, the Seer of Lublin," in *Jewish History: Essays in Honor of Chimen Abramsky*, ed. A. Rapoport-Albert and S. Zipperstein (London: Peter Halban, 1988): 393–455; Mendel Piekarz, "The Descent of the Tsadik to Geheynom and His Descent from His Spiritual Rung in this World," *BiYemey Zmikhat HaHasidut* (Jerusalem:

Mosad Bialik, 1978), 280–305 [Hebrew]; Yoram Jacobson, *Toratah shel HaHassidut* (Tel Aviv: Misrad Habitachon, 1985), 139–140 [Hebrew]; and Mor Altshuler, *HaSod HaMeshikhi shel HaHasidut* (Tel Aviv: Zmora-Bitan, 2002), 258–70 [Hebrew]. On the relationship of the zaddik to Hasidim, see Israel Koren, "Buber's Dialogic Interpretation of the Doctrine of Tzimzum," in *Mystery of the Earth*, 275–314.

82. Buber compared it to the psychoanalytic theory of "sublimating the libido." See Buber, "The Founding Stone," in *Origin and Meaning of Hasidism*, 83. For Buber's discussion of redemption and descent and elevation of sparks, see Buber, *Hasidism and Modern Man*, 101–8. See also Piekarz, *BiYemey Zmikhat HaHasidut*, 282.

83. Buber thought of *tikkun azmi* (self-improvement) as the way toward *tikkun olam* (mending the world). See Martin Buber, "Beginning with Oneself," in *The Way of Man: According to the Teaching of Hasidism* (New York: Kensington, 1994), 31.

84. Cited in Bernard Susser, *Existance and Utopia: The Social and Political Thought of Martin Buber* (Rutherford, NJ: Fairleigh Dickinson University Press, 1981), 12. Cited in *The Legend of the Baal-Shem*, trans. Maurice Friedman (New York: Harper Brothers, 1955), 19. It appears also in Buber, *Tales of the Hasidim: The Early Masters* (New York: Schocken, 1991), 277. Susser does not connect this idea with the doctrine of the descent of the zaddik in Hasidism.

85. On the Hasidic and Sabbatian "descent for the sake of ascent," see Elliot R. Wolfson, "Light through Darkness: The Ideal of Human Perfection in the Zohar," *Harvard Theological Review* 81, no. 1 (1988): 73–95. His references on this topic in footnotes 42 and 84 are especially useful.

86. Yoram Jacobson, *Toratah shel Ha-Hassidut* [The Hasidic Thought] (Tel Aviv: Misrad Habitachon, 1985), 139–40 [Hebrew].

87. The zaddik in Hasidism is said to be teaching in a holistic manner, not only theoretically. Buber refers to this method in "Teaching and Deed," in *The Writings of Martin Buber*, ed. Will Herberg (New York: Meridian Books, 1963), 317–24. Gershom Scholem explains: "The new ideal of the religious leader, the Zaddik, differs from the traditional ideal of rabbinic Judaism, the *Talmid Hakham* or student of the Torah, mainly in that he himself 'has become Torah.'" See Gershom Scholem, "The Living Torah," in *Major Trends in Jewish Mysticism* (New York: Schocken Books, 1995), 344.

88. Gershom Scholem, *On the Mystical Shape of the Godhead: Basic Concepts in the Kabbalah*, ed. Jonathan Chipman and trans. Joachim Neugroschel (New York: Schocken Books, 1976), 138.

89. Buber, "Life of the Hasidim," 91.

90. Buber, *Origin and Meaning of Hasidism*, 50–51.

91. On Buber's relation to the Jewish Law, see Leora Batnizky, "Revelation and 'The New Thinking': Rethinking Rosenzweig and Buber on the Law," in Zank, *New Perspectives on Martin Buber*, 149–64; Admiel Kosman, "'Ehyeh Asher Ehyeh': The Importance of the Biblical Passage (Exodus 3)

for Understanding the Buber-Rosenzweig Dialogue Regarding the Place of Halakhah in Modern Jewish Life," in *Ehyeh Asher Ehyeh*, ed. David Birnbaum and Martin S. Cohen (New York: Matrix, 2019), 329–80; Ron Margolin, "The Implicit Secularism of Martin Buber's Thought," *Israel Studies* 13, no. 3 (2008): 64–88; Sam Berrin Shonkoff, "Metanomianism and Religious Praxis in Martin Buber's Hasidic Tales," *Religions* 9, no. 12 (2018): 399; and Yemima Hadad, "'Ich Habe Nicht Geantwortet': Hermeneutics of Secrecy, Religious Silence, and Dialogvergessenheit in Martin Buber's Exchange with Franz Rosenzweig about Halakha," *Naharaim* 14, no. 1 (2020): 103–32. For more on the Buber-Rosenzweig debate on the Halakha see Benny Kraut, "The Approach to Jewish Law of Martin Buber and Franz Rosenzweig," *Tradition: A Journal of Orthodox Jewish Thought* 12, no. 3/4 (1972): 49–71. See also Joseph Turner, *Faith and Humanism: A Study of Franz Rosenzweig's Religious Philosophy* (Tel Aviv: Hakibbutz Hameuchad, 2001), 121–31 [Hebrew]; Yehoyada Amir, *Daat Maamina: Iyyunim be-mishnato shel Franz Rosenzweig* (Tel Aviv: Am Oved, 2004), 289–307 [Hebrew]; Maurice Friedman, "Rosenzweig and the Law," in *Martin Buber's Life and Work* (Detroit: Wayne State University Press, 1988), 40–49; and Arnold M. Eisen, "Buber, Rosenzweig, and the Authority of the Commandments," *Rethinking Modernity: Ritual Commandment, Community* (Chicago: University of Chicago Press, 1998), 188–215.

92. Gender statement: Since most of the figures that are mentioned in this article, such as the judge, king, prophet, Hasid, zaddik, etc., were men, I continue to use the male form in the section "The Leader to Come" in order to not confuse the reader by using a different gender. That does not mean that the figure of the leader has a specific gender or that it has to be male. Buber wrote about dominant women and women in the Bible. However, he did not pay special attention to the fascinating question of women's leadership. Ultimately, I see no reason to determine or suggest from Buber's characteristics of the leader that this figure is attached to a specific gender. On Buber and his female interlocutors, see Paul Mendes-Flohr, *Martin Buber: A Life of Faith and Dissent* (New Haven, CT: Yale University Press, 2019); see also Yemima Hadad, "Feminism, Femininity and Women: The Presence and Contribution of Women in Shaping Martin Buber's Thought: Reflection on Paul Mendes-Flohr's *Martin Buber: Life of Faith and Dissent*," *Alpaim Plus* 3 (2020): 151–165 [Hebrew]. On the exchange between Martin Buber and Bertha Pappenheim, whom he called "a female Moses," see Abigail Gillman, *A History of German Jewish Bible Translation* (Chicago: University of Chicago Press, 2018), 200–207.

93. Buber, *Kingship of God*, 40.
94. Ibid., 14.
95. Buber, "Prophecy, Apocalyptic, and the Historical Hour," *On the Bible*, 172.
96. Buber, *Kingship of God*, 14.

97. Ibid., 40.
98. Schaeder, *Hebrew Humanism of Martin Buber*, 306.
99. Buber, *Origin and Meaning of Hasidism*, 107.
100. Buber, "Life of the Hasidism," 47.
101. "The 'commonwealth without government' is thought of . . . as a commonwealth for which an invisible government is sufficient" (Buber, *Kingship of God*, 75).
102. Buber, *Origin and Meaning of Hasidism*, 43.
103. Ibid., 43.
104. See Kosman and Hadad, "Societal Role of the Man of Spirit according to Martin Buber."

PART III

ZIONISM AND BINATIONALISM

SIX

EXILE AND ALIENATION IN MARTIN BUBER'S PHILOSOPHICAL ANTHROPOLOGY

WILLIAM PLEVAN

ARNOLD EISEN HAS NOTED THAT spiritual Zionist writers and leaders, Martin Buber among them, sought to "universalize" their concept of exile because they believed that the Zionist aspiration of a Jewish return to the homeland could not be spiritually or morally justified if it did not serve humanity.[1] In Buber's case, the task of Zionism is for the Jewish people to renew the biblical aspiration to realize the "sovereignty of God" through the form of genuine community in which every individual can realize their whole personhood. This community, while situated in the land, is to serve as a model of such a community for all of humanity. And just as Jewish homecoming models a universal human aspiration, so too does Jewish exile—or, more precisely for Buber, the Jewish understanding of the meaning of exile—serve as a model for all people for how to contend with exile and alienation as a spiritual and social condition. Buber's transformation of the concept of exile is thus characteristic of his Hebrew Humanism as a project of bringing the classic teachings of the Jewish tradition to bear on the contemporary spiritual condition of the Jewish people and of humanity as a whole.

In this chapter, I look at Buber's philosophical anthropology as an additional site of his universalization of a Jewish understanding of exile. Various authors have noted the connection between Buber's Zionism and his philosophical anthropology through the centrality of his ideal of community and his interest in social theory.[2] Indeed, Buber's dialogical philosophy and his concept of the between, or the interhuman, serve as tools for social criticism for both the modern West and the Zionist project in measuring the achievement of genuine community. More specifically, Laurence Silberstein has suggested reading Buber's philosophy of dialogue as a response to the problem of alienation in modern society.[3] Buber attributes the alienating conditions of modern society to the greater measure of relationships of utility rooted in practical rationality—that is, "I-It" relationships—and prescribes returning to relationships of mutual caring and openness among humanity, nature, and God. However, Silberstein does not give significant attention to Buber's readings of Jewish religious texts on the meaning of exile and how they shed light on his philosophical anthropology and his diagnosis of the spiritual crisis of the modern West.

Buber treats exile on the national level and alienation on the individual level as paradigmatic forms of suffering. The spiritual challenge of exile and alienation is both how to endure them and to recognize what they demand of us, again, on the national and individual levels. To ignore the reality of such suffering is to be inured to the concrete realities of human existence. At the same time, viewing such suffering as a permanent, irrevocable, or immutable feature of existence would be to deny the possibility of meaningful hope for our earthly, embodied life. In his writings on Judaism, Buber associates the first position with what he calls "pagan" religiosity and the second view with what he calls "Gnostic" religiosity, and the limitations of both these views are, he argues, central to the failures of modern Western thought to address the spiritual and social crises of modern societies. Buber's interpretation of Judaism and his philosophical anthropology are both efforts to present a worldly, dialogical form of religiosity as an alternative source for addressing these crises. Just as Buber's Zionism cannot be understood apart from its universalizing aspects, his philosophical anthropology, I argue, cannot be fully appreciated without greater attention to his particular claims about how Jewish sources interpret the meaning of exile.

In what follows, I examine the parallels between Buber's critique of how some modern Jews, particularly in Reform Judaism, have interpreted the meaning of exile and his critique of philosopher Max Scheler's (1874–1928) understanding of the human condition. In both cases, Buber views these responses to modern social and religious life as recapitulations of ancient Gnostic thought and hence insufficient responses to the crises of modern societies because they fail to provide a sense of meaning or significance of the particular experience of the one who suffers, either the nation or the individual. In the first part, I examine Buber's critique of Reform Judaism's understanding of exile and how he contrasts that view to the one he finds in classical Jewish sources. In particular, I use his reading of Rabbi Judah Loew's (ca. 1525–1609) theology as a source for Buber's understanding of exile as a spiritual and social experience that both must be endured and may be overcome through spiritual and ethical action. In drawing on this tradition, Buber also looks to rebuke political Zionism's rejection of the spiritual significance of exile and its confidence that exile can be overcome through political achievement alone. In the second part, I will show how Buber interprets Scheler's philosophical anthropology as following the Gnostic model by spiritually capitulating to the alienating conditions of modern society. This Gnostic capitulation, as Buber sees it, both denies the individual the capacity to resist forms of domination and overlooks the universal spiritual significance of the unique suffering of each individual.

I

The theme of exile looms large in Buber's Jewish writings from the beginning of his turn to dialogical thinking. In his 1918 lecture "The Holy Way," Buber explains that after becoming a community in exile in different parts of the world, "the [Jewish] people were forced to realize that in fact not only they alone but also the *shekhina*, the divine Presence dwelling within the human element, had gone into exile. For the *shekhina* is at home only where there dwells a potent will for a covenant with God and an equally potent striving for realization of such a covenant, only where man endeavors to live within the sight of the unconditional. When the covenant is relaxed, when the striving slackens and man loses sights of the unconditional, the *shekhina* is in exile."[4] The notion of the *shekhina* in exile originated with the rabbis of the Talmud, who used it to make the comforting assertion that the divine presence once found in the Holy Temple was still with the people when they were sent into exile.[5] Buber adopted and universalized this classical rabbinic claim that the physical, political exile of the people is mirrored by the spiritual exile of the divine presence by giving it a distinctly humanistic interpretation. For Buber, the *shekhina* is the divine aspect that potentially dwells within any human community, not just Israel. Thus, any person who strives "to live within the sight of the unconditioned" is striving to overcome the exilic conditions experienced in different ways by all human beings in an effort to be connected to community.

Buber's writings on dialogue, beginning with *I and Thou* (1923), represent his attempt to articulate these Jewish teachings in a philosophical idiom rather than through an interpretation of classical Jewish sources.[6] "I-You" relationships are the kind of relationships that create and enact a genuine community, as opposed to "I-It" relationships, in which people are merely measured and categorized for their usefulness for social, economic, or political purposes. As Paul Mendes-Flohr has argued, Buber develops the philosophical concept of "the interhuman," which he also called "the between," to identify the a priori conditions for genuine community.[7] The creation of such a community overcomes alienation and exile as a spiritual and social condition that can be experienced by all human beings. Buber alludes to the Jewish provenance of this idea in the "The Holy Way": "Judaism therefore is not concerned with a God who lives in the far beyond, for its God is content to reside in the realm between one earthly being and the other, as if they were cherubim on the Holy Ark; nor is it concerned with a God who dwells in things, for it is not in the being of things that He abides but only in their perfection."[8] This passage suggests that Buber's later development of this idea of the between or interhuman in his philosophical anthropology grows out of his interpretation of classical Jewish teachings on the *shekhina*, the dwelling presence of God. Buber's central philosophical claim is that even when we do not see it or realize it, the between is *already there*, waiting for human beings to make its reality apparent though action. Buber's rendering of Jewish teachings about the divine presence is the same, as is illustrated in the Hasidic teaching of the Kotzker Rebbe (1787–1859), to which he attached great importance: "Where is the dwelling of God? ... God dwells wherever man lets (God) in."[9] On Buber's interpretation, the divine presence is available to those whose actions within the world make it possible for the divine to dwell "between one earthly being and the other."

To be clear, there is more to Buber's humanistic interpretation of exile than the Jewish people serving as a model for non-Jews. More significantly, Buber's humanism defines the standards for success of the Zionist project from within. For Buber, as Eisen notes, the collective Jewish return to the land of Israel does not in and of itself end all aspects of exile.[10] Entering the land is essential in allowing the Jewish people to reconnect to concrete material work, but the complete fulfillment of this physical return comes in realizing a genuine community as defined by his dialogical philosophy. Thus, while Buber's discussions of exile in his Jewish writings are directed at rival versions of Judaism or Zionism, they share the same analysis of the problem of human spiritual realization as his writings on philosophical anthropology. This is an important methodological point for this chapter as I aim to show that his writings on Judaism can inform our understanding of his philosophical project and vice versa.

To understand the connection between Buber's Jewish writings and his philosophical writings, I draw attention to the way he contrasts Judaism to other ancient ideas within Western thought. Buber presents these contrasts in a triadic form, where Judaism stands against Gnosticism on the one hand and heathen or pagan religion on the other. What is at stake for Buber in this contrast is the ways these different religious ideas deal with the relationship between the spiritual and the material. Buber introduces this tripartite structure in "The Holy Way," where he argues that Judaism's conception of community stands in contrast to an "Occidental dualism" that posits an irreparable breach between matter and spirit. In contrast, Judaism, on Buber's reading, teaches that the spirit can transform concrete material existence. In later lectures, Buber associates Gnostic thinking with the idea that spiritual realization requires a denial of material life and "heathen" or pagan thinking with the idea that material things have already achieved perfection and can be objects of worship. Whereas Judaism seeks to hallow the material through transformative action, Gnosticism denies the spiritual value of the material, and paganism glorifies the material.

As in "The Holy Way," Buber sometimes used this tripartite structure of Jewish/Gnostic/pagan without referring to it as such. This is the case in "The Jew in the World," a lecture from 1934 where Buber discusses his view of exile. Buber's main objective in this lecture is to argue that two modern Jewish ways of rethinking the Jewish experience of exile, that of liberal or Reform Judaism and that of mainstream political Zionism, are actually a problematic departure from what he takes to be the genuinely Jewish understanding of exile. As I will explain, Buber's analysis of the two Jewish views he opposes correspond to the schema he used to contrast Gnostic and pagan ways of thinking to Judaism.

The version of Zionism Buber attacks in "The Jew in World" is what we may call "secular political Zionism" that follows in the tradition of Theodor Herzl (1860–1904).[11] Although Buber worked closely with Herzl and was active in promoting Jewish settlement in Palestine, he came to distinguish his Zionism from that represented by Herzl and his successors. In some of its more vehement articulations, secular political Zionists promoted the view that accepting the condition of exile was inherently degrading and that a return to national sovereignty in their homeland was the sine qua non of a viable Jewish existence in modern conditions.[12] To a large degree, this aspect of Zionism was tied to a rejection of Jewish religious orthodoxy, which, according to this view, promoted acceptance of exile as a punishment from God. While mainstream Zionism sought to provide physical security to Jews through political activity, Buber drew on what he took to be the prophetic view that for Israel, genuine security could only come through its spiritual realization of the kingship of God in genuine community.

In "The Jew in the World," Buber argues that both secular political Zionism and religious liberalism (exemplified by Reform Judaism) represent a set of false choices modern Jews face between identifying themselves as either a "nation" or as a "religion," as if the two are mutually exclusive. The temptation facing modern Jews, as Buber sees it, is that in order to "fit in" in modern social and political life, they must abandon Judaism's unique understanding of community. The reason these categories are so appealing to the Jewish people is a byproduct of the people's exilic condition. What modern Jews are seeking in defining themselves as either nation or religion, Buber claims, is a sense of "security," both spiritual and physical. The Jews who define Judaism as a religion seek the security of national citizenship in the Western nation-states in which they reside. Jews who define Judaism as a nation like all other nations hope to build a nation state that will provide for the people's collective security. In both cases, these forms of security are mirrored by the clarity of identity that Jews achieve in the eyes of the nations and in their own eyes. In "The Jew in the World," Buber indicates that the desire for security is not only dealt with on an individual human level but on a collective level as well. Collective human entities, such as national or religious communities, seek to define themselves and their place in the world through some cosmic image of the world.[13] By accepting the categories of either religion or nation, modern Jews define their place both in the cosmos and in society.

Buber's argument in "The Jew in the World" is that the choice between religion and nation is a false choice rooted in the rejection of Judaism's distinctive teachings of human social life. In the Bible and later Jewish sources, he claims, there is no distinction between religion on the one hand and nation on the other. Rather, the world is divided into peoples, meaning national groups that are governed together and share all aspects of spiritual life, including common values, language, and religious rites. The modern categories of "religion" as primarily a matter of individual conscience and "nation" as identifying a collective entity based on common language, culture, and territory are both abstractions from what Buber claims is the more basic reality of peoplehood. The peoplehood framework does not assume the problematic distinction between religion and nationality that in Buber's estimation divides the soul of modern Western humanity, the Jewish people in particular.

The issue of self-definition is crucial to modern Jews, Buber acknowledges, because each answer—nation and religion—offers a way for Jews to overcome the indignities of exile by adopting one of these categories and the organizational program each one suggests. In the case of liberal Judaism, being a religion allows Jews to be full citizens of their home nation-states. In the case of Zionism, Israel's existence as a nation entitles them to build a state in their historic homeland. Buber's aim in "The Jew in the World" is, in part, to explain how Jews have misunderstood their own exilic condition by adopting the standpoint of "the nations" rather than that of the Jewish tradition. From the standpoint of the nations, Israel's exilic condition of powerlessness and dispersion looks unnatural or unhealthy. Buber states the problem as follows: "Ever since [the

Bar Kochba revolt, after which Jews were exiled from Jerusalem completely], [the Jew] has represented to the world the insecure man. Within that general insecurity which marks human existence as a whole, there has since that time lived a species of man to whom destiny has denied even the small share of dubious security other beings possess. . . . It is this inescapable state of insecurity which we have in mind when we designate the Jewish Diaspora as *galut*, i.e. as exile."[14] According to Buber, Israel's exilic state is deemed essentially problematic from the standpoint of the nations. To the nations, Israel appears as a specter, a ghostlike reality, because it does not fit into the standard categories of national life, having neither collective national power nor a common area of land on which to live. Buber remarks, "This state of affairs provides a basis of truth for the observation that anti-Semitism is a kind of fear of ghosts."[15] What provokes hatred of Jews, according to this line of thinking, is that the Jewish people appear frightening because they are something that should not exist: they appear to be a living people, with a meaningful communal existence, a sense of shared past and destiny, but their lack of land and collective power suggests, again from the standpoint of the nations, that they should not be living people. The "ghostly appearance" of the Jews comes from the paradox of their continued existence and even their spiritual vibrancy despite their exilic condition.[16]

Buber contends that viewing the Jewish people as ghostly fails to account for the Jewish tradition's own teachings, as he interprets them, of what gives life to a national and cultural group, namely, its realization of dialogical relations in its communal life. Buber's philosophical anthropology is directed precisely at this question, which, as I am arguing, he draws from his interpretation of Jewish sources. Here, Buber calls the "ghostly" view of Judaism a mere "appearance" and not the true reality of Jewish existence.[17] In order to understand the essence of Jewish existence, he claims, one must adopt what he calls "the way of faith." By this, Buber means Israel embracing its true calling to realize the kingship of God in realizing a genuine, dialogical community.[18] Ultimately, these categories will not fully suit the nations either, but because of their unique task, the Jewish people will lose their capacity to realize their historical task if they allow themselves to be categorized as a religion or as a nation, whereas other nations would simply be as they have typically been and not be spiritually damaged as a result.

The fact that the Jewish people had been able to continue to exist in exile is attributable, Buber contends, to their commitment to being a people of God who take no security in anything other than God's commandment and protection. The full realization of this mission should ultimately result in the transformation of all of humanity:

> When the prophets say that there is no security for Israel save that in God, they are not referring to something unearthly, to something "religious" in the common sense of the word; they are referring to the realization of the true communal living to which Israel was summoned by the covenant with God, and which it is called upon to sustain in history, in the way it alone is capable of. The prophets call upon a people which represents the *first real attempt at "community"* to enter world history as a prototype of that attempt. Israel's function is to encourage the nations to change their inner structure and their relations to one another. By maintaining such relations with the nations and being involved in the development of humanity, Israel may attain its unimperiled existence, its true security.[19]

Here, Buber inverts the assumptions of the nations as to what constitutes security and insecurity. What the nations view as security, particularly in the form of collective national power, is a sham. Likewise, the prophetic call is not to merely be a religion but to be a people of God. Israel, despite its exilic condition, has more security than the nations because it strives to realize its mission to be a community under God's rule. To be sure, being in exile diminishes Israel's capacity to realize this mission, but Buber argues that the genuine cause for the degrading character of their exilic existence is not the same cause given by "the nations" and modern Jews who subscribe to their thinking.

In Buber's view, Zionism cannot fulfill its purpose unless it eschews this Western conception, that of "the nations," of the meaning of exile. His version of Zionist aspiration stands in direct opposition to Herzl's notion that the Jewish people should become a "normal" nation-state. Rather than strive for the so-called normalcy of the nations, the Jewish people should settle the land and build it up as an outgrowth of their mission to create a true community under divine rule as a model for the nations of the world. As Buber interpreted Jewish teachings, the nations would eventually turn to Israel and look to its "way of faith." But in the interim, the nations would go on living according to their usual way. Israel, according to Buber, cannot afford this choice. Being Israel is predicated on self-consciously striving to complete this mission, and falling away from that mission into the comfort of being merely a "nation" or merely a "religion" would mean an abandonment of the Jewish people's existence in any meaningful sense. Again, the importance and urgency of Zionism for Buber was that it provided a modern framework for renewing the ancient Jewish commitment to Israel's mission in a time when the disintegration of prior autonomous forms of diaspora Jewish life left Jews without the live options for realizing the kind of communal life that at least acknowledged and approached the prophetic ideal he espouses.

For Buber, both Reform Judaism and political Zionism misunderstand the classical Jewish understanding of the meaning of exile and return to the land. Buber developed his interpretation of the centrality of the land in Judaism in his 1944 lectures *On Zion*, where he argues that Jewish spiritual leaders throughout the nineteen centuries of exile have viewed living in the land of Israel as representing the highest potential for spiritual fulfillment. But that spiritual fulfillment must emerge as a process of spiritual growth from within the condition of exile. Reform Judaism denies the value of striving to live in the land as a form of spiritual growth, while political Zionism ignores both the spiritual value of exile and the need for spiritual growth as part of the settlement of the land.

Buber's most significant discussion of the spiritual value of exile in *On Zion* comes in his treatment of Rabbi Liva ben Betzalel, or Judah Loew (ca. 1512–1609), also known as the Maharal of Prague and perhaps best known as the rabbi associated with the tales of the Golem. Buber seems to find in Rabbi Loew an example of a Jewish religious critic of the predominant Western view of exile that anticipates his—that is, Buber's—own view that Judaism has a spiritual conception of exile that is distinct from that of the other nations. Buber discusses Loew alongside his contemporaries Calvin, Grotius, and Machiavelli to argue that the great rabbi presented a sophisticated philosophy of history and nationalism that rivals the more well-known gentile figures'. Those three thinkers, Buber notes, all link the essence of national existence to the achievement of statehood on contiguous land. Without one or both, they aver, a cultural group fails to be a historical nation. Buber finds an alternative to this view in Loew's thought: "As against all these conceptions R. Liva affirms the nation as such, to which it is true that, so long as the world order is not disturbed, its own territory and independence appertain, but which, if it has lost both, may be regarded merely as having fallen ill, as handicapped in its functioning, not as having been robbed of its essence and made incapable of fulfilling its specific tasks."[20] The difference between "merely having fallen ill" and being "robbed of its essence" is a crucial distinction for Buber. Buber thinks that the strain of modern political thought embraced by mainstream Zionism concludes that the Jews, by virtue of being denied sovereignty and territory, have not been a nation at all since the first century CE. Buber sees the Jewish people as having been a genuine nation, albeit one that has not been able to fulfill its potential and has been ill. The "specific tasks" Buber refers to encompass Israel's mission to live under the divine rule. Exile has served as an impediment to fulfillment of this task in its fullness, particularly because of Israel's alienation from its land and the ability to work and hallow it. Nonetheless, exile does not completely rob the Jewish people of the ability to fulfill this mission in its life as a community.

According to Buber, Loew's philosophy of history is based on the idea that Israel has both the characteristics that make it a nation like all the other nations and is unique for its covenantal relationship with God. In so far as it has a common history, language, and culture, the Jewish people are entitled to their historic homeland, as any other nation would be. At the same time, the people's relationship to that land is determined by the terms of the covenant with God that stands outside the natural rights of nations. Israel's success or failure as a nation and its ability to hold on to its land depend on its fidelity to the covenant and thus to God's providence. If Israel fails in its covenantal relationship, it will lose possession of its land as a consequence. However, this unique relationship to God does not negate Israel's status as a nation like other nations. Buber summarizes Loew's position as follows: "The reason why God withholds [its right to its land] from Israel is not because it is less but because it is more than a nation: for in addition to being a nation it is also Israel."[21] Israel retains the characteristics and aspirations of any nation to achieve self-rule in its own territory, but its realization of these aspirations is determined by its covenantal fidelity.

Buber does not endorse the classical formulation of this covenantal theology, as he does not believe that Israel's exile is the result of direct divine intervention in historical events. However, he does embrace the idea that Israel's success as a nation depends on its fulfillment of its mission to be a people of God. He looks to Loew's philosophy of history as model for how the Jewish people should see itself as a unique people with a mission articulated by the biblical prophets while also possessing some characteristics of the other nations, such as a common language and attachment to a particular land. The problem with secular Zionism, as Buber sees it, is that it follows the dominant strands of the Western political tradition in holding that Jewish exile had effectively ended Jewish nationhood. From this perspective, exile is an unnatural condition and Jewish peoplehood in exilic conditions has no validity or genuine reality. To use Buber's phrase from "The Jew in the World," Jewish existence in exile is ghostlike.

In Loew's covenantal philosophy of history, however, exile does not represent the antithesis of nationhood but a moment in the life cycle of a nation in its relationship with God. Loew follows a Jewish tradition in which the punishment of exile is a purification of the people for their return to the land.[22] In Buber's rendering of Loew's metaphors, "the sufferings of exile smelt the ore and separate the precious metal from the dross, they crush the olives and separate the water from the waste."[23] Exile is a place of darkness, but it is this inevitable time of darkness that serves as a prelude to the light of redemption. In exile, the Jewish people must work to maintain their unity and become stronger as a nation, preparing them to return to the land to serve God in the fullness of national life. Should they fail in the next opportunity, the cycle will repeat itself. But exile does not negate Israel's existence as a nation; it rather affirms the covenantal character of their realization of national life.

Buber's critique of secular political Zionism's understanding of exile also extends to its view of the return of the people to the land. Here, we must take note of Buber's understanding of messianism as the ever-approaching but never fully realized aspiration for perfection.[24] For Buber, exile can be fully overcome only when the people achieve genuine perfection in their service of God, but claiming that such perfection has been achieved automatically undermines the credibility of the claim and hence should be discredited. Here, Buber fits into a Jewish tradition of what might be called "anti-messianic messianism." Messianic aspiration serves as an ideal that is kept out of reach out of skepticism that the ideal can be achieved within human history. Nonetheless, the ideal serves as an orienting goal for the community. This is the way Buber views overcoming exile. Secular political Zionists, following Herzl, might claim that moving all the Jews to Palestine would "overcome exile." For Buber this would be a false secular messianic claim tantamount to saying that the people had no need for continued moral or spiritual growth. At worst, Buber believed, claiming that the exile had been overcome completely could vouchsafe a self-righteous and potentially totalitarian Jewish nationalism.

For Buber, as we saw previously, the real meaning of exile is that one is in exile from God and from the service to God of building genuine community. Since one cannot claim, Buber believes, that one has perfected their service to God, then one cannot claim to fully overcome exile. It would seem that Buber has transformed the classical covenantal theology and its claim that exile stands as an eternal possibility as a punishment for Israel's sins without fully rejecting it. For Buber, exile is not an ongoing divine punishment but rather a condition inherent in the constant striving for perfection and realization. The extent to which we fail in the service to God is the extent to which we are still in exile. Thus, while Jewish settlement in the land is a necessary aspiration for the Jewish people to regain their strength as a people, simply moving people into the land or the achievement of sovereignty does not, in Buber's view, fully overcome the reality of exile with finality.

This view of exile fits with Buber's notion of Judaism as the striving to realize holiness within the everyday, by which I understand Buber to mean embodied material existence. For the Jewish people as a nation to participate fully in striving for holiness, they must do so in their particular land, the land that originally shaped their unique character as a people. Buber's *On Zion* lectures devote a great deal of attention to how Jewish thought since the Bible asserts that the land has shaped the people of Israel as a people of God. I will not review Buber's claims about the significance of the land here. My emphasis is on the fact that for Buber, the Zionist project of settling the land is only a precondition for the effort of spiritual realization within the material. The land is the "everyday" within which the Jewish people strive to realize holiness, but merely living in the land does not suffice for achieving this reality.

If Buber viewed political Zionism as reflecting the pagan tendency to glorify material and social reality, then Reform represents the Gnostic tendency to capitulate to exilic conditions. Buber views both as a denial of the classic Jewish view of exile as potentially transformative. For Gnostic and Reform thought, exile cannot be overcome, and both, in Buber's view, take this assumption as a point of departure for understanding the goal of spiritual realization. In the case of modern liberal Jewish thinkers, they argued that Jews should embrace their dispersion and view themselves as a religion of individual conscience and not as a national group. The problem with this view for Buber is that it ultimately denies the Judaism and the Jewish people a meaningful place in everyday material existence and robust social reality. Rather than entering into everyday life, Judaism on this model, remains merely religious and limited to the isolated realm of individual salvation. In classical Gnostic myth as Buber understood it, a person can only find individual spiritual realization by withdrawing from material existence and human community. Buber saw traces of this understanding of spiritual realization in Max Scheler's philosophical anthropology, to which I now turn. The parallels between his critique of Scheler and his critique of Reform Judaism's understanding of exile suggest that his philosophical anthropology can be read in part as a universalization of the Jewish understanding of exile.

II

Buber's 1938 lectures on philosophical anthropology, entitled "The Problem of the Human Being," should be understood as a continuation of his engagement with German social theory and sociology that shaped *I and Thou*. In particular, Buber emphasizes the significance of Kant's philosophy in setting the terms for modern philosophical inquiry on the meaning of human existence and the implications of that inquiry for the social sciences and humanities. In this respect, Buber follows his earlier teachers, Georg Simmel (1858–1918) and Wilhelm Dilthey (1833–1911), the latter of whom he refers to as his teacher in these lectures.[25] It is their interpretation of Kant's philosophy that interests Buber and shapes his understanding of the anthropological question.

For Buber, the salient feature and principal weakness of Max Scheler's anthropological thought is his recapitulation of an ancient Gnostic conception of human realization. While Buber does not say so explicitly, his critique of Scheler, as with his critique of Martin Heidegger, is meant to contrast the weakness of this Gnostic thinking to the worldly, communally oriented, and biblically rooted thinking of his own philosophical anthropology. Buber's critique of Scheler's approach to alienation in the human condition, I am arguing, parallels his critique of Reform Judaism in so far as they both accept alienation and exile without seeking to transform or overcome it. In Reform Judaism's case, this acceptance of exile is expressed in this movement's rejection of any claims to national status and embracing the status of religion, which Buber understands to be an individualistic category. In eschewing any aspiration to the land, Reform Judaism, in Buber's view, limits the potential for the Jewish people to realize a genuine community. Likewise, Scheler, in Buber's view, understands the alienated condition of modern humanity as an essential feature of the human condition that cannot be overcome. In viewing the human condition this way, Scheler rejects the possibility for a genuine human connection to overcome the existential loneliness and create meaningful communal life.

Buber's critique of the anthropology of Scheler in the penultimate lecture of "The Problem of the Human Being" revolves around an interplay between two key dichotomies in Buber's thought, one between spirit and body and the other between philosophy and religious thinking. Buber's central argument is that Scheler's philosophical account of the human spirit takes the modern state of alienation as a permanent reality and not something that can be overcome. For Buber, Scheler's metaphysics is "a consequence of the divorce between man and man" because it takes for granted the sociological reality of social disconnection as a permanent feature of reality.[26] Scheler exemplifies the tendency of the Western philosophical tradition to engage in abstract thinking when they claim that the spirit can only be realized in a state of detachment. In Scheler's case, he draws attention to detachment from the body.

Buber's critique of Scheler focuses on the latter's claim that the ground of being consists of two primary attributes: spirit and impulse.[27] In Scheler's metaphysics, spirit is a powerless godhead (*deitas*) that is the source of values and ideas, and the impulse is the unbridled energy of the flux of life. Impulse contains all images and imagination but is not guided by any purpose or meaning.

Scheler's philosophical anthropology depicts the human being as the place in all of existence where these two attributes of the ground of being interact with each other and have the potential to cooperate. Indeed, for the spirit's values and ideas to have any impact in the world, they must find some way to work through the impulse and its life energy. Humanity's significance for Scheler, then, is that it provides a meeting point for the spirit to attach itself to the power of impulse. Human self-realization is the culmination of this meeting of spirit and impulse in the distinctly human creation of culture.

Buber sees the dualism of Scheler's metaphysics as a recapitulation of the Gnostic myth of the deity separated from the embodied world of material existence. Buber notes a difference between the two, namely, that in classical Gnostic thinking, there are two distinct metaphysical entities: the genuine deity and the world of matter. In Scheler's metaphysics, these two aspects of reality are two attributes within the ground of being itself. But Buber understands this difference to be of minimal significance in its implications for the philosophical anthropology that emerges. As Buber reads him, Scheler's concept of the spirit is thoroughly Gnostic in that it is alien to the material world and powerless to master it in any consistent way. The most the spirit can do is offer its guidance to the material impulse, the attribute with genuine power.

Buber also rejects Scheler's claim that the latter has refuted the biblical account of creation ex nihilo by positing a powerless spirit. Buber does not see the biblical account of creation as entailing creation out of nothing, which is a phrase that comes from later medieval theology. Rather, Buber associates the conjuring of something from nothing with the magic trick performed by the Babylonian god Marduk in ancient creation myths.[28] The genuinely biblical teaching, Buber says, is that the process in which the world moves from being "unformed and void" to an ordered cosmos remains shrouded in mystery. According to Buber, the Bible and postbiblical Jewish tradition teaches that God can only be known through God's actions of kindness toward humanity but that God's essence cannot be known.[29] Buber concludes that Scheler's notion of the "'world's ground'... is only one of the countless gnostic attempts to strip the mystery from the Biblical God."[30] What Buber means here is that Scheler's notion of a powerless spirit seems to offer metaphysical knowledge of God by positing two aspects of reality, the spiritual and the material. The problem with this picture is felt most deeply in the anthropological picture that emerges from this division in reality that, according to Buber, becomes depicted by Gnostic teachings like Scheler's as a division within the human condition.

Buber understands Scheler's conception of the spirit to mean that the spirit cannot attain any influence in the world without giving itself over to material impulses or instincts. Buber's characterization of Scheler is similar to his characterization of Plato and Hegel as thinkers who present a conception of the spirit where the spirit capitulates to the prevailing power structures of "historical reality."[31] In Scheler, the capitulation of spirit to power becomes both a metaphysical dynamic in the ground of being and an anthropological condition for human self-realization. On Scheler's view, for a human being to achieve spiritual realization, the spirit must resign itself to embodied impulses and take strength from them, as the spirit itself lacks any of its own power. Buber does not think this account captures the essence of humanity but rather, like Gnostic lore, depicts "a certain kind of man, namely that in which the sphere of the spirit and the sphere of the instincts have been made so separate and independent from one another that the spirit from its height can bring before the instincts the fascinating magnificence of ideas, as in gnostic lore the daughters of light appear to the mighty princes of the planets in order to make them burn in love and lose the force of their light."[32] The human being of Scheler's anthropology, Buber suggests, is already so alienated from their own instincts that they cannot imagine maintaining their strength of spirit ("force of their light") without giving in to the power of the embodied instinct ("the daughters of light").

Buber's use of Gnostic myth to explain Scheler's view should not be taken as a claim about the sources of Scheler's ideas. Rather, Buber's critique is aimed at showing why Gnostic ideas have become attractive to philosophers living in the time of crisis of humanity that Buber has described. Buber's critique of Scheler, like his critique of Heidegger, is perhaps best understood as a diagnosis: he reads their philosophical anthropologies as an extension of the sickness that already pervades humanity in the modern West, a sickness due to the factors of social disintegration and alienation from technology and work. Buber concludes that "the powerlessness of the spirit which Scheler considers to be original is always an accompanying feature of the disintegration of community."[33] The modern period is just another moment, like the waning days of the Roman Empire, when Gnostic myth becomes attractive again because of social disintegration and spiritual alienation.

Buber's diagnosis of the sociological background to Scheler's Gnostic dualism parallels his own claims about the social dimension of spiritual realization. Buber contends that "the divorce between spirit and instincts is here [in Scheler's work], as often, the consequence of the divorce between man and man."[34] For Buber, spiritual realization occurs through genuine relationships with others. The separation of these two aspirations—the social and the spiritual—originates in the tendency of human beings, and philosophers in particular, to view the dichotomies of individual/community and spirit/body as distinct metaphysical entities. In the hands of philosophers, the abstraction of these entities from genuine reality results in theories of how these entities interact that sever these theories and the people who follow them from genuine reality. Buber's claim, however, is that both community and individuality, on the one hand, and body and spirit, on the other hand, are rooted in the original interhuman relational realm that Buber believes genuinely characterizes human existence. The spiritual aspect of life is not alienated from embodied life but exists in a dynamic tension with it. The spirit, as Buber understands it, can guide embodied life and both spirit and body are realized together in their fulfillment of the whole human being.

As Buber understands it, Scheler's account of the relationship between spirit and instinct is rooted in the idea that spiritual realization, especially as expressed in humanistic achievement such as art or philosophy, occurs as the result of an ascetic act whereby the body denies itself to make room for the spirit. Scheler's account also views the instincts almost demonically, as a source of temptation that would lead a person away from the spirit. In this depiction, Buber sees an element of Gnostic and Christian dualism. The problem with this account, Buber argues, is that it misinterprets the multiplicity of dynamics between spirit and instincts that takes place within the life of the artist. While some philosophical or artistic work requires acts of asceticism, these acts are not, Buber suggests, complete denials of the body but rather a "two-sided carrying out of an original contract which assures to the spirit unassailable mastery and which the instincts now fulfill—in individual instances grudgingly but in most actually with pleasure."[35] Indeed, artists may face temptations that they may need to overcome, and this process of overcoming may require acts of asceticism. But Buber believes it oversimplifies things to view these temptations as the essence of the instincts, as if the spirit and instincts are always at war with one another as one might find in Gnostic lore or some Christian theology. The instincts and spirit, Buber believes, seek their fulfillment in relationship with each other, making spiritual realization compatible with bodily pleasure.

Buber also views the separation of body and spirit in Scheler's anthropology as characteristic of the philosophical mind. Elsewhere, Buber characterizes philosophy as thinking that abstracts from concrete reality.[36] Philosophers in this specific sense can generate new forms of knowledge by setting themselves at a distance from concrete reality and seeing that reality as if they do not participate in it. The spiritual danger of philosophical thinking is for philosophers to lose a sense of contact with the concrete reality from which they abstract knowledge or concepts. In philosophical anthropology, the pitfall of this abstract distancing is particularly intense, as the philosophers, in distancing themselves from their chosen object of study, are distancing themselves from their own personalities.

Buber sees this phenomenon at work in Scheler's account of pain. For Buber, the weakness of his account is that Scheler asks what pain is as an abstraction of one's own actual pain. Scheler distinguishes between the human faculty of intelligence, which asks how the pain "has arisen and how it can be removed," and the spirit's perspective of a particular pain as indicative of an aspect of reality as a whole—namely, that pain and suffering are features of being itself—and asks how and why this could be the case. As Buber describes Scheler's account, "man's spirit abolishes the character of reality of the empirical pain which the man has felt." Buber concludes that this mode of reflection on pain may generate "all sorts of brilliant thoughts about pain" but not "the nature of pain."[37] The "brilliant thoughts" of philosophers may seem like impressive products of the intellect but they do not, Buber believes, penetrate the essence of pain as an aspect of human existence.

In a genuine consideration of pain, Buber continues, "the spirit does not remain outside and strip off reality, it casts itself into the depth of this real pain, takes up its abode in the pain, gives itself over to the pain, permeates it with spirit, and the pain itself in such nearness as it were discloses itself."[38] To give a genuine account of human existence, the philosopher must account for their own experience of human existence and not strip humanity of its concrete reality. As Buber puts it in his discussion of Scheler, "Pain—and every real happening of the soul—is to be compared not with a drama but with those early mysteries whose meaning no one learns who does not himself join in the dance."[39] The philosopher who treats reality at a distance cannot provide an adequate account either of that reality or of the source of their comprehension of that reality.

In Buber's rhetoric, the opposite of the philosophical tendency to abstract from concrete reality is the religious tendency to participate in and penetrate concrete reality. For Buber, genuine human religiosity confronts reality in its embodied material existence. Indeed, Buber characterizes genuine religiosity as a form of direct confrontation with suffering: "Man does not begin where God is sought, but where God's farness means suffering without the knowledge of what is causing it."[40] I take it that Buber means that a religious person views all human suffering as an instance of God's distance. But where God may be distant, the religious person does not distance himself from his suffering but confronts it and gives voice to his pain as *his* pain and not as "pain in general," that is, pain separate from this particular instance of pain. A religious person wants to be relieved of pain as any person would be, but in addition to this desire he experiences pain as an absence of meaning. Thus, the religious person also desires to be relieved of the perplexing distance from meaning and fulfillment experienced in solitude and despair.

Scheler himself, Buber notes, was once a religious person who gave up Christian theism for his metaphysics of the becoming God. In the process, Scheler elevated the philosopher as the spiritual type par excellence, producing what Buber takes to be this mischaracterization of the spirit as a separation from embodied, material, "organic" life. For Scheler, humanity's superiority in practical and theoretical intelligence over other animals is merely a difference in degree, not in kind. What differentiates humanity from animals for Scheler is this distancing from life that Buber describes as characteristic of the philosopher and leads us to create metaphysical accounts of existence.

In contrast to Scheler, Buber argues that the spirit is a "happening" or event that occurs without expectation.[41] What makes an event spiritual is that it emerges from an uninhibited *participation* in concrete, embodied reality, not a calculated, premeditated withdrawal from that reality. The spirit emerges in humanity in an instinct to language evident in children who describe the world in mythic terms. This is not the place to discuss Buber's remarks on language in general, but it is sufficient to note here that he regards the human instinct to speak as an indication of the priority of dialogical relations in human existence, as he describes in *I and Thou*.[42] Language in its most "primitive" form, as Buber would put it, reflects human beings' essential tendency to participate in the world rather than distance themselves from it as the philosopher tends to do.

In Buber's schematic contrast of religion and philosophy, choosing to embrace this philosophical tendency to the exclusion of the religious tendency involves severing the connection between the human spirit and concrete embodied reality. In Scheler, the alienation from embodied material existence reflects the alienation experienced in social life. At the heart of Scheler's philosophy is the same problem that Buber argued faced modern Jews: a lack of security from not having a sense of home. If I understand the meaning of Buber's critique, Reform Judaism denies the problem of exile by asserting that the Jews are at home in the lands of their dispersion, but in doing so it asserts that the life of the spirit, namely religion, is inherently exilic. In this articulation, classical Reform Judaism is a Judaism of no particular place. Likewise, Scheler denies the meaningfulness of the quest for home that Buber sees as the fundamental question of human existence and the pervasive question in the history of anthropological thought. Scheler takes for granted the lack of security from social bonds he sees in modernity and posits that the spirit does not belong to any concrete aspect of reality, including an individual person's concrete existence.

In Buber's analysis, to be spiritual for Scheler is to see oneself as not a concrete person but as an example of a generalized metaphysical reality. In Buber's view, Scheler's philosophy of existence fails on this point because it cannot deliver any genuine possibility of self-realization because an individual has no personal connection or stake in his vision of spiritual realization.

III

In both "The Jew in the World" and "The Problem of the Human Being," Buber is addressing a social and spiritual crisis in the modern West, in one place as it pertains to the situation of the Jewish people and in the other as it pertains to humanity's self-understanding. In both cases, Buber is arguing that the classical Jewish understanding of exile represents a compelling alternative to predominant Western ways of thinking about exile, alienation, and suffering. On Buber's reading, the classical Jewish view of exile affirms the meaningfulness and significance of embodied material existence both in the form of the full social life of a nation and the genuine vulnerability and suffering of the individual. Both Reform Judaism and the philosophical anthropology of Scheler seek refuge from the travails of worldly suffering in an abstract conception of spiritual realization that Buber finds ultimately fails to provide the basis for meaningful human connection in the form of genuine community.

I have suggested that Buber's philosophical anthropology be viewed as a universalization of his Jewish theology of exile. In saying this, I am not merely suggesting that his philosophical writings provide a universalistic parallel to his Zionism and Jewish religious thought. In his philosophical anthropology, Buber provides a philosophical picture of how the universal emerges from the particular, whether the particular is a national group that endures exile or whether it is a concrete individual who suffers. The Gnostic tendency of the Western philosophical tradition, Buber argues, has been to seek the universal in a realm outside of concrete material reality, often in abstract philosophical theory. Buber's central claim in his philosophical anthropology is that such theories do not account for the embedded, embodied life people actually live in real dynamic social interaction with others, facing their vulnerability along with others, and potentially sharing their suffering with them.

Buber's critique of Scheler (and Heidegger) provides him with a point of departure for introducing the notion of "the between" as the aspect of reality in which dialogue takes place. In Buber's reading of both philosophers as neo-Gnostic, people must separate themselves from reality, either social or organic, in order to achieve spiritual realization. For Buber, in contrast, spiritual realization takes place through *participation* both in the lives of others and in the embodied life of concrete material existence. Such participation in life together is the basis for genuine community. Buber places his ontology of the between as the grounding for such community in contrast to individualism and collectivism as rival theoretical frameworks for understanding both human realization and social regeneration. The hope for the realization of such a community is a hope that Gnostic-oriented thought abandons, a hope for being at home, returning from exile, and ending alienation.

The cultivation of the hope for genuine community is central to Buber's Zionism and his philosophical anthropology. If Zionism's mission is to model the ideal of true community for the nations, then Buber's philosophical anthropology can be seen as an effort to show the way in which the intellectual tradition of the West fails to provide a philosophical basis for such community. Thus, Buber's efforts to counter the spiritual legacy of paganism and Gnosticism in his philosophical reflections on spiritual and social life open the door to Jewish ways of thinking about spiritual realizations without explicit reference to Jewish sources, as he does in many places, most famously, of course, in *I and Thou*. No matter the language or the context, Buber's humanism is always *Hebrew* Humanism.

NOTES

1. Arnold Eisen, *Galut* (Bloomington: Indiana University Press, 1986), 88.

2. Cf. S. Daniel Breslauer, *The Chrysalis of Religion: A Guide to the Jewishness of Buber's 'I and Thou'* (Nashville: Abington, 1980); Laurence J. Silberstein, *Martin Buber's Social and Religious Thought: Alienation and the Quest for Meaning* (New York: New York University Press, 1989); and Paul Mendes-Flohr, *From Mysticism to Dialogue: Martin Buber's Transformation of German Social Thought* (Detroit: Wayne State University Press, 1989).

3. "A careful reading of Buber reveals his ongoing concern for the meaningless, fragmented quality of life in the modern world. His books and lectures reflect his concern for the modern person's estrangement from nature, from other persons, from God, and from his or her own essential being" (Silberstein, *Martin Buber's Social and Religious Thought*, 18).

4. Martin Buber, "The Holy Way" (1918), in *On Judaism*, ed. Nahum N. Glatzer (New York: Schocken, 1967), 128–29.

5. Babylonian Talmud, Tractate Megillah 29a.

6. While the style of *I and Thou* is certainly more evocative and poetic than a typical work of philosophy, it is nonetheless a book that makes philosophical claims about the nature of humanity and the divine.

7. Mendes-Flohr, *From Mysticism to Dialogue*, 40.
8. Buber, "Holy Way," 111.
9. Martin Buber, *Hasidism and Modern Man*, ed. and trans. Maurice Friedman (Atlantic Highlands, NJ: Humanities Press International, 1988), 167–68.
10. Eisen, *Galut*, 86.
11. This term is meant to distinguish Herzl and his ideological successors from cultural or spiritual Zionists in the tradition of Ahad Ha'am (1856–1927) and religious Zionists, who embraced the aims of the Zionist program within an orthodox religious framework.
12. Jacob Klatzkin (1882–1948) offers perhaps the clearest presentation of this view. See Arthur Hertzberg, ed., *The Zionist Idea* (Philadelphia: Jewish Publication Society, 1997), 322–25.
13. Martin Buber, "Nationalism" (1921), in *Israel and the World: Essays in a Time of Crisis* (Syracuse, NY: Syracuse University Press, 1997), 215.
14. Martin Buber, "The Jew in the World" (1934), in *Israel and the World*, 167.
15. Ibid., 168. He is presumably referring to the observation of the early Zionist ideologue Leon Pinsker (1821–91). See Hertzberg, *Zionist Idea*, 184–86.
16. Buber takes the view that in exile the Jewish people still have had a spiritual vibrancy while still believing that the fullest realization of Jewish spirituality can take place only on the land.
17. Here, Buber anticipates his own distinction between being and seeming as he elaborates in "Elements of the Interhuman," in *The Knowledge of Man: Selected Essays*, trans. Maurice Friedman and Ronald Gregor Smith (Amherst, NY: Prometheus Books, 1998), 65–68.
18. The Hebrew *malkhut*, here translated as "kingship," could also be translated with the word "rule."
19. Buber, "Jew in the World," 170.
20. Martin Buber, *On Zion: The History of an Idea*, trans. Stanley Godman (Syracuse, NY: Syracuse University Press, 1997), 79.
21. Buber, *On Zion*, 89.
22. Buber does not cite the source of this tradition.
23. Buber, *On Zion*, 84.
24. Buber discusses this view in "Two Foci of the Jewish Soul" (1930), in *Israel and the World*, 34–35.
25. Martin Buber, "What Is Man?" (1938), in *Between Man and Man*, trans. Ronald Gregor-Smith (New York: Macmillan, 1965), 126. For a treatment of Buber's engagement with neo-Kantian social thinkers, see Mendes-Flohr, *From Mysticism to Dialogue*, 25–47.
26. Buber, "What Is Man?," 197.
27. Ibid., 185. Buber notes the similarity of Scheler's view to Spinoza's doctrine of attributes of being but also notes that for Spinoza these attributes are merely

two among the infinite attributes, whereas Scheler's metaphysics assumes only these two.

28. Ibid., 188.

29. Buber discusses this view in his essay "Imitatio Dei" (1926), in *Israel and the World*, 72–76.

30. Buber, "What Is Man?," 189.

31. Martin Buber, "The Demand of the Spirit and Historical Reality" (1938), in *Pointing the Way: Collected Essays*, trans. Maurice S. Friedman (Amherst, NY: Humanity Books, 1999), 182–85.

32. Buber, "What Is Man?," 189.

33. Ibid., 198.

34. Ibid., 197.

35. Ibid., 190.

36. Martin Buber, *Eclipse of God: Studies in the Relation between Religion and Philosophy* (Atlantic Highlands, NJ: Humanities Press International, 1988), 38–41.

37. Buber, "What Is Man?," 191–92.

38. Ibid. The use of the word *depths* is likely an illusion to Ps. 130:2, "Out of the depths I call to You, Lord."

39. Buber, "What Is Man?," 191–92.

40. Ibid., 195.

41. Ibid., 193.

42. Martin Buber, *I and Thou*, trans. Ronald Gregor Smith (New York: Simon and Schuster, 1970), 69–73.

SEVEN

MARTIN BUBER, METAPHYSICS, AND THE AESTHETICS OF BINATIONALISM

ZACHARY BRAITERMAN

IN THE FOLLOWING REFLECTIONS I want at once to hold apart and tie together two distinct but not separate things—the aesthetic and the political as they appear in the writing of Martin Buber about Palestine, Israel, and the idea of binationalism. To begin, there is Buber's own more than happenstance immersion in the art and aesthetics of fin de siècle and German modernism. More basic to Buber's complete oeuvre is the impact of Nietzsche, art nouveau, expressionism, and neue-Sachlickeit on Jewish philosophy as a form of visual thinking about Jews, Jewishness, and place. Setting aside the philosophy of dialogue for which Buber is most well known, I will argue that the idea of unity is a "metaphysical" topos that Buber never left behind. Its forms only mutated, and we see its afterlife in the binational idea. As forms of first philosophy, seeing and imagining were and are the prism with which to think through critically the binational idea. Then, there is the imbrication of politics and aesthetics as distinct modes of being and the constellation of political thinking and projects around images. This imbrication brings to mind trenchant questions about what is real and what remains "irreal" in relation to aesthetics and politics, especially as they come together and fall apart in the imagining of utopian political visions. Finally, ideas about spirituality, the image of land and the Orient, and Jews in the Middle East center my discussion about Israel and Palestine.

Assuming that Buber was first and foremost a visual thinker, my purpose in this chapter is to consider the binational project as it appears in his thought in view of its pictorial aspect. The argument in these pages assumes additionally that the Zionism promoted by him was theo-aesthetic, not theo-political per se. This hunch about the combination of art and religious philosophy in Buber's thought is predicated on the claim that a picture constitutes a form of visual thinking and that thinking is itself a visual act. This basic contention is the one made by Rudolf Arnheim in *Visual Thinking*, his classic study from 1966. Visual thinking was understood to be the act of drawing out essential features in combination with contexts and changes in contexts, filling in gaps and identifying structures, and, in the process, paying attention and discovering what matters. Arnheim's notion was that visual experience already constitutes a type of thought that involves the organization of a perceptual field via concepts and categories. Rather than present visual information as prior to or foreign to thought, visual activity is constituted as a basic form of intellectual processing, while thought is grasped in relation to acts of making and reading patterns. Buber's philosophy of religion and spiritual Zionism confirms Arnheim's view that more than a datum of cognitive awareness, every visual image is a proposition about human existence.[1]

Invested in the imagination, visual thinking lends itself to dimensions that outstrip simple empirical existence and conventional common sense. Both in the concrete and in the abstract, visual thinking is basic to the dialogical constitution of the physical and the metaphysical, of politics and religion, of the real and the unreal—as separate figures of thinking, but also in relation to each other. Our investigation of the binational idea as a topos of Buberian philosophy will support Arnheim's contention that perception is always already intellectual and normative, while intelligence and normative value are always already visual. This includes the visualization of theoretical concepts, particularly in the absence of physically constituted objects, presenting the visage of a natural object in a "thoroughly unnatural constellation, not realizable on our gravity-ridden earth." Objects are reduced to a "few essential flashes of direction or shape" in both nonrepresentational painting and in abstract thought.[2]

For their part, the history of Zionism and the question of Palestine will be recognized as constituted as stylized objects of visual thinking and performance. The formation of both national communities depended on the formation of discrete imaginary communities out of larger regional and international confluences.[3] In Zionist circles, the most radically utopian platform was and remains the binational idea—the idea of creating on an equitable basis a shared political compact between what in the 1940s would have still been called Palestinian Jews and Palestinian Arabs. But what was the binational idea? Was it a practicable political solution to the conflict between Jews and Arabs over historical Palestine? How is one to gauge concrete struggles over geographical place and the construction of historical memory and cultural consciousness? Was binationalism just an idea? Was it a picture? Should we see in it a type of pictorial and picturesque visual thinking? And if so, on what kind of vision did that picture depend? Was that vision political, religious, or even "metaphysical" in its own unique way? As utopian, was it, per Arnheim, a "thoroughly unnatural constellation, not realizable on our gravity-ridden earth"?

In the pulling together of my thoughts for this chapter about the relation between Buber's early religious philosophy and his support later in life for the binational idea, I have depended heavily on Israeli geographer Meron Benvenisti's more recent book on the impact of Zionism on sacred Palestinian landscapes, *Sacred Landscape: The Buried History of the Holy Land since 1948*, and also on resources cited in that study. Buber's first Zionist writings and Benvenisti's promotion of binationalism are separated by only a little less than one hundred years. What separates them obviously is the historical havoc that sits between today and yesterday—the 1948 Israeli War of Independence; the Palestinian refugee catastrophe, or *Nakba*; and the Israeli occupation and colonization of the West Bank and Gaza following the Six-Day War in 1967, which Palestinians call the *Naksa*, or setback. Despite that distance, their thinking is characterized by a strange convergence. Buber, of course, was renowned as the philosopher of dialogue and mutuality and a lifelong Zionist. But against the Zionist political establishment, he opposed the creation of a Jewish state in Palestine even as late as the 1940s. He promoted instead the principle of Arab-Jewish coexistence and the creation of a binational polity. For his part, Benvenisti was among the first and most prominent exponents of the binational project in contemporary Israeli culture and politics. He was already arguing in the 1980s that Israeli settlements in the West Bank made impossible the partition of the land into two separate countries. Less interested in the empirical claim made by Benvenisti and many others today, I want to consider his appeal to old Arab Palestine as a sacred landscape. I hope to show that Buber, the philosopher, was no less a spatial thinker than was Benvenisti, the geographer, while Benvenisti's thought was no less "spiritual," no less bound to "our gravity-ridden earth," than was Buber's.

In my remarks for this volume, "binationalism" is not understood "simply" in terms of a project built on political ideas and ethical-utopian traditions, which, of course, for Buber it was. But reading through the lens of this foundational thinker of the binational idea, I conceive it in a spiritual dimension invested in images and the imagination, "art" and Orientalism, religion, and metaphysics. After quickly introducing Buber as a quintessential visual thinker, I will cut straight to comments about pantheism made by Benvenisti and to the work from the 1920s he cites by the Palestinian orientalist Tawfik Canaan (1882–1964). I do so in order to reconsider the project of a binational compact between Arabs and Jews in Palestine as at once aesthetic and metaphysical. In this reading, Benvenisti's remarks offer the cue with which to grasp retrospectively how Buber's mature formulation of the binational idea was prefigured in his first mystical or metaphysical speculations. By "metaphysical" I mean the image of an overriding principle of unity as the truer form of being than the duality and division out of which it emerges. In this inverted and anti-Platonic metaphysic, nonseparation was for Buber the "realization" of spirit nestled in the foundation of a primary and unifying sensual root.

My own critical contention is that the aesthetic-cum-metaphysical concept of unity in Buber's early addresses on Judaism underscores problems that dog binationalism as a political project. Against Buber, my more positivist assumption is that what first defines politics as "political" as opposed to "aesthetic" or "metaphysical" is the deliberate immersion into the very divisions and polarities, the vicissitudes and fractures, eschewed by Buber as an aesthetic and religious thinker. The argument here stands against the idea of "theopolitics" as Buber would have understood it in the 1930s (not as the transfer of the religious into the political as in "political theology" but rather the submersion of the political into the religious).[4] For the particular purpose of these specific reflections, I will rather try to split the two sets (politics and theology, on the one hand, and politics and art, on the other hand) instead of fusing them. The point here is to argue that binationalism was and remains a project steeped in the visual imagination and in a peculiar group of visual figures. The metaphysical structure of the binational picture is based on the principle of underlying, undergirding unity, not the overlay of divisions and decisions by which we might ordinarily understand political compacts. A metaphysical figment, the picture of binationalism has always been more aesthetic than political.

I

The idea of unity that was the basic concept of Buber's earliest philosophical reflections is the key term with which to understand his promotion of binationalism. But this requires one to understand that arguments about Buber and binationalism require one to look past the lenses of epistemology, ethics, dialogue, and politics through which his thought is usually viewed. The alternative picture of Buber as a visual thinker builds on one that I have presented elsewhere, the main lines of which are as follows. His thought saturated by visual figures, Buber was a "Jewish Renaissance" thinker whose work embraced the history of religion, the history of Jewish religion, philosophical anthropology, prophecy, mysticism, Hasidism, Zionism, and the utopian political tradition. Lost in the usual impression and scholarly interpretation of his work is how steeped it was in the aesthetics of form (*Gestalt*) and space. Oscillating between form and formlessness as the flow and the patterning of perception, a visually rich form of synesthetic thinking defined Buber's early oeuvre and would continue to bear on his thinking.[5]

I touch on some of that in the discussion that follows. But for now I want to provide a sharper conceptual frame with which to understand Buber's dialogical worldview, particularly in regards to time and space in relation to the aesthetic structure of the binational project. I start with what is more obvious. In terms of time and space, Buber's overall philosophy of dialogue would have seemed to be more naturally conditioned on the form of temporal sequence that a conversation would have to follow. In the course of a dialogue, first one speaks and then the other. Overlooked is that the *Gestalt*-frame for dialogue was, for Buber, always the spatial arrangement predicated on an almost static logic of simultaneous presence—I and You and the space in between. The structure is not unlike the one in painting by which multiple figures occupy the same space not in sequence but simultaneous to each other. This aspect of space as an open configuration would explain Buber's glancing interest in *I and Thou* and elsewhere to creaturely figures (a tree, a chip of mica, a human fetus, a cat, a horse). More than merely decorative, these are figures of thought that should be set alongside other figures, like the dancer Nijinsky and the Isenheim altar from a group of very early essays written around the time of Buber's 1913 *Daniel: Dialogues on Realization*, as well as alongside the image of biblical prophets and Hasidic masters that would continue to inform Buber's thought for the rest of his life.

The upshot would be that Buber was not able to imagine Jewish political and spiritual renewal outside a spatial *Gestalt*. Place was the necessary if not sufficient condition for the renewal of the Jewish people, and for the renewal of Jewish life as an expression of concrete life. This contention appears throughout Buber's early Zionist writing and also in his letter to Gandhi in which Buber defended the Zionist project after the rise of Hitler in Germany.[6] But what kind of place? On the one hand, he defended a real place, a physically tangible place, and, on the other hand, not just any kind of place. Throughout the larger body of Buber's work there is the idea not just of *Gestalt*, not just the idea of the image, but also of perfected form, the perfected image, and perfect life. Perfection was central to the way Buber understood the life of Hasidism as well as Zionism, his interest in both stemming back to the same time in the first decade of the twentieth century. The mature vision of Buber's binationalism would reflect an ongoing commitment to Palestine, to the project of perfected place. Viewed in relation to Buber's larger pattern of thinking, the commitment to Palestine as a political project would be to imagine it as structured as a correlate to the image of perfected space.

To be sure, Buber was not a philosopher of "totality" as understood by philosopher Emmanuel Levinas. But for all the close and essential attention given to individual figures in tension and in dialogue, it remains true that Buber thought in terms of large compositional blocs and fluid patterns. In this, Buber's philosophy of dialogue "looks" more like a modernist *Gesamtwerk*, an abstract composition by a painter such as Wassily Kandinsky, a complex totality with no single center. In the modernist composition, associated by Kandinsky with nothing less than "the spiritual in art," what happens is not the overwhelming of the particular by the whole. Quite the opposite, it is the individual element—be it a color fragment or a tone—that determines the visage or the sound of the larger whole, or *Gestalt*, of the compositional sense and structure. Regarding Buber's thought about place and space, the energy here owes itself to the thought of his time—to philosophical vitalism, *Lebensphilosophie*, and German expressionist art. In this conception, place does not appear as dead matter to be simply shaped and reshaped. The binational idea depends on a kind of landscape, conceived not as a dead or passive block of territorial space but as infused by a live and living charge. Perceived as foundationally fluid, place is not simply subject to binary division. As in contemporary affect theory, Buber's politics is predicated on the capacity to perceive or to sense matter as alive and buzzing. As a seer, this is what Buber hoped to see.

II

Interested in religion, one should have already made note of the very title of Meron Benvenisti's text, *Sacred Landscape: The Buried History of the Holy Land since 1948*. With an eye on the principle of restorative justice, Benvenisti's book, published in 2000, is a tragic lament to the destruction of Palestine as a human landscape and physical space.[7] Stretched over the place of the old Arab landscape, Benvenisti follows the historical mapping of Jewish Palestine and the creation of modern Israel. His study begins with a chapter titled "The Hebrew Map" and then proceeds to examine, in "White Patches," the Zionist Yishuv before chapters devoted to the Arab-Palestinian exodus and ethnic cleansing and then the uprooting and planting of the new Jewish-Israeli state as a territorial configuration. More meditation than political study, Benvenisti's work shows Arab topographies as organic, slow-tempoed and evolutionary, unmediated, authentic, aesthetic-poetic. In contrast, Jewish topography marks itself (or is marked by the author) in terms of rupture, sudden tempo, and synthetic spatial framing and as bureaucratic, brute, and ugly.

At issue are two points, one relating to the history of style and design, the other relating to the metaphysics of place and identity, both in relation to colonialism and violent conflict. The claims in other words, are not simply political. The Arab-Palestinian landscape is given the lush contours characteristic of romantic and neoromantic Orientalism, whereas Jewish settlements, both urban and rural, are presented in terms of modernism. (The iconography is not unusual; forgotten, though, in this representation is the memory of Arab Yaffa, with its own adaptations to architectural modernism in the 1920s.) On top of that is the metaphysical claim, the feel for what Benvenisti calls "metaphysical belonging" to the whole of the land. Benvenisti argues that the Zionists claimed this for themselves and denied it to the Palestinians, who were said to be immersed only in particular local places. Viewed metaphysically, the conflict is not so much to whom the land belongs as much as who belongs to the land.

Looking past the retelling of political history, Benvenisti hits his own groove when he turns to write about the old sacred landscape signposts of Muslim memory, about saints, peasants, and holy sites. No mere turn of phrase, the very title *Sacred Landscape* evokes the author's own feel for the spiritual wholeness of the land. A good antiquarian, Benvenisti expresses a special fondness for Arab-Palestinian folklore studies from the 1920s and 1930s with a particular nod to Tawkif Canaan's study *Mohammedan Saints and Sanctuaries in Palestine* (1927). Benvenisti notes that Canaan was criticized by later Palestinian nationalist writers in the 1980s for not writing about national identity or about resistance to Britain and to Zionism. But Benvenisti reads this and other older studies with a sense of sorrow, for "this innocent, in terms picturesque, and pristine world that has disappeared, never to return."[8]

What catches our own interest is the particular language with which Benvenisti describes "the demise of the pantheistic cult of sacred trees and healing springs."[9] In this, Benvenisti is clearly relying on Canaan's study. Already in 1927, Canaan laments how the "primitive features of Palestine"—what he characterizes romantically as simple, crude, uncontaminated, patriarchal Palestine—are fading before a "more sophisticated but more unnatural" European civilization.[10] To set the scene for the investigation of Muslim sanctuaries and shrines, Canaan depicts the Palestinian landscape as one of bald hills with gardens and orchards here and there, solitary trees, and groups of trees. In this telling, every place, every "shrine, tomb, tree, cave, spring, well, rock or stone" was "invested with some religious reverence." Called superstitious and in opposition to orthodox Koranic strictures, this describes the local folk religion of high places and other landscape features marked out by acts of devotion at innumerable sacred shrines, in every village, on every mountain, and in every valley, field, and stream, a landscape populated by spirits, demons, and saints.[11]

From the Mediterranean Sea to the Jordan River, Palestine is presented as an integrated geographical-spiritual matrix and immemorial temporal frame. With constant reference to the Hebrew Bible, Canaan is convinced that the Palestinian *fellahin* (peasant farmers) of his day are heirs and "in some respects descendants of—heathens, Jews, and Christians."[12] What one notes in Benvenisti's appeal to Canaan is the sense of his own attachment to an organic notion of land and spatial wholeness. With Benvenisti, the metaphysical pantheist model of bonding to particular site-places is more self-consciously naive. It is as if it is this pantheistic cult, which Benvenisti wants to join. Poignant, this metaphysical desire for an undergirding unity and sense of belonging suggests that binationalism as a critical Zionist project remains indelibly metaphysical, the aching and sentimental character of which has been ignored as such by political actors who fought and fight across both sides of the hard surface to the conflict.

Attempting to see past the impasse over landscape and memory, Benvenisti contrived his own set of cartographical redrawings. *Sacred Landscape* is in part a family drama, the author recalling trips through the countryside of Mandatory Palestine with his father, himself a geographer and cartographer. Feeling at home in the land and with his own eye of Canaan's study, Benvenisti remapped the area based on ideas that are just as staked in the imagination as those of any other orientalist. Having traced the way official Zionist organs drew a new and national Hebrew map over the old Arabic place names, Benvenisti would, in his own project, set out to denationalize the land and its landscapes. The concluding remarks to *Sacred Landscape* recommend the restoration and maintenance of old Palestinian holy sites and historical places such as castles, khans, mills, and olive presses. As part of a basic cartographical and narrative restructuring, Benvenisti calls the attention of his fellow Jewish Israeli nationals to the Arab geographical stratum underpinning the country that they claim as their own.

To draw out the notion of the old Palestinian landscape as a living organism, Benvenisti draws not so much directly from Canaan as from Israeli novelist Y. Z. Yizhar and Meir Shalev. It is in their work that one finds more clearly not just the tension between historical-cultural strata, but a bubbling life that roils underneath the surface, a sacred landscape as nature pantheism. That is the particular impression made by a passage cited by Benvenisti from Shalev's novel *Roman Russi* (*Russian Novel*, translated into English as *The Blue Mountain*, 1988). The novel chronicles the settlement of the Jezreel Valley in Israel across three generations. For our purposes, we will keep our attention on Baruch, a third-generation member of a cooperative village and the novel's first-person narrator, and Pinness, introduced as the "old schoolteacher" of the local cooperative village established by Baruch's grandfather during the 1920s.

The central protagonist in Shalev's novel is undoubtedly the land itself, represented as a deep and vital force over which the Zionist pioneers have only a tenuous grasp. Two scenes call our immediate attention. In the first, the one cited by Benvenisti, the novel recalls an episode when archaeologists from London were brought to explore a prehistoric cave discovered by Pinness when he was a still a young man during the British Mandate for Palestine. The site of archaic human remains—*Homo sapiens palestinaeus*, it is quipped—the cave uncovers the subterranean depths over which the new Jewish settlement was fabricated. An uncanny figure, the cave is the site of a disorienting revelation: "Stepping back out of the cave, [Pinness] sat in on the entrance looking down on the broad, obeisant, fertile Valley at his feet. The humble cabins of the village, its infant streets and young shade trees, suddenly seem to float on the fallow, long-historied earth, bobbing on its countless strata. The first geometric fields of the pioneers looked like so much patchwork, mere cobwebbery. [Pinness] was still a young man, and the thought of vast epochs swinging over the Valley like pendulums induced in him a feeling of vertigo."[13] In this passage, the one cited by Benvenisti, the novel reflects on the uncovering of the prehistorical past of the place, the sense of deep time that unmoors the present tense from any firm basis in reality. As revelation, the cave allows one to see the history of Jewish settlement in the valley as nothing but thin tissue.

A second scene from Shalev's novel, which Benvenisti does not cite, makes the same point. But here it is the biological past of the place, not the historical past, that calls the Jewish settlement into question as a surface phenomenon. Baruch, the grandson, is presented desperately at work on rooting out a wild native plant spreading like a rhizome over the vegetable garden and the hut of the now deceased family patriarch. The root is described as thickening and diving into the ground. The root Baruch finally pulls it out of the ground is as if ripped out from the bowels of the earth. Digging a trench, cutting through corn and clover and the ruins of old British military positions, his tearing out of the root leaves a deep hole. As described by Baruch in the first person: "A great hole remained in the ground, and from it rose a milky pestilent vapor thick with swarms of mosquitoes. Peering down into it, I saw the dense, murky water of the past swirling slowly, little grubs clinging to its surface and breathing patiently through their short air tubes. . . . A deep gurgle sounded from the hole. Shut up by the founders in the bowels of the earth, imprisoned in the trunks of the eucalyptus trees they planted, the soughing swamp began to surge toward me as it was touched by the sun's rays."[14] Representing a depth dimension beneath the surface of the historical present, the land itself is an undergirding, vital living form that confounds the feeble attempts by the Zionist founders to transform the place into an image of their own making. The power of nature as a living ensemble of forces is the same one captured by the thundering, "ear-blinding" roar of cicadas in the summer, clinging to jasmine bushes and olive branches, drinking fresh sap from the plants, "immemorially." Describing this nature-cacophony with a no uncertain biblical turn of phrase, Pinness likens the cicada song to "the true song of this country," "an obstinate trill that has no melody or notes, no beginning or end, nothing but the jubilant and admonishing proclamation of Existence that says, 'Here I am!'"[15]

While himself critical of the way in which Shalev obscures in his novel the Arab Palestinian landscape, what Benvenisti draws from poets and from fiction is the statement from Palestinian poet Mahmoud Darwish, "The geography within history is stronger than the history within geography." Benvenisti then continues to cite the call by Yizhar to hear the land as "growling, an un-forgetting silence, unable also to forget even when it has already been plowed and has already brought forth fair, new crops. Something within it knows and does not forget, cannot forget."[16] Land is not simply a material basis or substratum with which to support a superstructural ideological overlay, which might shape that land either this way or that. With its own memory, land is its own gnosis and expressive agency. Is this just a figure of speech? It is hard to tell the degree to which a writer not known to be "religious" is invested in such flights of fancy. And yet this appeal of Palestinian sacred landscape evokes the depth dimension of human dwelling. Only by integrating into its strata—forming an integral part of it, not as an alien invader—Benvenisti insists, can "the Israeli feel truly to be an 'image of his homeland's landscape."[17] Spanning nearly the entire twentieth century, for Jewish proponents of the binational idea, the political vision turns on a metaphysical image—spiritual and pantheist, the vision of the whole, the Israeli Jew in the image of his land, the secularization of the image of God in man. A composite picture bifurcated between a thin surface and primordial foundations, the model is metaphysical before it is political—aesthetic and spiritual, not strictly empirical.

III

The emphasis on the living character of what Benvenisti calls the sacred landscape—its underlying integrity and unity, not division—and the reference to nature pantheism and to the deep-seated desire to belong bring us back to Buber's early writings on Judaism. For the young Buber, it was a peculiar metaphysics combined with a feel for deep sensation that served as the basis of the modern Jewish political project. As promoted by Buber, the Jewish Renaissance–Zionist Renaissance relied on affective roots and primary acts of human cognition understood in terms of seeing, hearing, and touching. National and spiritual renewal was founded on the renewal of perception. It should be no surprise that we find this interest in his 1901 speech, "Address on Jewish Art," at the Fifth Zionist Congress; there he railed against "ghetto sentimentality" in the face of an exile that had robbed the Jews of "the ability to behold a beautiful landscape and beautiful people."[18] Zionism was going to cultivate a new Jewish art, a "new, strange, never before seen garden," the movement serving as a teacher for a living perception of nature and people, by means of which "we will behold and recognize ourselves."[19]

The erotic visual figure of the Orient was vividly pictured already in French romantic, pre-Raphaelite and symbolist–art nouveau paintings, in works of art by Dante Gabriel Rosseti, John Roddam Spencer-Stanhope, Odilon Redon, Frantisek Kupkl, and George Barbier. Relative latecomers to this tradition were nineteenth-century and fin de siècle Jewish artists such as Maurycy Gottlieb, Lesser Ury, E. M. Lilien, Ze'ev Raban, and Reuven Rubin. Add to the list as well the dark-haired Jewish oriental beauties, dappled in gold and jewel-like patterns in works by Gustav Klimt. The Shulamite from the Song of Songs was an especially beloved figure in this art tradition that found its way into modern Jewish thought, most notably in Franz Rosenzweig's the *Star of Redemption* (1921). The Orient was always evoked in these paintings and letters in bright colors, representing the beautiful and the sublime, sex and sexiness, and everything associated with it, including death, a figure with generative power opposed to the age of degeneration in the modern Occident and the ugliness of Jewish exile.

Buber provided a philosophical frame to this discourse, the fusion of politics of cultural Zionism and aesthetics assuming a more systematic bent in his first three addresses on Judaism, the *Drei Reden* (1910s). A theoretical structure, the metaphysic provided a fundamental orientation that was to limn the difference between unity and division. In the first address, "Judaism and the Jews," Jewish life in exile is inorganic. Judaism and the Jews are split between the external world and the inner world. None of these things cohere: the world of our impressions versus the world of substance, the external experience of the world and its native surroundings, language, and mores versus the internal experience of the individual Jewish soul represented as a part of a "blood community" binding past and contemporary generations together into a single assemblage. But what does unification mean? In the second address, "Judaism and Mankind," the perspective broadens past the particular divisions that mar and make ugly Jewish life in exile. Unification means not the expulsion but rather the organic combining of polar elements striving for psychological, social, political, ecological, and theological unity. Unity represents no lost Eden, no original ontological state but goal, redemption, and renewal. The demand for unity is born out of one's own duality. A Kabbalistic figure of thought in its psycho-theological isomorphism, it is existence itself that is rent and sundered. This includes the reality of God's being sundered from God's indwelling. Not simply political, the goal of renewal is the ontological redemption from duality, the very reunification of the godhead. In the third address, "Renewal of Judaism," Buber drove home the point that this striving for unity is an innate human and cosmic tendency exemplified within the Jewish soul. Now, unity is aligned with the undifferentiated, the absolute, and the unconditional. Renewal is the creative synthesis of purified tendencies into a united and organic whole.[20]

My own purpose in this essay is to read these ideas forward in order to situate conceptually what was to become Buber's mature binationalism, in particular his rejection of plans to partition Palestine into a Jewish state and an Arab state. With that in mind, I note the way in which the unity principle, as a peculiar form of religious-metaphysical thinking, was from the very start inflected by art and landscape painting. One of Buber's first published pieces was an essay on painter Lesser Ury (1861–1931) published as part of a series of Jewish artists sponsored by the Zionist Congress. Central to Buber's thinking about art was the rejection of any fixed and rigid boundary. What drew him to this artist in specific was the erasure of line by strong color in Ury's impressionistic landscape painting. More than an arbitrary aesthetic choice in respect to the history of style, this kind of art is held to represent an idea of cosmic reality, nothing less than a toppling of the picture of the Newtonian cosmos writ large.

In contrast to what Buber will later embrace in terms of *Gestalt*, the idea of a living and unifying form pattern, in this essay *Form* represents the antipode to life. As a rigid structure, "Form does not say anything about reciprocal relations, the reciprocity of things. . . . Form separates, color unites. Only color can tell about air and sun, fog and shadows: it puts the thing in context."[21] We see here an anticipation of relationship being more than an interpersonal ethical orientation, but as bearing all the marks of strong color and color fields. "Here, all is given in the natural-material as mutual effect [*Wechselwirkung*]," and the "soul of the landscape . . . reveals itself in the reciprocal effect [*Auseinanderwirken*] of its elements, in the reciprocal shadings, mistings, intensifications, and deepenings." Already thinking about landscape and soul, Buber sees in Ury's art a visualization of that "moment in which one thousand life streams mix," a view of the world with its fluid and dynamic exchange of reciprocating energies.²² More than the biblical characters who inhabit and the settings that locate Ury's biblical painting, one would look instead for principles like the "struggle of boundlessness," "world unity," and "infinity without rest." These are the elements that identify Ury's art as "Jewish."²³

All of the component figures from the essay on Ury—landscape, soul, religiosity, the infinite, sensation—come together only a little over ten years later in "The Spirit of the Orient and Judaism," published in *Vom Geist des Judentums* (*On the Spirit of Judaism*, 1916), another collection of essays from the same period as the *Three Addresses* (*Drei Reden*) and with which the first three addresses were later incorporated. While it would be fair to say that Buber, at this point in his career as a writer, was not disinterested in racial difference, one should note that he states quite clearly that he was more interested in what he called "supra-racial structures." The geographical object of analysis is not just this or that individual nation but rather "complexes of nations," in particular the great single complex of so-called oriental nations stretching across from the corner of Southwest Asia across to its far east.²⁴ Flying in the face of European anti-semitism and bourgeois German Jewish taste, the point is to embrace openly the oriental aspect of what we today would call "Jewish identity."

While ostensibly about spiritual geography—Buber maintained with great polemical force that none of the great world religions owe their origin to the West—the essay was at base an exercise in synesthetic thinking. Inverting all the dominant axiological binaries between "occident" and "orient," the essential and spiritual difference as posed by Buber was one between a motor-type personality versus a "sensory-type." The essay builds on a crude binary opposition between the occidental type of consciousness dominated by vision and the oriental motor personality for which the world is perceived in motions. In the Orient, sight is not sovereign. There is instead a close connection of all the senses, and these with the "dark life of the organism." Interconnected, an impression made on one sense passes through all of them. Rather than in a perception of single things as separate, the oriental type of person perceives the world in aggregate nodal points with an infinite motion flowing through him. The oriental type of person, one who senses rather than perceives, can be called a "subject" in a very restricted and weak sense.²⁵ This is the reason why all of the great world religions grew out of oriental soil. To the essence of the orient belongs the realization (the making actual) of a unified image of the world as "disclosure of the world's inner substance."²⁶

In this apologetic for Zionism, the Jew is found in the Orient not as a foreign interloper but in the spirit of kinship and spiritual belonging, part of a larger transracial ecosystem. Buber thus restructured the entire conception of

Judaism. Against the abstractions of the German idealist tradition and liberal Judaism, Buber was one of the first thinkers to turn attention back to the mythic dimension in Jewish religion. In "Myth in Judaism," as well as in *Vom Geist des Judentums*, Buber laments the sublimating spiritualization in prophetic literature by which God is divested of sensual reality. YHVH is turned into the God of the universe, the God of humanity, the God of the soul who no longer walks to and fro in physical concourse with human beings and material reality.[27] While Buber would not have expressed it this way, the god who appears in this essay and in "The Spirit of the Orient and Judaism" is pagan in its attachment to land and landscape. As Buber himself insists, the biblical text is itself filled with images of field, garden, and vineyard, the soil itself standing in as an object of divine threat and promise. God is painted as lord of the field, of agrarian festivals, of a "nature bound life." The Bible's is not a world-conquering message, but one at home in native land, finding there on the scanty Canaanite soil a place on which to build a model community, to which the human experience in exile (*galut*) compares as an unnatural and fenced-in space.[28]

Against the expression of aesthetic thinking that substitutes for politics, what anarchist-socialist Gustav Landauer (1870–1919) wrote to Buber on Buber's support of the German war efforts apply equally to this kind of writing about myth, the spirit of the orient, and Judaism. For Landauer, such thoughts were "very painful ... very repugnant, and border on incomprehensibility. Object though you will, I call this manner aestheticism and formalism and I say that you have no right ... to try and tuck these tangled events into your philosophical scheme [*schönen und weisen Allgemeinheiten*]: what results is inadequate and outrageous."[29] In his letter to Buber, he argued, "Historical matters can only be talked about historically, not in terms of formal patterns [*formalem Schematismus*] ... I gladly grant that behind this is the desire to see greatness; but desire alone is not sufficient to make greatness out of a confused vulgarity."[30] In relation to Zionism, Landauer's criticism would have been posed in terms of a sharp reaction to the kind of aestheticism that might only have obscured the dense historical and political knots that tangle Arab-Jewish conflict in Palestine. What remains an open question is whether binationalism was a political solution to that tangle or, understood aesthetically and metaphysically, its antithesis.

In this particular case, rather than follow Paul Mendes-Flohr in his classic study of Buber's turn away from the "mysticism" rejected by Landauer to "dialogue," I would suggest modulating the idea of a radical split between the early and mature Buber.[31] When all is said and done, these early mystical thoughts on unity and dualism remained the metaphysical basis on which Buber built his vision of the binational idea. The metaphysical indeed transferred over into the political for Buber, leading to considerable confusion. Buber's entire philosophical apparatus was built on a conception that begins with the need to orient the human body in abysmal space, both ontologically and politically as represented by a form of modern crisis consciousness. The dream of a binational, Jewish-Arab confederation in Palestine was drawn out of this same conceptual root. Buber's mature thought developed and modified that earlier orientation. The life of dialogue was meant to draw the most diverse gathering of people possible into a perfected common space free from domination. The idea is not distinct from the earlier writing on community.

By the end of the 1920s, Buber's mature thought had turned from the cozy *Gemeinschaft* idea to a more modern, more complex *Gesellschaft* point of view. This too was a shift brought to bear on his understanding of Zionism. In the late essay "Two Peoples in Palestine" (1947), he proposed economic-technical and political-spiritual action. *Politics* refers to the platonic sense according to which one "builds and gives form to society and state." *Technical* signifies the spiritual will to create an "all-encompassing, fruitful, and lasting peace among the peoples on the face of the earth." As a way to stimulate "the whole of Palestine," Buber viewed economic development, especially a huge irrigation enterprise, as the way to increase arable land and supply energy to local industry: "From being a divided territory made up of a dynamic Jewish element and an Arab element that is still fundamentally static, it would come to be a united land humming with intense productivity."[32] A land that hums—the image presupposed a sonorous plastic form. It is a machine image but vaguely pagan, this technical project whose end was meant to sustain two people in one elastic place. The turn to technology, the expansion of space, the unification of a space around national difference, the creation of international institutions as a way to settle conflict were all together thought to constitute nothing less than a design for the earthly form of the kingdom of God.

Buber was aware that refusing to enter into relationship will collapse the struggle for "perfect space" back into the nonspace of violent chaos. In light of the increasing threats to Jewish life in Europe, his political prognosis for Palestine missed the mark, but the diagnosis did not. He vociferously rejected the tragic view of two irreconcilable national claims, understanding that the ultimate success of Zionism requires peace with the Arab world. A binational state would have guaranteed free Jewish immigration and Arab rights simultaneously in the same place. The particular scheme was doomed from the start, given Arab opposition to unrestricted Jewish immigration. As one British commentator observed, "I personally think Buber's solution, the so-called bi-national State is the figment of the constitutional imagination. If [Jews and Arabs] work together, you don't need it, and if they don't work together the constitution doesn't work."[33] It was never going to happen. For Prime Minister David Ben-Gurion and the rest of the Zionist leadership, open Jewish immigration was a nonnegotiable Jewish political interest that the Arabs of Palestine, as they were called at the time, were simply unable to accept.

Throughout almost the entirety of Buber's literary oeuvre, his thinking about the kingship of God, politics, and political community was based on a metaphysics of undergirding unity combined with art, design, proportion, figments, imagination, and fabrication. This was the rich conceptual soil out of which grew one of the most important and influential expressions of binationalism as a resolution to the Arab-Jewish conflict in Palestine. Reading Buber alongside Benvenisti and Canaan, the point should have been obvious from the very start. The binational idea was always already a religious idea, steeped in religious ideas. One is surprised only to find this metaphysical root in Benvenisti or binationalism so early in Buber. Both thinkers sought to locate the Jewish people vis-à-vis an integrated sacred landscape, an oriental landscape, vital and growling and humming, a landscape that resists duality and partition. What both feared and hoped to resolve on an equitable basis was the reality of historical collision, clashing sacred cartographies, and political violence.

IV

Viewing its object from a historical distance, *Sacred Landscapes* is caught up in reverie and memory, on recalling old Arab-Muslim place names and their religious associations, almost all erased out in the countryside by the Zionist project. Like Tawfik Canaan, who once held the office of the president of the Palestine Oriental Society, Benvenisti's is an Orientalism committed to sympathetic claims regarding indigenous place and presence. Indeed, Benvenisti's analysis sheds almost no light on the basic question about the location of a Jewish place vis-à-vis larger Arab space, in both Palestine and the larger Middle East, except to observe that a long time ago, traditional Jews and Muslims were welcome at each other's holy sites. Ironically, Buber's binational idea—steeped in artificial constructs of Jewish cultural memory, the Bible and art, and Jewish political exigencies in relation to Europe—has the more complicated relationship to Orientalism. Touching on the relationship between the Orient as actual and imagined place, the aspect of Orientalism of interest here in relation to Buber and to the question of modern Jewish identity is more theoretical than the Orientalism of empire and bayonets.

If Orientalism as a scopic regime was dependent on a dominant point of view, the point of view of the Jewish orientalist was bound to be more complex. On the one hand, not unlike Benvenisti's, Buber's view of the Orient was from the intruding subject position of a Western observer. On the other hand, unlike the native-born Benvenisti's, the viewpoint positioned by Buber was European, even if from the underside of Europe. While the political Zionism espoused by Theodor Herzl and inherited by Ben-Gurion played the colonial card, the motivating cause of Zionism was not European empire but the vulnerability of Jewish belonging, especially in the face of European antisemitism. Like most Zionist writers enmeshed in colonial patterns of thinking, Buber was unable to see Arab culture on equal terms. But for Buber and others like him, the point of view sought was not supposed to be that of the place from above. While the binational idea in Zionism might have had something to do with what philosopher Jean-Luc Nancy calls "the community of a people" in relation to the idea of landscape, for them this had nothing to do with nationalism and patriotism per or with the idea of possession and ownership.[34] A critic of political Zionism, Buber expressed the desire to locate the Jewish people and Judaism "in" the country, not over it.

Should it come as a surprise that Buber couched his own Orientalism against the occident or that Jews and Judaism should be seen as such ambiguous figures by Jews and non-Jews in a larger scholarly discourse saturated by antisemitic overtones? As part of what is a much broader mapping of an entire field of scholarship, Jews and Judaism appear as frequent objects of racial orientalist antisemitism, particularly among German Indologists interested in Aryan origins. That is one basic conclusion from Suzanne Marchand's study *German Orientalism in the Age of Empire*. But Jews and Judaism also appear as participants in and objects of orientalist discourse at its best. Marchand pays a great deal of attention to the great practitioner of the art Ignaz Goldziher, for whom Islam was a "living, breathing, malleable tradition" and for whom the sympathetic study of Islam worked in tandem with the project of mid-nineteenth-century liberal Judaism.[35] And then there were the next generation of what Marchand calls the "furor orientalists" of the 1890s, whose interests were not historical per se but rather aesthetic, religious, philosophical, and critical-political. This generation of German orientalists was committed to cultural and spiritual renewal, to the intertwining of Europe with the people of other continents, and to the truth and superiority of art, ideas, and wisdom from the East. Countercultural, flamboyant, and antibourgeois, they made a decided break with liberal, nineteenth-century Eurocentric conventions modeled on classical Greek and Roman antiquity. Among these neo-Romantics Marchand includes Buber, without much discussion, along with Franz Rosenzweig, Abby Warburg, Ernst Troeltsch, Rudolf Bultmann, C. G. Jung, and Gershom Scholem. German Zionism is also included as part of this little cultural constellation.

Against the German Jewish liberal century, the embrace of a stylized image of "the Orient" by a new generation of German Jewish intellectuals represented a "self-affirmation" one could identify as "auto-Orientalism."[36] What makes Jewish auto-Orientalism a unique and peculiar form of Orientalism is that it was not a discourse of the Other as much as it was a discourse of the self, of the self as Other to the self. With a predilection for East European *Ostjuden* and mysticism, German Jewish cultural performance from this period would show not a little dress-up and masquerade, photographed in oriental drag. Jewish auto-Orientalism would have involved not the imposition of an alienating grid mapped over and on top of an Other but rather an animating mask, a fictitious claim to an "identity" that would have been perceived at the time as one's own true self by the very people already marked off as "oriental" and "Semitic" by members of the "Aryan" majority. What we are calling "auto-Orientalism" is actually another modern variation of Jewish identity formation identified by Asher Biemann in *Dreaming of Michelangelo*, a book whose subject is Jewish cultural affinities with Rome, art, sculpture, and the Italian Mediterranean by an earlier generation of German Jews. In both Biemann's book and Marchand's study, what one sees is the finding of oneself through the critical lenses perceived through distant mirrors, the self as it becomes Other to itself, transforming itself in the process, as the poet or the subject comes to life before colorful images.[37] Michelangelo and the Mediterranean, or the Orient and Palestine, were the erotic geographical figures transforming German Jewish thought and culture.[38]

What should any of this spiritual alienation from Europe have had to do with "the real Orient" in which actual people already lived in place? In a technical sense, these German Jewish performative peregrinations were "unreal." The auto-oriental Jew—the self as the object of auto-Orientalism—turns out to be more virtual than real. In this, we follow Marchand when she quotes critic of Orientalism Edward Said, mainly because she wants to argue against him. First, she contends that Said was too quick to reduce the entire project of Orientalism to imperialism; second, to do so, Said had to ignore the Germans (including Germanophone Jews, especially Goldziher), who would further complicate the politics of cultural Orientalism in ways that complicate Said's political model. But the following remark by Said quoted by Marchand is for us the most important one. As if conceding Marchand's point, Said writes, "There was nothing in Germany to correspond to the Anglo-French presence in India, the Levant, North Africa." And this is the upshot, Said's conclusion being that "moreover, the German Orient was almost exclusively a scholarly, or at least a classical, Orient: it was made the subject of lyrics, fantasies, and even novels, but it was never actual."[39] Said continues to claim that German Orientalism was not original, that it just worked off techniques learned from the British and French. This was to miss what was strange and exotic, and also powerful, not about the Orient itself, but about German Orientalism and the particular case of German Jewish auto-Orientalism, including German Zionism, as identity formation.

Said's remark about the nonactuality of German Orientalism stands in the face of Buber's embrace of the spirit of the Orient as predicated on "realization"—that is, the making real (*Verwirklichung*) of a unifying impulse. As a performance, there was something deeply nonactual, or virtual, more real than real, in the images of the Jewish East in Poland and the Hebrew Orient in Palestine that captured our German Jewish auto-orientalists. Readers of Jewish philosophy might recall something similar about ideas and reality in the discussion of prayer by the philosopher Hermann Cohen in *Religion of Reason*. An idealist, Cohen understood prayer in terms of lyric poetry (an only slightly different variant than the lyric identified by Said) as the dialectical deidealization whose purpose is to suffuse the real with ideality. In the fuller-blooded German Jewish philosophy of "furor orientalists" such as Buber and Rosenzweig, figures like "the orient" or "the Shulamite" from the biblical Song of Songs are supposed "to realize" their object with physical presence. The Orient gives Jewish life its special character. The energy of its light and revelation makes the object more "real" and in the world, as opposed to ideal.

In this dialectic, a virtual Judaism realized in figures drawn from the Orient works against the principle of "realization" for which they were employed because these figures make the projects of liberal Judaism or postliberal German Jewish Renaissance all the more nonactual, fantastic, and lyrical. German Jewish philosophers sought to situate figures of Jewish life or religious life, to situate even the idea or presence of God, in the real, physical world of space and time. But what comes out in the end is just how steeped in the nonactual the actual actually is. In Buber's case, the more real he tried to be, the less real was the result. This is endemic to the image-work of utopian thinking. It is the unreality of the real in this type of thinking that continues to complicate the project of binationalism in the spirit of aesthetic performance and religious renewal. That this might come to impact destructively the fate of the Arab indigenous people in Palestine was barely perceived and beyond Buber's imagination in the early 1900s, when this discourse first emerged, along with political Zionism, out of the vortex of European antisemitism.

V

Looking past both Benvenisti and Buber, the entire question about binationalism in Palestine would hang not on the reality and unreality of politics and metaphysics but on powerful biopolitical dynamics that the idea of binationalism would be unable to contain. To push the conversation into twenty-first-century theoretical parameters would be to consider models in which two subjects of sovereign power—subjects of and subjected to sovereign power—no longer assume the status and function of individual moral subjects (e.g., the geographer, the philosopher, the novelist, the Jew, the Arab). No longer interested in the local, we would have to look past the state form itself as a national and nationalist identity structure toward the organization and regulation, the protection or destruction of populations and organic life itself. In this global view—as such no longer a local or subject-bound expression of political thinking—the bio-political maps astringent and unforgiving political dynamics unmoored by ethics, individual responsibility, solidarity, and other subjective frames essential to the ethical orientation in politics represented by binationalism.

Rather than enter into the biopolitical itself, I want to conclude these reflections with a type of visual thinking we could point to as "landscape thinking." Common to Buber, Benvenisti, Shalev, and Canaan is an ongoing interest in land. In particular is the way in which the subjective presence of human figures and human cultures assume a place vis-à-vis land. As it has appeared in these pages, the land itself already enjoys and suffers what theorist Jane Bennet calls a "vital materiality."[40] Surging underneath the thin veneer of the Zionist project, the land itself is a growling, singing, humming force. Combining characteristics drawn from mysticism, folklore, political geography, technology, and literature, these characteristics are meant by our writers here to buttress thinking about Palestine, belonging, and the binational idea. In the process, they complicate the picture by combining human and inhuman categories of experience and thought, along with the political and the mystical.

Almost all of the authors touched on in this essay are humanists who understand land as an inhuman presence in relation to human belonging and to problems of human belonging—indigenous and Palestinian-Arab, indigenous and pagan, oriental and Hebrew, Israeli and modern. Against the thin veneer of duality, under this or that surging picture of "unity," individual and collective human figures and compacts are meant to occupy an abiding presence not just on the land, but in and with the land. In their urgency, what none of these discussions capture is the central point made by Jean-Luc Nancy in *The Ground of the Image* about the uncanny nature of landscape itself. Against the humanist tradition in art, landscape is ultimately recognized by Nancy in its purely inhuman dimension as a void that overwhelms any trace semblance of human presence.

While I will shy away from Nancy's analysis, I want to stay with it in the interim. In ways that will remind us of Buber, Benvenisti, Canaan, and Shalev, Nancy's discussion of the landscape is broken into three parts: location, occupation, and representation. Reading this essay on landscape painting, particularly in relation to the *paysan* or peasant, our own fretful thoughts are with mental pictures of the orient, imaginary constructs of the Palestinian *fellah* (tiller) and the Jewish ḥalutz (pioneer).

1. *Location or Country (Pays).* What is the country? The "country," any country, a country such as Palestine, is a corner, a corner cut out of indistinct expanse, out of an expanse like "the Orient." As per Nancy, the country is "the space of a land considered from a certain corner or angle, a corner delimited by some natural or cultural feature: a row of trees or a road, a river or a ridge, etc."[41] Suggestive of the notion of primordial indigenous space, the country as understood by Nancy is without and prior to administration or the invocation of property. At this initial point in its presentation, "the country," a country such as Palestine, escapes clear geographical, juridical, political determination. Such as it first appears, the human figure is manifested as belonging to and in relation, being attached, holding and being held. One is "in it" in a relatively simple way.[42]

2. *Occupation/paysan.* As a dimension of landscape painting, the *paysan* is defined by the indigenous tiller, whose presence is defined in terms of the occupation of place, occupied by or with belonging, taken up with time and space. One could think of *The Harversters* (1556), the famous landscape by Pieter Bruegel the Elder, with its human figures at work, at rest, and eating in a yellow field with its hilltop view receding into the distance. As presented by Benvenisti and Canaan, the *paysan* represents the type of belonging that "the Arab" in Palestine enjoys as if naturally. As projected by the early Buber, it represents the mythic condition of primal innocence that Zionism would restore to the Jewish people. As confirmed by Canaan, this occupation of the land is understood by Nancy as profoundly pagan. As per both Buber and Canaan, this spiritual disposition is deeper than any monotheism and orthodoxy, Jewish or Islamic. It reflects the

folk religion of local gods present "in each corner of the field, at each limit of the domain, or in the spring, etc." Inside the landscape, the *paysan*'s life is lived in the continuous presence of the gods, occupied as much with the gods as with sowing, bulls and thunder.[43]

3. *Representation/landscape/paysage*. Nancy's final point would be one that escapes Buber and Benvenisti, Shalev or Canaan. Unlike Nancy, they fail to see the uncanny capacity of landscape to absorb and dissolve all presences into itself. The peasants, princes, and gods who do appear "in" the landscape disappear, reduced to a diminutive presence to be entirely given over and lost under the vast dome of sky and before the receding horizon. Nancy's analysis should strike with terror anyone invested politically and emotionally in Zionism and the question of Palestine. The peasant (Palestinian farmer or Jewish pioneer) can be just as easily replaced by anyone, by travelers or by walkers. Disinterested in their presence, the landscape, as such, contains no presence: "It is itself the entire presence." All that remains there is "immensity itself, the limitless opening of place as a taking place of what no longer has any determinate place." The bigger view corresponds neither to "determinate figures, circumstances, or actions" nor to anything human. No longer sacred, the landscape "opens onto the unknown" as profound dislocation and disappearance.[44]

With its overarching sense of sacred landscape, the metaphysics of unity and presence that undergirds the binational idea in Benvenisti and Buber feeds unwittingly into the nihilism marked out by Nancy in the landscape tradition in painting. Myth and folk religion, binationalism, a connected sense of place and of belonging to place—all that to which Buber and Benvenisti hold dear would seem to shrink before an inhuman dimension in relation to which human figures fade away into insignificance. As Canaan himself feared in the preface to his study, what Benvenisti calls the sacred landscape can hold for only so long. The same warning was called out by Buber against the impact of colonialism at the end of his essay "The Orient and the Spirit of Judaism." Geological and topological segments remain indifferent as the gods take flight or before the expulsion of a human presence, indigenous or otherwise. In our view, the imagination of any shared human compact in Israel and Palestine would have to step away from the landscape pattern of thinking, a nihilism without God or the gods that lends itself to nothing less than the country's depopulation.

As per Nancy, Israel and Palestine represent landscapes that "[open] onto the unknown." With Jewish settlements thickly rooted throughout the Palestinian West Bank, the country today appears to a great many people inside and outside Israel and the Palestinian territories to be on the cusp of an unequal and nightmarish form of apartheid binationalism. Today, it might very well be the case that Buber's vision, which struck many in the 1940s to be a hopeless fiction, turned out to be prophetic after all. Assuming that neither national community will actually dispossess the other, Buber's general conception continues to hold after the passage of so many years. Regardless of the precise future territorial configuration, that conception would be one that is *expansive*. It is expansive in the refusal to bifurcate person from person, community from community, morality from politics, and spirit from power. At the same time, his is a *narrowing* conception, in that each party to this space makes do with basic needs, forfeiting the surplus that comes at the other's expense.

In perhaps his most clear-eyed political thinking, *Paths in Utopia* (1947), Buber was to plot the "image of perfect space" in a now unmetaphysical way. Like a draftsman working in virtual space, he drew out this image with lines that allow no fixed definition, allowing the scheme to recalibrate the shifting zone between the individual and collective according to the free creativity of its members. Buber described, "The relationship between centralism and decentralization" as a "problem which ... cannot be approached in principle, but ... only with great spiritual tact, with the constant and tireless weighing and measuring of the right proportion between them." A "social pattern," utopia was based on a constant "drawing and re-drawing of lines of demarcation."[45] An "experiment that did not fail," the Jewish Village Commune in Palestine (i.e., the *kvutza*, kibbutz, and *moshav*) owed their success to the pragmatism with which its members approached the historical situation, their inclination toward increased levels of federation, and the degree to which they established a relationship with the society at large. Single units combined into a system or "series of units" without the centralization of state authority.[46] "Nowhere ... in the history of [the] Socialist movement were men so deeply involved in the process of differentiation and yet so intent on preserving the principle of integration."[47] They discovered "the right proportion, tested anew every day according to changing conditions, between group-freedom and collective order."[48]

Setting aside this or that particular proposal (all the varieties of either a one-state or two-state option), this image of a mobile patterning of lines would be the model with which to structure an equitable-basis Arab-Jewish, Israeli-Palestinian compact or system of cohabitation in Israel and Palestine. Scaled up from the commune to the country as a whole, the utopian path is constituted out of bifurcating and intersecting lines; a sense for proportion and constant rebalancing; getting right the relation between centralization and decentralization, between integration and differentiation; the combining of single units and series of units into larger working patterns that maintain the integrity of the individual component piece. Subject to shift and flux, there is no metaphysical or messianic tendency toward unity and unification, no appeals to the orient or to any sacred landscape, and no tendency to the dangers that such appeals to autochthony inevitably invite. With no secure basis or guarantee, Zionism and the question of Palestine hang together over a catastrophic abyss. About this, Buber was right.

Another model with which to imagine the political future in Israel and Palestine is the more rooted expression of what I would also call "auto-Orientalism" emerging out of Ammiel Alcalay's *After Jews and Arabs: Remaking Levantine Culture*.[49] Published in 1993, Alcalay's text explores the systemic marginalization of Mizrahi Jewish cultures in mainstream Jewish and Zionist discourse, both popular and academic. It should be clear now more than ever that, philosophically, this marginalization has distorted the very concepts with which we think Jewish politics and culture, not just in Israel, where the problem is most acute, but also in the United States, where "all of a sudden" we are now having to rethink Jewish-Muslim relations and the phenomenon of race in Jewish culture. A literary scholar who works in Arabic and Sephardic Jewish literature, Alcalay shows what happens when signifiers like "Jews" and "Arabs" get hardened and homogenized by their respective nationalisms. If this was not so clear in 1993, it is painful and obvious today. The author presents Levantism as an alternative perspective with which to carve out a capacious common space for a diversity of peoples, most urgently in the modern Middle East. At work here is the critique of the Eurocentric nature of the entire Zionist project, its inability to deal with others (not just Arabs and Palestinians, but also Sephardic Jews, religious Jews, and diaspora Jews).[50]

In 1993, the critique was more new than it is today, now practically mainstream in academe. What is unique to Alcalay is that unlike most forms of post-Zionism or anti-Zionism, he actually takes it for granted that Jews are not a foreign, European implant into the Middle East, based on the experience of Sephardic/Mizrahi Jews in opposition to mainstream Zionist discourse. Placing Jews as always and already in the East, Alcalay loosens up the conceptual field of Jews and Arabs, especially today when these formations seem so calcified, first by nationalism and now by religion. At the same time, Alcalay's text puts under question the stylized picture of nomadic placelessness with which the Jews and Judaism are figured in so much postmodern and critical theory.

Alcalay would represent a post-European and a non-European expression of Jewish identity and cultural placing of Jews and Jewish culture. Contrasting the Levantine writers to Kakfa, Alcalay writes about "their concrete and sensual attachment to the fact and memory of a native space." In relation to the future of Israel and Palestine, that this picture could lend itself to either this or that practical outcome and political arrangement is precisely its strong point. In this image is the understanding that Jews belong to the Middle East and that Israel is a Middle Eastern country. It surpasses, as such, the theoretical models of exile and homecoming offered by Martin Buber from a hundred or so years ago on which he sought to trace a path to utopia.

NOTES

1. Rudolf Arnheim, *Visual Thinking* (Berkeley: University of California Press, 1969), 296. On secondary literature relating to Buber as an aesthetic thinker and to aesthetics in the German Jewish Renaissance, see Zachary Braiterman, *The Shape of Revelation: Aesthetics and Jewish Thought* (Stanford: Stanford University Press, 2007); Martina Urban, *Aesthetics of Renewal: Martin Buber's Early Representation of Hasidism as Kulturkritik* (Chicago: University of Chicago Press, 2008); and Asher Biemann, *Inventing New Beginnings: On the Idea of Renaissance in Modern Judaism* (Stanford: Stanford University Press, 2009).

2. Arnheim, *Visual Thinking*, 113, cf. 128.

3. On early Zionist aesthetics, especially in relation to Jugendstil art, see Michael Berkowitz, *Zionist Culture and West European Jewry before the First World War* (Chapel Hill: University of North Carolina Press, 1993). On the construction of a unified Palestinian identity, see Rashid Khalidi, *Palestinian Identity: The Construction of Modern National Consciousness* (New York: Columbia University Press, 1997).

4. On the invaluable distinction between political theology versus theopolitics as relating to Carl Schmitt and Buber, respectively, see Samuel Hayim Brody, *Martin Buber's Theopolitics* (Bloomington: Indiana University Press, 2018), especially 62–64.

5. Braiterman, *Shape of Revelation*, especially the introduction, but see also the first chapter, "Form," and the fifth chapter, "Space."

6. See Martin Buber, "A Letter to Gandhi," in *Land of Two Peoples: Martin Buber on Jews and Arabs*, ed. Paul Mendes-Flohr (New York: Oxford University Press, 1983), 111–26.

7. Meron Benvenisti, *Sacred Landscape: The Buried History of the Holy Land since 1948* (Berkeley: University of California Press, 2000), 5.

8. Ibid., 253.

9. Ibid., 252–53.

10. Taufik [sic] Canaan, *Mohammedan Saints and Sanctuaries in Palestine* (London: Luzak & Co, 1927), v.

11. Ibid., especially 1–5.

12. Ibid., 278–79, 280. One could read the constant reference to the Hebrew Bible in Canaan's account to what contemporary Bible scholars today credit as the Canaanite origins of biblical religion. Much of Canaan's account reads like crude early twentieth-century theory of "primitive religion," which is interesting as a reflection of Canaan's own thinking. More pertinent historically is how later in the text, Canaan points out how the establishment of Muslim shrines in Palestine were part of the attempt, after the Crusades, to secure parts of the countryside with large Muslim populations, by locating shrines at such strategic junctures as Jerusalem, Ramleh, Gaza, and Acre (see ibid., 299). This is part of the backdrop behind the ethnographic account of the Nebi Musa Festival around Easter, starting and concluding in Jerusalem. One notes that it is here and later in the text that the biblical references drop out of the book's discussion for a more clearly Islamic milieu.

13. Meir Shalev, *The Blue Mountain: A Novel*, trans. Hillel Halkin (New York: HarperCollins, 1991), 268.

14. Ibid., 250.

15. Ibid., 316.

16. Ibid., 340.

17. Ibid.

18. Martin Buber, "Address on Jewish Art," in *The First Buber: Youthful Zionist Writings of Martin Buber*, ed. and trans. Gilya G. Schmidt (Syracuse, NY: Syracuse University Press, 1999), 48.

19. Ibid., 51, 52.

20. Martin Buber, *On Judaism*, ed. Nahum N. Glatzer (New York: Schocken, 1967), chaps. 1–3.

21. Martin Buber, "Lesser Ury," in Schmidt, *First Buber*, 65.

22. Ibid., 67–68.

23. Ibid., 83.

24. Matin Buber, "Spirit of the Orient and Judaism," in *On Judaism*, 56.

25. Ibid., 58–9, 64.

26. Ibid., 60–2.

27. Martin Buber, "Myth in Judaism," in *On Judaism*, 102.

28. Martin Buber, "Spirit of Judaism," in *On Judaism*, 70–74.

29. Martin Buber, *The Letters of Martin Buber: A Life of Dialogue*, ed. Nahum N. Glatzer and Paul Mendes-Flohr, trans. Richard Winston, Clara Winston, and Harry Zohn (New York: Schocken, 1991), 189.

30. Ibid., 190–91.

31. Paul Mendes-Flohr, *From Mysticism to Dialogue: Martin Buber's Transformation of German Social Thought* (Detroit: Wayne State University Press, 1989).

32. Martin Buber, "Two Peoples in Palestine," in *Land of Two Peoples*, 200.

33. Ibid., 206.

34. Jean-Luc Nancy, *The Ground of the Image*, trans. Jeff Fort (New York: Fordham University Press, 2005), 53.

35. Suzanne Marchand, *German Orientalism in the Age of Empire: Religion, Race, and Scholarship* (New York: Cambridge University Press, 2009), 330.

36. Ibid., chap. 5, especially 212–27.

37. Asher Biemann, *Dreaming of Michelangelo* (Stanford: Stanford University Press, 2012), xv, 5, 43–44.

38. Cf. Paul Mendes-Flohr, "Fin de Siècle Orientalism, the *Ostjuden*, and the Aesthetics of Jewish Self-Affirmation," in *Divided Passions: Jewish Intellectuals and the Experience of Modernity* (Detroit: Wayne State University Press, 1991), 77–132.

39. Edward Said, *Orientalism*, (New York: Vintage Books, 1979), 17, 19, quoted by Marchand in *German Orientalism in the Age of Empire*, xviii.

40. Jane Bennett, *Vibrant Matter: A Political Ecology of Things* (Durham, NC: Duke University Press, 2010).

41. Nancy, *Ground of the Image*, 51.

42. Ibid., 53–54.

43. Ibid., 55–57.

44. Ibid., 58–59.

45. Martin Buber, *Paths in Utopia* (Syracuse, NY: Syracuse University Press, 1996), 137. The material in this paragraph has been taken and revised from my discussion in Braiterman, *Shape of Revelation*, chap. 5, to make better sense, in particular, of the binational idea in Buber's mature thought.

46. Ibid., 142–48.

47. Ibid., 145.

48. Ibid., 148.

49. Ammiel Alcalay, *After Jews and Arabs: Remaking Levantine Culture* (Minneapolis: University of Minnesota Press, 1992).

50. On the relation between nationalism, ethnicity, and religion, see Yehouda Shenhav, *The Arab Jews: A Postcolonial Reading of Nationalism, Religion, and Ethnicity* (Stanford: Stanford University Press, 2006).

PART IV

PHILOSOPHY

EIGHT

CHAOS, ABGRUND, AND *WIRBEL*

On Buber's Notion of
Ambivalence

ASAF ZIDERMAN

IN THIS FAMOUS TESTIMONY, WRITTEN in 1917, Martin Buber reflects back on his acute and unsettling condition as a teenager:

> So long as I lived with [my grandfather], my roots were firm, although many questions and doubts also jogged about in me. Soon after I left his house, the whirl [*Wirbel*] of the age took me in. Until my twentieth year, and in small measure even beyond then, my spirit was in steady and multiple movement, in an alternation of tension and release, determined by manifold influences, taking ever new shape, but without center and without growing substance: it was really the "Olam-ha-Tohu," the "World of Confusion," the mythical dwelling place of the wandering souls. Here I lived in versatile fullness of spirit, but without Judaism, without humanity, and without the presence of the divine.[1]

When young Martin was three years old, his mother eloped to remarry in Russia. His father entrusted the child's upbringing and education to his own parents, and Martin grew up at their farmhouse in the rural outskirts of Lemberg (today's Lviv in Ukraine). At the age of fourteen, Martin abandoned his grandparents' observant upbringing and moved to his father's townhouse. Then, at the age of eighteen, he started his academic training in the cultural mélange that was fin de siècle Vienna.[2] In the passage quoted previously, he describes the loss of direction and confusion that accompanied the two major shifts in his early life. Young Martin was pulled in different directions by various cultural currents and was unable to fully and unwaveringly commit to one of them. As such, he felt the absence of a stable core, of a "center" and "substance." He was a "wandering soul" in a "world of confusion." In short, Martin was in a deep state of ambivalence.

While Buber the person managed to overcome this acute state of ambivalence in his early twenties, Buber the scholar was preoccupied with it throughout his career. In his first venture as an independent thinker—his three addresses on Judaism, delivered in 1909-11 to the young German Jewish intelligentsia—Buber restages the personal malaise of his youth as a universal problem of humanity.[3] He considers ambivalence to be the essential cause and catalyst of Western humankind's—and particularly the exilic Jew's—most urgent problem: the state of self-disintegration.[4] With the dialogical turn that came to fruition in his foundational book *I and Thou* (1923), Buber came to view the illness of the age as the lack of interpersonal relations (*Beziehungen*). However, the state of self-disintegration (and, inter alia, of ambivalence) continued to play a crucial role in his understanding of the human predicament. The main goal of this chapter is to draw the contours of the notion of ambivalence in Buber's writings.[5]

The theme of ambivalence in Buber's writings is prevalent but does not emerge at first sight. In a manner typical of his writing, Buber often refers to the phenomenon of ambivalence but rarely moves beyond this mere reference to unpack and describe its various components and dynamics. Moreover, even Buber's mere references to the state of ambivalence are not easily transparent. Buber does not use the German term *Ambivalenz* or any other straightforward term to refer to it. True, he has coined two suggestive phrases—"holy insecurity" and "narrow ridge"—to refer to the notion of ambivalence, and these are widely used in some of Buber's secondary literature. Having identified the centrality of the state of ambivalence in Buber's writings, it was Maurice Friedman who adopted these coinages and devoted a central role to them in his presentation of Buber's thought; through his work, they entered into the Buberian discourse. Nevertheless, these phrases appear in a mere handful of places in Buber's own oeuvre, while the references to the state of ambivalence are extensive.[6] Another term that alludes to the state of ambivalence in Buberian scholarship is "demarcation line." However, it refers less to the actual state of ambivalence and more to how one should decide in the face of ambivalence. In this case as well, the centrality of the term has been amplified by Buber's commentators, most notably Ernst Simon.[7]

The way in which Buber *does* refer to the state of ambivalence, constantly and in a strikingly consistent manner, is—I claim—via two sets of metaphors used abundantly throughout his writings: "chaos" (*Chaos*) and "abyss" (*Abgrund*), on the one hand, and "vortex" or "whirlpool" (*Wirbel*)—and the related imagery of a swirling or whirling motion—on the other.[8] Buber's use of these metaphors is remarkable in that he uses them consistently for almost sixty years. Also, in almost all cases, he makes do with the metaphoric description of ambivalence and does not add much further literal explanation to it. These two facts are instructive. They indicate that, for Buber, these metaphors sufficiently capture the meaning of the state of ambivalence. As such, they also indicate that deciphering their inner workings is essential for our understanding of Buber's notion of ambivalence. Moreover, they indicate that a valid reconstruction of Buber's notion of ambivalence, as it arises from his few and brief discussions of it, must parallel the image of the state of ambivalence portrayed by these metaphors.

Deciphering the metaphors of "abyss" and "chaos" is a relatively straightforward task. We will reconstruct their meaning from the cosmogenic myths in which they appear and that Buber clearly relies on, as well as from their use by other thinkers and discourses known to have influenced Buber. Deciphering *Wirbel*, however, is another story. As a metaphor for the state of ambivalence, it is Buber's original and idiosyncratic creation, which, unfortunately here too, he does not take the time to define. As is the case with many of his original and idiosyncratic concepts, instead of defining, he applies it in different contexts and lets the reader pick up its meaning intuitively.[9]

Notwithstanding, there is one striking exception to some of what has been said here. In "Images of Good and Evil" (1952), Buber goes beyond mere referencing the state of ambivalence or merely mentioning its metaphors and discusses the state of ambivalence at relative length, making extensive use of the *Wirbel* metaphor and, as we will see, also adding some literal explanation to it. This is perhaps the only place in Buber's writings that provides us with a firm ground from which to reconstruct the *Wirbel* metaphor's meaning and inner workings. In this regard, the essay is key to our understanding of Buber's notion of ambivalence.[10]

Due to the centrality of "Images of Good and Evil" to our overall argument, a clarifying note is in order before moving on. This essay is generally considered part of Buber's biblical writings, and there is a justified tendency in Buberian scholarship to beware of relying on his biblical and Hassidic writings in reconstructing his dialogical philosophy. However, Buber himself certainly considered the essay part of his core dialogical writings. This is clear from the preface to the second volume of his main philosophical essays translated into Hebrew, where he presents "Images of Good and Evil" as the central text in which his dialogical philosophy is applied to the field of ethics.[11] Likewise, the centrality of "Images of Good and Evil" is quite apparent in Buber's writings after 1952 (the year "Images of Good and Evil" was published), in that when addressing the question of ethics, he constantly refers back to and even quotes from it.[12]

Somewhat confusingly, Buber's conception of ambivalence evinces not only a negative depiction but also a positive one. In some places, he describes the state of ambivalence not as harmful but as constructive. More specifically, he views ambivalence as a necessary precursor to all decisions and, as such, the seedbed of authentic human activity. It is, therefore, another goal of this chapter to resolve the seeming contradiction between ambivalence's positive and negative depictions. This will be done via existential-humanist psychologist James F. T. Bugental's distinction between sequential and simultaneous states of ambivalence.

The remainder of this chapter is organized as follows. In section 1, we reconstruct both Buber's negative and positive depictions of the state of ambivalence as they arise from his few and (mostly) brief discussions of it. Next, in section 2, Buber's metaphoric code is deciphered and correlated to our previous reconstruction. Finally, in section 3, the tension between the negative and positive depictions is resolved, providing further insight into Buber's conception of the state of ambivalence.

1. ENCOUNTERING THE SWIRLING CHAOS

As said, in "Images of Good and Evil," Buber depicts the state of ambivalence at some length and mostly in negative terms. A person in ambivalence is surrounded by a plentitude of optional courses of action and is tempted by, fantasizes on, and toys with them. One becomes "possessed by the play of the phantasy with potentialities, of plunging in this possession upon that which offers itself."[13] This state of fantasy, temptation, and desire becomes quickly unnerving if prolonged—if "the ebb that leads to familiar normality does not make its appearance." It becomes a revolving "vortex," a "dizzy whirl," a "swirling chaos." Anyone stuck in a prolonged state of the swirling chaos is "bowled over" and "overwhelmed" by the plentitude of potentialities and pulled in different directions by conflicting passions.[14]

Lingering in such a state, Buber says, is unbearable and can eventually lead the person into a pathological state of self-doubt or mania. The more we try to resolve such a state and the more we fail to, the greater our frustration and fear. Furthermore, prior unresolved moments of swirling chaos accumulate and affect future ones: they "do not remain in [one's] self-knowledge a series of isolated moments of non-decision... [but] merge into a course of indecision, as it were into a fixation in it."[15] We drag into the new moments our past failings and frustrations in dealing with them. We then narrate to ourselves a history of failures. Finally, we view it as part of our identity and develop a "fixation" over it. This is perhaps the deepest entrenchment in the state of the swirling chaos, from which one can escape only by extreme measures. Hence, the state of swirling chaos—or ambivalence, as I suggest calling it—is an escalatory process: the more one dwells in it, the more she becomes entrenched in it and the harder it is to exit from it.

Ia. Ambivalence and Destabilization

One should ask why a state of ambivalence is so destabilizing in Buber's aforementioned descriptions. Buber partially addresses this question through the notion of "confirmation" (*Bestätigung*).[16] As human beings, we are "incessantly enveloped by possibilities," the "category of possibility" being fundamental to us. We can choose and, through our choices, affect the course of our life for good or bad. Hence, we need continuous confirmation that our choices are right: "'Yes' must be spoken to [us], from the look of the confidant and from the stirrings of [our] own heart, to liberate [us] from the dread of abandonment." In most places where Buber discusses confirmation, he describes it as the need to be confirmed by another, and does not raise the option of self-confirmation. This is also the case in the secondary literature on Buber. However, as we have seen in the previous quote, the option of self-confirmation is also present in his writings. In fact, between the two, the latter is more essential: "At a pinch, one can do without confirmation from others if one's own reaches such a pitch that it no longer needs to be supplemented by the confirmation of others. But not vice versa: the encouragement of his fellow-men does not suffice if self-knowledge demands inner rejection, for self-knowledge is incontestably the more reliable."[17] The state of ambivalence is unnerving because it prevents one from confirming oneself, and ultimately one cannot live without confirmation.

Beyond the lack of confirmation, the dynamics of the swirling chaos harbor other elements of distress. Buber does not convey them explicitly, so in order to flesh them out let us determine the precise type of ambivalence to which Buber refers. Buber deals with a *pragmatic* ambivalence, that is, an inability to decide between various courses of action. It is not merely an affective ambivalence—a state of contradictory emotions—nor is it a mere intellectual ambivalence, a state of opposing ideas on a certain issue.[18] As these two latter cases involve no more than theoretical dilemmas, we can simply set them aside and carry on with life leaving the (emotional or intellectual) ambiguity unresolved.[19] However, in a pragmatic ambivalence, this is not an option. One can postpone a decision for a while, but in the end, the moment of decision will come knocking. Moreover, and more importantly, "carrying on" or "not deciding" are themselves resolutions. If in the midst of a state of ambivalence we decide to "do nothing," we are still making a decision. Leaving things as they are is a decision not to interfere in the course of reality. Procrastination is a decision.

As we have seen, Buber describes the swirling chaos as an escalatory process, and this is true of pragmatic ambivalence as well: the more we try to resolve a pragmatic dilemma and the more we fail to do so, the greater our frustration and fear. We ponder one option, but then move to others, and finally find ourselves pondering the first option again. We come to be frustrated by this interminable and futile process. Furthermore, the closer the final moment of decision the more anxious we become, and the realization that lingering is a continuous choice not to decide only deepens our frustration. Lastly, as we have seen, this exacerbating frustration is carried over into future states of ambivalence, progressively eroding our confidence.

Before moving on, note that Buber does not explain what is in fact so difficult in escaping the swirling chaos. Furthermore, if such an escape is truly a remarkable feat, how in the end does one actually accomplish it? We shall return to this question in section 3.

Ib. Negative and Positive Ambivalence

While the portrayal of the state of ambivalence in "Images of Good and Evil" is the clearest and most detailed in Buber's writings, it is nevertheless one-sided. Since the main subject of that essay is not ambivalence but the notion of evil, Buber discusses the former only to the extent that it serves to explain the latter. Accordingly, he portrays the state of ambivalence by and large in negative terms, as a psychologically destabilizing danger zone. Contrarily, elsewhere in his writings we find positive depictions of the state of ambivalence. Throughout his writings Buber stresses that, at a crossroads, uncertainty is a virtue. When faced with a moment of decision and unable to rely on preconceived knowledge, criteria, or rules of thumb; at such a moment, all preconceptions fail. In "Dialogue" (1929), for example, Buber stresses that in the moment of decision, "nothing that he believed he possessed as always available would help him, no knowledge and no technique, no system and no program; for now he would have to do with what cannot be classified, with concretion itself." Reason and deliberation, Buber claims, are insufficient for a person faced with a moment of decision. In a true moment of decision, one deals with "concretion itself," and concretion "cannot be classified."[20]

Hailing ambivalence and the futility of applying preconceived knowledge at moments of decision and deeming such an attempt as an escape from truly facing the abyss of ambivalence are recurring themes in Buber's writings. It is frequently referred to in *Daniel: Dialogues on Realization* (1913), which is where he terms the state of ambivalence (positively) as "holy insecurity." Buber deems the use of rationalization when faced with a decision an inauthentic act of "orientation," of escaping ambivalence.[21] Later, in "Symbolic and Sacramental Existence" (1935), Buber defines the uniqueness of the Hasidic *devotio* in that it can have no rules. Here too, when faced with a concrete situation and called on to respond to it, "the man of sacramental existence has no acquired rules and rhythms, no inherited methods of working avail, nothing 'known,' nothing 'learned'; he has to withstand ever again the unforeseen, unforeseeable moment."[22] For Buber, "it is precisely in stopping short, in letting [one]self be disconcerted, in deep knowledge of the impotence of all 'information,' of the incongruence of all possessed truth, in the 'holy insecurity,' that Hasidic piety has its true life."[23] In "On National Education" (1939), Buber diagnoses the disease of the generation as one of clinging to preconceived knowledge and solutions when facing a moment of decision.[24] Finally, in *Philosophical Interrogations* (1964), he defines his most basic standpoint as one that defies the reliance on criteria.[25] In fact, leaning on preconceived knowledge is a strategy to avoid concretion and the need to cope with ambivalence and thereby avoid a true decision. In other words, ambivalence is a necessary precursor of all true decisions and actions. This is why Buber at times extols the state of ambivalence, and why he coins for it such glorifying terms as "holy insecurity" and "narrow ridge."

Buber's negative and positive depictions of the state of ambivalence seem to contradict. In its negative depiction, ambivalence is a danger zone, which one should try to overcome and escape. While perhaps unavoidable, one should try to limit one's exposure to it as much as possible. In its positive depiction, ambivalence is where the agent who is about to make a decision enters and holds her ground. It is not where one is forced to enter and leaves in haste, but where one chooses to dwell and endure. We can rephrase this tension as a question: If the state of ambivalence is two-sided, how does one get on its "good" side? How does one handle it so it becomes not an accelerating downward spiral into destabilizing self-doubt but a foundation for decisions and actions? This, too, will be addressed in section 3.

II. BUBER'S METAPHORS OF AMBIVALENCE

As mentioned previously, Buber uses two sets of metaphors to refer to the state of ambivalence: "chaos" (*Chaos*) and "abyss" (*Abgrund*), on the one hand, and "vortex" or "whirlpool" (*Wirbel*), on the other. Through the former metaphors, I suggest, Buber conveys the disorientation and danger experienced in the state of ambivalence. Through these same metaphors, however, he also conveys the positive aspect of this state, as a pool of human potential and source of action. The origin of the abyss metaphor is the biblical *tehom*, which antedated all creation (Gen. 1:2). In many instances in Buber's writings, the term *abyss* alludes directly to this cosmogony: "When all 'directions' fail there arises in the darkness over the abyss the one true direction of man, towards the creative Spirit, towards the Spirit of God brooding on the face of the waters."[26] In many other instances, it alludes to others' rendering of that biblical creation myth. For example, in his early Hasidic writings Buber uses the abyss metaphor—in a manner typical of the fin de siècle critique of language (*Sprachkritik*) discourse—to denote ordinary language's inability to describe reality or express meaning.[27] Likewise, Buber alludes to Jakob Böhme's and Meister Eckhart's "abyss," which is the source of all being, the home of creativity, and the sphere where God and person merge.[28] Notwithstanding, the primary allusion of this metaphor is to Kierkegaard's *Dyb* or *Afgrund*, which denote the absence of any certain knowledge with which one can decide, and the anxiety that such lack of grounding evokes. However, and similar to Buber, the concept of abyss has a positive meaning as well. In Kierkegaard's case, it denotes not only danger and despair but also the place where one encounters God's forgiveness.[29]

These different facets of *abyss* highlight the various dynamics of the state of ambivalence. The danger of the bottomless pit parallels the psychological danger of ambivalence and the anxiety it evokes. The abyss metaphor also conveys the problem of escaping the state of ambivalence: once in the abyss, as it is bottomless, one cannot climb back up. Similarly, as we have seen, the more one dwells in the abyss of ambivalence, the more entrenched one becomes in it and the harder it becomes to escape. The groundlessness of the abyss also conveys a sense of disorientation, of having no foundational knowledge with which to decide: one has no sure ground to stand on. Finally, through the allusion to Kierkegaard and Böhme, Buber is able to convey the double-sidedness of ambivalence. As mentioned, Kierkegaard's abyss is not only a place of despair but also of divine forgiveness. Böhme's abyss denotes the source of all being, the pool of potentiality where God and person merge. These conceptualizations echo Buber's positive depiction of ambivalence as a source of great hope: only by descending into the abyss of ambivalence can one truly decide on a course of action.

Akin to abyss, chaos ($\chi\acute{\alpha}o\varsigma$) refers in Greek mythology to the primordial state of formlessness and disorder that preceded the ordered cosmos ($\kappa\acute{o}\sigma\mu o\varsigma$). Buber clearly often alludes to this cosmogonic myth, as well as concurrently alluding to the biblical one.[30] Through the metaphor of chaos, I suggest, Buber conveys the disorientation one feels in a state of ambivalence. This is evident from the way Buber translates the biblical term for chaos—*tohu va-vohu*—as "confusion and desolation."[31] It is also evident from the way Buber translates "olam-ha-tohu," the Kabbalist rendering of the biblical precreation chaos, as "world of confusion."[32] The state of ambivalence is chaotic because one does not control the potential courses of action that offer themselves but is rather controlled by them. As with *abyss*, however, Buber uses the term *chaos* to allude not only to the dangerous aspect of ambivalence but also to its positive role as the source of human creativity and action. The term *chaos* connotes "cosmos," the creation that proceeds from it.

Both "chaos" and "abyss" allude to myths of creation. While the latter metaphor is richer in content and allusions, Buber's juxtaposition of it with "chaos" sharpens the allusion specifically to the creational myths. According to Buber, chaos and abyss are more than just good metaphors for the state of ambivalence; they are, in fact, humans' projection of the psychological state of ambivalence onto the canvas of myth: "Human life as a specific entity, which has stepped forth from nature, begins with the experience of chaos as a condition perceived in the soul. Only through this experience and as its materialization could the concept of chaos, which is to be derived from no other empirical finding, arise and enter into the mythic cosmogonies."[33] Human beings externalize their internal state of ambivalence and project it on the cosmos by describing the world (in its origin) as chaotic. As such, chaos and abyss are not simple metaphors: they are not merely "borrowed" from the world of myth to describe a psychological state. Rather, they have been forged out of the very core of the human experience of ambivalence. They are thus paradigms, albeit mythical, of the state of ambivalence. Furthermore, God's creation of the world serves Buber as a mythical paradigm for human action. The upshot of this is that by linking humans' internal chaos to the myth of the primordial chaos, Buber is able to convey also the strong linkage between human ambivalence and human action: just as divine creation proceeds from chaos, so does true human action proceed from a state of ambivalence.

The third metaphor Buber uses to refer to the state of ambivalence is "whirlpool" or "vortex" (*Wirbel*), together with imagery of circular and centrifugal acceleration, such as "dizzy whirl" and "swirling chaos."[34] The metaphor and imagery are distinct from "abyss" and "chaos," as Buber does not borrow them from well-known myths or authors. As seen in this chapter's opening quote and elsewhere, this is Buber's preferred way of relating to the personal state of ambivalence he experienced in his youth.[35] Furthermore, Buber considers the metaphor of *Wirbel* to be so basic to the state of ambivalence that he rewrites it into the mythical paradigm of ambivalence by describing the biblical abyss and chaos as swirling, even though there is no textual justification for it. This set of metaphors also differs from the former in that it is one-sided: it does not denote any positive feature of the state of ambivalence.

In "Images of Good and Evil," Buber explains a partial element of this metaphor and says that what revolves around the person are not "things" but the possible courses of action "of joining and overcoming them."[36] Buber felt the need to clarify this point, due to a change of position he had through the years.[37] While he does not go any further in decoding this metaphor, this is enough to provide us with a firm ground from which to start. We hear a clear statement regarding this metaphor: it denotes a dizziness caused by being surrounded by revolving potential courses of action. The imagery of circular motion, I suggest, corresponds to several elements in the Buberian description of ambivalence. First, the circular motion conveys the sense of being surrounded from all directions by multiple potential courses of action and being overwhelmed by and submerged in them without being able to see beyond them. Second, the circular motion alludes to the nonfinite and impotent form of deliberation inherent to the state of ambivalence: one starts by toying with a potential course of action, leaves it, and moves on to the next, and then to the next, until one comes full circle and finds oneself faced once more with the first. This accounts for the interminableness of this situation and the resulting sense of frustration and dizziness. A whirlpool is characterized by its centrifugal acceleration and gravitational pull. These features correspond, I suggest, to two more characteristics pointed out previously. The first is its escalation: the more one is in a state of ambivalence, the more unnerving it becomes. The whirlpool's pull, moreover, parallels the growing difficulty of escaping ambivalence.

To conclude this section, we have seen that the metaphors Buber uses to refer to the state of ambivalence fit the various facets of our reconstruction of ambivalence in section 1. Regarding *abyss* and *chaos*, this elegant fit is due not to an accidental resemblance to ambivalence. Rather, the myths of the abyss and chaos were, according to Buber, originally forged as a projection of the human psychological state of ambivalence. Furthermore, analysis of these metaphors shows that they echo the double-sidedness of Buber's depiction of ambivalence. In the following section, we shall further explore this two-sidedness.

III. SEQUENTIAL AND SIMULTANEOUS AMBIVALENCE

We have two questions left open: Why is it so difficult to escape the state of ambivalence? And how can we resolve the tension between its negative and positive depictions? To answer these questions, let us examine more closely the positive depictions of ambivalence. In the following passage, Buber describes a decision-making process in which a dilemma arises: to what extent should one go forcibly against the grain of a given unjust situation, and to what extent should one be more pragmatic? Buber describes this state of ambivalence in positive terms:

> You stand before a political decision.... You are driven by the command of justice and, your heart stirred by it, you look into the depths of a situation, there from where the contradiction looks back at you. You make present to yourself, as strongly as you possibly can, all: once again and from the ground up, what you have already known and the new, what now presents itself to be known. You do not spare yourself, you let the cruel reality of both sides inflict itself on you without reducing it. You, theater of war and judge, let the battle be fought out unchecked. And now, in the midst of the struggle, rather, in the moment of an unforeseen standstill, something happens. I may not say: always, I say truly: again and again. It happens that you perceive with surprise, at times positively overpoweringly, what of truth and justice can be realized in this situation. You perceive, you have perceived how much must be given to life in order that life accept the justice. And in just this moment—not always, but again and again (that is your chance)—the forces of your soul, which even now were striving against one another, concentrate, they concentrate as into a crystal.[38]

Reading in this passage the positive portrayal of the state of ambivalence, we see a striking difference between it and the negative portrayals. Recall that in the latter Buber describes the ambivalent agent as trapped in a whirlpool of potential courses of action and unable to choose among them. Conversely, here the agent does not switch allegiances between the various options. Rather she lets the different opinions within her fight each other, letting "the battle be fought out unchecked." To clarify, it is not as if she is oblivious to the drama unfolding within her. On the contrary, she fully embraces its various aspects, despite the pain this entails: "You do not spare yourself, you let the cruel reality of both sides inflict itself on you without reducing it." Thus, rather than a revolving vortex, there is here a "sudden standstill," out of which a resolution suggests itself and enables one to become a unified whole, "a crystal."

This dynamic, of embracing simultaneously contradicting poles and a unification that results from it, is a prevalent theme in Buber's writings. Buber calls it "polarity," as famously described in *Daniel*:

> He takes the tension of the world upon himself so that it is lived by his soul as its own. He takes upon himself, say, the tension of spirit and matter, and the soul experiences world-wide its own freedom and its own bondage, its own spontaneity and its own being conditioned, its own bearing and its own being borne. It is no longer so that the one pole is present, the other only

known about, but in it there takes place simultaneously the full polarity in undiminished brilliance and strength.... Thus the world lives its duality from within: in the man who wills to create the unity. He creates it by bringing together in himself the tension that he has taken upon him: by awakening the I of this tension.[39]

The person described here in *Daniel* is not trying merely to solve a practical dilemma but to unify the world. He does so by interiorizing the world's polar dualities and living both simultaneously "in undiminished brilliance and strength." Through this embracing of the interiorized polarity, he unifies himself and consequentially the world. Setting aside the mystical content of this passage regarding a cosmic unification, ideas subsequently repudiated by Buber himself, we see a similar structure to that of the decision-making process described in the previous passage: a state of ambivalence that is negotiated not by *alternating* between contradictory elements but by embracing them all simultaneously and encompassing their polarity.[40] Furthermore, negotiating ambivalence in this manner results in self-unification. Thus, the positive depiction of the state of ambivalence differs from its negative counterpart in that one is not trying to escape it but is willing to live through and endure it. Moreover, one is not drawn alternately to the various choices but fully embraces them all, together with the tension and pain that such an embrace entails.

In order to better understand the dynamics of the state of ambivalence in its positive depiction and its relation to the negative, let us employ the important distinction made by James F. T. Bugental between sequential and simultaneous ambivalence: "In sequential ambivalence we experience first one and then the other of two conflicting intentions, but we do not feelingfully know both at the same time. While one is dominant in awareness, the other is perceived only abstractly or detachedly."[41] Engaging in a sequential ambivalence is frustrating, as it involves futile repetitions of clutching at one option, abandoning it, and seizing another. Bugental offers the example of a woman, Mable, who needs to decide between continuing her relationship with her husband, Greg, and terminating it for the sake of a relationship with Hal: "Thus Mable, for a time, when she was at home with Greg would be very aware of how rich her life was with him and would wonder that she could be tempted to overturn it with all the pain, guilt, and disruption of her own and his futures that would be involved. Then when she was with Hal or perhaps just away from Greg, she would be swept by anguish as she knew how vital was her feeling for Hal and her yearning for the different life she would have were she to go to him."[42] According to Bugental, when engaging in sequential ambivalence, one repeatedly suppresses and denies all other options but one and hence no real choice is ever made. In simultaneous ambivalence, on the other hand, "one confronts the conflict of intentions directly" and experiences them simultaneously and with "all of his feelingful awareness." Here there are no suppressions or denials, and the person needs to deal with the full effect of the existential anxiety of choice, which includes "fear, exasperation and great pain."[43]

Deciding between two contradictory options, especially when they are momentous, is harsh and traumatic because the deliberating agent fully realizes that they necessarily involve loss and, in Mable's case, a tragic one, no matter what she decides. Sequential ambivalence is a neurotic strategy through which she avoids truly facing this "dread of the existential anxiety of choice."[44] Deciding between options entails honest consideration of both, and in sequential ambivalence, the agent does not actually deliberate but yields each time anew to one while suppressing the other. This is why, according to Bugental, in order for one to overcome ambivalence and make a decision, one needs to shift from sequential to simultaneous ambivalence.

Bugental's distinction is illuminating in our context. First, his concepts of sequential and simultaneous ambivalence clearly mirror Buber's negative and positive depictions of ambivalence. Buber's swirling chaos is Bugental's sequential ambivalence. In both, there is constant rapid *movement* of the agent between the various options; in both, a decision is never reached, and the state of ambivalence is never resolved. Similar to the dynamics of the entrapped in the swirling chaos, Mable keeps clutching one option (Greg), rejecting it for another (Hal), and goes back to the first rejected option only to reject it again for the second. And Bugental too views this dynamic *pathologically* as a neurosis. Conversely, Bugental's simultaneous ambivalence mirrors Buber's positive depiction of ambivalence as a "standstill," where one stops alternating from one option to another and rather faces them all at once.[45] Similar to Buber's process of self-crystallization, Bugental too views simultaneous ambivalence as a transformational moment. And Bugental too views such a standstill positively, not as neurotic, but as *existential* ambivalence.

Second, the comparison with Bugental's sequential and simultaneous ambivalence helps sharpen a crucial difference between Buber's negative and positive depictions of ambivalence. In the case of Mable, it is not that she first *chooses* Hal over Greg and goes over to his apartment and then chooses Greg over Hal and comes home. Rather, she shifts between them undecidedly. She meets Hal and comes home to Greg without truly deciding on each of these actions. Rather than truly deciding, she drifts with the options that the world or her momentary passions press on her.[46] When she *finds* herself at home with

Greg, she would then feel the richness of her life with him. Likewise, when she finds herself with Hal, she would be "swept away by anguish." The sequential attending of each option is brought on the *passive* Mable by her sweeping passions.[47] The same is true of Buber's person entrapped in the swirling chaos. It is not only that she entertains only one option at a time. While entertaining that one option, she is not truly considering it. Rather, she lets her passion sweep her toward *savoring* it. To recall, the whirlpool starts as a moment of temptation and fantasy, as a "surge of... enticements," of "[all-encompassing] temptation," of "[all-encompassing] passion."[48] If it continues for long, the swirling chaos becomes unbearable, but its character as passion remains: it is a state of "undirected surging passion," in which to ponder over an option means to "clutch at [it] ... and cast one's passion upon it."[49]

Third, Bugental's distinction now clarifies both why, according to Buber, it is so difficult to exit the swirling chaos and how one ultimately achieves such a difficult feat. It is difficult, because one finds herself in a swirling chaos *exactly because* one shies away from deciding. Hence, one needs first to come to terms with the tragedy and loss involved in making the decision and face the existential anxiety and dread involved. In Bugental's terms, in order to make a decision, one needs first to transform sequential into simultaneous ambivalence; in Buber's, one needs to transform the swirling chaos into a standstill, a polarity. According to both, this involves fully embracing all options simultaneously.

In conclusion, let us resolve the tension between Buber's seemingly conflicting depictions of ambivalence by setting them in the wider context of Buber's anthropology. The positive and negative depictions do not refer to the *same experience*. They refer to two different experiences, each arising from different strategies of coping with the *same fact* of the human condition: the openness to possibilities and the freedom and responsibility to choose from them. According to Buber, a defining feature of the human condition is that our existence is not limited to facticity, to what already is. The human sphere of existence is one in which the potential borders on and envelops the factual. Through our ability to imagine, we are exposed to the potentiality of our acts, to optional worlds that are yet to be determined.[50] This exposure, however, reveals the inescapable facts of choice, of the possibility of making mistakes, and one's sole responsibility for them, all of which necessitate confirmation, as discussed previously. A person finds herself entrapped in a revolving vortex when trying to escape from this human predicament, of facing the potential and the inescapabilty of choice and loss. Escaping from agentic responsibility, the passions kick in and sweep the person to various and changing options. On the other hand, a person who truly embraces these predicaments and attempts to choose, while putting all preconceived criteria and information aside, will experience the "polarity" of the moment. He may even experience, "again and again," the transformational process of self-crystallization.

NOTES

This article is dedicated to the memory of my dear student, Tal Bahat, who in life and death courageously championed the dynamics of ambivalence. I thank Dustin Atlas, Karma Ben-Jochanan, Zachary Braiterman, Menachem Fisch, Daniel Herskowitz, Ron Margolin, Benjamin Pollock, and Sarah Scott for reading and commenting on various versions of this article. In addition, I thank the School of Philosophy at Tel Aviv University, Rosenzweig Center at the Hebrew University, Dialogik Foundation, Fulbright Foundation, Center for Jewish Studies at Harvard University, and Department of Literature, Language and the Arts at the Open University of Israel for the support during the years in which this article was written.

1. Martin Buber, "My Way to Hasidism" (1917), in *Hasidism and Modern Man*, ed. and trans. Maurice Friedman (New York: Horizon Press, 1958), 56.

2. On this time period for Buber, see Maurice Friedman, *Martin Buber's Life and Work: The Early Years, 1878–1923* (New York: E. P. Dutton, 1981), 3–4, 15–25; Grete Schaeder, "Martin Buber: A Biographical Sketch," in *The Letters of Martin Buber: A Life of Dialogue*, ed. Nahum N. Glatzer and Paul Mendes-Flohr, trans. Richard Winston, Clara Winston, and Harry Zohn (New York: Schocken, 1991), 7; and Gilya Gerda Schmidt, *Martin Buber's Formative Years: From German Culture to Jewish Renewal, 1897–1909* (London: University of Alabama Press, 1995), 5–11.

3. Buber's three addresses were "Judaism and the Jews," "Judaism and Mankind," and "Renewal of Judaism," all in *On Judaism*, ed. Nahum N. Glatzer (New York: Schocken, 1967). On the three addresses, see Zohar Maor, *A New Secret Doctrine: Spirituality, Creativity, and Nationalism in the Prague Circle* (Jerusalem: Zalman Shazar, 2012), 101–53 (Hebrew); Friedman, *Early Years*, 124–47; and Scott Spector, *Prague Territories: National Conflict and Cultural Innovation in Franz Kafka's Fin de Siècle* (Berkeley: University of California Press, 2000), 147–51. On the impact of these lectures on German-speaking Jewish youth, see Friedman, *Martin Buber's Life and Work*, 145–47; and Hannah Arendt, "A Guide for Youth: Martin Buber," in *The Jewish Writings*, ed. Jerome Kahn and Ron H. Feldman (New York: Schocken, 2007).

4. Buber, "Judaism and the Jews," 18–19; "Judaism and Mankind," 23–29; and "Renewal of Judaism," 42–43. This notion is repeated in other essays from that time period: "He and We" (1910), in *The First Buber: Youthful Zionist Writings of Martin Buber*, ed. and trans. Gilya G. Schmidt (Syracuse, NY: Syracuse

University Press, 1999), 168–70; and "Jewish Religiosity" (1915), in *On Judaism*, 81–83. On the notion of self-disintegration in the dialogical phases of Buber's thought and its relation to ambivalence, see chapters 4 and 5 in my forthcoming book, *The Act of Love*.

5. As far as I know, there is no secondary literature analyzing the state of ambivalence in Buber's writings. Friedman often uses the expression "holy insecurity" to describe that state and discusses the meaning of that term in several places. See, for example, Maurice Friedman's translator's introduction, in Martin Buber, *Daniel: Dialogues on Realization*, trans. Maurice Friedman (New York: Holt, Rinehart and Winston, 1964), 25–34. However, these discussions hardly explain the notion of holy insecurity beyond recapitulating Buber's own words. Avraham Shapira presents the centrality of the concept of *Wirbel* and highlights some of its various functions in Buber's writings over the years; see Avraham Shapira, *Hope for Our Time: Key Trends in the Thought of Martin Buber* (New York: SUNY Press, 1999), especially chapter eight. Finally, Andrea Poma discusses Buber's description of the chaotic in light of postmodern sensitivities; see Andrea Poma, "Unity of the Heart and Scattered Self: A Postmodern Reading of Buber's Doctrine of Evil," in *New Perspectives on Martin Buber*, ed. Michael Zank (Tübingen, Germany: Mohr Siebeck, 2006), 165–74.

6. Contrary to common perception, Buber rarely uses these two coinages. "Holy insecurity" appears in *Daniel*, 95–99; "Symbolic and Sacramental Existence" (1935), in *The Origin and Meaning of Hasidism*, ed. and trans. Maurice Friedman (New York: Horizon, 1960), 179; and "Interrogation of Martin Buber," conducted by M. S. Friedman, in *Philosophic Interrogations*, ed. S. and B. Rome (New York: Holt, Rinehart and Winston, 1964), 58. The "narrow ridge" appears in "What Is Man?" (1938), in *Between Man and Man*, trans. Ronald Gregor-Smith (London: Routledge, 2002), 218–19. Other instances of "narrow ridge," albeit without clear allusion to the state of ambivalence, may be found in "What Is Man?" 243, and "The Question to the Single One" (1936), in *Between Man and Man*, 64.

7. See Ernst Simon, "Martin Buber, the Educator," in *The Philosophy of Martin Buber*, ed. Paul A. Schlipp and Maurice Friedman (La Salle, IL: Open Court, 1991), 571–76. In Buber's writings this expression appears in "Comments on the Idea of Community" (1931), in *A Believing Humanism: Gleanings*, trans. Maurice Friedman (New York: Simon and Schuster, 1967), 88 (and also in the reprint of this text in *Paths in Utopia* [Boston: Beacon Press, 1958], 134); "Society and the State" (1951), in *Pointing the Way: Collected Essays*, trans. Maurice S. Friedman (New York: Harper and Brothers, 1957), 175; "The Validity and Limitation of the Political Principle" (1953), in *Pointing the Way*, 217; and "Replies to My Critics" (1961), in *Philosophy of Martin Buber*, 722. Only in the last source does Buber refer to the line of demarcation as a conceptual term of his thought, by way of positive reaction to Ernst Simon's usage.

8. Instances in Buber's writing where "chaos" serves as a metaphor for the state of ambivalence may be found in "The Life of Hasidim" (1908), in *Hasidism and Modern Man*, 84–85; *Ecstatic Confessions* (San Francisco: Harper and Row, 1985), 1–2; *Daniel*, 56–57, 78, 134, 142; "Herut: On Youth and Religion" (1919), in *On Judaism*, 168; "The Holy Way" (1919), in *On Judaism*, 138; "Religion as Presence" (1922), in *Buber's Way to "I and Thou": The Development of Martin Buber's Thought and His "Religion as Presence" Lectures*, by Rivka Horwitz (Philadelphia: Jewish Publication Society, 1988), 90; "Dialogue" (1930) in *Between Man and Man*, 45; "What Is Man?" 172, 234; "Guilt and Guilt Feelings," in *The Knowledge of Man: Selected Essays*, trans. Maurice Friedman (New York: Harper and Row, 1965), 140; "Distance and Relation" (1950), in *Knowledge of Man*, 71; "Healing through Meeting" (1950), in *Believing Humanism*, 140; "Images of Good and Evil," in *Good and Evil: Two Interpretations* (New York: Charles Scribner's Sons, 1953), 125–26; and "Interrogation of Martin Buber," 17.

Instances in Buber's writing where *abyss* serves as a metaphor for ambivalence include "Life of the Hasidim," 106; *Ecstatic Confessions*, 2, 6; *Daniel*, 86–99; "Jewish Religiosity," 82; "My Way to Hasidism," 67; "Holy Way," 114, 137; *I and Thou*, trans. Ronald Gregor Smith (Edinburgh: T&T Clark, 1937), 52, 70; "Education" (1926), in *Between Man and Man*, 121–22; "What Is Man?" 173; "Healing through Meeting," 139–40; "Religion and Modern Thinking" (1952), in *Eclipse of God: Studies in the Relation between Religion and Philosophy* (New York: Harper and Row, 1952), 73; and *Meetings: Autobiographical Fragments* (New York: Routledge, 1967), 34.

The *Wirbel* metaphor is used almost exclusively to describe states of ambivalence. See *Ecstatic Confessions*, 1–2; "The Teaching of the Tao" (1910), in *Pointing the Way*, 34; *Daniel*, 56–57; "Brother Body" (1914), in *Pointing the Way*, 21–22; "My Way to Hasidism," 56; "Religion as Presence," 90; *I and Thou*, 56; "Education," 121; "The Faith of Judaism" (1929), in *Israel and the World: Essays in a Time of Crisis* (New York: Schocken, 1948), 18; "Spinoza, Sabbatai Zvi, and the Baal-Shem" (1935), in *The Origin and Meaning of Hasidism*, 102–3; "The Question to the Single One," 92; *Two Types of Faith: A Study of the Interpretation of Judaism and Christianity*, trans. Norman P. Goldhawk (New York: Macmillan, 1951), 63; "Images of Good and Evil," 89, 92–93, 126–28; and *Meetings: Autobiographical Fragments*, 34.

9. This is the common way in which Buber introduces concepts in many of his early writings. In this regard, see Gustav Landauer's response to Buber's drafts of the book *Daniel*:

> But I feel somewhat like a student who has unfortunately missed the early classes and who gathers from the definite tone that these are established terms which cannot be amended; but he has no experience with them or examples of them and yet is supposed to keep up and build on the basis

of this. This is one of the idiosyncrasies of your mentality to which I've called attention so often before. You work something out inside yourself until it has a certain roundedness and completeness, and then you do not communicate the route by which you reached your results.

See Buber, *Letters of Martin Buber*, 137.

10. A second important text in which Buber discusses the state of ambivalence is his 1913 *Daniel*, 88–93, 95–99. However, the notion of ambivalence in these pages is presented idiosyncratically, reflecting Buber's still premature and vague conception thereof.

11. See Martin Buber, author's preface to *Penei Adam* (Jerusalem: Bialik, 2012).

12. See, for example, Buber, "Guilt and Guilt Feelings," 136; "Replies to My Critics," 720–21; and "Interrogation of Martin Buber," 105, 111–14.

13. Buber, "Images of Good and Evil," 134. In *I and Thou*, we find another vivid description of the preliminary state of ambivalence caused by the plentitude of options: "The fiery stuff of all my ability to will seethes tremendously, all that I might do circles around me, still without actuality in the world, flung together and seemingly inseparable, alluring glimpses of powers flicker from all the uttermost bounds: the universe is my temptation" (Buber, *I and Thou*, 51–52).

14. Buber, "Images of Good and Evil," 125–27. See also Buber, *Ecstatic Confessions*, 1, and Buber, "Herut," 150.

15. Buber, "Images of Good and Evil," 134.

16. The concept of confirmation (*Bestätigung*) is central to Buber's late writings, particularly "Distance and Relation," 67–68, 71; "Guilt and Guilt Feelings," 134; "Dialogue between Martin Buber and Carl R. Rogers" (1957), in *The Knowledge of Man*, 181–82; and "The Unconscious" (1957), in *The Knowledge of Man*, 242–43. On the notion of confirmation in Buber's writings in general, see Maurice Friedman's introduction to *The Knowledge of Man*, 11–16; Laurence J. Silberstein, *Martin Buber's Social and Religious Thought: Alienation and the Quest for Meaning* (New York: New York University Press, 1989), 147–49, 159–60; and Kenneth Anderson and Rob Cissna, *Moments of Meeting: Buber, Rogers, and the Potential for Public Dialogue* (New York: State University of New York Press, 2002), 54–56, 88–89, 149–52.

17. Buber, "Images of Good and Evil," 135–36. See also Buber, "Guilt and Guilt Feelings," 134.

18. This tripartite division is a reworking of Eugen Bleuler; see Eugen Bleuler, *Dementia Praecox or the Group of Schizophrenias* (New York: International Universities Press, 1950), 374. Bleuler employed it in his analysis of schizophrenia, but here I use it more loosely. I have also changed the name of the first kind of ambivalence to "pragmatic" rather than the original "volitional," given the fact that Bleuler was concerned only with internal psychological states,

while I am employing his tripartite division to describe the broad sphere of human activity.

19. In his early writings, especially *Daniel*, Buber's notion of ambivalence denotes not only pragmatic but also theoretical ambivalence. At that time, Buber was under the influence of aesthetic enthusiasm, which made him view the world as much more chaotic than in his subsequent writings. Buber thought one could actually let go of Kantian categories and perceive the world as chaotic. Hence, he felt a more urgent need to resolve theoretical ambivalences in order to survive the world's chaos.

20. Buber, "Dialogue," 19.

21. Buber, *Daniel*, 88–99.

22. Buber, "Symbolic and Sacramental Existence," 171.

23. Ibid., 179.

24. Buber, "On National Education," 163. Likewise, Buber discusses how to find the middle path between the individual and the in-group's need for self-assertion, on the one hand, and the others' right for self-assertion, on the other hand. He emphasizes the inability in such a case to rely on fixed criteria for demarcating the line between them. See Martin Buber, "Nationalism" (1921), in *Israel and the World*, 216.

25. Buber, "Interrogation of Martin Buber," 58. Relatedly, in the 1950s, both in "Healing through Meeting" and in "Guilt and Guilt Feelings" Buber asserts the psychologist's need to transcend all methods and tools of trade in order to properly address the abyss of the patient. See, for example, "Guilt and Guilt Feelings," 131.

26. Buber, "Education," 121–22. The expression "the Spirit of God brooding on the face of the waters" refers to Genesis 1:2. See also Buber, "Faith of Judaism," 20, 27.

27. For Buber's involvement in the *Sprachkritik* discourse, see Martina Urban, *Aesthetics of Renewal: Martin Buber's Early Representation of Hasidism as Kulturkritik* (Chicago: University of Chicago Press, 2008), 76–93; Paul Mendes-Flohr, "Buber's Rhetoric," in *Martin Buber: A Contemporary Perspective*, ed. Paul Mendes-Flohr (Syracuse, NY: Syracuse University Press, 2002), 10–15; and Asher Biemann, "Einleitung," in Martin Buber, *Martin Buber Werkausgabe 6*, ed. Paul Mendes-Flohr and Peter Schäfer with Martina Urban (Berliner Akademie der Wissenschaften / Israel Academy of Sciences and Humanities, 2003), 9–68. For this use of *abyss* in Buber's writings see, for example, "The Life of the Hasidim," 106; *Ecstatic Confessions*, 6; "The Spirit of the Orient and Judaism" (1915), in *On Judaism*, 68; and "Interrogation of Martin Buber," 17.

28. Buber wrote his dissertation on Jakob Böhme (and Nicholas of Cusa). On the "abyss" in Buber and Böhme, see Urban, *Aesthetics of Renewal*, 77–78, and Sarah Scott, "The Ethics of Perception: Martin Buber's Study of Nicholas

of Cusa, Jakob Böhme, Art and Aesthetics" (PhD diss., New School for Social Research, 2011), 67–68. As both Urban and Scott point out, there are striking similarities between Böhme's "abyss" and the Kabbalistic *Ein-Sof*. Certainly in his Hasidic writings, and perhaps also in others, Buber alludes concurrently to the latter as well. However, the origin of this meaning of "abyss" is in Meister Eckhart's writings, in which Buber was also fluent from very early on (see his testimony in "What Is Man?" 219). Furthermore, throughout his writings, Buber often refers to Eckhart but hardly to Böhme. On Eckhart and the "mysticism of the ground," see Bernard McGinn, *The Mystical Thought of Meister Eckhart: The Man from Whom God Hid Nothing* (New York: Crossroad, 2001), 35–52. For further discussion regarding the concepts of *Wirbel* and *Abgrund*, in the context of Buber's Bible translation, see Ghilad Shenhav, "Between Abgrund and Urwirbel: The Story of One Word in the Buber-Rosenzweig Bible Translation," *Naharaim* 14, no. 1 (2020): 83–102.

29. Simon D. Podmore, *Kierkegaard and the Self before God: Anatomy of the Abyss* (Bloomington: Indiana University Press, 2011), chap. 4. On Buber's link to Kierkegaard, see Helmut Kuhn, "Dialogue in Expectation," in Schlipp and Friedman, *The Philosophy of Martin Buber*, 647–48. On the meaning of "abyss" in Kierkegaard's writings, see Podmore, *Kierkegaard and the Self before God*, 1–9.

On the anxiety produced by lack of grounding, see Buber, "What Is Man?" 173: "No dialectical guarantee keeps man from falling; it lies with himself to lift his foot and take the step which leads him away from the abyss. The strength to take this step cannot come from any security in regard to the future, but only from those depths of insecurity in which man, overshadowed by despair, answers with his decision the question about man's being." See also *Daniel*, 86–99; "Jewish Religiosity," 82; "My Way to Hasidism," 67; "Herut," 159; "Holy Way," 114, 137; "Healing through Meeting," 139–40; "Right and Wrong" (1952), in *Good and Evil*, 60; and "Religion and Modern Thinking," 73.

30. In some places the allusion to the Greek cosmogonic myth is explicit, for example, *Daniel*, 55, and "Education," 110. In other places it is implicit in Buber's use of the contrasting terms *chaos* and *cosmos*, for example, "The Question to the Single One," 87; "What Is Man?" 234; "Images of Good and Evil," 129; and "Guilt and Guilt Feelings," 140. On its allusion to the biblical myth, see, for example, "Myth in Judaism," in *On Judaism*, 102, and "Images of Good and Evil," 126.

31. Buber, "Images of Good and Evil," 126. In the German original, Buber translates *tohu va-vohu* as "Irrsal und Wirrsal." See "Bilder von Gut und Böse," in *Martin Buber Werkausgabe 10*, ed. Paul Mendes-Flohr and Peter Schäfer with Judith Buber Agassi (Berliner Akademie der Wissenschaften / Israel Academy of Sciences and Humanities, 2008), 61. The same appears in Buber and Rosenzweig's translation of the Bible. See Genesis (1:2) in *Die Schrift*, trans. Martin Buber with Franz Rosenzweig (Deutsche Bibelgesellschaft, 1992).

32. Buber, "My Way to Hasidism," 56.

33. Buber, "Images of Good and Evil," 125. In "The Life of Hasidim," we also find the identification of primordial chaos with human ambivalence: "God governs men as He governed chaos at the time of the infancy of the world. And as when the world began to unfold and He saw that if it flowed further asunder it would no longer be able to return home to its roots, then he spoke, 'Enough!'—so it is that when the soul of man in its suffering rushes headlong, without direction, and evil becomes so mighty in it that it soon could no longer return home, then His compassion awakens, and he says, 'Enough!'" See Buber, "Life of Hasidim," 84–85.

34. Buber, "Images of Good and Evil," 126.

35. See, for example, Buber, *Meetings: Autobiographical Fragments*, 34.

36. Buber, "Images of Good and Evil," 126.

37. In his early writings, Buber does hold that the objects themselves revolve in the vortex; see, for example, Buber, *Ecstatic Confessions*, 1. This is in line with a more general tendency in his later writings to accept the facticity of the world, and so to downplay the idealistic conception prevalent in his early writings of one's control over the constitution of exterior realities.

38. Buber, "Replies to My Critics," 722–23.

39. Buber, *Daniel*, 141–42. On polarity in Buber's thought, see Maurice Friedman, translator's introduction to *Daniel*, 15–20; Shapira, *Hope for This Hour*, 23–29; and Phil Huston, *Martin Buber's Journey to Presence* (New York: Fordham University Press, 2007), 152–62, 174–75.

40. On the repudiation of a cosmic unity, see, for example, Buber, *I and Thou*, 85–88.

41. James F. T. Bugental, "Intentionality and Ambivalence," in *William James: Unfinished Business*, ed. Robert B. MacLeod (Washington, DC: American Psychological Association, 1969), 94.

42. Ibid.

43. Ibid., 95.

44. Ibid., 95.

45. Buber, "Replies to My Critics," 723.

46. On the category of drifting, see Edna Ullmann-Margalit, "Big Decisions: Opting, Converting, Drifting," in *Political Philosophy*, ed. Anthony O'Hear (Cambridge: Cambridge University Press, 2006), 157–72. As in our case, the drifter is not fully aware of her in fact trying escape from making a decision.

47. Bugental, "Intentionality and Ambivalence," 95.

48. Buber, "Images of Good and Evil," 126–28.

49. Ibid., 139, 127.

50. Ibid., 91–93, 125, 135; Buber, "Distance and Relation," 71.

NINE

THE ELOQUENT MUTENESS OF CREATURES

Affect and Animals in Martin Buber's Dialogical Writings

DUSTIN ATLAS

IN *THE OTHER MARTIN BUBER*, a work of recollections seemingly selected to paint an unflattering portrait, we nonetheless find the following depiction of Buber's office by Schalom Ben-Chorin: "There were cats in the room and Buber would speak to them. In the summer the window was open and the cats would jump in and out. Once a cat jumped in and Buber asked it, 'Where did you come from, I haven't seen you for quite a while.' I felt as if the cats understood what Buber said to them."[1] Martin Buber spoke with animals, and his philosophical and religious writings (if we may so divide them) reflect this fact. This is part of a larger tendency: at key points in his work, we find phenomenological "vignettes," where major claims are supported by philosophical stories about encounters with nonhumans. Several of these, such as his confrontation with a tree, are repeated throughout his oeuvre, changing depending on the argument they are positioned within. Some, like an encounter with a cat in *I and Thou* (1923), occur only once but as part of a central argument. If these were mere examples, the literary exorbitance of a Viennese aesthete, they would be of little interest. But, as Hugo Bergmann noted with some exasperation, this is not the case: "[It] is certainly the most difficult but fundamental fact of Buber's theory—that the I-Thou relationship exists between people and objects of any kind. It comes about at the moment the object—be it a cat, a horse, or tree—becomes a Thou." As Bergmann reads Buber, "there is no reason why the thing I get to know need be human; it can be an animal, a plant or a stone."[2] This claim is overly simplistic—Buber holds that different types of objects are encountered differently, that my encounter with a cat is not the same as my encounter with a stone. But Bergmann nonetheless gets at something important: Buber does not merely allow for the *possibility* of encountering a nonhuman animal but goes further, claiming that there are some things we learn *only* in nonhuman encounters. Specifically, and of interest for this chapter, Buber claims that there are fundamental affects and emotions that open up only when we talk with animals: such as forms of anxiety and melancholy that express basic structures of our relationships.[3]

However, despite their stated importance, Buber's philosophical articulation of nonhuman encounters is frustratingly underdeveloped. This chapter hopes to partly change that, by focusing somewhat narrowly on Buber's dialogical work and asking how it is possible to talk with animals and what we learn when we do. I suggest that one way to make sense of Buber's animal vignettes, and the claims he makes about them, is to extrapolate and augment his writing with affect theory. Affect theory—itself concerned with the movement and circulation of affects and feelings—is well placed to help us understand relationships that are dialogical but occur without language.[4] An affect-driven inquiry into these animal relations not only fleshes out Buber's dialogical thought but also helps position it within a larger discussion of the limits of humanism, language, and rational autonomy, a discussion to which his work (and religious studies, in general) still has much to contribute. While interpreters have tended to pass over this aspect of his work in embarrassed silence, understanding how and why Buber thinks we can speak to animals both broadens the reach of his dialogical works and helps us understand the centrality of nondiscursive feelings (specifically anxiety, but also melancholy) in them. These feelings, opened up when we talk to animals, are not mere illustrations or accompaniments to dialogue but express dialogical structures that hold even in the absence of language.

This chapter begins with a brief foray into the question of whether it is reasonable, or useful, to use affect theory to understand Buber. It then engages in a reading of a passage in *I and Thou* (the three "spheres" of relation) to understand the human/animal distinctions Buber begins with and the role of language in marking this difference. This is followed by an articulation of the elements of affect theory that I believe will help us make sense of human/animal dialogue. Human/animal dialogue takes place against the backdrop of nature (as it functions in Buber's work); what Buber means by "nature" is elucidated through a reading of *Daniel: Dialogues on Realization* (1913), which also gives us an opportunity to explore some of Buber's earlier forays into affect-thinking. Finally, after noting the ways in which the older Buber complicates this youthful romantic vision of nature, I end with a close reading of the section of *I and Thou* where Buber talks to a cat. In this section, the apparatus constructed by the rest of the paper is put to the test, and the adequacy, or inadequacy, of an affect-reading becomes apparent.

Throughout each of these sections, the goal remains the same: to see how thinking about affect can help us understand Buber's animal dialogues. However, the chapter's focus is not affects in general but two key affects: anxiety and melancholy (as Buber defines them). Buber claims these key affects are discovered in animal dialogue—in his case, talking to cats. Thus, when I say that the goal is to understand human/animal dialogue, I do not mean only "how is it possible for Buber to say we can dialogue with animals" (although I hope to do that, as well). The goal is *also* to understand what specific affects Buber discovered in his animal dialogues and what they tell us about the structure of dialogue in general.

I. WITH WHAT RIGHT?

It is fair to ask, With what right do I use affect theory to read Buber?[5] One answer comes from *The Philosophy of Martin Buber*, where Buber's contemporaries interpreted and critiqued his work and he was invited to respond. Many asked him to define himself: is he "a philosopher or a theologian or something else?"[6] Buber rejected all these categories, calling himself an "atypical" man looking to express his "decisive experiences." While these experiences were irreducible and singular, he felt that their transmission should be general and, in theory, able to reach anyone. For this reason, he claimed his *"communication* had to be philosophical ... to relate the unique and particular to the 'general' ... to express what is *by its nature incomprehensible* in concepts that could be used and communicated."[7] This goal (expressing unique encounters in general language) not only allows but also requires continual philosophical elaboration, because the "general" is constantly shifting and expanding as systems of thought transform. Further, theoretical elaboration or transposition has to continually self-correct to ensure it does not crush the incomprehensible element of the experience that provides the occasion for elaboration.

This dance between theoretical extrapolation and the singularity of the experience being extrapolated led Buber to suggest "it is incumbent upon [philosophical elaboration] to *logicize the superlogical*, for which the law of contradiction does not hold valid."[8] Philosophical elaboration should aim for consistency (or "logicize") in order to help transmit ideas and experiences but must not "sacrifice" or distort for the sake of this consistency.[9] This puts us in an odd position: when we elaborate ideas and experiences that seem to contradict basic philosophical principles (such as the law of noncontradiction), we are asked to engage in the paradoxical practice of "logiciz[ing] the superlogical" sooner than violate the experience.[10] I suggest that affect theory, with its careful consideration of the contradictions and tensions involved in feeling, can help us do exactly this: philosophically elaborate Buber's animal encounters without imposing false consistency.

Finally, Buber's character and tone make him a ready fit for this approach. I have been told on several occasions that he is too "touchy-feely" or overly sensitive for a philosopher.[11] While this was meant as an insult, I consider it a strength: Buber's sensitivities allowed him insight into regions many conventional philosophers ignored and make him an ideal candidate for a conversation with affect theory.

II. HUMAN/ANIMAL DISTINCTIONS

Despite the openness to nonhumans suggested by his encounters with wild Jerusalem cats, in his philosophical vignettes Buber generally follows what he takes to be a Hasidic example, stressing encounters with *domesticated* animals, implying a relation of subservience (however disavowed).[12] Similarly, while punctuated by encounters with nonhumans, Buber's work has an unabashedly anthropological focus, one that sometimes bleeds into anthropocentrism with sometimes frustrating results.[13] Indeed, Buber postulates—but does not argue for, let alone demonstrate—a categorical distinction between human and nonhuman animals.[14] This paper will neither seek to explain nor to excuse the troubling ways Buber carves up the human/animal difference except where it relates to dialogue. And where dialogue is concerned the problem is not nearly so complicated as an undemonstrated metaphysical distinction or as troubling as a relation of domesticity. The problem with animal dialogue is simple: animals do not talk.

It is a simple problem but a big one for a philosophy where dialogue is a central relationship. Arguably, the point of Buber's dialogical philosophy is that when we talk *to* someone we are in a very different relationship than when we talk *about* them and, further, that this second-person relationship is too-often obscured. "Dialogue," "speaking to," "living speech," or the famous "I-You" relation: these are all terms Buber uses to argue that the second-person standpoint reveals things of philosophical importance that are missed by a third-person position.[15] Simply put: when I "talk about" someone in the second-person, they appear "over-there," like an object, composed of particulars (the infamous "I-It"); when I "talk to" someone in the second-person, they are present with me (the famous "I-You").[16] This is not merely an epistemological claim—that the third-person misses things—there is a therapeutic and religious element, as well. As is well known, Buber claims that the *types* of relationship we establish with other things and other people transform not only how things *appear* but also who we are.

One can read much of Buber's work as a series of attempts to resist unthinking lapses into the third person and capture the insights of the second person. Buber was preoccupied with the shortcomings of the third-person position and sought to overcome these with a number of tactics, running the gamut from indexing (pointing), through philosophical vignettes and phenomenological exercises, to philosophical argument. *I and Thou*, the text we are most concerned with here, presents his most famous attempt: recasting our most important relationships as forms of dialogue.[17] And when it comes to relationships between humans, this tactic is remarkably successful. After all, speaking to another human is a commonplace occurrence and a good ground for understanding our larger relationship. Things get more complicated when we interact with nonhumans, of which animals are a privileged class. It is difficult to see how far we can get with casting our relationship with nonhuman, nonspeaking beings, as dialogue. And yet if the second-person stance, or dialogue, is an essential type of relationship, then a world where we cannot dialogue with animals and other things is impoverished and narrow.

Buber is aware of this difficulty and so carves up the dialogical situation into three "spheres" of relation to differentiate between the various difficulties that dialogue entails.[18] Here a long passage is helpful to understand what is at stake in viewing different relationships as dialogue and how we can position animals within this broader picture.[19] There are three spheres in which relation can occur:

> The first: life with nature. Here the relation vibrates in the dark and remains below language. The creatures stir across from us, but they are unable to come to us, and the You we say to them sticks to the threshold of language.
>
> The second: life with men. Here the relation is manifest and enters language. We can give and receive the You.
>
> The third: life with spiritual beings. Here the relation is wrapped in a cloud but reveals itself, it lacks but creates language. We hear no You and yet feel addressed; we answer—creating, thinking, acting: with our being we speak the basic word, unable to say You with our mouth.[20]

As humans, we begin in the middle, the interhuman world (sphere 2), the world where dialogue is, if not effortless, at least explicable, because most everyone you meet in this sphere is capable of talking (even if you do not understand their language). This interhuman world is constituted by language but is also delineated by language: it has edges, and the edges are the places where you try to talk to, or dialogue with, nonhumans. If we peer over one edge of the interhuman world, we find "nature": plants, animals (the concern of this paper), and other objects (sphere 1). If we move to the other side (sphere 3), we find religious and cultural objects. In other words, if we go to either edge of the anthroposphere and engage nonhumans (creatures or works of art), we are ejected from sphere 2. And in these other spheres, we run into problems for the very simple reason that we are opening a dialogue with beings that do not, strictly speaking, speak. Thus, despite being on opposite sides of the anthroposphere (2), there is a hidden relationship between spheres 1 and 3: when you approach either, language "breaks down"—and this breakdown is what lets you know you have left the human world. In a sense we could say that these spheres are constituted *by* this breakdown (in one, language breaks down and clings to the "threshold"; in the other, it "lacks but creates"). The spheres are thus defined not so much by their objects as by the way language functions or, rather, *does not* function, in them.

Is dialogue possible in the absence of language? Can I talk meaningfully with a cat, a tree, a sculpture, or a coat? While it might seem that this is a case of overstretching a metaphor or figure (dialogue), Buber is committed to the belief that something like dialogue with all beings, including silent ones, is possible.[21] Dialogue with a silent being is not an exceptional case for Buber—it is integral to his thinking. If we could not, then meaning would be confined to the very narrow interhuman realm. Silence permeates his notion of dialogue, as seen in the fact that I can dialogue with a person, without using language: "Just as the most eager speaking at one another does not make a conversation . . . so for a conversation no sound is necessary, not even a gesture. Speech can renounce all the media of sense, and it is still speech."[22] Thus, much as we can dialogue with a mute being, we can mutely dialogue with a speaking one. This paper is not the place to try to understand what Buber is referring to or how a silent dialogue is possible (he is emphatic that he is not referring to a lover's reverie or a mystical state), but I would suggest this silent speech is something like a shared "intentional stance." It is sufficient to note that Buber himself was of the opinion that a silent dialogue was possible, a dialogue independent not only of speech but also of all transmitted content: "Human dialogue, therefore, although it has its distinctive life in the sign, that is in sound and gesture . . . can exist without the sign, but admittedly not in an objectively comprehensible form. On the other hand an element of communication, however inward, seems to belong to its essence. But in its highest moments dialogue reaches out even beyond these boundaries. It is completed outside contents, even the most personal, which are or can be communicated."[23] In other words, it is possible to have a bare dialogical relationship where nothing is "transmitted," a form of second-person intimacy without content. This empty relation may not be "objectively comprehensible," but it occurs nonetheless.

However, it seems that speechless dialogue between two silent humans differs from that between a human and an animal—there are different kinds of silence. Human dialogue, even in the emptiest, quietest form, always has the *potential* to be "realized," or concretized, in speech—this relation can in theory be made into a "thing" and transmitted by articulating it in "signs." But this cannot happen in sphere 1: no matter what, my cat will not answer me in language I can understand. Our silences are concretized, or realized, differently: human silence is realized (potentially) in speech; animal silence can never achieve completion in the sense of being realized in an object. This, I believe, is why Buber uses the figure of sticking to the threshold of language: interhuman dialogue may choose to remain silent; interanimal dialogue *must* be silent. So how do we articulate and understand this necessarily unspeaking dialogue? How to make sense of it?

That animal dialogue presents a problem for Buber's thought should surprise no one. If we take dialogue as a central relation, then it is impossible to dismiss animal dialogue without dismembering the world, and yet it is an undesirable problem because the terms at play (*animal* and *dialogue*) make for a very uneasy fit. As Jay Geller has noted, the question of the animal follows the question of the human like an "uncanny guest."[24] Despite the anxieties of his students and the first few generations of Buber interpreters (many made uncomfortable by the notion that Buber thought we could dialogue with animals), the question of the nonhuman You follows the human You with an almost natural necessity.[25] Near the end of his life, Buber admitted to Helmut Kuhn that he had never sufficiently dealt with "the relationship of the human person to nature" and suggested this would be a worthwhile project: to elucidate how it is possible to have a dialogical relationship with an animal while sustaining the "unconditionality of the distinction" between the second- and third-person perspectives.[26] In other words, to explicate the relationship to a natural being within the bounds of the second-person, or I-You. Affect theory can help us think of an alternative to speech when we try to understand dialogue with nonhuman animals, or "creatures" (*die Kreaturen*)—where, to iterate, we remain on the border, or threshold (*Schwelle*) of language.[27] I suggest that if we wish to follow Buber, and view relations to nonhumans as a kind of dialogue, *we find something that requires affect to explicate it*: a communication formed out of feelings and movements rather than words.[28]

III. AFFECT AND COMMUNICATION

This approach assumes (correctly, I think) that humans and nonhumans are creatures of affect. In plainer language: animals feel and sense many of the same things we do—and many we do not—and form language-like relationships which express and share these affects. But an affect reading cannot rest content with noting commonalities in affective *content*—such as common-feeling, shared experience, or overlap between affective worlds—if only because Buber is quite clear that there are feelings we do *not* share with nonhumans, and there are key affects we only access in animal dialogue. I propose that when dialoguing with animals, *both* form and content—the "subject" of dialogue *and the manner of expression*—should be read through affect theory.[29] While I have made the case for reading the difference between spheres 1 and 2 as a difference in the role language plays—indeed, this is Buber's explicit claim—one can also read this difference as a difference in affect. Here things get a little odd: there are affects we only have access to in sphere 1 (human-animal dialogue), but these affects teach us about, or express, relationships that hold in all the other spheres. To give away the plot: the affect of anxiety is found only in sphere 1 but articulates (affectively!) a formal structure found in all relationships.

This particular affect will be elucidated in this paper's final section, concerning the dialogue with the house cat. However, before reaching this passage, a brief excursion into affect theory is necessary. My goal here is to employ a slightly eccentric form of affect theory, one modified by distinctions laid out by pragmatist philosopher Charles Sanders Peirce (1839–1914), to read Buber's repeated (and vague) claims that animal communication approaches the threshold of language. Because of spatial limitations, this will be an extremely truncated discussion and easily contested: I do not intend to claim that this is what affect theory is, or should be, but only that some of the tools it provides can help us understand what is going on in Buber.[30] There are two interrelated things I want to get out of affect theory. First, affects can be viewed somewhat independently of any particular way of mediating them; in other words, an affect of anxiety or anger can exist independently of any particular expression, articulation, or even feeling of it. Second, these independent affects are nonetheless capable of mediation and can move between bodies and creatures in a way that transforms these very same creatures—not unlike the way language functions in Buber.

The overall goal here is to think of affects as potentially independent of language and yet able to function in a language-like manner. As discussed, dialogue, for Buber, *can* occur independently of language, and yet language and dialogue have a tense relationship. Arguably, the same is true for affect—but if so, we would expect affect to (like language) be in some sense separable from the dialogical situation. Affect theory is itself replete with debates about the "separability" of specific affects: are affects distinct from emotions? embodiment? language? More abstractly, we can say that these are all debates about the *degree of mediation* that affects involve. The basic question underlying these discussions seems to be "can affects exist in-themselves, or must they always be mediated?"[31] This question exists in proximity to one that plagues Buber interpreters: Buber seems to require something prelinguistic, or at least alinguistic, for his thinking to "work."[32] And while much critical and literary theory is hostile to the notion of the nonlinguistic, affect theory has, if anything, been downright enthusiastic about this potential.[33] This potentially nonlinguistic element (affect), which nonetheless exists in proximity to dialogue, is the part of affect theory that is most valuable for this paper. And so my employment of affect theory will move between those positions that sustain the independence of affect *and* those that stress the ways in which affect is mediated between bodies (that are themselves formed and transformed by this process).

The "unmediated affect" position finds a (rather extreme) representative in the work of Brian Massumi. For Massumi, affects are a kind of unmediated pure intensity, and emotion is what happens when that intensity is captured: "Affect is autonomous to the degree to which it escapes confinement in the particular body whose vitality, or potential for interaction, it is. Formed, qualified, situated perceptions and cognitions fulfilling functions of actual connection or blockage, are the capture and closure of affect. Emotion is the intensest (most contracted) expression of that capture—and of the fact that something has always and again escaped.... That is why all emotion is more or less disorienting, and why it is classically described as being outside of oneself."[34] While the affect/emotion distinction cannot quite be mapped onto Buber's own work, there is value in the distinctiveness that Massumi seeks—seeking to identify "feels" or affects independently of the structures that mediate them. Massumi is useful because I want to draw a distinction between an affect and the various ways it can be mediated, including language, if only to allow for dramatically different ways of mediating the same affect that might differ across species. For Massumi, emotions are one way of mediating, or capturing affects—and his project hinges on differentiating the "pure" affect from its capture in an emotion. Here, my goal is slightly different: to identify something that is at least *potentially* prelinguistic (affect) that can be articulated, felt, and expressed differently by different creatures. Anxiety, as an autonomous affect, may have a *quality* that is shared but may be mediated completely differently and, therefore, felt completely differently by different species.

However, rather than sticking with Massumi's stark division, I suggest that we take the impetus for his project (affect's autonomy) but redraw the distinction on Peircean lines, employing the assembled text in the *Collected Papers of Charles Sanders Peirce* entitled "The Phenomenology" as a guide.[35] Peirce's work sustains the distinction developed by Massumi—the autonomy of affects—while also providing multiple logics of mediation (whereas Massumi, in his valorization of "untamed" affect, tends to denigrate all forms of meditation and capture). In other words, Peirce lets us think about affect as something that can *both* be considered independently or as part of a mediating structure and, just as importantly, provides us with logical systems to address both. This is unlike Massumi, who in his exuberance, seems to want affect to rupture, or transgress, logic. Peirce, ever the logician, is more careful, and more helpful, when thinking about the potential autonomy of feelings.

Read through Peirce's works, an affect is an instance of "firstness." Peirce calls these firsts "feelings": "Among phanerons [the substance of phenomenology] are certain qualities of feeling, such as the color of magenta... the quality of the emotion upon contemplating a fine mathematical demonstration, the quality of feeling of love, etc. I do not mean the sense of actually experiencing these feelings, whether primarily or in any memory or imagination. That is something that involves these qualities as an element of it. But I mean the qualities themselves which, in themselves, are mere may-bes, not necessarily realized. The reader may be inclined to deny that."[36] Here is the first instance where I find Peirce valuable: he claims that we can, at the very least, think about feelings that exist even if no one is feeling them. These firsts, or pure feelings, are independent of the linguistic mind or, indeed, of any mind. Peirce is claiming that there is no logical reason to assume anger cannot exist independent of a mind feeling it or its concretization in an emotion.[37] A feeling, in this sense, "is what it is" whether it is "felt" or not: it "involves no analysis, comparison or any process whatsoever, nor consists in whole or in part of any act by which one stretch of consciousness is distinguished from another, which has its own positive quality which consists in nothing else, and which is of itself all that it is."[38] Using Peirce, we can redraw the affect-emotion distinction thus: an affect is a pure feel (a "first"), while an emotion is when this feeling is felt (as a "second"). I can "be" angry without "feeling" angry, and it may well be visible to my partner long before I feel it myself. I may well angrily insist I am not angry—I may not feel my anger—but I am angry nonetheless, and it is visible to those around me. Another way of carving up this distinction is to think of a depressing room. An affect theorist could argue that a room can "be" depressing even if no one is in it—it only "feels" depressing once someone enters it.[39] But an unfelt affect is only a potential, or first—it becomes real, or encountered, only after it is taken up by a creature as an emotion, or second. Once this occurs, it is now part of a heavily mediated communicative system.[40]

Unlike Massumi's "intensity," Peirce's "feeling" is an affect-structure that has *qualities*, and these qualities can then be felt, thought about, or taken up into diverse systems, frameworks, consciousnesses (or unconsciousnesses), or organisms. The human animal often takes up (or, in Massumi's more macho framing, "captures") this affect in an emotion and, from there, as a linguistic (symbolic) cognition. Thus, affects are shared: "I know very well that my dog's musical feelings are quite similar to mine though they agitate him more than they do me. He has the same emotions of affection as I, though they are far more moving in his case. You would never persuade me that my horse and I do not sympathize, or that the canary bird that takes such delight in joking with me does not feel with me and I with him." But they are nonetheless mediated differently:

> As for the senses of my dog, I must confess that they seem very unlike my own, but when I reflect to how small a degree he thinks of visual images, and of how smells play a part in his thoughts and imaginations analogous to the part played by sights in mine, I cease to be surprised that the perfume of roses or of orange flowers does not attract his attention at all and that the effluvia that interest him so much, when at all perceptible to me, are simply unpleasant. He does not think of smells as sources of pleasure and disgust but as sources of information, just as I do not think of blue as a nauseating color, nor of red as a maddening one.[41]

Peirce lets us have our cake and eat it afterward: he sustains the distinction between affect and emotion (as with Massumi), but he also lets us think about the way these affects participate in mediating systems (as with Sara Ahmed). And so he is useful for understanding Buber's work, where feeling also play these two roles, albeit in a woefully undertheorized manner.

But why not give up on the distinction entirely, as has been the case in much recent affect theory? The advantage of sustaining the analytic distinction between affect and the ways it is mediated is that it allows for a set of shared affects, or feels, but allows for radically different ways, perhaps even incommensurable ways, of taking them up into a system or organism. Of humans, we might well say (and I will say) with Sara Ahmed that sensations are always mediated, and this mediation is bound up with signs and our sign systems (which Peirce calls "thirds").[42] But maintaining a distinction between affects and the systems that mediate them allows us to assume that nonhuman animals might have parallel affects, but radically different mediation systems—ones that may approach language (as our own affects do) but are distinct from it. At minimum, this framework allows us to more cogently interpret Buber's animal passages and understand how it is that we can dialogue with animals who cannot speak—because there are other forms of communication available to them.

Here Ahmed's work on affect and surfaces is germane to my reading of Buber. Ahmed's work spends little time on defining or confining affects and emotions but rather asks, "What do emotions do?"[43] Her multiple answers to this question include two of importance for understanding Buber's work: (1) they circulate, and (2) they form "surfaces" (and this in turn allows for something like interiority to emerge).[44] The first illuminates the language-like manner in which affect functions: affects can move between bodies like words. The second answer suggests how different affective "relationships" might constitute different surfaces and interiors, much as the "basic words" do for Buber (where the I changes depending on the relationship it is in): Because "emotions create the very effect of the surfaces and boundaries that allow us to distinguish an inside and an outside in the first place ... *emotions are not simply something 'I' or 'we' have*. Rather, it is through emotions ... that surfaces or boundaries are made: the 'I' and the 'we' are shaped by, and even take the shape of, contact with others."[45] In other words, I am suggestion a connection between this claim of Ahmed's and Buber's more gnomic statement: "basic words do not state something that might exist outside them; by being spoken they establish a mode of existence ... There is no I as such but only the I of the basic word I-You and the I of the basic word I-It."[46] Ahmed's mobilization of affect theory provides a way for us to understand how we can dialogue with animals who do not speak: through the movement and circulation of emotions between us and our animal dialogue partner, a movement that does not pass between us like real estate, or a property, but constitutes our surfaces (and in so doing, our interiorities). Affect, like language in Buber, not only transmits, but also transforms.

This is not to suggest that we want to "plug a leak" in Buber's work with affect theory or that we can, or should, reread Buber's animal vignettes replacing the word *dialogue* with *affect*. The goal is not to take Buber's "strange" articulation of animal dialogue and render it ordinary—far from it: what I would like to do is articulate these strange encounters in sharper detail, which, if anything, will increase their seeming contradictions as we "logicize the supralogical." As Buber articulates it, it is the strange aspects of the animal encounter—those that resist easy assimilation into human language, or refuse to "cross the threshold," and so remain somewhere between the affective and the discursive—that are the most philosophically interesting. This uneasy fit between the two "spheres,"

IV. THE NONHUMAN OTHER (DANIEL'S TREE)

Daniel is a useful text for this study because it is very much concerned with affect and emotion and the role they play in communication with nonhumans. While *Daniel* does not treat animal dialogue it is very much concerned with relations to nonhumans, or nature (the rest of sphere 1). It is useful to dwell on it for a moment, if only because animal dialogue must be differentiated in two directions: from humans and their use of language and from other natural beings, such as plants or rocks. In terms of the development of Buber's work, *Daniel* sets the stage for his later work on animal dialogue, because it is only after he ceases to view nature as an undifferentiated body and begins to start drawing distinctions within the sphere of "nature" that he is able to take animal dialogue seriously. Finally it is worthy of note that Buber claims the concept of dialogue first occurred to him in relation to a nonhuman being (a tree). This occurs in the preface, with the following unselfconsciously phallic description: "I pressed my stick against a trunk of an oak tree. Then I felt in twofold fashion my contact with being: here, where I held the stick, and there, where it touched the bark.... *At that time dialogue appeared to me.* For the speech of man, wherever it is genuine speech, is like that stick; that means: truly directed address."[47] Here we see a premonition of the structures that underlie *I and Thou*: direction, address, dialogue. I will suggest it's not a coincidence that this structure "appears" to him outside of a conversation with another human. These theoretically productive encounters with nonhumans recur throughout Buber's work, cresting in *I and Thou*'s conversation with the cat: encounters with nonhuman creatures elucidate and clarify the boundaries of dialogue in a way that interhuman conversation does not. In this case, it is presented as an accident of biography, and no grander claims are made. Further, there is no affective component, and it is barely an interaction: everything seems to occur in his head. This changes a few pages later, in the body of the text, when the eponymous hero Daniel encounters another tree, this time with an attentiveness to its specific affects and feelings.

> Look at this stone pine. You may compare its properties with those of other stone pines, other trees, other plants.... And now seek to draw near to this stone pine itself. Not with the power of the feeling glance alone.... Rather, with all your directed power, receive the tree, surrender yourself to it. Until

you feel its bark as your skin and the springing forth of a branch from the trunk like the striving in your muscles.... until you are transformed. But also in the transformation your direction is with you, and through it you experience the tree so that you attain in it to the unity.[48]

Despite the conscientious investment in the tree, and the division between a fragmented relation and a unified one that is reminiscent of *I and Thou*, this example is more interesting as a *failure* to develop a dialogical relationship than anything else. As the passage continues, it becomes evident that Daniel's relation to the tree is one of absorption rather than conversation, one that reads more like a form of consumption than encounter.[49] When Daniel says of his encounters, "The directed soul alone *rules* here," it is hard to interpret his transformation as much more than a human ego appropriating "nature," what Buber will later critique as "inner experience": a kind of use or spiritual tourism.[50] To paraphrase Phil Huston, in *Daniel* one "absorbs" the tree by surrendering to it—but this is a "guided" surrender; throughout his ecstatic merging, Daniel remains firmly in control.[51]

Daniel's relation to the tree exists somewhere in the middle of the "mysticism to dialogue" periodization of Buber advanced by Paul Mendes-Flohr.[52] It is not "mysticism" in the sense of *uncontrolled* surrender, but neither is it dialogue. The duality of the participants is preserved, which is indicative of a dialogical relation, but surrender is not avoided *for dialogical reasons*—say, for fear of trespassing on the tree or absorbing it. Rather, surrender is avoided because it is a threat to the ego. When Daniel's interlocutor ("The Woman"—the only female in the book and the only figure without a proper name) suggests that Daniel should have more fully abandoned himself to the tree or sought some variant of *unio mystica*, Daniel replies that anyone who "surrenders" (*überantwortet*) to ecstasy is torn apart like Dionysus.[53] This fear of being torn apart by an ecstatic surrender governs the relationship to the tree (as it does for much of *Daniel*). Buber seems to want the feeling of union without the violence (being "torn apart") that comes with it. So independence is sustained out of fear and is maintained by a gentle domination of the tree and the way it feels. This is why Daniel feels "like" the tree or "as" the tree feels: it is not a communication of affects but an appropriation of them. His fear is the dominating affect, and so there is no circulation or construction of a between space where Daniel encounters the tree.[54] The "surface" the affect constructs is one of enclosure: enclosing the tree within Daniel, such that they share the same skin.

It bears noting that, despite the self-possessed fear of ecstasy, Buber is nonetheless attentive to the tree's affects, to the feel of the tree, and how the tree feels.⁵⁵ Even if the "self-directed" Daniel "sets the rule" for the encounter, breaking the conditions for a proper dialogue, we see here something like the affective *content* of a dialogue, the communication of "feels" and feelings, even if the form, or matter of expression, is lacking. However, the tree is ultimately too passive to challenge the young Buber's "I." It takes a more dynamic animal, in particular, the ornery cat, to call Buber's ego into question and develop a space where affect is shared rather than consumed.⁵⁶

V. COMPLICATING NATURE

As Buber aged his understanding of "nature," or sphere 1, grew more diverse. A key moment in this transformation occurred in 1923 with the entry of the cat into his *I and Thou*; a second key moment in occurred in 1957, with *I and Thou*'s afterword: Buber's relationship to animals and plants became less absorptive, more variegated, and more attentive to the singularity of his nonhuman interlocutors. He ceased to treat nature en bloc and recognized—despite the somewhat simplistic "spheres" passage quoted previously—that different nonhumans had to be approached differently. By the time he died, Buber seemed convinced that dialogue with animals was different *in kind* from dialogue with trees and stones. Thus, the manner in which we dialogue with beings in sphere 1 operates on two different tracks: with nonanimals, dialogue occurs in the realm of sensuality, an interesting story in its own right but one that cannot be told here; with animals, dialogue occurs in a space of circulating affects, moving between two animals, one human, one not.⁵⁷

This brings us to a tension in Buber's work, one that is perhaps irresolvable. After *I and Thou*, the "You"—including the nonhuman You—is engaged not as a member of a "species" but as a singular being.⁵⁸ But as Buber's work developed and the attention paid to singularity increased, there was a simultaneous increase in attentiveness to species difference. A conflict arises between these two intertwined impulses in Buber's dialogical work: a desire to engage each entity as a singular individual independent of its attributes and membership in groups (openness to dialogue wherever it may be found), and, simultaneously, a recognition of the radically different ways in which dialogue occurs (not all dialogue is like human speech).

Buber's work sustained both sides of this conflict, and so an increasing attentiveness to individual animal encounters did not expunge the human/nonhuman distinction. If anything, as Buber aged this distinction became more deeply inscribed: Buber eventually posited a categorical distinction between dialogue with human animals and dialogue with nonhuman animals. As Buber put it in a late work, the human has a "special way of being."⁵⁹ Thus, it is odd when Maurice Friedman claims that Buber, in a private conversation, suggested "were he to write *I and Thou* again, he would feel compelled to find terminology that would sharpen the distinction between the I-Thou relationship with one's fellowman and that with nature."[60] Friedman, perhaps the most apologetic of all of Buber's interpreters, is surely telling the truth, but it is hard to imagine a deeper distinction than an ontological difference. Buber's published statements on the issue suggest that rather than this "categorical" distinction (one largely accomplished), he was more interested in strengthening distinctions *within* nature and not simply between "man and nature."

This is, in fact, what he calls for in the afterword to *I and Thou*'s 1957 edition.[61] Buber notes, "Instead of considering nature as a single whole, as we[!] usually do, we must consider its different realms separately."[62] Here he divides sphere 1 into two groups: animals, who exist at the threshold, and nonanimals, who remain "before the threshold."[63] These two subgroups—more are implied—are differentiated by several characteristics, all of which relate to "reciprocity": *animals and nonanimals reciprocate differently*. Animals (quite literally) "turn toward" us and are "spontaneous."[64] The moving, dynamic animal ("stir[ring] across from us") is distinguished, by this movement, from the rest of nature. This is a distinction between beings like cats that can actively transmit affects (through spontaneous motion, sounds, their gaze) and those like trees that cannot—where affect transmission is dictated by what they are (what Buber calls their "being"), not what they do.[65] Animals can reply, even if only affectively, and plants and rocks cannot. Over the course of the afterword, it becomes clear that what was once called the sphere of nature (sphere 1), now really applies only to animals; there is no explicit correction of the earlier position, but the use of the term *threshold* has shifted. The dialogue that "sticks to the threshold" now applies only with moving animals—nonanimals no longer make it to the threshold. This position is repeated in the *Philosophy of Martin Buber* (1967), where, in a passage that comes close to plagiarizing *I and Thou*'s afterword, Buber more explicitly differentiates between our relationships with animals and plants.[66] Thus, one can safely say that as Buber ages, he develops a firmer distinction not only between humans and nature, but also within nature, between animals and other creatures. And sphere 1, once applied to "nature," ends up applying only to animals: spontaneous beings that exchange affects with us on the threshold of mutuality.

VI. ANXIETY: I AND MEOW

To iterate: the spheres of dialogue are explicitly delineated by the way language functions, or does not function, in each. Both spheres 1 and 3 are defined by a breakdown in language. But this breakdown is not merely diagnostic, a way of finding the edge of the sphere: it can teach you things. In this final section, I will engage the section in *I and Thou* where Buber encounters a cat to explore one such thing we can learn from a breakdown in language. In this case, the cat opens us up to the affect of anxiety. *Pace* Massumi, this affect is not a form of intensity but is better seen as an intense form. It is a highly structured affect: part of the structure of the dialogical situation itself, *both* reflecting and forming the structure of dialogue. In a word, anxiety is simultaneously the form and content of the dialogue with the cat. But this affect can be philosophically extrapolated on: anxiety expresses and is the fundamental uncertainty that inheres in all dialogue, and leads into melancholy, the necessary end of all immediate relationships. Anxiety is thus part of the dialogical encounter's structure; in Ahmed's language, it textures and shapes the surfaces and relations of the bodies in dialogue.[67] Anxiety shapes the relationship between Buber and the cat as much as it expresses this relation.

When Buber claims that anxiety must be learned from an animal, that animals *alone* are capable of "opening" us to the "anxiety of becoming [*Bangigkeit des Werdens*]," he is claiming, a few short years before Martin Heidegger's *Being and Time* is published, that a fundamental affect—one with serious philosophical implications—is available only through nonhuman animals (in his case, a cat).[68] This notion of anxiety (*Bangigkeit*) is antithetical to Heidegger's much better known theory of *Angst*, which is seemingly available only to humans and is arguably a solitary, monological condition.[69] It is not opened up by dialogue and certainly not by dialogue with a cat. I do not intend to take the Heidegger/Buber comparison too far: *Angst* and *Bangigkeit* do very different work for each respective author's "systems," and the two concepts, while overlapping, differ semantically in that the former suggests a fear with an unclear object, and the latter is closer to an embodied uneasiness.[70] But *Angst* and *Bangigkeit* are alike in that they emotionally open us to an essential structure (one ontological, the other dialogical), which informs much of their respective author's works.

A reading of the cat passage suggests that it is precisely because of the animal's difference from us, and the fact that the communication is affective and not linguistic, that we are able to feel and understand this key affect (*Bangigkeit*). As we peer over the edge of sphere 2, the interhuman world, and encounter a nonhuman animal, we are exposed to affects that force us to realize things about relation and dialogue. This is because, and not despite, the fact that this interaction "remains at the threshold" of language: in our anxious relation to the cat this threshold is drawn with greater intensity than is possible in human intercourse. As Mikhail Bakhtin has noted, the threshold is an anxious space.[71] From this anxious threshold dialogue, we can then extrapolate that this affect (anxiety) defines and articulates the unstable boundaries that exist in all forms of dialogue, even if it is made obvious, or "opened" to us, only in dialogue with animals.

Again, in *I and Thou*, Buber is committed to interpreting all forms of presence through the lens of dialogue, and this requires that he interpret nonhuman relationships as being in some sense language-like: "The eyes of an animal have the capacity of a great language. Independent, without any need of the assistance of sounds and gestures . . . they express the mystery in its natural captivity, that is, in the anxiety [*Bangigkeit*] of becoming. *This state of the mystery is known only to the animal, which alone can open it up to us*—for this state can only be opened up and not revealed [*eröffnen, nicht offenbaren*]."[72] Despite, or rather because, of the "categorical difference" between us and nonhuman animals, animals are able to communicate (express) this otherwise unknowable affect. Buber only admits two formal differences between us and nonhuman animals: language and distancing. Humans use conventional language, and humans set things at a distance. The latter distinction is not developed (in print at least) until much later, in "Distance and Relation" (1951). In this late anthropological text, Buber claims humans are categorically different from nonhumans because they can set things at a distance and *then* relate to these "distanced" objects. In this manner, humans cocreate a world (*Welt*) that they both are and are not a part of, whereas nonhuman animals lack the ability to "distance" objects and are more completely "stuck" in an "environment" (*Umwelt*).[73] It seems that Buber borrows language from the biologist Jakob von Uexküll (1864–1944) to understand how human beings can both be involved with natural things while simultaneously maintaining a degree of alienation from them (having a world). The animals' "worldlessness," by contrast, seems largely intended to cast the privileged status accorded to humans in a sharper light.[74] Buber's other formal difference (between humans and animals) is less contentious: humans use conventional language, while nonhumans do not.[75] I suggest that the cat passage—and most of *I and Thou*—is more concerned with language than distancing. But both distinctions (distancing and language) are key moments in what Buber calls "actualization": making things actual, or transforming fleeting encounters, no matter how "authentic," into concrete objects and actions. Language, for instance, can be used to actualize a dialogical relation, channeling the elusive, perhaps silent, dialogical relation into a concrete, transmittable (and replicable) semiotic form. Distancing similarly turns an encountered other into an object, by giving it a solid place in the world rather than having it be part of an encounter or a "stream of consciousness." And both these forms of actualization are unavailable to animals.

But there is a cost to actualization, a cost the animal does not have to pay and that gives it access to affects that escape us. The "trick" is to see that actualization—be it through distancing, articulation in language, or some other method—makes things actual but, simultaneously, disrupts the dialogical relation. Actualization establishes stability and concreteness, but in so doing, something is lost or obscured. It is precisely because neither form of actualization is available to a cat that it has access to a kind of anxiety and can in turn share this affect with us. This sharing is, of course, not done in language, not only because the cat cannot speak, but because speaking would actually diminish the affect's intensity. This is corroborated by Buber's claim that anxiety can only be "opened" up but not "revealed."[76] In addition to the religious overtones, this distinction operates something like the difference between "exposing" and "showing": the animal communicates the actual feeling of the anxiety affect itself rather than isolating it and indexing it via a semiotic system or language. To reveal, show, explain, describe, or articulate the anxiety would involve Peircean seconds and thirds: "capturing" and transmitting the affect. Instead, here, we are "opened," brought into the same insecure and exposed state of the animal.

To continue: "The language in which this is accomplished *is what it says:* anxiety—the stirring of the creature between the realms of plantlike security and spiritual risk. This language is the stammering of nature under the initial grasp of spirit, before language yields to spirit's cosmic risk which we call man. But no speech will ever repeat what the stammer is able to communicate."[77] Here, as elsewhere, Buber echoes Aristotle's hierarchy of souls.[78] Buber's addition is that the *position* of the nonhuman is anxious: there are two types of security offered here—plantlike immobility and language—and the animal has neither. The plant's security is in its immobility: it takes no risks and is immediately connected to its nutrients. Language, the opposite extreme, is a form of security because it allows us to capture, or anchor, our affects and experiences: it is security in mediation. The animal is neither fully immediate nor mediated: the cat cannot speak, but it still expresses something. Unlike the day-to-day talking with cats that introduced this paper ("Where did you come from, I haven't seen you for quite a while . . ."), in this passage a fundamental affect is expressed—fundamental because it is an expression of the animal's "position"—in particular, its position vis-à-vis us, in dialogue. Hence, Buber's seemingly odd claim that here the "language" "is what it says"—odd because, more-or-less all of the time, language is *not* what it says: it is a sign system that points at something or performs something. A word refers to a thing; it is not that thing itself. To use an oversimplified Peircean nomenclature: conventional language is a semiotic system, composed of thirds, or symbols that interpret, index, and *reveal* things other than themselves. Here, speaking to an animal, the "language" is a first; it is, like an icon, the very thing it is expressing.[79] Again, humans are *opened* up to this affect (made to feel it) by the animal (in this case, a cat), not shown it:

> I sometimes look into the eyes of a house cat. The domesticated animal has not by any means received the gift of the truly "eloquent" glance from *us*, as a human conceit suggests sometimes; what it has from us is only the ability—purchased with the loss of its elementary naturalness—to turn this glance upon us brutes.... Undeniably, this cat began its glance by asking me with a glance that was ignited by the breath of my glance: "Can it be that you mean me? Do you actually want that I should not merely do tricks for you? Do I concern you? Am I there for you? Am I there? What is that coming from you? What is that around me? What is it about me? What is that?!"[80]

I is here a paraphrase of a word of I-less self-reference that we lack. *That* represents the flood of man's glance in the entire actuality of its power to relate. Despite the passage's vagaries, Buber makes a few things quite clear: the cat does not receive its ability to communicate from us (if anything, dialogue with us makes the cat anxious); the cat in question does not trust us to remain present; each species lacks something the other has (we lack the cat's form of self-reference and are forced to "paraphrase" this strange self-reference as an "I," while the cat lacks the stability of the human relation, a stability owed to language); and each species (cat and human) "opens" the other to something. Our concern here is that the cat opens us up to anxiety or allows us access to an anxiety that we normally do not feel, precisely because of the security afforded us by language, which stabilizes, and anchors our relations and feelings in symbolic relations. The cat has no such anchor; when we dialogue with a cat, we actually intensify its anxiety.[81]

There is a lot going on in the cat dialogue, so it might help to summarize before moving to the next stage in Buber's conversation. There are four points in particular I hope to highlight: first, the animal dialogue is insecure because it cannot be stabilized in language; second, the animal dialogue is formed out of affects, and so there is a one-to-one relationship between the signs that circulate and what they convey (hence, things are opened, not shown, and the dialogue "is what it says"); third, these affects function like the "basic words" (I-It and I-You) shaping the participants as well as the structures by which they appear to each other (each participant in this dialogue transforms the other "I"); fourth, and finally, the animal-human dialogical *situation* is nakedly expressed in this dialogue, obscured neither by actualization or reference.[82] It is prelinguistic and, for this reason, necessarily anxious and insecure.

In writing, "Do I concern you? Am I there for you? Am I there?" Buber nicely indexes this anxiety in the vignette. But there is something of this anxiety in all dialogical situations (as theorized by Buber). As mentioned, there is an interplay in Buber between immediacy and mediacy, between dialogue and actualization. The first terms in each of these pairs (immediacy, and dialogue) are anxious: they are fragile and easily shattered. Again, Buber says that this anxiety is something we learn only from the animal, because the animal's relation to language is *fundamentally* anxious. But the affect of anxiety that the animal opens us up to applies well beyond the human-animal encounter: human-human encounters also partake of anxiety; we just often manage to ignore it.[83] We learn about anxiety from the animal, but this lesson has a general application.

Buber tells us the story of the cat not to illustrate what happens when we talk to cats but to give us a "decisive experience" from which we can philosophically extrapolate. He has something very specific in mind: "*No other event has made me so deeply aware of the evanescent actuality in all relationships* to other beings, the sublime *melancholy* of our lot, the fated lapse into It of every single You. For usually a day, albeit brief, separated the morning and evening of the event; but here morning and evening merged cruelly.... At least I could still remember it, while the animal had sunk again from its stammering glance into speechless anxiety, almost devoid of memory."[84] Talking to cats not only opens us up to a fundamental affect (anxiety) that we are normally protected from but also allows us to extrapolate from this anxiety and learn something else about the general structures of dialogue: all dialogue is compelled to end—not from an outer compulsion, but from an inner, structural necessity.[85] Buber's term for this compulsion is *melancholy* (*Schwermut*). Melancholy is twinned to anxiety, and while he does not say that melancholy (like anxiety) can *only* be learned from animals, he is explicit that *he* learned about it from cats. Melancholy, like anxiety, is a structure as much as it is an affect. Where anxiety is the fragility of the dialogical situation—the fact that it is insecure and *can* break at any instant—melancholy is the affective articulation of the fact that all dialogue *will* break: it is doomed.

This is not the place to dwell on the role that melancholy plays in Buber's thought—one that is often misunderstood, in part because the word itself (*melancholy*) seems to imply depression. Indeed, both of these words (*anxiety* and *melancholy*) suggest a darker picture of the world than Buber intends to paint. Much as anxiety is part and parcel of the tender fragility of intimate presence, melancholy is part and parcel of the singularity of dialogue. Because dialogue, at its most intense *is not a thing*, it is also, in a basic sense, not actual: it is seemingly too singular to relate to, or be brought into contact with, anything else. However, if a dialogue is important, or valuable, it *should* be brought into connection with the other things in your life. But it can only have contact with other things after it *becomes* a thing. To refer again to the former brief discussions of "actualization" and silence: dialogue in its most intense, unmediated sense is not objectively actual because it is not an object. This pure dialogue is doomed, not because something will come from the outside to destroy it (although this can happen—hence, anxiety) but because eventually, out of an inner necessity, it should be made actual. Otherwise, you are stuck in a dialogical la-la land, moving between a series of glorious but ultimately meaningless encounters. Without realization—which ends dialogue by making it a real thing in the world—dialogue is an affair for beautiful souls. This is undesirable because it is a betrayal of the encounter: the only way to remain true to a meaningful dialogue is by bringing it into contact with the rest of your life, which means, ending it. But it is nonetheless true that there is something sad about the end of an encounter (even if that end is the development of a more stable, more nurturing, more concrete relationship). And this sadness is made visible when the mechanism of deferral we use to protect ourselves from anxiety and melancholy—language—is unavailable: "Here morning and evening merged cruelly."[86] Without language, there is no escape and no way to delay the inevitable or hang on once the moment has passed: we are exposed to the bare affective content of the dialogical relationship, which, at least in the case of Buber's cat, is anxiety and melancholy.

Buber relates the story of talking to the cat, "this minute occurrence that happened to me more than once," not because he likes cats, but because certain essential affects are opened there, affects that expose the structure of dialogue. It is thus the case not only that affects allow us to understand how animal dialogue is possible but, conversely, that animal dialogue helps us understand the role certain affects play in all dialogue.

VII. CONCLUSION

From *I and Thou* onward (if not before), Buber consistently held that we can, and should, engage in dialogue with nonhumans. This fact, which troubles some commentators, is not extraneous to his thinking but is an integral element of it: dialogue refers to far more than a thing we do when we share a language or play with words. It is nonetheless hard to understand what it means to engage in dialogue with beings who lack language. This chapter has sought to address one aspect of this much larger problem: how to dialogue with nonhuman animals. Affect theory allows for a form of nonlinguistic communication and provides a way of thinking about the shape, and content, of this strange form of dialogue.

Despite Buber's at times problematic treatment of animals, he consistently holds that communication between humans and nonhumans is not only possible but also desirable. At the very least, as we have seen, there are fundamental affects and concepts that apply even in interhuman dialogue that are discovered, or opened, only in dialogue with animals. I have suggested that certain tools taken from affect theory can help us understand how this is possible and how we can interpret these affects that shape the dialogical situation.

NOTES

I thank Elliot R. Wolfson, M. Gail Hamner, Zachary Braiterman, Jeremy Fogel, Ron Margolin, and, most especially, Sarah Scott for the criticism, editing, and support needed to develop this chapter.

1. Schalom Ben-Chorin, quoted in Haim Gordon, ed., *The Other Martin Buber: Recollections of His Contemporaries* (Athens: Ohio University Press, 1988), 163.

2. Samuel Hugo Bergman, *Dialogical Philosophy from Kierkegaard to Buber*, trans. Arnold A. Gerstein (Albany: State University of New York Press, 1991), 231. Emmanuel Levinas shares Bergman's exasperation, and, if anything, amplifies it, suggesting that the fact that "the I-Thou is possible in relation to thing" discredits the ethical value of Buber's entire enterprise. Following Peter Atterton, I would suggest that this is a strength of Buber's work. See Peter Atterton, "Face-to-Face with the Other Animal?," in *Levinas and Buber: Dialogue and Difference*, ed. Peter Atterton, Matthew Calarco, and Maurice Friedman (Pittsburgh, PA: Duquesne University Press, 2004), 262–81.

3. Hereafter, when I refer to *animals*, I mean "nonhuman animals" and by *human*, I mean "human animal." Thus, the "human/animal distinction" can be taken as the "human animal/nonhuman animal" distinction.

4. A key text for any attempt to use affect theory to help elucidate the relationship between animals and religious thought, which inflects this entire paper, is Donovan O. Schaefer, *Religious Affects: Animality, Evolution, and Power* (Durham, NC: Duke University Press, 2015). For two recent attempts to develop Jewish studies in relation to critical animal studies, see Jay Geller, *Bestiarium Judaicum: Unnatural Histories of the Jews* (New York: Fordham University Press, 2017), and Mira Beth Wasserman, *Jews, Gentiles, and Other Animals: The Talmud after the Humanities* (Philadelphia: University of Pennsylvania Press, 2017), chap.

2. The present paper diverges from these excellent studies, in that it is concerned not as much with the "figure" of the animal (literary or otherwise) as with Buber's attempts to engage actual animals. However, the gap between literary figures and phenomenological reports is not always so wide, and the present paper is much indebted to their works.

5. This question could be asked of any philosophical analysis or explanation he was unacquainted with. Andrea Poma's delightful essay on Buber and postmodernism provides an excellent model for employing Buber's work in critical fields that were developed after his death, one that I will echo here. If some kind of partial agreement can be found between Buber and the body of theory "then it should be possible to consider Buber's position without trying to blunt his thought in the attempt of adapting it.... The opposite may in fact be the case, namely, if it can be shown that the premises of Buber's philosophy emerge fully only once we interpret them under the presupposition of [this other theoretical] sensibility." See Andrea Poma, "Unity of the Heart and Scattered Self: A Postmodern Reading of Buber's Doctrine of Evil," in *New Perspectives on Martin Buber*, ed. Michael Zank (Tübingen, Germany: Mohr Siebeck, 2006), 172.

6. Martin Buber, "Replies to My Critics," in *The Philosophy of Martin Buber*, ed. Paul Arthur Schilpp and Maurice Friedman (La Salle, IL: Open Court, 1967), 689.

7. Ibid.

8. Ibid., 690, emphasis added.

9. In some cases, it may even be necessary to challenge Buber's own articulations and theories if they fall short of the mark or obscure the experience in question. See Jochanan Bloch, "The Philosophy of Dialogue," in *Martin Buber: A Centenary Volume*, ed. Haim Gordon (New York: Ktav, 1984), 49. For a precise instance of this logicizing the supralogical, see the paradoxical account of personhood in Elliot R. Wolfson, "Theolatry and the Making-Present of the Nonrepresentable: Undoing (A)Theism in Eckhart and Buber," *Journal of Jewish Thought and Philosophy* 25, no. 1 (2017): 5–35.

10. It is perhaps for this practice that Buber is often considered a mystic, despite his protestations otherwise, for instance in Gershom Scholem, "Martin Buber's Concept of Judaism," in *On Jews and Judaism in Crisis* (New York: Schocken, 1978), 151–52. Israel Koren amplifies Scholem on this point, writing, "Buber is not a philosopher" in *The Mystery of the Earth* (Leiden, Netherlands: Brill, 2010), xi, 3. This is perhaps true, but not being a philosopher does not make Buber a mystic.

11. This dismissal has a dismal history behind it. See Gershom Scholem's (perhaps fanciful) recollection: "We argued about Buber from various points of view. [Walter] Benjamin said that Buber represented feminine thinking.... Benjamin meant it as a condemnation" (Gershom Scholem, *Walter Benjamin: The*

Story of a Friendship, trans. Harry Zohn [Philadelphia: Jewish Publication Society, 1981], 38).

12. The presentations of animals in Hasidic tales often emphasize the importance of not treating animals cruelly and, further, suggest that one can in fact speak to animals, as shown, for example, in the lesson from Louis I. Newman's *Hasidic Anthology: Tales and Teaching of the Hasidid* (New York: Schocken Books, 1963): "When Rabbi Wolf Zbarazer was on a journey, he would not permit the driver to beat his horses, saying to him, 'You would have no need even to scold them, if you knew how to address them properly'" (12)—a story Buber repeats in *The Life of Hasidism*. That said, the human/animal hierarchy is rarely questioned, and neither is the right of humans to subjugate, or slaughter, nonhuman animals. In *Hasidism and Modern Man*, Buber makes use of the notion of the "divine sparks" to illustrate human-animal relations (one where the human elevates the animal's spark through relation), implying not only that one *can* have intimate relations with nonhumans but also that one should. Again, however, the frame of domination and use is not questioned. In sum: Buber's employment of the Hasidic frame encourages close relationships with nonhumans and forbids cruelty but does not challenge human superiority. See Martin Buber, *Hasidism and Modern Man*, ed. David Biale, trans. Maurice Friedman (Princeton, NJ: Princeton University Press, 2015), 9, 11, 49, 56, 59.

13. For instance, at no point (that I know of) does he address the ethical, or unethical, work that the human/animal distinction does—the distinction between murdering and killing, where human death is murder and nonhuman death is mere killing, or slaughter. On this, see Donna J. Haraway, *When Species Meet* (Minneapolis: University of Minnesota Press, 2007), 4, 78.

14. Martin Buber, "Distance and Relation," in *The Knowledge of Man: Selected Essays*, trans. Maurice Friedman (New York: Harper and Row, 1965), 59–61.

15. The second-person stance has become something of a minor topic in contemporary ethical thought. Buber's interests are (much to the chagrin of many interpreters) significantly broader than that: ethics is neither central, nor determinative, for him. For the central text, see Stephen Darwall, *The Second-Person Standpoint: Morality, Respect, and Accountability* (Cambridge: Harvard University Press, 2009). For a "look at the field," see Naomi Eilan, ed., *The Second Person: Philosophical and Psychological Perspectives* (New York: Routledge, 2017).

16. Bloch, "Philosophy of Dialogue," 50. It is conventional, but incorrect, to refer to the You as a "subject." Buber himself almost never uses this term.

17. Martin Buber, *I And Thou*, trans. Walter Kaufmann (New York: Touchstone, 1971), 54.

18. Buber's work is replete with spheres and maternal figures, which call for a critical analysis that has rarely been attempted, with few exceptions, such as Mara Benjamin, "Intersubjectivity Meets Maternity: Buber, Levinas, and the

Eclipsed Relation," in *Thinking Jewish Culture in America*, ed. Ken Koltun-Fromm (Lanham, MD: Lexington Books, 2013).

19. Sarah Scott, in one of the few studies to take Buber's relationships to nonhumans seriously, carves up different relational objects differently than I do, viewing them in terms of "degrees of personhood." See Sarah Scott, "An Unending Sphere of Relation: Martin Buber's Conception of Personhood," *Forum Philosophicum* 19, no. 1 (2014): 12. This is a more useful frame where ethics and animal are concerned, but as my interest here is communication, I believe the "spheres of language" approach is more fruitful.

20. Note that a more concise variation of this passage occurs in section 3: "Three are the spheres in which the world of relation is built [*baut*]. The first: life with nature, where the relation sticks to the threshold of language. The second: life with men, where it enters language. The third: life with spiritual beings, where it lacks but creates language." See Buber, *I And Thou*, 56, 150. I explore the three spheres from an anthropological perspective, with an emphasis on relation to objects, in my "How to Do Things with Things: Craft at the Edge of Buber's Philosophical Anthropology," *Images: Journal of Jewish Art & Visual Culture* 12, no. 1 (2019): 134–47.

21. Martin Buber, "Dialogue," in *Between Man and Man*, trans. Ronald Gregor-Smith (New York: Routledge, 2002), 12. Levinas writes: "One of the most interesting positions of the philosophy of Buber is to show that truth is not a content and that words do not contain it." See Emmanuel Levinas, *Proper Names*, trans. Michael Smith (Stanford: Stanford University Press, 1997), 19. While Levinas then goes on to almost aggressively misunderstand Buber, this is an important observation. Language might realize truth, by giving it a stable form in the world, but it does not contain it.

22. Buber, "Dialogue," 3.

23. Ibid., 5.

24. Geller, *Bestiarium Judaicum*, 10.

25. Eva Jospe is a notable early exception here. While her interpretation is understandably dated, she devotes several pages to Buber's concern with animals. See Eva Jospe, *Encounters in Modern Jewish Thought: The Works of Eva Jospe*, ed. Raphael Jospe and Dov Schwartz (Brighton, MA: Academic Studies Press, 2013). As noted, Atterton, in a piece that is largely concerned with Levinas and *ethical* considerations, nonetheless sees Buber's animal-relations as a "major strength" of his philosophy. See Atterton, "Face-to-Face with the Other Animal?," 263.

26. Martin Buber, "Interrogation of Martin Buber," conducted by M. S. Friedman, in *Philosophic Interrogations*, ed. S. and B. Rome (New York: Holt, Rinehart and Winston, 1964), 21.

27. Buber, *I And Thou*, 56.

28. At the risk of a stretched homology, with animals, silence would mean dialogue without motion or affect, not dialogue without words.

29. Buber's understanding of movement and motion would require another paper, if not a book. From the early *Daniel* to the late "Man and His Image Work," Buber is preoccupied with movement.

30. My rehearsal of affect theory leans very heavily on Schaefer, *Religious Affects: Animality, Evolution, and Power*. I do not come to the same conclusion he does, but it would be impossible for me to advance this argument without his work. As will be obvious, this chapter is also deeply indebted to Sara Ahmed, *The Cultural Politics of Emotion*, 2nd ed. (New York: Routledge, 2014).

31. This debate is well summarized in Schaefer, *Religious Affects: Animality, Evolution, and Power*, 24.

32. This alinguistic element can be, and has been, used as evidence of his lack of seriousness: after all, if anything has characterized the last forty years of theory, it was an attentiveness to language's inescapability.

33. See the seminal Eve Kosofsky Sedgwick and Adam Frank, "Shame in the Cybernetic Fold: Reading Silvan Tomkins," *Critical Inquiry* 21, no. 2 (1995): 496–522. For an important feminist corrective, see Clare Hemmings, "Invoking Affect," *Cultural Studies* 19, no. 5 (2005): 548–67. For a critical interrogation of the way affect theorists have employed scientific documents, see Constantina Papoulias and Felicity Callard, "Biology's Gift: Interrogating the Turn to Affect," *Body & Society* 16, no. 1 (2010): 29–56.

34. Brian Massumi, "The Autonomy of Affect," in *Deleuze: A Critical Reader*, ed. Paul Patton (Cambridge: Wiley-Blackwell, 1991), 228. Ahmed astutely notes that there are political and ethical problems with Massumi's notion of affect, one that has the potential to discredit, if not denigrate, experiencing, political, bodies, writing, "But this [Massumi's] model creates a distinction between conscious recognition and 'direct' feeling, which negates how what is not consciously experienced may still be mediated by past experiences." See Ahmed, *Cultural Politics of Emotion*, 40. While I have philosophical objections to the notion that everything is mediated, Massumi's affects are too pure for this world. In addition to several important political and ethical critiques of this division: if one casts the line between affect and emotion as "intensity," or a kind of phallic-romantic "freedom from capture," then it is hard to see how we can say much about any affect other than the fact that it is "intense."

35. The *Collected Papers of Charles Sanders Peirce* are, by any assessment, a mess, but the chronological edition is incomplete and does not cover the late Peirce's phenomenological writings. For a very different, more politically focused attempt to develop a Peircean theory of affect, see Lara Trout, *The Politics of Survival: Peirce, Affectivity, and Social Criticism* (New York: Fordham University Press, 2013).

36. Charles Sanders Peirce, *Collected Papers of Charles Sanders Peirce* (Cambridge, MA: Harvard University Press, 1931), sec. 1.304. The passage continues, gently mocking those who would deny the separability of these feelings (at least in the phenomenological position).

37. Ibid., sec. 1.305.

38. Ibid., sec. 1.307.

39. For an evocative meditation about affect and space, see Teresa Brennan, *The Transmission of Affect* (Ithaca, NY: Cornell University Press, 2004), chaps. 1 and 3.

40. Peirce's own work provides several formulations for the ways in which the pure firsts of phenomenology are incorporated into real minds, bodies, and languages. There are few thinkers who have spent more time on the "threshold" of language, and a study of Peirce and affect would be very desirable.

41. Peirce, *Collected Papers of Charles Sanders Peirce*, sec. 1.314. For a study of Peirce's semiotics and evolutionary distinction, see Terrence W. Deacon, *The Symbolic Species: The Co-Evolution of Language and the Brain* (New York: W. W. Norton & Company, 1998).

42. Ahmed, *Cultural Politics of Emotion*, 25, 194.

43. Ibid., 4.

44. Ibid., 10.

45. Ibid., 4.

46. Buber, *I And Thou*, 53.

47. Martin Buber, *Daniel: Dialogues on Realization*, trans. Maurice Friedman (New York: Holt, Rinehart and Winston, 1964), 47.

48. Ibid., 54.

49. Ibid., 55. For a more sympathetic take on Buber's philosophy of unification, see Elliot R. Wolfson, "The Problem of Unity in the Thought of Martin Buber," *Journal of the History of Philosophy* 27, no. 3 (1989): 423–44.

50. More kindly, one might see a parallel in what Buber calls the "elementary relational processes" of so-called primitive peoples (Buber, *I And Thou*, 56, 70).

51. Phil Huston, *Martin Buber's Journey to Presence* (New York: Fordham University Press, 2007), 116.

52. Paul Mendes-Flohr, *From Mysticism to Dialogue: Martin Buber's Transformation of German Social Thought* (Detroit: Wayne State University Press, 1989).

53. Buber, *Daniel*, 55. A gender analysis of the following passages, perhaps along the lines of Mara Benjamin's previously cited paper, would be as desirable as it would be depressing: beginning with the need for direction, it ends "You come to the mother not otherwise than through the son" who is then compared to a sheath on a sword.

54. This between space is developed throughout Buber's works and in the end is positioned as the basic structure of sensuality; see Buber, "Distance and Relation."

55. Buber, *Daniel*, 54.

56. The tree contributes to our relation to it, but it contributes "sensation." This is no small thing, but it is not nearly so affective, or disruptive, as what mammals are capable of. Specifically, it is a horse, and later, the cat, that challenge Buber. For the encounter with a horse, see Martin Buber, *Meetings: Autobiographical Fragments* (New York: Routledge, 2002), 32.

57. Buber develops a completely different understanding of our relations to nonhuman animals, one that depends not on the I-You relationship but, rather, on the "co-working" that occurs in sensation. See Martin Buber, "Man and His Image Work," in *Knowledge of Man* and Dustin Atlas, "How to Do Things with Things: Craft at the Edge of Buber's Philosophical Anthropology," *Images: A Journal of Jewish Art and Visual Culture* 12, no. 1 (2019): 134–147.

58. "A thing's 'presence' means its particular being, its 'So-Sein'—this tree, this rock, this animal, not just any member of a given species. And to become aware of this presence means to recognize a personal quality in that thing" (Jospe, *Encounters in Modern Jewish Thought*, 21).

59. Buber, "Distance and Relation," 60.

60. Maurice Friedman, "Walter Kaufmann's Mismeeting with Martin Buber," *Judaism* 31, no. 2 (1982): 233.

61. Sarah Scott draws attention to the new levels of variegation added in this afterword in Scott, "Unending Sphere of Relation: Martin Buber's Conception of Personhood," 12.

62. Buber, *I And Thou*, 172.

63. Ibid., 173. Atterton is the only writer I have found other than Scott who takes these distinctions seriously, but his reading is overly concerned with ethics and slips up by identifying spiritual and human beings. See Atterton, "Face-to-Face with the Other Animal?," 264.

64. Buber, *I And Thou*, 173.

65. "It is part of our concept of the plant that it cannot react to our actions upon it, that it cannot 'reply.' . . . We find here . . . a reciprocity that has nothing except being" (ibid., 174).

66. Buber, *Philosophy of Martin Buber*, 708.

67. Ahmed, *Cultural Politics of Emotion*, 194.

68. Buber, *I And Thou*, 144, emphasis added.

69. Martin Heidegger, *Being and Time*, trans. Joan Stambaugh, rev. ed. (Albany: State University of New York Press, 2010), 178.

70. For a study of the later encounter between Heidegger and Buber, see Paul Mendes-Flohr, "Martin Buber and Martin Heidegger in Dialogue," *Journal of Religion* 94, no. 1 (2014): 2–25.

71. Mikhail Bakhtin, *Problems of Dostoevsky's Poetics* (Minneapolis: University of Minnesota Press, 1984), 63.

72. Buber, *I And Thou*, 144, emphasis added.

73. Kohanski summarizes the distance and relation dyad well (in an otherwise problematic text): "Buber wants to avoid splitting the world into two realms ... as, for example, Kant did. [Therefore,] he starts with man [sic] as a being endowed with a double movement, one of distancing and the other of relation. In the first movement man sets things over against himself as separate existents, and in the second he establishes a relationship with them" (Alexander Sissel Kohanski, *Martin Buber's Philosophy of Interhuman Relations* [Rutherford, NJ: Fairleigh Dickinson University Press, 1981], 21).

74. Buber, "Distance and Relation," 59–61. Hans Jonas takes up this world-creating distancing but makes it a matter of degrees, with more complex organisms creating more "distanced" worlds. See Hans Jonas, "To Move and to Feel: On the Animal Soul," in *The Phenomenon of Life: Toward a Philosophical Biology* (Evanston, IL: Northwestern University Press, 2001).

75. Deacon argues on Peircean lines for allowing nonhumans complicated semiotic systems composed of Peircean firsts and seconds that are nonetheless not "language" (which is a network of thirds). Whether one goes this route or not, it seems that language is the one human/nonhuman distinguishing characteristic that has been problematized but not erased. See Deacon, *Symbolic Species*.

76. There is a religious distinction operating here as well, and one can read a homologous difference in *Two Types of Faith* between following and imitating. See Martin Buber, *Two Types of Faith: A Study of the Interpretation of Judaism and Christianity*, trans. Norman P. Goldhawk (New York: HarperCollins, 1951), 96.

77. Buber, *I And Thou*, 144, emphasis added. However, in Buber's work, the animal soul's position—between the security of the plant and the realization of it—is anxious.

78. Aristotle, *De Anima*, trans. C. D. C. Reeve (Indianapolis: Hackett Publishing Company, 2017), secs. 2.1–4; Abraham Bos, "Aristotle on the Differences Between Plants, Animals, and Human Beings and on the Elements as Instruments of the Soul," *Review of Metaphysics* 63, no. 4 (2010): 821–41.

79. An icon is the sign that operates like a first: "An Icon is a sign which refers to the Object that it denotes merely by virtue of characters of its own, and which it possesses, just the same, whether any such Object actually exists or not. It is true that unless there really is such an Object, the Icon does not act as a sign; but this has nothing to do with its character as a sign. Anything whatever, be it quality, existent individual, or law, is an Icon of anything, in so far as it is like that thing and used as a sign of it" (Peirce, *Collected Papers of Charles Sanders Peirce*, secs. 1.369, 2.247).

80. Buber, *I And Thou*, 145, emphasis added.

81. This is, of course, not to suggest that cats are always anxious or inculcate a state of anxiety. As I write this, my cat is curled up on my foot, and I believe we are comforting each another. The anxiety Buber refers to occurs only in the dialogical situation and, even then, only occasionally. I do not believe that Buber, who, again, routinely talked to cats, meant to imply that dialogue with a cat is always anxious. It would be interesting to see how he would write about dogs, whose relation to language is rather unlike that of cats (dogs obey commands and respond to words) and whose anxieties are, it seems to me, completely different.

82. Ahmed, *Cultural Politics of Emotion*, 4.

83. Anxiety in this sense is not "negative" but a consequence of immediacy: intimacy is fragile, and perhaps beautiful, and the more intimate something is— the fewer abstractions and actualizations to distract us—the more anxious.

84. Buber, *I And Thou*, 146.

85. This paper is not the place to treat this basic aspect of Buber's thought— that every I-You relationship must end. It suffices to note that in order to be "made real" the relationship must be in some sense objectified, and so, if an I-You encounter is to be more than an airy possibility, if it is to be realized, then it must end and transition into a thing in the world. On this, see Bloch, "Philosophy of Dialogue," 56; Friedman, "Walter Kaufmann's Mismeeting with Martin Buber"; and Dustin Atlas, "Out of the In-Between: Moses Mendelssohn and Martin Buber's German Jewish Philosophy of Encounter, Singularity, and Aesthetics" (PhD diss., Rice University, 2013), 202–5. As Buber writes, "Every You *in the world* is compelled by its nature to become a thing for us or at least to enter again and again into thing-hood" (Buber, *I and Thou*, 147, emphasis added). Apparently, God is exempted from this rule.

86. Buber, *I And Thou*, 146.

TEN

MONOLOGUE DISGUISED AS DIALOGUE

Almodóvar's *Talk to Her* and Buber
on the "Lovers' Talk"

SARAH SCOTT

IN HIS 1929 "DIALOGUE," MARTIN Buber writes of eros that he knows of no other realm in which dialogue and monologue are so mingled and opposed.[1] The terms dialogue and monologue go back to Buber's 1923 *I and Thou*, which laid out the distinction between "I-Thou" or dialogic modes of existence and "I-It" or monologic modes of existence. Because it identifies just two basic modes of being—namely, that which responds to the self and other as whole, unique, spontaneous beings in relation and that which takes the self and other as mere objects of experience—*I and Thou* has been criticized for presenting a simplistic understanding of human relationships.[2] This point was not lost on Buber, who, while never leaving behind the scholar's penchant for taxonomy and conceptual distinctions, dives into the messy, "real world" problems of relationships in later works that explore topics as wide ranging as the relationships of teacher-student, therapist-patient, political or religious leader-community, and lover-lover.

In "Dialogue," Buber elaborates his philosophy of dialogue and identifies three basic forms of what is commonly, but often mistakenly, called "dialogue." Besides the "genuine dialogue" of I-Thou relations, there is also "technical dialogue," which is a turning toward the other to establish objective understanding that usually entails an exchange of the findings of observation, and "monologue disguised as dialogue."[3] He explains that in monologue disguised as dialogue interlocutors are engaged with their own experiences, not with the address of the other. They "dialogue," "without the men that are spoken to being regarded in any way present as persons. A *conversation* characterized . . . solely by the desire to have's own self-reliance confirmed by marking the impression that is made, or if it has become unsteady to have it strengthened; a *friendly chat* in which each regards himself as absolute and legitimate and the other as relativized and questionable; a *lovers' talk* in which both partners alike enjoy their own glorious soul and their precious experience."[4] Because this takes place between friends and lovers—relationships not typically thought of as being marked by viewing the other as a mere "It"—monologue disguised as dialogue can be harder to recognize and more pernicious than straightforward monologue. While monologue disguised as dialogue may be a subset of his initial category of I-It relations, Buber's shift from a simple dualism to thinking about multiple moral phenomena and the ways a category can masquerade as another category paves the way for a more nuanced and productive moral philosophy—albeit one that forces us to confront our own practices of and encounters with category disguise.

This chapter explores monologue disguised as dialogue, particularly as it emerges in the "lovers' talk," by bringing Buber's philosophy of dialogue into relation with Pedro Almodóvar's 2002 film *Talk to Her* (*Hable con ella*).[5] In reconstructing Buber's account of monologue disguised as dialogue, we shall see that Buber uses examples of deeply embodied relations, for example, sexual or violent encounters, to describe the seeing of the other that takes place in genuine dialogue. At the same time, he is concerned that relationships, particularly erotic relations, are often plagued by monologue disguised as dialogue. I use *Talk to Her*, which follows the failed romantic endeavors of Marco and Benigno, to illuminate Buber's claims. Marco and Benigno, who meet in a hospital ward while tending to Lydia and Alicia, their respective comatose love interests, illustrate how dwelling in memory and fantasy may lead one to fall into monologue even as one believes they are engaged with the presence of the other. Indeed, throughout the film Benigno appears to be a paragon of the virtue of "talking to," that is, the virtue of being able to enter into dialogue, yet ultimately, he is shown to be incapable of forming genuine relationships. Despite the fact that Benigno rapes his comatose patient, commentators have referred to his relationship with Alicia as a tragic romance in which Benigno practices supererogatory devotion. It is my view that this illustrates the successful disguise of monologue as dialogue that permeates the film and human relations in general.

In order to explore the phenomenon of monologue disguised as dialogue, I first lay out the salient features of the film and the way Alicia's rape has been characterized as an act of care. I then introduce three models of sexuality used by contemporary philosophers: forceful-seduction, contractual, and communicative. Drawing on *Talk to Her*, I propose a fourth model of sexuality—romantic-care—and argue that this model is especially pernicious as it is a paradigmatic case of monologue disguised as dialogue. To clarify the monologic danger of the romantic-care model, I contrast it to Buber's requirements for genuine dialogue. In my reconstruction of Buber's requirements I focus on imagining the real (*Realphantasie*) and mutuality, which I argue can give a foundation for communicative sexuality. I end by considering tragic limitations to dialogue and the importance of basic category distinctions, particularly when facing categories that disguise themselves as other categories.

I. THE VIRTUE OF TALKING TO

Almodóvar is known for creating films that undermine traditional patterns of thinking through the use of category violation.[6] His attempts "to show that the human facts are ambivalent and contradictory" often force his viewers to undergo a sort of moral education.[7] We typically assume harmony between the moral worth of an agent's mode, that is, intention or orientation, her action, and the consequences of her action. *Talk to Her* separates these insofar as a morally ambiguous mode (Benigno's pathological "love" for his patient) leads to a condemnable action (rape of his patient) and a praiseworthy consequence (miraculous awakening of his patient upon her birth of their stillborn child), thereby forcing viewers to reflect on their pattern of moral assessment.[8] Because *Talk to Her* leads viewers to identify with Marco and Benigno, viewers are often unclear if Benigno should be categorized as villain or hero, his attentiveness categorized as assault or care, or his talking to categorized as monologue or dialogue. Putting viewers in the uncomfortable position of sympathizing or even identifying with a rapist forces us to confront cultural and historical frameworks or models for sexual relations and our own struggle to separate monologue disguised as dialogue from genuine dialogue.

Almodóvar uses two dance performances to frame the film. In the first, a male dancer frantically attempts to move obstacles out of the way of a closed-eyed, erratic female dancer.[9] Marco sits in the audience weeping. In the scenes that follow, we learn that he is a writer doing a story on Lydia, a rare female bullfighter. They have a romantic relationship until a goring by a bull leads to her coma and ultimate death. Flashbacks show that from the beginning of their relationship Marco interprets Lydia as a desperate woman in need of saving. In so doing he relives the pattern of his last failed relationship, in which he attempted to save an underage heroin addict. He even says to Lydia, "She was the same as you." We infer that Marco cries during the film's opening dance sequence because he identifies with the male dancer, who attempts to rescue a woman—close-eyed, moved by her own inner torment, and unaware of the dangers of her environment—trapped in her own private reality. The contrast between the male and female dancer initially sets Marco up as a savior and romantic hero.[10] However, as the film progresses, we learn he never really saw Lydia, only the memory he created of his last girlfriend, projected onto Lydia. Although Marco identifies with the attentive, perpetually rescuing male dancer, because he is caught up in the analysis and projection of his own memories, he is actually as monologic and blind as the female dancer. In his last conversation with Lydia, he excitedly explains that he is finally over his former relationship. At the end of his speech, Lydia says, "We should talk." "We've been talking for an hour," he replies. "You have, not me," she answers. Unbeknownst to Marco, not only does Lydia not need saving, but she has decided to leave him to return to her former lover.

Benigno, a nurse tending to the comatose Alicia, who is at the same facility as Lydia, initially functions as a foil to Marco. While Marco engages in monologic behavior, Benigno beseeches him to "talk to her." Because of Benigno's unusually attentive nursing, he is chosen by Alicia's father to be her primary caretaker. He has done this for four years, which Benigno describes as the "most complete years of my life." Besides *talking to* Alicia, Benigno often *speaks of* her in the first-person plural saying, for example, "we're reading" and "we're getting around." He also interprets her wishes and directly *speaks for* her, saying, for example, "She likes it a lot." As the film proceeds Benigno is shown to be far from benign, for we learn that he stalked Alicia prior to her accident. He believes he is in a romantic relationship with her and tells Marco he wants to marry her, prompting Marco to call his relationship "crazy monologue." Unbeknownst to Marco, Benigno has recently raped Alicia. Rather than show the viewer the rape, Almodóvar shows Benigno describing a movie he has seen to Alicia. Believing that Alicia is a fan of silent films, Benigno watches films and afterward tells her "what she has seen" through his eyes. In *Shrinking Lover*, a scientist drinks a shrinking potion, climbs inside his lover's vagina and "stays inside her forever." Almodóvar cuts from the black-and-white scenes of *Shrinking Lover* to a close-up of red lava lamp fluid, and we could easily miss the fact that a rape has just occurred were it not for Alicia's subsequent pregnancy. Almodóvar explains his choice to disguise the rape: "Benigno had become like a friend of mine, although I wrote the character. Sometimes, you don't want to see things that your friends do. I didn't want to show Benigno doing what he did in the clinic. I also did not want to show the audience that image. So I put the silent movie in there to hide what was happening."[11] Ultimately the birth process causes Alicia to wake up, while the jailed Benigno, believing Alicia is still in a coma and fearing he will never see her again, kills himself in an attempt to place himself into a coma so that he can rejoin her.

Because Almodóvar initially presents Benigno as the benign, indeed virtuous, foil to Marco and shows Benigno's stalking, obsessive care, and rape from Benigno's point of view (as well as the sympathetic point of view of Marco, who alternates between viewing Benigno as a friend, a virtuous person to learn caretaking from, and a troubled person in need of care), "reviewers continually refer to Benigno and Alicia as a couple and to their relationship as a love affair."[12] His obsessive nursing and rape are viewed as a sacrifice, with Benigno tragically dying not knowing he has healed the woman he loves. No such empathetic identification with Alicia is encouraged; her perspective is consistently erased, even to the point that her rape is disguised as a silent film out of loyalty to Benigno. Viewers are thus encouraged to reenact the ways Marco and Benigno silence the reality of others, as men identifying with one another—in "dialogue" with each other but in monologue with women.[13]

Along these lines, Robert B. Pippin interprets Benigno's behavior as demonstrating what it means to respond to the other as a person, that is, as a being with moral value: "the last thing Benigno has done (within, let us say, the frame of relevance, salience and moral import created by Almodóvar and Benigno) is to treat Alicia merely as an object, a thing to be used for his pleasure."[14] While Pippin acknowledges this frame of relevance is problematic and likely created by Almodóvar with the goal of causing viewers to question standard moral categories, other viewers become so pulled into the frame created by Almodóvar and Benigno that they seem to forget that the silent film within the film that hides the rape does not depict reality but is a fantastical film that serves to shore up Benigno's own fantasy. C. D. C. Reeve, for instance, acknowledges that intercourse with one's sleeping spouse is morally and legally problematic but then interprets the scene of the shrunken lover climbing inside his spouse as the fulfillment of her (not his) unarticulated desires: "A shot of her face shows us that she is aroused, even while asleep. Speaking its own natural language, the soft animal of her body has spoken its consent."[15] Reeve then uses this ostensible ability of the animalistic nature of a body to consent using natural language to offer a rationalization of Benigno's rape of Alicia: "When Marco says to Benigno that 'Alicia can't say with any part of her body "I do,"' the odd formulation he employs focuses us on something he overlooks. Alicia is ovulating or close to it: she gets pregnant. As a result there will be more mucus than usual in her vagina. We can imagine Benigno discovering this and (mis-)interpreting it."[16] In the confusion produced by Almodóvar, viewers can fall prey to the same delusion Benigno suffers from: the reading of one's own inclinations into the appearance of an other, rationalized by a mistaken epistemology that takes automatic bodily changes to be an objective communication of the desire and will of a subject, such that a nonconscious body can consent without the subject herself actually consenting.

II. MODELS OF SEXUALITY

Ethicists and legal scholars working on the problem of rape have vigorously condemned the notion that the body has a "natural language," such that explicit consent is unnecessary. Indeed, several jurisdictions have adopted affirmative consent policies, which is a shift from a "no means no" to a "yes means yes" model of consent.[17] While a shift to affirmative consent may be an improvement, I believe that consent laws require the clear and ongoing communication in intimate encounters described by Lois Pineau in "Date Rape: A Feminist Analysis" to be effective. Pineau explores two interrelated sexual mythologies that make it very difficult to successfully prosecute (and prevent) instances of rape: the notion that women desire forceful sex and/or a compelling seduction and the notion that sexual relations are like contractual agreements. The "forceful-seduction model" assumes women cannot be trusted to honestly express or even know their own sexual desires.[18] While shifting one's framework to a "contractual model" is an improvement insofar as it assumes sex ought to be practiced by consenting adults (that is, rational and autonomous agents), it is also potentially dangerous. A contractual model assumes each participant has his or her respective ends set at the outset. As in other contractual relationships it is common for one party to have less negotiating power, with women often being presented merely with the option to "opt out"—or under affirmative consent, to "opt in"—as opposed to being equally empowered to articulate and seek their own desires. Moreover, the common understanding of contractual obligation allows for a party that has changed his or her desires and breaks the contract to be forced to uphold his or her side of the contract or receive suitable punishment. While the forceful-seduction model can lead one to believe that women secretly desire date rape, the contractual model can lead one to believe that women deserve date rape.[19] In both models (which often work in tandem), there is an epistemic and moral failure on the part of the assailant to ascertain and attend to the victim's present desires.

To combat this failure, Pineau offers "communicative sexuality" as an alternative framework. In contrast to the forceful-seduction model, communicative sexuality relies on the articulation of and responsiveness to desire. She explains, "Persons engaged in communicative sexuality . . . will be sensitive to the responses of their partners. They will, like good conversationalists, be intuitive, sympathetic, and charitable."[20] As in the contractual model, consent is paramount. However, unlike the contractual model, consent is seen as an ongoing dialogic process that requires each partner to be fully present to and engaged with the other.[21] Moreover, communicative sexuality suggests that at least one of the ends of the encounter is the cooperative relationship itself.[22] A similar proposal is made by Michelle J. Anderson, who uses the term "negotiation model." She calls our attention to the ways negotiation is a more robust moral and legal requirement than both negative and affirmative consent, which are both undermined by the pitfalls of contractual sexuality: "Under the No Model, he may legally penetrate her because she failed to object verbally. Under the Yes Model, he may legally penetrate her because she engaged in kissing and heavy petting, a functional 'yes' in his imagination. Under the Negotiation Model, he may not penetrate her, no matter the kissing and necking shared, nor his hopeful interpretation thereof, until he breaks out of his solipsistic universe and engages the girl—another human being whose desires and boundaries matter—in a conversation."[23]

Given these proposals for communicative sexuality as a means for ascertaining if one has fulfilled epistemic and moral obligations toward one's sexual partner, it is striking that Benigno tries to show Marco how to "talk to her" (Lydia) and yet ultimately rapes Alicia. It is relatively easy to recognize when forceful-seduction and contractual models lead to monologic engagement in one's own fantasy or desires. It can be harder to recognize the moral harm that occurs when something that looks like communicative sexuality distorts into monologue. George Wilson's analysis of Benigno illustrates the potential difficulty of recognizing the peculiar moral harm of monologue disguised as dialogue. Wilson describes Benigno "as the chief exemplar of a kind of fundamental human virtue... [the virtue of 'talking to':] the virtue of establishing or trying to establish some fundamental mode of communication."[24] He explains, "'Talking to her,' understood in the appropriate expanded sense, is a prime instance of and a metonymy for the activity of taking care of another person with unquestioning love, without any condition and without expectations of reward or immediate response."[25] In his view, Benigno shows "supererogatory devotion" and "empathetic openness to signs from the other of what they need and want."[26] Although he condemns the act of rape, Wilson defends the perpetrator Benigno as "a caring, intensely devoted man, acting out of a welter of confused passions."[27] Wilson's understanding of the virtue of talking to lends itself to a rationalization of Alicia's rape as driven by Benigno's empathetic openness to the need of Alicia's ovulating body to be inseminated, and supererogatory willingness to face social and legal punishment in order to meet her needs, despite the fact that she is incapable of reciprocating his love.

In Wilson's account, Benigno fits neither the forceful-seduction nor the contractual models of sexuality but instead is an example of what I call the "romantic-care model." This model is built around the romantic notion that true love inspires self-sacrifice and need not be requited. This is also how Almodóvar understands Benigno's actions:

> In terms of utopian love, I think that if you look at Benigno and Alicia, it is a real relationship. Or at least in Benigno's mind it is a real relationship because he feels absolutely compensated by taking care of this woman and being with her every moment of the day.... for there to be a loving relationship it is only necessary for one person to love. For there to be communication within a couple, it is enough for there to be only one person who communicates or who really wants to communicate. Even though a couple consists of two people, if one of the people in a couple puts all their effort into moving a couple along they will move along. All of this relates to pure romanticism.[28]

I am troubled by Almodóvar's views on relationships and communication and concerned that *Talk to Her* conflates the virtue of talking to applied to sexual relationships, that is, the communicative model of sexuality, with what I identify as the romantic-care model.

I take this conflation to illustrate a broader problem. If viewers have a hard time interpreting Benigno, it is not just because Almodóvar ruptures expectations by coding attacker as benign and villain as hero. It is because we struggle with distinguishing dialogue from monologue. Perhaps because it is hard to distinguish dialogue from monologue, perpetrators, victims, and onlookers alike can also have a hard time distinguishing care from violence. Benigno's hair brushing and massages suddenly become violent gestures once we see him as a stalker turned rapist. Benigno's case illustrates that one way the monologue of the romantic-care model disguises itself as dialogue and hence protects itself from accusations of force is by putting on the superficial trappings of communicative sexuality. Pedophiliac "grooming" and deceptive "care" practices similarly illustrate just how dangerous romantic-care sexuality and monologue disguised as dialogue can be.[29] By breaking down the distinction between hero and villain and the distinction between care and violence, *Talk to Her* shows us that the romantic-care model actually overlaps most closely with the forceful-seduction model. This overlap is possible insofar as each model normalizes and champions monologic relationships.

III. GENUINE DIALOGUE VERSUS MONOLOGUE

While Pineau and Anderson advance our understanding of sexual ethics in important ways, they are primarily legal scholars, and do not provide a full account of the ontological, epistemological, and moral underpinnings of dialogic relationships. I argue that Buber does, and that without working our way down to these foundations it is not possible to identify what exactly is wrong with the monologic practices we seek to dismantle, nor is it possible to illuminate when we are successfully building new practices and not just reconstructing old monologic structures under a new disguise. In order to make clear the hidden monologic nature of the romantic-care model I will now flesh out Buber's distinction between dialogue and monologue, and then use Buber's philosophy of dialogue to distinguish a Buberian communicative model of sexuality from the romantic-care model of sexuality.

The young Buber planned to write a monograph on sex for the forty-volume Die Gesellschaft series he edited but set the project aside after publishing *Die Erotik* by Lou Andreas-Salomé as a part of the series in 1910.[30] In later years, Buber often used erotic encounters to illustrate dialogic relationships in general. In "Dialogue," he writes:

> That inclination of the head over there—you feel how the soul enjoins it on the neck, you feel it not on your neck but on that one over there, on the beloved one, and yet you yourself are not as it were snatched away, you are here, in the feeling self-being, and you receive the inclination of the head, its injunction, as the answer to the word of your own silence.... The two who are loyal to the Eros of dialogue, who love another, receive the common event from the other's side as well, that is, they receive it from the two sides, and thus for the first time understand in a bodily way what an event is.[31]

A few years earlier (1925), Buber gave a talk in which he gave another positive description of an erotic encounter: "A man caresses a woman, who lets herself be caressed. Then let us assume that he feels the contact from two sides—with the palm of his hand still, and also with the woman's skin. The twofold nature of the gesture, as one that takes place between two persons, thrills through the depths of enjoyment in his heart and stirs it. If he does not deafen his heart he will have—not to renounce the enjoyment but—to love."[32] Lovers possess an unusual potential for knowing the entirety of their partner—not just the minds and public acts of the other, but also their bodies and private existence. By asserting that understanding in "a bodily way what an event is" gives us access to common reality, Buber counters the rejection of embodiment and suspicion of feeling typical of philosophic analysis.

A comparison to Kantian views shows the distinctiveness of Buber's orientation. Given Kant's emphasis on autonomy and freedom of contract, Kantian ethics initially seems a good foundation for a contractual model of sexuality.[33] But Kant himself maintains that while all desire-driven acts are amoral, sex is especially immoral because, other than cannibalism, it is the only use of the other to satisfy desires where the other is rendered a mere physical object (and not a rational subject whose knowledge, talent, or goods we are using).[34] Kantian worries about sex might be assuaged if we conceive of good sexual relations as a form of "moral friendship." However, moral friendship is characterized by mutual respect rather than feeling, and Kant thought sexual relationships were too intimate, too lacking in respectful distance, to possess moral friendship.[35] As his descriptions of erotic encounters indicate, Buber would agree with Kant that such relations are unusually intimate and filled with desire and embodied experience. Yet we shall see that Buber maintains that what is needed between persons is not moral respect for autonomous individuals with preset ends—not a revisionist account of Kantian ethics that would defend a contractual model of sexuality—but the moral exercise of the imagination to dynamically relate to a unique, dynamic other in their embodied totality, which could provide a foundation for communicative sexuality.

While Buber's embrace of embodiment and intersubjectivity redeems sex from the suspicions of much of philosophy, because he does not elaborate on his erotic illustrations of dialogue, they can misleadingly suggest he advocates the romantic-care model. Indeed, Benigno would seem to identify with Buber's examples of the person who sees in the inclination of a head "the answer to the word of his own silence" and the man caressing a woman who feels (so he imagines) the contact from both sides and is filled with love. This raises the question of how Benigno's attentiveness to Alicia's body and fantastical interpretation of the signs of her body differs from the practices of Buber's dialogic lover, especially given that the lover's partner is strikingly silent or passive in both of the previous examples. Yet despite the one-sided nature of his descriptions, Buber uses language as harsh as that of Kant to describe monologic eros: "Dialogic is not to be identified with love. But love without dialogic, without real outgoing to the other, reaching to the other, and companying with the other, the love remaining with itself—this is called Lucifer."[36] Turning to Buber's analysis of the barriers to genuine dialogue helps identify the central features of "love remaining with itself."

The three great barriers to genuine dialogue identified by Buber—"the invasion of seeming," "the inadequacy of perception," and "imposition"—are all interrelated.[37] In general monologue is characterized by inward turning reflection (*Rückbiegung*).[38] Dialogue requires us to be present to the other. But we can find ourselves preoccupied with manufacturing a certain image of ourselves, and this "invasion of seeming" keeps us from being fully present. This invasion of seeming is not to be confused with "genuine seeming," as when, for example, a youth sincerely imitates his hero and in sincere imitation comes to actualize his own potentialities.[39] Insincere seeming is rather an act of disengagement and manipulation, such that others are reduced to "mirrors" that are only valued insofar as they reflect an image of ourselves back to us.

> The kingdom of the lame-winged Eros is a world of mirrors and mirrorings.... There a lover stamps around and is in love only with his passion. There one is wearing his differentiated feelings like medal-ribbons. There one is enjoying the adventures of his own fascinating effect. There one is gazing enraptured at the spectacle of his own supposed surrender. There one is collecting excitement. There one is displaying his "power." There one is preening himself with borrowed vitality. There one is delighting to exist simultaneously as himself and as an idol very unlike himself. There one is warming himself at the blaze of what has fallen to his lot. There one is experimenting. And so on and on—all the manifold monologists with their mirrors, in the apartment of the most intimate dialogue![40]

Instead of being with the other, which Buber understands as a state of spontaneity and lack of reserve, we are preoccupied with our fantasy of our self and desire to ensure the other receives that fantasy image. This makes it difficult for our interlocutor to adequately perceive us and, given that we are engaged with our own image and not with the other, makes it difficult for us to adequately perceive the other.

While the manipulation of our image is one form of imposition, there are myriad ways in which we may be so focused on imposing something on another that we miss adequately perceiving and responding to her. For example, education can involve the imposition of the teacher's own norms and beliefs. Insofar as this is an imposition, the educator is really a propagandist: "the propagandist, who imposes himself, does not really believe even in his own cause, for he does not trust it to attain its effect of its own power without his special methods."[41] In contrast, the genuine educator influences her charge to unfold his unique person without attempting to shape that person according to the educator's own desires: "in education, then, there is a lofty asceticism: an asceticism which rejoices in the world, for the sake of the responsibility for a realm of life which is entrusted to us for our influence but not our interference."[42] This "ascetic" refusal to impose or interfere plays a decisive role in separating monologue from dialogue.

Buber's philosophy of dialogue takes us to be interdependent with other creatures. As such, our identity is neither static nor passively received but dynamic and emergent from ever changing relations with others. To adequately perceive others, such as occurs in genuine dialogue, we have to recognize them as similarly dynamic and interdependent beings, which means we have to be open and receptive to being surprised by others. Conversely, "he who is living the life of monologue is never aware of the other as something that is absolutely not himself and at the same time something with which he nevertheless communicates."[43] In monologic or I-It relations our ability to conceptualize beings overtakes our ability to recognize what is new and unique and we see the people we meet as static categories. Without seeing others for who they really are—unique, dynamic, spontaneous particulars—we form relationships not with actual persons but with concepts in our own mind. Buber contrasts this monologic withdrawal to dialogic presence. I take the dual temporal and spatial meaning of "presence" to suggest two basic forms of monologic absence: withdrawal into monologue that is driven by temporality, such as a preoccupation with memory or future goals, and monologue occasioned by a distortion, so to speak, of the "spatial" aspects of relationship, for example, not extending one's imagination to include the other's point of view or overidentifying with the other and hence closing all distance. In *Talk to Her*, Marco illustrates temporal absence while Benigno illustrates spatial absence.

Buber's *I and Thou* repeats the refrain "in the beginning is the relation," thereby suggesting a sort of state of nature for man. This prehistory lives on in our "innateness of the longing for relation [*Ursprünglichkeit des Beziehungsstrebens*]."[44] However, Buber then describes a sort of "fall" of humanity into a historical mode.[45] Our desire for the security of a permanent relationship appears to be threatened by the spontaneity and transience of the creatures to which we form relations. This moves us to use memory to shape what we encounter into controllable and permanent entities. Memory "educates itself" and transforms our relations from unmediated encounters to encounters mediated by the concepts we create of the other, actions, and our own self.[46] Although this work of memory stems from our desire to relate, an excess development of our ability to place things in the past counterproductively undermines our ability to enter into relations with others since their uniqueness and ability to surprise us is no longer recognized. The character of Marco is just such a temporal monologist. When he looks at Lydia, instead of gaining entrance into a shared reality, he sees the reflection of his own past experiences and his own image as a savior.

While both Marco and Benigno are driven by the "innateness of the longing for relation," Benigno falls into monologue not from the undue influence of memory but from a distortion of imagination. Buber writes, "*Phantasie . . .*

is the drive to turn everything into a You, the drive to pan-relation [*Trieb zur Allbeziehung*]—and where it does not find a living active being that confronts it but only an image or symbol of that, it supplies the living activity from its own fullness."⁴⁷ Benigno projects romantic and sexual reciprocity onto Alicia's inert body from the fullness of his own imagination. This excessive use of imagination is apparently his dominant mode of relating. When Marco visits Benigno in prison, Benigno tells him that in the absence of having Alicia to fixate on, he has been living vicariously through Marco's travel articles: "I became one with those people that have nothing and invent everything," he explains. His attempts at relating suffer from a lack of distance and an excess of empathetic identification; he loses himself in his object, just like the shrunken lover. While this initially seems benign and even virtuous, he not only diminishes himself but also diminishes his partner insofar as he is excessively aesthetically absorbed in her. He cares for or curates her as if she were an art object, whose sole purpose is to occasion his monologic play with his own internal imaginative states. By presenting this monologic play as the loss of his own self, he is able to shirk responsibility for the role he plays in the relationship. He truly believes his victim "asked for" his "care."

IV. IMAGINING THE REAL

With this contrast between dialogic and monologic sexuality brought into preliminary view, we are now in a position to think through the epistemological foundations of communicative sexuality. Although Buber's phrase "adequate perception" suggests a sensory or perhaps cognitive act to be contrasted to the inadequate perception occasioned by an overgrowth of memory or imagination, by adequate perception Buber also has in mind an act of the imagination, which he calls "imagining the real" (*Realphantasie*).[48] An important aspect of imagining the real is "inclusion" (*Umfassung*), which is the inclusion or embrace of the subjective point of view of the other without giving up one's own subjective point of view. This use of the imagination to generate, so to speak, binocular vision, gives us access to intersubjective reality. Inclusion requires:

[1] a relation between two persons

[2] an event experienced by them in common, in which at least one of them actively participates

[3] the fact that this one person, without forfeiting anything of the felt reality of his activity, at the same time lives through the common event from the standpoint of the other.[49]

This living in common through an act of the imagination provides the foundation for the giving and receiving of genuine self that is the dialogic relation. The connotation of perception as a merely sensory or cognitive act is further undermined by Buber's characterization of making the other present to oneself through imagining the real as a deeply embodied epiphany of intersubjectivity. In Buber's writing, embodiment does not come up because he wishes to understand eros; rather, eros comes up because he uses perspicuous examples of embodiment, such as sexual and violent encounters, to explain dialogic relationships and what it means to live through a common event together.

One of the most striking examples of imagining the real is shared in psychologist Carl R. Rogers's 1957 interview with Buber, when Buber addresses how he came to develop his understanding of people and relationships. He first describes having an initial attraction to psychiatry and the sense he had to let himself be willing to be changed by others and then describes the impact of World War I and subsequent death of his friend, the anarchist-socialist Gustav Landauer (1870–1919), who was brutally stomped to death by Freikorps:

> I could not resist to what was going on, and I was just compelled to, may I say so, to live it. You see? Things went on just in this moment. You may call it "imagining the real." Imagining what was going on. This is—this imagining, for four years, influenced me terribly. Just when it was finished, it finished by a certain episode in May nineteen when a friend of mine, a great friend, a great man, was killed by antirevolutionary soldiers in a very barbaric way, and I, now again once more—and this was the last time—I was compelled to imagine just this killing, but not in an optical way alone, but may I say so, just with my body.[50]

Buber's story illustrates the way we can become aware of the other's bodily experience in and through our own bodies, even when we are separated by a great distance (indeed, death) and are not actually physically sensing them. Nevertheless, Buber wants to make clear that we do not feel with our own bodies the profound pain and pleasure of another body in such a way that we lose the sensation of our own body and collapse the distinction between self and other.

Although his reaction to Landauer's death may appear to be an involuntary empathetic response, Buber insists that instead he was imagining the real. The key distinctions here are *imagining* versus feeling or conceptualizing, accessing *the reality of the other qua Other* versus identifying with or respecting the other qua sameness, and that this is a *practice* versus an involuntary response. After Buber recalls the effect on him of World War I and the death of Landauer, Rogers describes this as a state of feeling. Buber corrects him, replying the word *feeling* was not strong enough; this was rather a "living with" the people wounded and killed, and with Landauer in particular.[51] Buber elsewhere denounces empathy (*Einfühlung*) as the abdicating of one's own perspective for aesthetic absorption in another: "[Empathy] means the exclusion of one's own concreteness, the extinguishing of the actual situation of life, the absorption in pure aestheticism of the reality in which one participates. Inclusion is the opposite of this. It is extension of one's own concreteness, the fulfillment of the actual situation of life, the complete presence of the reality in which one participates."[52] Insofar as it collapses the distinction between self and other, empathy is monologic. Like the romantic-care model of sexuality it is especially dangerous because it often disguises its aesthetic absorption as dialogue.

Nor is imagining the real the conceptualization of what pleasure or pain are as a general category, as occurs with the use of reason and memory in acts of technical dialogue. Rather, imagining the real is living through an event with the other such that the lives of the two partners become, at least for the moment, lived in common, so that at least one of the partners leaves his enclosed, private reality and enters into an intersubjective reality, rendering him able to grasp this specific pleasure or pain as it belongs to this specific person. In his 1951 "Distance and Relation," published just a few years prior to the Rogers interview, Buber writes: "I experience, let us say, the specific pain of another in such a way that I feel what is specific in it, not therefore, a general discomfort or state of suffering, but this particular pain as the pain of the other. This making present increases until it is a paradox in the soul when I and the other are embraced by a common living situation, and (let us say) the pain which I inflict upon him surges up in myself, revealing the abyss of the contradictoriness of life between man and man."[53] What Buber is trying to get at, through the use of terms such as *making present, imagining the real,* and *inclusion,* is the epistemic work needed to understand the other person as a novel, embodied particular.

The epistemic work that happens in *Realphantasie* cannot occur without what Buber calls "distancing." Distancing is the imagination's depiction of what we encounter as a distinct totality that exists for itself, independent of our own experiences and emotional and practical investment in it.[54] Buber's distancing exhibits Kantian aesthetic "disinterestedness," which helps ensure that we practice *Realphantasie* and not mere *Phantasie*. This disinterestedness creates the space for the other to be present to us as they really are and gives the foundation for the "ascetic" lack of imposition or interference discussed earlier. Note this is not the same as the Kantian moral notion of respect. Buber's insistence that this requires a particular sort of imagination makes it more similar to Kantian aesthetics, as detailed in Kant's *Critique of Judgment*, than to Kantian ethics. Indeed, as I have elsewhere shown, Buber's moral epistemology rests on the use of what Kant calls reflective judgment, not determinate judgment.[55] Unlike determinate judgment, which is the subsuming of a particular under a preestablished category, reflective judgment describes the process of judging a novel particular that cannot be captured by preexisting categories. This happens in the level of the imagination, not reason. Rather than use categories to subsume various phenomena under the mantle of sameness, it creates distance in order to fully embrace the particular, embodied other.

From this different epistemological foundation there emerges a different understanding of moral relationships. In this model of relationship, difference and uniqueness connect, rather than the mediation of the sameness of personhood: "Only by means of their difference, by means of the uniqueness of this man and the uniqueness of that one, can men participate in one another."[56] Because of this, self and other never merge and become lost. Buber insists, "No matter how all-embracing the relation of two beings to each other may be, it does not in any sense mean their 'unification.' If I posit a 'correlation,' it still in no way follows from that, that a 'totality' exists."[57] Kantian insistence on protecting symmetrical autonomy may seem to be a method of preserving difference. However, in Buber's view, because this relationship is mediated through sameness, it is a version of monologue disguised as dialogue. As we saw foreshadowed in the contrast I drew between Kantian contractual sexuality and Buberian dialogic sexuality, Buber's rejection of Kantian ethics in favor of Kantian aesthetics reorients our moral compass away from the protection of symmetrical autonomy and toward the reinforcement of intersubjectivity. Because it is predicated on the imagination's initial distancing in order to more authentically enter into relation, this intersubjectivity grasps difference in a way that respect for personhood cannot.[58]

V. MUTUALITY VERSUS SYMMETRY

With this epistemology in place, let us revisit the ethical criteria for genuine dialogue. Buber's warning of the danger of empathy and insistence on the need for distancing illuminate the epistemological failures that undergird the romantic-care model in general, and the *Shrinking Lover* fantasy of dissolving one's identity until one lives inside the other and Benigno's rape of Alicia in particular. Nevertheless, the reader may still be troubled that all of Buber's examples of imagining the real specify an active partner who suddenly becomes aware of reality as it is experienced by a passive partner. One reading of Buber's philosophy of dialogue takes it to assume perfectly reciprocal relationships, under the mistaken assumption that dialogue entails symmetry. For instance, Steven T. Katz writes: "The freedom of *I-Thou* entails the total autonomy of both dialogical partners. To act in accordance with external rules is heteronomy, and this violates the premised freedom of the 'other' as *Thou* as well as of the self as *I*. As *I-Thou* encounter is an intersubjective relation between equals, at least in terms of their relation to each other for the duration of the encounter, this relation is characterized by mutuality. This is an especially important feature of *I-Thou* meeting. The symmetry of the relation is a basic premise of the whole dialogical life."[59] In this passage the notions of equality, mutuality, and symmetry run together, perhaps due to a mistaken attempt to fit Buber's philosophy of dialogue into Kantian ethics. Buber, however, separates these notions. Against those who assume he only leaves room for symmetrical relationships, Buber often writes of asymmetrical relations, for example, therapist-patient and teacher-student, and his examples of imagining the real are all strikingly one-sided. This raises the troubling question if Buber is asserting, as Almodóvar states, that "only one need actively participate" in dialogic relationships, indeed, if this one-sided relationship might be the height of love as the romantic-care model proposes.[60]

I believe that distinguishing between the moral requirement of mutuality and the moral requirement of symmetry helps explain why, despite his frequent analysis of asymmetrical relations, Buber offers an alternative to the romantic-care model. As we have seen, genuine dialogue has as its minimum preconditions being (versus seeming), adequate perception, and, while influence is an integral part of intersubjectivity, the preclusion of imposition or interference. There can be no dialogue without the presence (meeting and seeing the other in the here and now) of both parties, and no dialogue without each party being open to receiving and being changed by the other. Buber's summation stresses the mutuality of this presence and influence: dialogue has "as its minimum constitution one thing, the mutuality [*Gegenseitigkeit*] of the inner action."[61] They must "no matter with what measure of activity or indeed consciousness of activity—have turned to one another."[62] But in recognizing different degrees of activity or consciousness of activity, Buber removes the requirement for symmetry. This is because he is interested not just in dialogue between human persons but in dialogic relations with different life forms (he writes, for example, of his meetings with cats and horses) and transcendent beings, particularly God. As Buber puts it in *I and Thou*, we give language to beings that are below the threshold of language, we enter into language and give and receive with each other, and we create language to express what we receive from the transcendent.[63] When he revisits this tripartite structure in his 1957 afterword to *I and Thou*, Buber recasts the thresholds as that of mutuality, not language, and discusses "the normative limits of mutuality [*Mutualität*]."[64] In general, "every I-You relationship in a situation defined by the attempt of one partner to act on the other one so as to accomplish some goal depends on a mutuality that is condemned never to become complete."[65] While all genuine relationships are characterized by a degree of mutuality, some relationships, for example, teacher-student and therapist-patient relationships, are and should be asymmetrical, while other relationships, for example, loving sexual relationships, may have the added requirement of symmetry. If properly employed, distancing and inclusion should help us recognize the level of (a)symmetry between us and the other we meet and accept the limits for relationship set by that level.

While Buber's dialogic ethics and the romantic-care model both recognize the fact of and occasional necessity for asymmetry, the romantic-care model differs from Buber's dialogic ethics because it refuses to recognize the more foundational requirement of mutuality. By ignoring, indeed prohibiting, mutuality under the guise of providing asymmetrical care, the romantic-care model of sexuality is a paradigmatic case of monologue disguised as dialogue. Unlike Benigno, Buber's exemplary caretakers—the teacher, the therapist—vigilantly exercise distancing and avoid imposition in order to mitigate the projection of their desires on to the persons they are charged with helping. Their "lofty asceticism" grants their charges the space to be themselves, to be present so that they can better see what they really need. Because they recognize "the participation of both partners is in principle indispensable," they expect and are attuned to receive and react to the responses of their charges, even though they do not expect to receive symmetrical care in return.[66] As the figure of the caregiver turned rapist shows, once mutuality is discarded as the foundation of a relationship, ostensibly moral asymmetrical devotion becomes free from the constraint of responding to the reality of the other person, which can cause caring to flip into imposing a twisted "symmetry" on the other, for example, by assuming and imposing an implicit contractual obligation for him to return "care" by giving sexual gratification.

There may be a virtue of talking to, but contrary to Wilson's description, I join Buber in insisting that it requires an expectation of and attunement to response.[67] We should be deeply concerned about the monologic self-deception that lies behind a "relationship" that does not expect a response, whether this be the fantasy of unrequited love, or equally as dangerous, and often concomitant, the fantasy of a purely unidirectional relationship of care. As Buber puts it, "wishing to understand the pure relationship as dependence means wishing to deactualize one partner of the relationship and thus the relationship itself."[68]

Ignoring the silence, freezing, or turning away of the other while we blithely or doggedly press forward in "talking to" indicates we are not adopting the intersubjective perspective of *Realphantasie* because we are preoccupied with responding to the contents of our own memory or imagination.[69] Buber describes the disturbing pseudo-attentiveness that purports to carefully analyze and react accordingly to the other but never actually attends to the responses of any particular other: "I can separate it into its component parts, I can compare them and distribute them into groups of similar phenomena; and when I have done all this I have not touched my concrete world reality. Inseparable, incomparable, irreducible, now, happening, once only, it gazes upon me with a horrifying look."[70] Conversely, if we were to use *Realphantasie*, we would be challenged to not simply categorize the other according to some preconceived notion of the "natural language" of the body but to put our entire being to work to know and respond to the present desires and language of this particular, embodied person. In other words, we would be moved to practice communicative sexuality.

Buber's philosophy of dialogue can give a foundation for the communicative sexuality feminists working decades later proposed as an alternative to models of sexuality that enable rape. Indeed, I believe the communicative model of sexuality must be grounded in Buber's philosophy of dialogue to be able to distinguish communicative sexuality from monologue disguised as dialogue. While the contractual model of sexuality is an improvement on the forceful-seduction model, it is flawed insofar as it presupposes a static self with preset ends, and that the ends of action are one's own private ends, not the relationship itself, such that one can seem justified in forcing the other to fulfill his part of the contract. The communicative model of sexuality, when grounded in Buber's philosophy of dialogue, corrects the contractual model by making it a requirement that we recognize others and ourselves as unique, dynamic particulars with desires that can and do change. Meeting this requirement entails developing our capacity to enter into dialogic relationships, that is, our ability to be present, imagine the real, and practice distancing and inclusion. The moral demand for symmetry implicit in the Kantian-inspired contractual model can be incorporated into the model of communicative sexuality, but Buberian communicative sexuality takes mutuality to be what is of utmost moral importance. Without this emphasis on mutuality, the romantic-care model can insidiously present itself as a viable alternative to the forceful-seduction or contractual models, when in fact it is a dangerous refusal to enter into mutuality that often uses legitimate asymmetrical relationships to mask and justify its monologic imposition.

VI. TRAGIC LIMITS AND THE PROBLEM OF CATEGORIES

Almodóvar considered two alternative titles for his film: *Loneliness, I Suppose* and *The Man Who Cried*.[71] We infer that Benigno is the lonely figure, since "loneliness, I suppose" is the answer he gives when a therapist asks him why he is seeking treatment (the therapist is Alicia's father and Benigno set up the appointment only to gain entry into Alicia's dwelling), and Marco is "the man who cried," since he is first shown to us crying while watching the opening dance scene. In the prison scene where Benigno says "I became one with those people" to Marco, Almodóvar subtly superimposes Benigno's face, reflected through the prison glass, on top of Marco's face. Is Benigno still trapped in monologue, fantasizing he is becoming one with Marco? Or is he practicing *Realphantasie* and seeing himself simultaneously from his point of view and that of Marco? Is Marco practicing imagining the real and finally seeing Benigno for who he really is? Or are both characters doomed to forever remain trapped behind the barriers they have constructed in their failed attempts to enter into relation, as symbolized by the prison glass that divides them? In what could be a description of these dynamics, Buber writes:

> Let us now imagine two men, whose life is dominated by appearance, sitting and talking together. Call them Peter and Paul. Let us list the different configurations which are involved. First, there is Peter as he wishes to appear to Paul, and Paul as he wishes to appear to Peter. Then there is Peter as he really appears to Paul, that is, Paul's image of Peter, which in general does not in the least coincide with what Peter wishes Paul to see; and similarly there is the reverse situation. Lastly, there are the bodily Peter and the bodily Paul. Two living beings and six ghostly appearances, which mingle in many ways in the conversation between the two. Where is there room for any genuine interhuman life?[72]

This will be the last meeting of Marco and Benigno.

In his interview of Buber, Rogers insists that there is occasional reciprocity in the therapist-patient dialogue. Buber replies very sharply to this, and in so doing reinforces the preconditions for and limitations of dialogue. The therapist-patient relationship should have moments of mutuality and genuine dialogue, but insofar as the two parties remain in their roles, this will never be a symmetrical exchange. This is not just an issue of the therapist practicing rigorous distancing in order to limit imposition and maximize adequate perception. Many patients may be unable to imagine the real. As Buber explains to

Rogers, "You can see it, feel it, experience it from the two sides.... He cannot do it at all.... He cannot be but where he is."[73] The therapist ideally adequately perceives the patient. Yet while the patient may see that the therapist is practicing distancing and inclusion, the patient will not be able to see the therapist's personhood outside of his limited role as someone who sees the patient. When Rogers suggests one can have reciprocity even with schizophrenic or extremely paranoid patients, Buber presses back, explaining he is interested in "the problem of limits." Extreme cases present "a limit set for dialogue."[74] This type of patient does not present the everyday case of a person unduly influenced by memory and imagination and hence overly involved in seeming and imposition: "He does not open himself and does not shut himself. He *is* shut. There is something else being done to him that *shuts him*. And this, the terribility of this fate, I'm feeling very strongly because in the world of *normal* men, there are just analogous cases, when a sane man behaves, not to everyone, but behaves to some people *just so*, being shut. And the problem is if he can, be opened, if he can open himself, and so on. [Buber sighs.] And this is a problem for humans in general."[75] Marco seems to present a character that has shut himself and hopefully has learned to open himself up to intersubjectivity. However, Benigno appears to simply be shut. Buber says of the person who is shut, "This is a man in hell. A man in hell cannot think, cannot imagine helping another. How *could* he?"[76] If Benigno is shut, then his monologic eros seems less that of "Lucifer" than that of a tragic figure. While this does not justify his actions—that a rape is performed by a criminally insane person brings it no closer to being a virtuous act—it does suggest a limit to the category of those we can reasonably expect to enter into dialogue.[77] Benigno's limitations help us understand Marco's moral failure: a person capable of dialogic relations behaving to some people as if he were being shut. In a sign of the ubiquity of this problem and Almodóvar's success in problematizing moral categories, viewers reverse the gloss: Marco's moral failure is used to erroneously normalize and valorize Benigno's "crazy monologue" as "romantic" and "virtuous." I take it that this seductive path through disguise, normalization, and finally championing of moral harm is what Buber meant when he called monologic eros "Lucifer."

In the last part of the film, Marco spends time learning how to be alone. We hope that this prepares him to be fully present to others as unique, spontaneous persons, as opposed to reinforcing his tendency to retreat into memory or fantasy and do away with difference, and that it prepares him to accept others without trying to save or fix them, because Almodóvar concludes the film by arranging for Marco to meet the now awake Alicia at a dance performance. Alicia's dance teacher sees Marco at the dance performance. "One day, we should talk," she tells him. "Yes, and it will be simpler than you thought," says Marco, who may or may not have learned the lesson that dialogue easily slips into monologue. "Nothing is simple," she replies. "I am a dancing teacher, and nothing is simple." Marco and Alicia see each other, and Almodóvar inserts the intertitle "Marco and Alicia." Unlike the first dance scene, in which one dancer is lost in her own world, while the other's excessive attentiveness points to the monologic underside of care, the dancers in the closing performance are true partners.[78] This, coupled with uplifting music and lighting, suggests the viewer has just watched a romantic comedy, in the sense of a plot in which sympathetic characters overcome misconceptions and setbacks to finally enter a successful romance. Yet Almodóvar inserted the intertitles "Lydia and Marco" and "Alicia and Benigno" before their stories, which turned out to be far from comedic.

The seeming, imposition, and inadequate perception that hinder dialogue may be moral flaws, but the limits of dialogue may also be tragic, that is, marked by an insurmountable failure or inability to relate to one another that we experience as fated or out of our control. Buber cautions us: "There is not only you, your mode of thinking, your mode of doing, there is also a certain situation—things are so and so—which may sometimes be tragic and even more terrible than what we call tragic. You cannot change this. [Buber sighs.] Humanity, human will, human understanding, are not everything. There is some reality we confront—is confronting us. We cannot—we may not—forget it for a moment."[79] It is tragic that Alicia falls into a coma and cannot respond, even negatively, to Benigno. Benigno attempts to overcome this tragic asymmetry by "talking to" Alicia, but his dialogue is mere fantasy. Marco attempts to overcome his tragic inability to help his former lover beat her addiction by "saving" his new lover, and that too is mere monologue. Viewers attempt to overcome Benigno's tragic inability to practice distancing and inclusion by empathetically entering his fantasy and recasting him as a virtuous caregiver or romantic hero. Almodóvar tries to hide what his "friend" Benigno did by obscuring the rape from the audience and concluding the film by coding it as a romantic comedy. Yet an integral part of exercising *Realphantasie* and not mere *Phantasie* is that we confront the reality of a person or situation and recognize when, despite all our attempts at presence—or maybe even because of our misguided attempts to impose presence—no manner of caring, empathizing, projecting, or attempts at saving or rationalizing will unlock or transform the person or the situation. Not all stories turn into comedies. Sometimes we do not want to recognize the normative limits of mutuality or see what caregivers, friends, or we have done, but we must look anyhow.

When we leave fantasy behind and accept the existence of moral failure and tragedy, Buber's careful assessment of what exactly is wrong with monologic relationships that at first glance appear to be morally admirable—for example, contractual and romantic-care sexualities—provides clarity. But what is helpful about Buber is that he provides *illumination*, not a rulebook to determine dialogue from monologue disguised as dialogue. Articulated epistemological and ethical features of dialogic relationships, such as the exercise of distancing (the recognition of others as dynamic and interdependent beings, "ascetic" refusal to impose or interfere, and receptivity to being surprised by others) and the requirement of mutuality (instead of symmetry), are attempts to elucidate what cannot be codified. When he specifies that mutuality is the minimum criteria for dialogue, Buber writes, "It is good to put this forward so crudely and formally. For behind the formulating question about the limits of a category under discussion is hidden a question which bursts all formulas asunder."[80] I take it that the hidden question that bursts all formulas asunder is not just what are the limits of this category but also, given the reality of difference, what are the limits of categories in general. Dialogue cannot be codified because it is a mode of existence that conditions experience and hence occurs prior to determinate judgment. The hard truth is that we cannot know once and for all if we are in dialogue, for any attempt to create stable criteria for dialogue is already working within the realm of I-It relations and closing us off from being able to recognize novel phenomenon. So long as we insist on stable criteria and only exercise determinate judgment, we run the risk of being blind to monologue disguised as dialogue.

Is Buber's project then tragically flawed insofar as it is an attempt to elucidate what defies conceptualization? As noted, Almodóvar's stated goal is to "show that the human facts are ambivalent and contradictory."[81] In making audiences sympathize and identify with a rapist and showing how care can actually be violence, he forces us to question simplistic patterns of moral assessment. But just because the distinction between tragic and morally flawed persons can be ambivalent, or dialogue can sometimes be revealed to actually be monologue, does not mean that we should give up on or collapse basic category distinctions. The collapse of basic category distinctions mirrors the collapse of the distinction between self and other that characterizes monologue and makes us complicit in I-It relations. It would have us shirk responsibility for moral judgment and assert that there is no difference between care and violence, hero and villain, or loving sex and rape. Conversely, recognizing the extent to which much of what we thought was dialogue was actually monologue disguised as dialogue forces us to confront the extent to which we have harmed others, been complicit in the harm of others, and been harmed ourselves by monologue. The reality of difference and the necessity of reflective judgment of novel particulars is not a barrier but the way to nuanced moral judgment, which includes recognizing what confronts us and when categories are disguised as other categories. As I quoted Buber previously, "There is not only you, your mode of thinking, your mode of doing. . . . There is some reality we confront—is confronting us. We cannot—we may not—forget it for a moment." That we cannot forget the reality of difference and the reality of the other is the actual moral education provided by *Talk to Her* and the key message of Buber's philosophy of dialogue.

NOTES

I thank Jordan Pascoe, Heidi Furey, and the anonymous reviewers for their helpful comments, and the students in my spring 2017 "Philosophers on Sex, Love, and Friendship" class at Manhattan College for their engaging discussions on many of the topics in this chapter.

1. Martin Buber, "Dialogue," in *Between Man and Man*, trans. Ronald Gregor-Smith (New York: Routledge, 2002), 5.

2. See, for example, Walter Kaufmann, "I and You: A Prologue," in *I and Thou*, by Martin Buber, trans. Walter Kaufmann (New York: Touchstone, 1996).

3. Buber, "Dialogue," 22.

4. Ibid., 23.

5. Pedro Almodóvar, dir., *Talk to Her* (Los Angeles: Sony, 2002), DVD.

6. For a summary of this feature of Almodóvar's plots, see Robert B. Pippin, "Devils and Angels in Almodóvar's *Talk to Her*," in *Talk to Her*, ed. A. W. Eaton (London: Routledge, 2009), 31.

7. Pedro Almodóvar, "Talk to Them: Pedro Almodóvar, Screenwriter," interview conducted by Bob Verini, *SCRIPT* 12, no. 6 (2006): 42–47.

8. Noël Carroll, "Talk to Them: An Introduction," in Eaton, *Talk to Her*, 7–8.

9. The first dance scene is from Pina Bausch's *Café Müller*.

10. The role of savior and romantic hero becomes solidified during their first meeting when Marco kills a snake that frightens Lydia.

11. Pedro Almodóvar, "Pedro Almodóvar," interview conducted by Jose Arroyo, *The Guardian*, July 13, 2002, www.theguardian.com/film/2002/jul/31/features.pedroalmodovar.

12. A. W. Eaton, "Almodóvar's Imoralism," in *Talk to Her*, 11.

13. This empathy is likely not merely the product of Almodóvar's filmmaking; Kate Manne coins the term "himpathy" to describe our culture's tendency to empathize with and defend men in general and male rapists in particular. See

Kate Manne, *Down Girl: The Logic of Misogyny* (New York: Oxford University Press, 2018), especially chapter 6, entitled "Exonerating Men."

14. Robert B. Pippin, "Devils and Angels in Almodóvar's *Talk to Her*," 33–34.

15. C. D. C. Reeve, "A *Celemín* of Shit: Comedy and Deception in Almodóvar's *Talk to Her*," in Eaton, *Talk to Her*, 98.

16. Ibid. Although he denounces the rape, Reeve dabbles in an obfuscation of rape that has long operated, namely, the false idea that pregnancy is nearly impossible under conditions of rape. On the use of this falsity to repudiate the right to choose an abortion, see Garance Franke-Ruta, "A Canard That Will Not Die: 'Legitimate Rape' Doesn't Cause Pregnancy," *Atlantic*, August 19, 2012, www.theatlantic.com/politics/archive/2012/08/a-canard-that-will-not-die-legitimate-rape-doesnt-cause-pregnancy/261303/.

17. California, Illinois, and New York, for example, have passed affirmative consent laws for their high schools, colleges, and/or states. New York Bill S5965 (2015) states: "Affirmative consent is a knowing, voluntary, and mutual decision among all participants to engage in sexual activity. Consent can be given by words or actions, as long as those words or actions create clear permission regarding willingness to engage in the sexual activity. Silence or lack of resistance, in and of itself, does not demonstrate consent."

18. Lois Pineau, "A Response to My Critics," in *Date Rape: Feminism, Philosophy, and the Law*, ed. Leslie Francis (University Park: Pennsylvania State University Press, 1996), 94.

19. Lois Pineau, "Date Rape: A Feminist Analysis," in Francis, *Date Rape: Feminism, Philosophy, and the Law*, 13–15.

20. Ibid., 19.

21. Pineau, "Response to My Critics," 97–98.

22. Pineau, "Date Rape: A Feminist Analysis," 19.

23. Michelle J. Anderson, "Negotiating Sex," *Southern Californian Law Review* 78, no. 6 (2005): 137–38.

24. George M. Wilson, "Rapport, Rupture, and Rape: Reflections on *Talk to Her*," in Eaton, *Talk to Her*, 46.

25. Ibid., 48.

26. Ibid., 66, 64.

27. Ibid., 64.

28. Almodóvar, "Pedro Almodóvar."

29. A paradigmatic case of this is Lawrence Nassar, who worked as a physician for USA Gymnastics and Michigan State University and was convicted in 2018 of sexual assault of minors. Over three hundred victims have come forward. Several stated the seemingly remarkably kind and unusually devoted doctor was able to commit sexual abuse even with parents of victims present in the room because neither victims nor onlookers were equipped to unmask his violence disguised as

care. Those who did report Nassar were consistently told by school authorities, law enforcement, and even parents that they must be mistaken.

30. Maurice Friedman, *Martin Buber's Life and Work* (Detroit: Wayne State University Press, 1988), 28.

31. Buber, "Dialogue," 34.

32. Martin Buber, "Education," in *Between Man and Man*, 114.

33. See, for example, Onora O'Neill, "Between Consenting Adults," *Philosophy & Public Affairs* 14, no. 3 (1985): 252–77.

34. Jordan Pascoe, "Kant and Kinky Sex," in *What Philosophy Can Tell You about Your Lover*, ed. Sharon M. Kaye (Chicago and LaSalle, IL: Open Court, 2012), 27.

35. Ibid., 30.

36. Buber, "Dialogue," 24.

37. Martin Buber, "Elements of the Interhuman," in *The Knowledge of Man: Selected Essays*, trans. Maurice Friedman (Amherst, NY: Prometheus Books, 1998), 72.

38. Buber, "Dialogue," 26–28.

39. Buber, "Elements of the Interhuman," 66.

40. Buber, "Dialogue," 34–35.

41. Buber, "Elements of the Interhuman," 73.

42. Buber, "Education," 112.

43. Buber, "Dialogue," 23.

44. Martin Buber, *I and Thou*, trans. Walter Kaufmann (New York: Touchstone, 1996), 77.

45. For the role Buber takes memory to play in human relations, including the way memory threatens our capacity to fully relate as persons and the way critical memory may restore our ability to relate, see Sarah Scott, "An Unending Sphere of Relation: Martin Buber's Conception of Personhood," *Forum Philosophicum* 19, no. 1 (2014): 5–25.

46. Buber, *I and Thou*, 72.

47. Ibid., 78.

48. See Buber, "Elements of the Interhuman," 71: "Some call it intuition, but that name is not a wholly unambiguous concept. I prefer the name 'imagining the real,' for in its essential being this gift is not a looking at the other, but a bold swinging—demanding the most intensive stirring of one's being—into the life of the other."

49. Buber, "Education," 115.

50. Martin Buber, *The Martin Buber–Carl Rogers Dialogue: A New Transcript with Commentary*, ed. Rob Anderson and Kenneth N. Cissna (Albany: State University of New York Press, 1997), 23.

51. Ibid., 25.

52. Buber, "Education," 115.
53. Martin Buber, "Distance and Relation," in *Knowledge of Man*, 60.
54. Ibid., 52.
55. Buber's critique of the moral danger of romantic aesthetic absorption goes hand in hand with a defense of the moral need for another type of aesthetics, namely, disinterested aesthetics. For the relationship between Buber's moral philosophy and his use of aesthetics, especially the relation of Kantian reflective judgment to Buber's moral epistemology, see Sarah Scott, "From Genius to Taste: Martin Buber's Aestheticism," *Journal of Jewish Thought and Philosophy* 25, no. 1 (2017): 110–30. As Zachary Braiterman argues in this volume, Buber is first and foremost an aesthetic thinker. I do not believe he ever leaves his early training in art history and philosophy of art behind, though he does leave romanticism behind.
56. Martin Buber, "Interrogation of Martin Buber," conducted by M. S. Friedman, in *Philosophic Interrogations*, ed. S. Rome and B. Rome (New York: Holt, Rinehart and Winston, 1964), 44.
57. Buber, "Interrogation of Martin Buber," 27. For Buber's critique of unity see Sarah Scott, "Knowing Otherness: Martin Buber's Appropriation of Nicholas of Cusa," *International Philosophical Quarterly* 55, no. 4 (2015): 399–416.
58. The key text to read on distance as a precondition for relation is Buber, "Distance and Relation."
59. Steven T. Katz, "Martin Buber's Epistemology: A Critical Appraisal," *International Philosophical Quarterly* 21, no. 2 (1981): 141–42.
60. If an emphasis on symmetry mistakes Buber for Kant, the reading of Buber that holds that a completely asymmetrical relationship is the height of moral response mistakes him for Emmanuel Levinas. A starting point for the differences between Levinas and Buber, which are beyond the scope of this paper, is Peter Atterton, Matthew Calarco, and Maurice Friedman, eds., *Levinas and Buber: Dialogue and Difference* (Pittsburgh, PA: Duquesne University Press, 2004).
61. Buber, "Dialogue," 9.
62. Ibid.
63. Buber, *I and Thou*, 57.
64. Ibid., 178.
65. Ibid., 179.
66. Buber, "Elements of the Interhuman," 65.
67. It is beyond scope of paper to determine if this is a virtue. My suspicion is that, for Buber, the ability and moral impetus to enter into dialogue is neither a Kantian maxim nor an Aristotelean virtue but a joining of will and grace to move the imagination.
68. Buber, *I and Thou*, 131.

69. Many victims experience peritraumatic paralysis and disassociation, such that the experience of the victim is often similar to that of the comatose Alicia, with the added horror of consciousness and memory. This is one of many reasons why consent models can be ineffective in stopping rape. See Anderson, "Negotiating Sex," 115–16.

70. Buber, "Dialogue," 15. Even close attention to body language is not enough if it is filtered through wishful imagination and misconceptions. Anderson points out that studies show men consistently interpret women's body language to be expressing sexual intent or consent when they are actually not. Women tend to not make the same mistake. See Anderson, "Negotiating Sex," 117–19.

71. Reeve, "*Celemín* of Shit," 103, 93.

72. Buber, "Elements of the Interhuman," 67.

73. Buber, *Martin Buber–Carl Rogers Dialogue*, 37–38.

74. Ibid., 54.

75. Ibid., 55, emphasis in the original.

76. Ibid., 59, emphasis in the original.

77. For Almodóvar, Beningo's limitations do confer moral innocence. See "Pedro Almodóvar": "The point about Benigno's character is that he is completely innocent, in the sense that he does not have experience. He lives in another world. This world is parallel to the real world but it has its own rules."

78. The final dance scene is from Pina Bausch's *Masurca Fogo*.

79. Buber, *Martin Buber–Carl Rogers Dialogue*, 38–39.

80. Buber, "Dialogue," 9–10.

81. Almodóvar, "Talk to Them: Pedro Almodóvar, Screenwriter."

CONTRIBUTORS

DUSTIN ATLAS is Director of Jewish Studies and Assistant Professor in the School of Religion at Queen's University, Canada.

ZACHARY BRAITERMAN is Director of Jewish Studies and Professor in the Department of Religion at Syracuse University. He is author of *The Shape of Revelation: Aesthetics and Modern Jewish Thought* and *(God) After Auschwitz: Tradition and Change in Post-Holocaust Jewish Thought* and editor of *The Cambridge History of Jewish Philosophy: The Modern Era*, and he contributes regularly to the blog jewishphilosophyplace.com.

SAMUEL HAYIM BRODY is Associate Professor in the Department of Religious Studies at the University of Kansas. He is author of *Martin Buber's Theopolitics* and editor of two volumes in the *Martin Buber Werkausgabe*: 15 (*Schriften zum Messianismus*) and 21 (*Schriften zur zionistischen Politik und zur jüdisch-arabischen Frage*), the latter edited with Paul Mendes-Flohr.

YEMIMA HADAD is Juniorprofessur für Judaistik at the University of Leipzig. She is Research Fellow at the Bucerius Institute for Research of German Contemporary History and Society at the University of Haifa and is currently working on a book on the weak God in Jewish sources and modern philosophy.

PETER A. HUFF is Chief Mission Officer and Professor of Theology at Benedictine University, Illinois. He has held endowed chairs at Xavier University and Centenary College of Louisiana. His books include *The Voice of Vatican II* and *Atheism and Agnosticism: Exploring the Issues*.

WILLIAM PLEVAN teaches Jewish thought at the Jewish Theological Seminary, the Reconstructionist Rabbinical College, and Gratz College. He is author of a chapter on Martin Buber's virtue ethics in a forthcoming volume, *Jewish Virtue*

Ethics and editor of the festschrift *Personal Theology: Essays in Honor of Neil Gillman*.

SARAH SCOTT is Professor and Chair of the Philosophy Department at Manhattan College. Her articles on Martin Buber include studies of his appropriation of Kantian aesthetics and Nicholas of Cusa and his concepts of grace and personhood.

CLAIRE E. SUFRIN is Associate Professor of Instruction and Assistant Director of the Crown Family Center for Jewish and Israel Studies at Northwestern University, Illinois. She is editor of *The New Jewish Canon: Ideas & Debates 1980–2015*.

ASAF ZIDERMAN is Postdoctoral Fellow at The Franz Rosenzweig Minerva Research Center at the Hebrew University of Jerusalem. He is currently completing a manuscript under the title *The Act of Love: Martin Buber's Dialogical Thought as a Philosophy of Action*.

INDEX

Abgrund (abyss), 7, 30, 182, 183, 187–89, 188, 197n8, 199n28
Achdut Ha'avoda, 77
actualization (Buber), 47, 80, 219–20, 222–23
adequate perception (Buber), 245–46
affect and affect theory, 218, 224n4; actualization (Buber), 219–20; anxiety (*Bangigkeit*), 200n29, 218–20, 222–23, 231n76, 232n81, 232n83; as basic words, 221; body language, 237–38, 239, 242, 260n70; Buber, Martin, 2, 21, 204–5, 209, 210, 225n5; emotions, 210–13; feelings (Peirce), 211–12; manner of expression, 209; of Massumi, 7, 210–11; mediation in, 210; the nonlinguistic in, 7, 209–12, 214, 216, 218–22, 232n81; Peirce on, 211; reading through, 209; Sara Ahmed on, 7, 212, 213, 218, 228n34; subject of dialogue, 209; trees, 7, 214–16, 230n56
affirmative consent policies, 238, 257n17, 260n69
Afgrund (Kierkegaard), 188
agentic responsibility, 192–95
agnosto theo sermon (Saint Paul), 21, 25
Ahad Ha'am, 149n11
Ahmed, Sara, 7, 212, 213, 218, 228n34
Alcalay, Ammiel, 174–75
Alicia (*Talk to Her* (*Hable con ella*)): Benigno's pathological love for, 235, 245; as comatose, 254; encounters with Marcos, 235–36, 253–54; erasure of, 237; objectification of, 237; pregnancy of, 236; rape of, 234–35, 236, 237, 239, 248, 250, 253, 254, 255; relations with Benigno, 234, 235, 236–37, 245, 253–54
Allegemeiner Deutscher Arbeiterverein (General Workers' Association), 87n7
Almodóvar, Pedro. See *Talk to Her* (*Hable con ella*) (Almodóvar)
ambivalence: *Abgrund* (abyss), 7, 182, 183, 187–89, 197n8, 199n28; application of preconceived knowledge, 186–87; the case of Mable, 192–94; circular motion describing, 190; as constructive, 183–84; decisions made in a state of, 185–86, 187, 191, 198n16; deliberation, 190; demarcation line, 7, 182, 196n7; described in *I and Thou* (Buber), 198n13; drifting, 193, 201n46; escape from, 186–87, 190–91, 194; as "holy insecurity," 186, 187, 196n5, 196n6; moral ambiguity in *Talk to Her* (*Hable con ella*) (Almodóvar), 235; myths, 188–89, 200n30; as "narrow ridge," 7, 86n2, 182, 187, 196n6; negative depictions of, 184, 186, 187, 191, 194; positive aspects of, 183–84, 186, 187, 190–91, 192, 194; potential courses of action, 190, 201n46; pragmatic ambivalence, 185–86, 198n18, 199n19; psychology of, 182, 184, 186, 189–90, 244, 253; sequential ambivalence, 192–94; theoretical ambivalence, 199n19; *Wirbel* (vortex), 7, 187–88, 189–90, 197n8, 201n37. *See also* Chaos

INDEX

anarchy: anarchism, 2, 69–70, 73–74, 77, 87n10, 91n41, 92n45; chaotic anarchy, 103, 120n44; religious anarchy, 97, 99, 100–101, 103, 114; temporary leadership, 113–14. *See also* Landauer, Gustav; theocracy

Anderson, Michelle J., 239, 240–41, 260n70

Andreas-Salomé, Lou, 241

Angst (Heidegger), 218

animal dialogue: anxiety, 218, 220, 221–22, 232n83; cats, 7, 202, 206, 209, 214, 216, 218–22, 232n81; ethical aspects of, 226n12, 226n13, 255; human interactions, 203–4, 205–6, 210–13, 217, 218–19, 226n12, 226n13, 250, 255; language absent from, 207, 208, 209–10, 221–23, 232n83; nonhuman You, 208

animals: anxiety (*Bangigkeit*), 200n29, 218–20, 222–23, 231n76, 232n81, 232n83; cats, 7, 202, 206, 209, 214, 216, 218–22, 232n81; as creatures of affect, 208; emotions of, 210–13; feelings of, 210–13, 212; in Hasidic tales, 205, 226n12; nonhuman v. human animals, 205–6; relation to language as anxious, 222–23, 232n83; use of term, 224n3

Anshey Ha-Ruach (people of spirit), 113

antisemitism, 2, 74–75, 90n31, 135, 163, 167

anxiety (*Bangigkeit*), 200n29, 218–20, 222–23, 231n76, 232n81, 232n83

Arab-Muslim place names: erasure of, 156–57, 158, 166

Arab-Palestinian folklore, 157–58

Arabs: on Jewish immigration to Palestine, 165–66

Arabs in Palestine, 91n41

Arendt, Hannah, 1–2

Ariel, Yaakov, 14

Arlosoroff, Chaim, 76, 91n41

Armstrong, Karen, 18

Arnheim, Rudolf, 152, 153

art, 151, 155, 156, 162, 163, 172

asymmetrical relationships, 249, 250, 252–53, 254

atheism, 4, 14–15, 21–26, 27–29, 34, 45

"Atheistic Theology" (Rosenzweig), 45

avdey Ha-Shem (the servants of God), 104, 105, 106

Avoda baGashmiyut, 111

Bakhtin, Mikhail, 218–19

Bakunin, Mikhail, 69

Bangigkeit (anxiety), 200n29, 218–20, 222–23, 231n76, 232n81, 232n83

Bar Kochba revolt, 135

Barth, Karl, 17, 74–75, 80

Bebel, August, 87n7

Ben-Chorin, Schalom, 202

Ben-Gurion, David, 77, 166, 167

Benedict XVI, Pope, 19, 20, 22, 28

Benigno (*Talk to Her* (*Hable con ella*)): appearance of, 234, 253, 260n77; as being shut, 253; dialogue as fantasy, 254; imagination of, 245; as longing for a relationship, 244–45; monologic behavior of, 237, 239, 252, 253, 254; objectification of Alicia, 237, 245; rape of Alicia, 234–35, 236, 237, 239, 248, 250, 253, 254, 255; relations with Marco, 236, 237, 245, 252, 253; reunion with Alicia, 253–54; spatial absence, 244; suicide of, 236–37; in therapy, 252

Benjamin, Walter, 79, 225n11

Bennet, Jane, 170

Benvenisti, Meron: Arab-Palestinian folklore, 157–58; geographies, transformations of, 158–60; Israeli authors cited by, 158–60; metaphysical belonging, 157, 158; Orientalism of, 166; pantheism, 153; the *paysan*, 171

Bergman, Hugo, 59n9, 202, 224n2

Bestätigung (confirmation), 185, 198n16

Biblical Politeia, 104, 105

Biermann, Asher, 168

binationalism: apartheid, 173; Arab-Jewish coexistence, 31–32, 85–86, 153; Brit Shalom (Covenant of Peace), 32, 91n41; Buber on, 85–86, 152, 154, 169–70, 173; dynamics of, 170; Jewish cultural memory, 166; Jewish statehood, 135–37, 153, 156; metaphysical belonging, 154, 172; and mysticism, 164–65; pictorial aspect of, 151; project of

perfected place, 155–56; unreality of the real, 169; visualization of, 153. See also *Sacred Landscape: The Buried History of the Holy Land since 1948* (Benvenisti)
Bleuler, Eugen, 198n18
Bloch, Ernst, 21
The Blue Mountain (Shalev), 158–60
Böhme, Jacob, 30, 188, 199n28
B-R Bible: *cola*, 4–5, 49; Genesis in, 49–50; German, 50–51; *Leitworte*, 5, 49, 50–51, 53, 54, 55; political aspects, 74; printed editions of/layout of, 50; revelation addressed in, 51
breath units (*cola*), 4–5, 49
Brit Shalom (Covenant of Peace), 32, 91n41
Bruegel, Pietr, 171
Brunner, Emil, 17
Buber, Martin: animal encounters, 202–3, 213–14; Arab-Jewish coexistence, 30–32, 85–86, 153; on atheism, 15, 24–25, 27–29; barriers to genuine dialogue, 242–43; Carl R. Rogers interview, 246–47, 252–53; cats, encounters with, 7, 209, 214, 216, 218–22, 232n81; in Christian thought, 17–21; on *Einfühlung* (empathy), 247, 248–49; factory worker, encounter with, 24, 28; *Gestalt* in works of, 155–56; Hebrew Humanism, 32, 66, 86n2, 129, 148; on Jesus, 31; letter to Gandhi, 155; life events, 26–27, 28–29, 30, 43, 54, 78, 181, 246; on monologic eros, 241, 242; on neo-Orthodoxy, 44; *Realphantasie* (imagining the real), 235, 245–46, 247–48, 251–52, 253–54, 258n48, 260n69; response to Wilhelm Stapel, 74–75, 90n31; on utopia, 77, 112–14, 169, 173; as visual thinker, 154–55; on women in the bible, 124n92; World War I, 44, 68, 71–72, 164, 246. See also binationalism; land and landscape; Landauer, Gustav; Zionism
—works of, see also *I and Thou*; "Address on Jewish Art," 160; "Address on Jewish Art," 160; *The Anointed* (*Der Gesalbte*), 67;
"Authentic Bilingualism," 32; "Believing Humanism," 32; *Daniel: Dialogues on Realization*, 7, 68, 186–87, 191–92, 196n5, 197n10, 199n19, 203, 214–16, 230n56; "Das Judentum und die wahre Gemeinschaft" ("Judaism and True Community"), 72–73; "Dialogue" (*Zwiesprache*), 65, 233–34, 241; "Distance and Relation," 247; *Early Addresses on Judaism*, 44–45; *Eclipse of God*, 15, 24, 28; eternal voice in, 48; "Genuine Dialogue and the Possibility of Peace," 32; Hasidism, 28, 68, 97–98, 109, 117n13; "The Holy Way," 131, 132–33; "Images of Good and Evil," 183, 184, 186, 190; "The Jew in the World," 133–38, 147; "Judaism and Mankind," 160–61, 195n3; "Judaism and the Jews," 160, 195n3; *Kingship of God* (*Königtum Gottes*) (Buber), 53–54, 55, 67–68, 73, 78–80, 82, 92n55, 97, 108, 117n12; *Between Man and Man*, 15, 16, 34; *Moses* (*Moshe*), 53–54, 55, 67, 78–80; "Myth in Judaism," 164; "On National Education," 187, 199n24; *Origin and Meaning of Hasidism*, 97–98, 117n13; *Paths in Utopia*, 77, 173; *Philosophical Interrogations*, 187; "The Problem of the Human Being," 140–41, 147; "The Question to the Single One," 32–33; "Religion as Presence" lectures, 44, 46–47, 48; sensual imagery, 48–49; "The Spirit of the Orient and Judaism," 163, 164; "Symbolic and Sacramental Existence," 108, 187; *Tales of Rebbe Nachman*, 68; *Tales of the Hasidim*, 109; "The Two Foci of the Jewish Soul," 31; "Two Peoples in Palestine," 165; *Two Types of Faith*, 31, 231n76; "Two Types of Faith," 31; *Vom Geist des Judentums*, 163; *On Zion: The History of an Idea*, 85, 96, 137–40
Buber, Solomon, 43
Buber-Rosenzweig translation of the Bible. *See* B-R Bible
Buckley, Michael, 22
Bugental, James F. T., 184, 192–93, 194
Bullivant, Stephen, 22

Bultmann, Rudolf, 168
burning bush (Exod. 3), 44, 47–49, 55–56, 57, 59n17

Camus, Albert, 24
Canaan, Tawfik, 6, 153, 157–58, 166, 170–71, 176n12
cartography, 156–57, 158–59, 166, 173
Catechism of the Catholic Church, 19
Catholic-atheist dialogue, 14–15, 22, 32–34
cats, 7, 202, 206, 209, 214, 216, 218–22, 232n81
Chaos, 182, 184–86, 187–88; in Kabbalah, 188–89; lack of successive leadership, 103; as metaphor for ambivalence, 183, 197n8, 199n19; in mythology, 188–89, 200n30; olam ha-tohu (Hasidic rendering), 188–89, 200n30; primordial chaos identified with human ambivalence, 201n33; sequential ambivalence, 192, 193; transformed into standstill, 194
charisma, 100, 102, 104–5, 106, 108–9
Cohen, Hermann, 71–72, 169
Cohen, Richard I., 42
cola (breath units), 4–5, 49
commentaries: biblical commentaries of Buber, 53–54; Documentary Hypothesis, 78; *Leitworte*, 5, 49, 50–51, 53, 54, 55; "Tradition Criticism" (Buber), 54
communicative model of sexuality, 234, 235, 238–40, 245, 251, 257n29
community: conceptions of, 132–33; formation of, 80–83, 117n12, 136–37, 152; the interhuman (Buber), 131–32; I-You relationships in, 131–32; Neue Gemeinschaft, 70; security of, 134–36; spiritual realization, 143–44. *See also* Israelites; leadership
community of a people (Nancy), 167
confirmation (*Bestätigung*), 185, 198n16
contractual model of sexuality, 234, 238–39, 241, 248, 251, 254
covenant, 32, 47–48, 56, 59n17, 91n41, 96, 107, 117n10
creation accounts, 47–48, 52–53, 57, 59n17, 142, 189

Critique of Judgment (Kant), 247–48
cultural Zionism, 73, 114, 160

Daniel: Dialogues on Realization (Buber): ambivalence, 186–87, 191–92, 198n10, 199n19; Buber's neo-Romanticism in, 7, 68; "holy insecurity," 7, 182, 186, 196n5, 196n6; on nature, 203–4; trees, encounter with, 7, 214–16, 230n56
Darwish, Mahmoud, 160
"Das Judentum und die wahre Gemeinschalt" ("Judaism and True Community"), 72–73
Deacon, Terrence W., 231n75
de Beauvoir, Simone, 1
deceptive care practices, 234, 237–38, 257n29
decision-making, 185–86, 187, 191–92, 194, 198n16, 199n24
Degania (kibbutz), 76
Dei Verbum, 19
"demarcation line," 173, 182, 196n7
Der Socialist (newspaper), 70
deus absconditus, 21
Deutsches Volkstum, 74
dialogue: alienation in modern society, 129–30; anxiety (*Bangigkeit*), 200n29, 218–20, 222–23, 231n76, 232n81, 232n83; Arab-Jewish understanding, 30–32, 85–86, 153; Bible as, 53–54, 79, 83–85; Buber's philosophy of, 7, 29–32, 65–66, 86n1, 86n2, 255; Catholic-atheist dialogue, 14–15, 22, 30, 32–33, 32–34; conditions for, 31, 155, 165, 210, 219, 242–43, 247, 250, 253, 255; distancing in, 219–20, 247–49, 250, 255; ethics of dialogical relationships, 250, 255; full engagement in, 243–44; genuine dialogue, 233, 234–35, 242–44, 252–53; *Gestalt* of, 155, 156, 162; in models of sexuality, 234, 235, 238–40, 245, 257n29; monologue disguised as, 7, 233–35, 239–40, 248, 251, 255–56; mutuality, 153, 235, 249–50, 252, 254–55; mysticism to dialogue, 68, 215; as non-linguistic, 7, 209, 214, 216, 218–22, 232n81; *Realphantasie* (imagining the real), 235, 245–46, 247–48,

251–52, 254, 258n48, 260n69; silence in, 207–8, 228n28; spheres of relations, 205–7, 208, 209, 214–16, 217–219, 226n15, 227n20; symmetry, 248–49, 251, 259n60; thresholds in, 217, 218–19, 250; virtue of talking to, 234, 236, 239; *Zwiegespräch* (dialogue), 79–80, 93n55. *See also* animal dialogue; *Daniel: Dialogues on Realization* (Buber); *I and Thou* (Buber); I-Thou (*Ich-Du*) (I-You); *Talk to Her* (*Hable con ella*) (Almodóvar); Vatican II
"Dialogue" (*Zwiesprache*) (Buber), 65, 233–34, 241, 242
Diamond, Malcolm, 16, 21
Die Kreatur (journal), 30
Dignitatis Humanae, 19
Dilthey, Wilhelm, 141
direct theocracy, 99, 101–4, 120n44
disinterested aesthetics, 247, 248, 259n55
"Distance and Relation" (Buber), 219
distancing, 219–20, 231n73, 246, 247–49, 250, 254, 255
divine sparks, 109, 121n52, 226n12
Does God Exist? (Küng), 29
Drei Reden (Buber), 160–61, 163
dualism and duality 2, 154, 162, 164, 166, 170, 192, 215, 234; Gnostic dualism 143, 144; Occidental dualism 132
Dyb (Kierkegaard), 188

Ebert, Friedrich, 69, 77
Eckhart, Meister, 188
Eclipse of God, 15, 24, 28; eternal voice in, 48
ego, 47, 59n14, 98, 216
"ehyeh asher ehyeh" (Exod. 3:14), 47–48, 51, 55–56, 59n17
Einfühlung (empathy), 247, 248–49; as "himpathy" 256n13
Eisen, Arnold, 129, 132
Eisner, Kurt, 72, 89n24
emotions, 210–13, 212, 213, 246–47. *See also* affect and affect theory; empathy
empathy (*Einfühlung*), 247, 248–49; as "himpathy" 256n13
Erdozain, Dominic, 22

Erfurt program (SPD), 69
eros, 233, 242, 246, 253
Die Erotik (Andreas-Salomé), 241
ethics, 183, 226n13, 247–48, 250, 255
eved Ha-Shem (the servant of God), 104, 105, 106
evil, 25, 30, 183, 184, 186. *See also* Lucifer
exile (*galut*): Buber on, 96, 117n7, 130, 133, 160, 161–62, 182; Jewish art in, 160–62; Jewish existence in, 129, 135, 138–39, 149n16; Judah Loew on, 137; and national identity, 134; political Zionism on, 130–31; as purification, 96, 117n7, 138–39; reduction of the holy, 108; Reform Judaism on, 141, 146; and return to the land, 132, 137–38, 139–40, 146; security in, 134–36; self-disintegration in, 182; *shekhina* (divine Presence) in, 131; space of, 164; ugliness of, 161–62; Zionism on, 95–96, 130–31, 133–34, 138

forceful-seduction model of sexuality, 234, 238, 240, 251, 257n29
Form, 162
Francis, Pope, 19–20, 34
Freies Judisches Lehrhaus (Frankfurt), 5, 44, 46, 68
Freie Volksbühne, 69, 87n9
Friedman, Maurice, 30, 67, 86n1, 87n5, 182, 196n5, 217

galut. *See* exile (*galut*)
Gandhi, Mahatma, 155
Gaudium et Spes, 14, 19, 22
Geller, Jay, 208
genuine dialogue, 233, 234–35, 242–44, 252–53
genuine seeming, 242–43
geographies, transformations of, 159–60
German language, 44, 50–51, 74
German modernism, 151
German socialism, 69
Gestalt, 155, 156, 162
geula, 99
Gideon, speech of, 99, 100, 102
Gnosticism, 130, 132, 133, 140–43

God: of the ancestors, 47–48, 55–56, 59n17; atheism, 4, 14–15, 21–26, 27–29, 34, 45; in Catholic theology, 21; characteristics of, 26–29, 46–48, 55–56, 84–85, 101, 142; in creation account, 52–53, 142, 189; direct theocracy, 101–2; "ehyeh asher ehyeh" (Exod. 3:14), 47–48, 51, 55–56, 59n17; encounters with, 44, 48–49, 51–52; gift of land, 82–83; Hechsler's challenge to Buber, 27; kingship of, 54–55, 79–80, 97, 99, 117n12, 135; and nature, 164; nomination of king, 103–4; presence of, 46, 119n29; punishments of, 84; sensual reality, 164; as Thou, 28, 29, 100, 105; in the time of the Shoah, 25; YHVH, 31, 79, 83–84, 99, 104, 164; youth's relations with, 45.

Goldmann, Nahum, 76
Goldziher, Ignaz, 167
Gordon, A. D., 76
Gottlieb, Maurycy, 160
Guardini, Romano, 1, 19–20
Gunkel, Hermann, 54

Hamilton, William, 28
Ha'poel Ha'tzair (the young worker), 73–74, 76
The Harvesters (Bruegel), 171
Hasidism: abyss metaphor in Hasidic writings, 188; *Avoda baGashmiyut*, 111; Buber's works on, 68, 70, 97–98, 109, 117n13; chaos as "olam ha-tohu," 188–89, 200n30; communal life, 109; in Galicia, 43; Hasidic *devotio*, 187; Kingship of God in, 97; Kotzker Rebbe, 132; Levi Yitschak of Berditchev, 28; mutual elevation, 110; reunification of the holy and secular, 108, 111; works on, 68, 97–98, 109, 117n13, 205, 226n12; Zionism, 97, 98. *See also* zaddik
Hebrew Bible, 176n12; Buber's approach to, 43; burning bush (Exod. 3), 44, 47–49, 55–56, 57, 59n17; in Catholic thought, 21; Christian understanding of, 42; creation accounts, 47–48, 52–53, 57, 59n17, 142, 189; divine speech in, 47–48, 59n17; "ehyeh asher ehyeh" (Exod. 3:14), 47–48, 51, 55–56, 59n17; Moses, 44, 48, 52, 53–56, 78–82; Ohel Mo'ed (Tent of Meeting)(Exod. 25, 36), 47–48, 52–53, 57, 59n17; Sinaitic revelation, 44, 52, 56; youth's reading of, 45. *See also* revelation; sources (biblical) heading
Hebrew Humanism, 32, 66, 86n2, 129, 148
Hebrew University of Jerusalem, 54, 78
Hechler, William H., 27
Heidegger, Martin, 141, 143, 147, 218
Der Heilige Weg: Ein Wort an die Juden und an die Völker (*The Holy Way: A Word to the Jews and to the Nations*), 72–73
Herder, Johann Gottfried, 98
"Herut" (essay in *Early Addresses on Judaism* (Buber)), 45–46
Herzl, Theodor, 27, 133, 136, 139, 149n11, 167
Heschel, Abraham Joshua, 18, 20
hierarchy, 121n53
Hirsch, Samson Raphael, 44
Holocaust, 25, 30
"holy insecurity," 7, 182, 186, 196n6
human (use of term), 224n3
human body: natural language of, 238
Hurwitz, Rivka, 47
Husserl, Edmund, 1, 19
Huston, Phil, 215
Hyman, Gavin, 22

"I" (*Ich*), 47, 59n14, 213, 216, 221, 222, 249. *See also* ego; I-It (*Ich-Es*); I-Thou (*Ich-Du*) (I-You); the self, fantasies of, 236, 237, 243, 248
I and Thou (Buber), 1, 15, 26, 44, 117n16; ambivalence described in, 198n13; aspect of space in, 155; cat, encounter with, 218–22, 232n81; dialogue, 47, 66, 67, 87n6, 214–15, 233–34; "ehyeh asher ehyeh" (Exod. 3:14) in, 47–48; on language, 249; longing for relation in, 244; nature, 216–17; power of speech, 58; "Religion as Presence" lectures, 47; revelation in, 47, 51–52, 79; style of, 131, 148n6; on the transcendent, 249; word-pairs, 58; "You" in, 93n58, 100, 208, 216–18, 230n58

icon, 221, 232n79
Ihud (Unity), 32
I-It (*Ich-Es*), 1, 7, 24, 47, 59n14, 93n58, 130–31, 205–6, 233–35, 251, 255–56.
imagination, 152; adequate perception (Buber), 245; binocular vision generated by, 245; in Buber's work, 2; distancing, 247–48; living in common through act of, 245–46; in monologue, 244–45; *Realphantasie* (imagining the real), 235, 245–46, 247–48, 251–52, 253–54, 258n48, 260n69; *Shrinking Lover* imagery, 236, 237, 248
indirect theocracy, 103–4, 121n53
Industrial Workers of the World (IWW), 70
the interhuman (Buber), 131–32, 252, 253
invasion of seeming, 242–43
inward turning reflection (*Rückbiegung*), 242
Isaacs, Jules, 18
Islam, 167
Israel, land of: community building in, 136–37; Eretz Israel, 96, 97; Israeli novelists on, 6, 158–59, 160, 170; Jewish-Arab relations, 31–32, 85–86, 91n41, 153, 173–74; Jewish immigration and settlement, 91n41, 157, 159, 165–66, 173; metaphysical belonging, 157, 159–60; people of Israel, 96, 117n7; religious anarchy in, 97; return to, 132, 136, 137–38, 139–40, 146; spiritual growth in, 137; theocracy in, 98; world redemption, 96, 97–98; zaddikim in, 115. *See also* exile (*galut*)
Israelites: accountability of, 107, 122n72, 137–38; community formation, 80–81; election of, 80–81, 85; God's relationship with, 54–56, 67–68, 97, 100; Israelite monarchy (I Samuel 8), 73; kingship of God, 54–55, 97, 99, 117n12, 135; as *Mamlechet Kohanim*, 96–97, 100, 111, 120n38; Moses, 44, 48, 52, 53–56, 78–82; nationhood, 137–38; Ohel Mo'ed construction, 47–48, 52–53, 57, 59n17; polarization between religious and secular, 105–6, 107, 108; property ownership, 82–83; prophecy, 83–84; Sinaitic revelation, 44, 52, 56; their will of constitution, 79; theopolitical regime in Eretz Israel, 96, 97–98, 117n7; vocation of redemption, 101; YHVH, 83–84. *See also* exile (*galut*)
Israeli War of Independence (1948), 153
"It," Buber on, 26, 47. *See also* I-It (*Ich-Es*)
I-Thou (*Ich-Du*) (I-You), 1; affect theory 213, 221; as genuine community 131; as genuine dialogue, 233, 234; as *Gestalt* 155; as second-person standpoint 205, 208; God as Thou, 20, 28, 29, 46, 47, 67, 81, 100, 105; incompleteness 93n58, 232n85, 250; interpretations of, 117n16, 249; nonhuman encounters, 202–3, 208, 216, 224n2, 230n57; Ohel Mo'ed, building of, 47–48, 52–53, 57, 59n17; revelation, 48; Sinaitic revelation, 44, 52, 56; sources related to, 48–49, 59n17. *See also* "You"

Jeremiah (prophet), 83–84
Jesus, 16, 31
Jewish-Christian dialogue, 30–31
Jewish-Israeli state, 135–37, 153, 156
"Jewish People's Theology," 45
Jewish religious orthodoxy, 133
Jews, election of, 77
Jews in the Orient, 163–64
John Paul II, Pope, 19
John XXIII, Pope, 14
Jonas, Hans, 231n74
Jospe, Eva, 208
Jotham's fable, 99, 100, 113
Jubilee year, 93n62
judges (*shophtim*): antimonarchic period, 114; charisma of, 102, 104–5; in indirect theology, 107; Judges, book of, 101–3, 105; obligations of, 107; priesthood, 102; as theopolitical leader, 102; as vocation, 102, 107
Jung, C. G., 25, 168

Kabbalah, 99, 109, 121n52, 188–89, 199n28, 226n12
Kafka, Franz, 79, 175
Kandinsky, Wassily, 156

Kant, Immanuel, 259n60; on judgment, 247–48, 259n55; modern philosophical inquiry, 140–41; on sexual relationships, 241–42, 248; on world order, 199n19, 231n73
Kasimow, Harold, 21
Katz, Steven T., 249
Kaufmann, Walter, 16, 26
kellipot (husks), 109
kibbutz movement, 5, 68, 76–77, 83, 85, 92n45, 173
Kierkegaard, Søren, 188
King, Martin Luther, 17
kingdom-message, 80, 90n36
Kingdom of Priests (*Mamlechet Kohanim*), 96–97, 100, 111, 120n38
kings, 84; accountability of, 104–5; charisma of, 104–5; decline of divine theocracy, 106; as divine, 104; as *eved Ha-Shem* (the servant of God), 104, 105; in indirect theocracy, 104; judge compared with, 104; as *mamrim* (obstinate), 105; refusal of kingship, 99, 100, 102, 113; separation of sacred from the secular, 105; vocations of, 106–7
Kings: in Hebrew Bible, 102–3, 112
Kingship of God (*Königtum Gottes*) (Buber), 53–54, 55, 67–68, 73, 78–80, 82, 92n55, 97, 108, 117n12
Klimt, Gustav, 160
Kohanim (priests), 96–97, 100, 111, 120n38
Kohanski, Alexander Sissel, 231n73
Kook, Abraham Isaac, Rabbi, 75
Kotzker Rebbe, 132
Kracauer, Siegfried, 90n31
Kriegserlebnis, 71
Kropotkin, Peter, 69
Kuhn, Gabriel, 87n11
Kuhn, Helmut, 208
Küng, Hans, 29

land and landscape: in art, 161, 172; Benvenisti's notion of, 158; in biblical text, 164; erasure of landscape, 157–58, 166; folklore, 157–58; human dimensions of, 6, 170–71; immigration and settlement, 91n41, 157, 159, 165–66, 173; Jewish-Israeli statehood, 135–37, 153, 156; mapping of, 156, 157, 158–59, 173; metaphysical belonging, 157; Muslim memory, 157–58, 176n12; paganism, 164; property rights, 82–83; sabbatical year, 82, 93n62; as sacred, 160, 166, 172; in theopolitics, 97–98; as vital, living form, 159–60. *See also* exile (*galut*)
Landauer, Gustav: anarchism of, 69–70, 84–85, 87n9, 87n11, 164; background of, 68–69; Buber's support for, 72–74, 90n30, 91n41, 246; correspondence with Buber, 164; death of, 69, 246, 247; influence on Buber, 68, 70, 72–73, 88n12; on mysticism, 70, 164; responses to *Daniel*, 197n9; works of, 70, 73–74; on Zionism, 75–76, 77, 91n41
language: body language, 237–38, 239, 242, 260n70; conventional language of humans, 219; silence, 207–8, 223, 228n28, 236, 237; *Sprachkritik* (critique of language), 188, 199n27. *See also cola*, German language, *Leitworte*
Laplace, Pierre-Simon, 28
Lasalle, Ferdinand, 87n7
Laudato Si', 20
leadership: charisma, 100, 102, 104–5, 106, 108–9; direct servants, 102, 120n38; election of, 100–101; in Hebrew Bible, 5, 99, 100, 103; lack of succession, 45, 103; of man over man, 100–101, 102; of the messiah, 112–14; vocation of, 106–7. *See also* judges (*shophtim*); kings; zaddik
League for Jewish-Arab Rapprochement and Cooperation, 32
Leitworte, 5, 49, 50–51, 53, 54, 55
Levinas, Emmanuel, 1, 19, 156, 224n2, 227n21, 259n60
Levi Yitschak of Berditchev, Rabbi, 28
liberal Judaism, 44–45, 163, 167, 169
Liebknecht, Wilhelm, 87n7
Life of Jesus movement, 45
Lilien, E. M., 160
Loew, Judah, 96, 130, 137–39
Lucifer (monologic eros), 242, 253
Lumen Fidei (Pope Francis), 20, 21

Lumen Gentium, 19
Luther, Martin, 1, 50, 51
Lydia (*Talk to Her* (*Hable con ella*)), 234, 235–36, 239, 253–54

Mable (example of sequential ambivalence), 192–94
Macquarrie, John, 17
Maharal of Prague (Rabbi LIva ben Betzalel), 96, 130, 137–38
Mamlechet Kohanim (Kingdom of Priests), 96–97, 100, 111, 120n38
Manne, Kate, 256n13
Mapai, 76
mapping, 156–57, 158–59, 166, 173
Marchand, Suzanne, 167–68
Marco (*Talk to Her* (*Hable con ella*)): as being shut, 253; character of, 235–36, 244; the crying man, 252; learns to be alone, 253; as longing for a relationship, 244–45; meets Alicia at dance performance, 235–36; monologic behavior of, 236, 244–45, 252, 254; moral failure of, 253; relationship with Alicia, 236; relationship with Lydia, 234, 235–36, 239, 244, 253–54; relations with Benigno, 236, 237, 245, 252, 253; temporal absence, 244
marriage, image of, 32–33
Marx, Karl, 69–70, 87n7
Massumi, Brian, 7, 210, 212, 218, 228n34
McGrath, Alister, 18
melancholy (*Schwermut*), 223
memory: formation of relationships, 244, 258n45; of place, 157–59; *Realphantasie* (imagining the real), 235, 245–46, 247–48, 251–52, 254, 258n48, 260n69
Mendelssohn, Moses, 51
Mendes-Flohr, Paul, 30, 68, 131, 164, 215
Merkle, John, 21
Merton, Thomas, 18, 33
messianism, 75, 110, 112–14, 117n12, 139
metaphysical belonging (Benveniste), 157
Mizrahi Jews, 174
models of sexuality: communicative model, 234, 235, 238–40, 245, 257n29; contractual model, 234, 238–39, 241, 248; forceful-seduction model, 234, 238, 240, 251; monologue disguised as dialogue, 239–40, 242, 251, 254; negotiation model, 239; romantic-care model, 234–35, 240, 242, 247, 251, 254
monarchy. *See* kings
monologue: disguised as dialogue, 7, 233–35, 239–40, 248, 251, 255–56; empathy (*Einfühlung*), 247; I-It (*Ich-Es*), 1, 24, 47, 59n14, 93n58, 130–31, 205, 206, 255; imagination and, 244–45; models of sexuality, 234–35, 239–40, 242, 251, 254, 257n29; moral harm of, 239; partial engagement in, 243–44; *Rückbiegung* (inward turning reflection), 242–43; self-centeredness, 236; temporal absence, 244
Moore, Donald, 26
Moses, 44, 48, 52, 53–56, 78–82
Mohammedan Saints and Sanctuaries in Palestine (Canaan), 157
Munich lectures (Buber), 72–73
mutuality, 153, 235, 249–50, 252, 254–55
mysticism, 21, 68, 70, 164–65, 215, 225n10

Nakba (Palestinian refugee catastrophe), 153
Naksa (setback after Six-Day War), 153
Nancy, Jean-Luc, 6, 167, 170–71
"narrow ridge," 182, 196n6
Nassar, Lawrence, 257n29
nationhood, Jewish, 137–38, 140
Natorp, Paul Gerhard, 29
nature, 216–17. *See also* cats; land and landscape; plants; trees
negotiation model of sexuality, 239
neo-Romanticism, 68, 70, 84, 167–68. *See also* romanticism
Neue Freie Volksbühne, 87n9
Neue Gemeinschaft, 70
nevi'im (prophets). *See* prophets (*nevi'im*)
Nicholas of Cusa, 30
Niebuhr, Reinhold, 17
Nietzsche, Friedrich, 21, 70, 84, 151
Nolan, Ann Michele, 18
nonhuman dialogue, 202–3, 205–6, 208–9

nonverbal dialogue, 7, 209, 211–12, 214, 216, 218–22, 232n81
Noske, Gustav, 69
Nostra Aetate (Vatican II), 14, 19

occasionalism, 79, 84
occidental consciousness, 132–33, 163
Ohel Mo'ed (Tent of Meeting) (Exod. 25, 36), 47–48, 52–53, 57, 59n17
"olam ha-tohu," 188–89, 200n30
O'Malley, John, 34
Orientalism, 6, 153, 157–58, 160–61, 163–64, 166–71, 174, 176n12

paganism, 130, 132, 140, 164, 171
pain, 145–46, 247
Palestine: Buber on, 153, 155–56; erasure of landscape, 157–58, 166; geography of, 158; Jewish-Arab relations, 31–32, 85–86, 91n41, 153, 173–74; Jewish immigration and settlement, 91n41, 157, 159, 165–66, 173; mapping of, 156, 157, 158–59, 173; metaphysical belonging, 157; Palestinian *fellah*, 171; Palestinian refugees, 153; project of perfected place, 155–56; works on, 165. *See also* Zionism
Palestine Land Development Company, 76–77
Palestine Oriental Society, 166
pantheism, 153, 158, 160
Pascal, Blaise, 28
Paths in Utopia (Buber), 77, 173
Paul, Saint, 25
Paul VI, Pope, 14–15, 18, 20
paysan, 171–72
Peirce, Charles Sanders, 7, 209, 211, 212, 220–21, 229n40, 231n75
people of spirit (*Anshey Ha-Ruach*), 113
"People Today and the Jewish Bible" (Buber), 51–53, 54
personhood, 32–33, 258n45
phenomenology, 211, 229n40
philosophical anthropology, 129–32, 140–42. *See also* Scheler, Max
Pineau, Lois, 238–39, 240–41

Pinsker, Leon, 149n15
Pippin, Robert B., 237
plants, 7, 202, 214–16, 217, 220, 230n56
Platonic Politeia, 104
pneumatic reading of texts, 78, 92n49
political theology, 74–75
political Zionism, 130–31, 137, 140, 169–70
Poma, Andrea, 196n5, 225n5
pragmatic ambivalence, 185–86, 198n18, 199n19
Prague, 68, 73, 76
prayer, 25–26, 169
presence (term), 46, 79
The Prophetic Faith (Torat Hanevi'im) (Buber), 53–54, 67, 79, 83; Bible as great dialogue, 53–54, 79, 83
prophets (*nevi'im*): as *avdey Ha-Shem* (the servant of God), 104, 105, 106; charisma of, 106, 108–9; divine mission of, 105–6, 107, 122n72; Jeremiah, 83–84; Samuel, 73, 102–4, 105, 112; the spiritual in, 164; of YHVH, 83–84; zaddikim as, 108–9
Proudhon, Pierre-Joseph, 69

Raban, Ze'ev, 160
Ragaz, Leonhard, 74, 80, 81
rape, 234–39, 248, 250–51, 253–55
Ratzinger, Joseph, 19, 20, 22, 28
Realphantasie (imagining the real), 235, 245–46, 247–48, 251, 253–54, 258n48, 260n69
redemption, 96, 97–98, 101, 117n12
Reeve, C.D. C., 237, 257n16
reflective judgment (Kant), 248, 259n55
Reform Judaism, 6, 130, 133–34, 137, 140–41, 146, 147, 246
religious anarchy, 69, 97, 99, 100–101, 103, 114, 120n44
religious liberalism, 6, 130, 133–34
religious secularism, 26
religious socialism, 68, 74–75, 81
religious Zionism, 75, 98, 133, 149n11
"Renewal of Judaism" (Buber), 161, 195n3
revelation: biblical commentaries of Buber, 53–54; burning bush (Exod. 3), 44, 47–49,

55–56, 57, 59n17; as confrontation, 46–47; content to call of, 80; as divine presence, 48, 55, 79; "ehyeh asher ehyeh" (Exod. 3:14), 47–48, 51, 55–56, 59n17; human-divine encounters as, 44; Ohel Mo'ed as response to, 52–53, 57; responses to, 52–53; at Sinai, 44, 52, 56; subordination of anointed king through, 104; Wissenschaft des Judentums on, 45
Rogers, Carl R., 246–47, 252–53
Roman Russi (Shalev), 158–60
romantic-care model of sexuality, 234–35, 240, 242, 247, 248, 249, 251, 254
romanticism, 68, 70, 92n49, 118n17, 167–68, 234–35, 239–40, 259n55. *See also* neo-Romanticism
Rosenzweig, Franz, 2, 29, 44, 55, 79; "Atheistic Theology" (Rosenzweig), 45; Freies Jüdisches Lehrhaus (Frankfurt), 44; "Jewish People's Theology," 45; modern Jewish thought compared with Life of Jesus movement, 45; neo-romanticism, 168; on revelation, 45; Shulamite in Song of Songs, 160; *Star of Redemption* (Rosenzweig), 160; on translation methods, 49. *See also* B-R Bible
Rubin, Reuven, 160
Rückbiegung (inward turning reflection), 242–43
Ruppin, Arthur, 76

Sabbatianism, 110, 111
sabbatical year, 82, 93n62
Sacred Landscape: The Buried History of the Holy Land since 1948 (Benvenisti), 6, 153, 156–57, 166; cartographical redrawings of, 158–59; geographies, transformations of, 159–60; metaphysical belonging, 157; notion of land in, 158; Orientalism of, 166; pantheism, 153; the *paysan*, 171
Said, Edward, 168–69
Samuel, books of, 73, 102–4, 105, 112
SAPD (Sozialist Arbeiterpartei Deutschlands), 69, 77, 87n7

Sartre, Jean-Paul, 1, 24–25
Schaeder, Grete, 112
Scheimann, Richard, 92n55, 93
Scheler, Max, 149n27; Buber's critique of, 6, 130–31, 142–43; his Gnostic model, 131, 141; on the human condition, 130, 141; influence on Pope John Paul, 19; metaphysics of, 141–44, 146, 147; on pain, 145; philospophical anthropology of, 131, 140, 141–43, 147; spirit, conception of, 141–46, 149n27
Schmidt, Christoph, 95
Schmitt, Carl, 75, 80
Scholem, Gershom, 8, 79, 83, 92n49, 110, 123n87, 168, 225n11
second-person stance, 205, 206, 208, 226n15
Second Vatican Council. *See* Vatican II
secular political Zionism, 75, 133–34, 138–39, 149n11
the self: fantasies of, 236, 237, 243, 248. *See also* ego; "I" (*Ich*)
sequential ambivalence, 192–94
servants, 102, 104, 105, 120n38
sexual relationships: as moral friendship, 242. *See also* models of sexuality
Shalev, Meir, 6, 158–60, 170
Shapira, Avraham, 98, 196n5
shekhina (divine Presence), 131, 132
Shoah, 25, 30
shrines, Muslim, 157, 176n12
Shrinking Lover (film), 236, 237, 248
Shulamite in Song of Songs, 160, 169
Silberstein, Laurence, 129, 130
silence, 207–8, 223, 228n28, 236, 237
Simmel, Georg, 38n50, 58n4, 141
Simon, Ernest, 182, 196n7
simultaneous ambivalence, 192, 193
Sinaitic revelation, 44, 52, 56. *See also* Moses
Six-Day War (1967), 153
Smith, Ronald Gregor, 16, 34
Social Democratic Workers' Party of Germany (Sozialdemokratische Arbeiterpartei Deutschlands), 87n7
socialist Zionism, 76
soul, 162, 163

sources (biblical) related to: abyss metaphor (Gen. 1:2), 188; the covenant (Exod. 3, 19:5-6), 47–48, 56, 59n17, 96, 117n10; "ehyeh asher ehyeh" (Exod. 3:14), 47–48, 51, 55–56, 59n17; on the existence of God (Acts 17:22), 27; Gideon's speech (Judg. 19), 99; God's identification with ancestors, 47–48, 59n17; Israelite monarchy (I Samuel 8), 73; on kingship (Judg. 17:6 Ps. 2, 7), 103, 104, 120n45; land sovereignty (Lev. 25:23), 82; memory of slavery (Deut. 10:17-19), 31–32; Ohel Mo'ed (Tent of Meeting) (Exod. 25, 36), 47–48, 52–53, 57, 59n17; profanation of God's name (Exod. 20:7), 26; revelation, 44, 47–48, 52, 59n17; sabbatical year (Lev. 26:23), 82; Sinaitic revelation (Exod. 19), 51–52; the stranger (Deut. 10:17-19), 188

Sozialdemokratische Arbeiterpartei Deutschlands (Social Democratic Workers' Party of Germany), 87n7

Sozialistische Bund, 70

SPD (Socialist Democratic Party), 69, 77

Spinoza, Baruch, 149n27

spirit, 141–46

Sprachkritik (critique of language), 188, 199n27

Stapel, Wilhelm, 74, 80

Star of Redemption (Rosenzweig), 160

stranger: in biblical teaching, 31

suffering, 130, 145–46, 247

Summa Theologica (Aquinas), 21

Susser, Bernard, 99

Talk to Her (*Hable con ella*) (Almodóvar): dance scenes, 235–36, 253–54; monologic behavior in, 236, 237, 239, 244–45, 252, 253, 254; moral ambiguity in, 235, 240; rape in, 234–35, 236, 237, 239, 248, 250, 253, 254, 255; *Shrinking Lover* fantasy, 236, 237, 248; temporal absence, 244; viewers' sympathy with characters, 235, 237, 239, 240, 254, 255; virtue of talking, 235–36, 239, 240. *See also* headings for individual characters (e.g. Benigno (*Talk to Her* (*Hable con ella*)))

Tannenbaum, Marc, 14

technical dialogue, 233

tehom, 187–88

teshuva, 84–85

theocracy: religious anarchy, 97, 99, 100–101, 103, 114, 120n44

theopolitical commentaries, 53–54

theopolitics. *See* anarchy; God; Hasidism; Israelites; kings; theocracy; zaddik; Zionism

therapist-patient relationship, 233, 249, 250, 252–53

the servant of God (*eved Ha-Shem*), 104, 105, 106

third-person stance, 205, 206

Thomas Aquinas, Saint, 21

"Thou." *See* "You." *See also* I-Thou (*Ich-Du*) (I-You)

"Three Theses of a Religious Socialism" (Buber), 75

tikkun (repair), 99, 110

Tillich, Paul, 17, 24

Tolstoy, Leo, 71

trees, 7, 202, 214–16, 230n56

Troeltsch, Ernst, 168

Trumpeldor, Joseph, 92n44

Uexküll, Jacob von, 219

Umfassung (inclusion): in imagining the real, 245–46

Unitatis Redintegratio, 19

unity principle, 154–55, 160–62

Ury, Lesser, 160, 162–63

utopia and utopianism, 77, 82, 92n46, 99–101, 114, 169, 173

Vatican II: atheists, dialogue with, 14–15, 21, 22; Buber's impact on, 15, 18–20; dialogue, 13–14, 30, 34; *Gaudium et Spes*, 14, 22; Jewish-Catholic relations fostered by, 21; *Nostra Aetate*, 14, 19

visualization, 151–52, 157, 158–59, 166

Visual Thinking (Arnheim), 152

vocation, 106–7

völkisch, 87n11

Von Balthasar, Hans Urs, 21

Warburg, Abby, 168
Wellhausen, Julius, 99
West Bank settlements, 153, 173
Wilson, George, 239–40, 250
Winkler, Paula, 30
Wirbel (vortex), 7, 182, 184, 187–88, 189–90, 197n8, 201n37
Wissenschaft des Judentums, 43, 45
Wolf, Siegbert, 87n11
women: body language, 237–38, 239, 242, 260n70; in the bible, 124n92; myths of sexual desire, 238, 257n17; rescue of, 235–36; sexual desires of, 238
word-pairs (concept), 47, 58. *See also* I-It (*Ich-Es*); I-Thou (*Ich-Du*) (I-You)
word-roots, 50–51. *See also* Leitworte
World War I, 44, 68, 71–72, 164, 246

yeridat ha-zaddik (descent of the zaddik), 109–10
YHVH, 31, 79, 83–84, 99, 104, 164. *See also* God
Yizhar, Y. Z., 158, 160
"You," (*Du*) (Thou), 20, 28–29, 93n58, 100, 117n16, 131–32, 206, 208, 216–18, 222, 226n16, 230n57, 245; "you-saying," 93n58. *See also* I-Thou (*Ich-Du*) (I-You)

zaddik, 5, 95; charisma of, 108–9; as community builder, 111–12; elevation of the holy sparks, 121n52; Kotzker Rebbe, 132; in land of Israel, 115; leadership of, 104, 109–10, 114; Levi Yitschak of Berditchev, 28; as prophet, 108–9; teachings of, 123n87; in time of exile, 108; *yeridat ha-zaddik* (descent of the zaddik), 109–10
Zionism: Buber on, 31–32, 71–74, 85–86, 92n46, 114, 152, 153, 165; cartography, 158–59; community building, 129, 136–37, 148; economic development, 165; election of the people of Israel, 85; eurocentrism of, 174; on exile, 95–96, 130–31, 133–34; Hasidism, 97, 98, 114; kibbutz movement, 5, 68, 76–77, 83, 85, 92n45, 173; land and the Zionist project, 158–59, 170; Landauer on, 75–76, 77, 91n41; metaphysical belonging, 157, 158; national claims, 137, 165–66, 167; philosophical anthropology, 129–30; political Zionism, 130–31, 137, 140; rejection of concept of "the nations," 136; religious Zionism, 75, 98, 133, 149n11; secular political Zionism, 75, 133–34, 138–39, 149n11; technical development, 165; as theo-aesthetic, 151–52; Theodor Herzl, 27, 133, 136, 139, 149n11, 167; visual thinking, 6, 151–52; Zionist socialist movement, 73–74, 76
Zionist socialist movement, 73–74
Zunz, Leopold, 51
Zwiegespräch (dialogue), 79–80, 93n55

www.ingramcontent.com/pod-product-compliance
Lightning Source LLC
Chambersburg PA
CBHW021349300426
44114CB00012B/1149